Radio Audiences and Part[icipation] in the Age of Network Society

This book maps, describes and further explores all contemporary forms of interaction between radio and its public, with a specific focus on those forms of content co-creation that link producers and listeners. Each essay will analyse one or more case studies, piecing together a map of emerging co-creation practices in contemporary radio. Contributors describe the rise of a new class of radio listeners: the networked ones. Networked audiences are made up of listeners that are not only able to produce written and audio content for radio and co-create along with the radio producers (even definitively bypassing the central hub of the radio station, by making podcasts), but that also produce social data, calling for an alternative rating system, which is less focused on attention and more on other sources, such as engagement, sentiment, affection, reputation and influence. What are the economic and political consequences of this paradigm shift? How are radio audiences perceived by radio producers in this new radioscape? What's the true value of radio audiences in this new frame? How do radio audiences take part in the radio flow in this age? Are audiences' interactions and co-creations overrated or underrated by radio producers? To what extent can listener-generated content be considered a form of participation or "free labour" exploitation? What's the role of community radio in this new context? These are some of the many issues that this book aims to explore.

Tiziano Bonini is a Lecturer in Media Studies at the IULM University of Milan, Italy. Since 2005, he has also worked as a freelance radio producer for community, national commercial and public radio.

Belén Monclús is a Post-doctoral Researcher in the Audiovisual Communication and Advertising Department at the Autonomous University of Barcelona, Spain, and researcher at the Image, Sound and Synthesis Research Group (2014SGR1674). Since 2007, she has been the coordinator of the Catalonia Radio Observatory (l'OBS, GRISS-UAB).

Routledge Studies in European Communication Research and Education

Edited by Nico Carpentier, Vrije Universiteit Brussel, Belgium and Charles University, Czech Republic, François Heinderyckx, Université Libre de Bruxelles, Belgium and Claudia Alvares, Lusofona University, Portugal.

Series Advisory Board: Denis McQuail, Robert Picard and Jan Servaes

ECREA
http://www.ecrea.eu

Published in association with the European Communication Research and Education Association (ECREA), books in the series make a major contribution to the theory, research, practice and/or policy literature. They are European in scope and represent a diversity of perspectives. Book proposals are refereed.

Radio Audiences and Participation in the Age of Network Society

Edited by Tiziano Bonini
and Belén Monclús

Routledge
Taylor & Francis Group

LONDON AND NEW YORK

First published 2015
by Routledge

2 Park Square, Milton Park, Abingdon, Oxfordshire OX14 4RN
711 Third Avenue, New York, NY 10017

*Routledge is an imprint of the Taylor & Francis Group,
an informa business*

First issued in paperback 2018

Library of Congress Cataloging-in-Publication Data
Radio audiences and participation in the age of network society / edited by
    Tiziano Bonini and Belén Monclús.
        pages cm. — (Routledge studies in European communication
research and education ; 6)
    Includes bibliographical references and index.
    1. Radio audiences—Europe.   2. Radio programs—Europe.   3. Radio
broadcasting—Europe.   4. Information technology—Social aspects—
Europe.   I. Bonini, Tiziano.   II. Monclús, Belén, 1974–
    HE8697.25.E85R33 2015
    302.23′44094—dc23
    2014030649

ISBN: 978-0-415-73915-3 (hbk)
ISBN: 978-1-138-54863-3 (pbk)

Typeset in Sabon
by Apex CoVantage, LLC

To Adria and Enrico.
To Herminia and Ricard

Hang the blessed DJ
Because the music that they constantly play
It says nothing to me about my life
(The Smiths, 1986)

Contents

Figures, Tables and Images

IMAGES

Preface

There's no doubt we're in the midst of a new and exciting age in radio's history. Audiences, it seems, are being given the chance—are actively seizing the opportunity—of a dramatically expanded share in determining what happens on air. Social media are at the root of this change. And as a consequence, social media will soon become an innate part of our understanding of what constitutes 'radio.' Texting, messaging, time-shifting, re-mixing, using Facebook or Twitter: all these provide new and potentially destabilising means of interaction between radio's producers and radio's consumers. Indeed, the enfolding of social media within the very fabric of radio—the emergence of what we might call 'social radio'—surely challenges that very distinction between 'producer' and 'consumer.' We are, as they say, all makers now.

Sometimes, as the essays gathered here make clear, this new, participatory world offers audiences a role that doesn't quite extend to full-scale co-creation of output. When we scratch the frantic, beguiling surface of interactivity, we often discover little more than what Tiziano Bonini in his introduction calls a 'sequence of action and reaction'—where those in the studio and behind the microphone still call the tune. But, as he goes on to argue—and as we recognise more and more as the book progresses—this is very much at the 'minimal' end of a vast spectrum of new behaviours. There are other examples—the collective production of a playlist, the crowdsourcing of a documentary and so on—where we can sense a rather more equal power relationship emerging.

It's right to be excited. But we also need to be wary. We should, for instance, remain mindful of the dynamic qualities of the past—which are often underappreciated. We also need to be mindful of the powerful restraints on change today—to retain a grasp of the larger political economy. Radio, now as much as ever, is a significant sector in the media industry. As a business, it remains prone to inertia, weighed down by vested interests, or force of habit, or the simple desire to play safe in the interests of profit. Different parts of the world will respond to innovation in different ways and at different speeds. Nevertheless, radio also has an insurrectionary side to its character: it is, and always has been, highly mutable, fleet-footed—a form of communication capable of taking risks, aesthetically, technically, editorially. Those who make it, study it, care for it, have long harboured anxieties about this 'old' medium being eclipsed by a succession of other, newer, more viscerally exciting media. Nowadays it is the Internet. Half a century ago it was television. Each new arrival has provoked a step-change in the character of radio. Indeed, it is quite possibly this nervy sense of existential threat that explains precisely why radio practitioners have always been trying harder than almost anyone else to reinvent their craft.

If we want to sort out the truly new from the superficially new, a strong sense of history is vital, then. In our own age of interactivity, we're sometimes too ready to assume that 'the listener' has been discovered—or rather empowered—for the first time. But the numbers of people communicating with their favourite radio station, seeking to express an opinion or challenge its decisions, have always been staggering—as Tiziano Bonini demonstrates vividly in his introduction. Now, it's true that many broadcasters, most notably the BBC under its founding father John Reith, were notoriously reluctant to pander to audience tastes.

As Reith himself saw it, the BBC's historic task was to lead and to shape public attitudes, not to follow them. Even so, none of these thousands upon thousands of letters was ignored entirely. Indeed, to eavesdrop on the decision-making process inside the BBC—as I have done myself through archival research—is to witness an organisation often pathologically concerned with the minute-by-minute opinions of its listeners.

Here, the distinction between commercial radio and public service radio—though never absolute—is still useful. For while commercial radio has always had an intrinsic interest in ratings and in aggregating listeners into 'demographics' or markets, public service radio has always claimed to be an ethical project: one in which 'audiences' are less important than the notion of 'the public.' It is a notion that refuses—has always refused—to see listeners as inert bodies and minds, passively waiting to be 'filled up' with what they are given. It assumes—has always assumed—that they are capable of growth and change. In this conception, radio has continually operated on the basis of a symbiotic relationship between broadcaster and listener. Indeed, those words 'service' and 'public' are not insignificant. Indeed, they say it all. Everything they do, they do for us.

Of course, one of the features of the interactive age is that we've decided we don't actually want them to do it all for us. We want to do it for ourselves. But even here, we need pause for thought. It's great if anyone and everyone can feel involved in the making and shaping of radio. But it's great too, sometimes, just to be allowed to listen—even to listen in what we think of as a 'passive' way. As Kate Lacey argues in her recent and profoundly important book, *Listening Publics: The Politics and Experience of Listening in the Media Age* (Cambridge: Polity, 2013), listening to others is just as important a part of the communicative process—and certainly just as important a part of the deliberative process in a modern democracy—as speaking to others. In this respect, keeping quiet and keeping still embodies a form of radical openness. We might also remember the concept of broadcasting articulated most clearly by writers such as Paddy Scannell and John Durham

Peters: as something freely given—scattered in the wind, as it were—without any formal expectation of response: in short, a gift. Then again, we might also remember that interactivity—even at the 'maximum' end of the spectrum of participation—does not always represent a form of real power or influence in the wider world. As those who have studied the role of social media in the Arab Spring—and in its dispiriting aftermath—have noted, interactivity can often distract from collective effort as well as co-ordinate it. Invest too much hope in it, and we shall be disappointed.

In reading these chapters, then, the crucial challenge for us is not just to see all these changes in radio delineated but also to understand them in a broader critical—and politically aware—perspective. How might they change the act of listening at a fundamental level? What, if anything, remains of the valuable notion of 'the public'? What is the intrinsic social or cultural value of the various forms of interactivity uncovered here? What are the affective powers of a more interactive form of radio—or, more specifically, how does it provide pleasure, joy, companionship, understanding, escape, relaxation or inspiration? And, perhaps most crucially of all: what guarantees are there that creativity—something which, after all, has long been associated with the work of the lone 'genius,' or at least the paid labour of the practised, professional radio 'craftsman'—is being preserved or enhanced as we shift inexorably towards a world of co-creation? In other words, how can we be sure we're not losing valuable dimensions of the radio experience as we gaze, mesmerized, at the shiny new ones?

To pose all these questions is not to doubt the force—or the advantages—of change. It is merely to suggest that as we read the fascinating essays in this edited collection, we should keep digging deep and occasionally do some standing back. Above all, it is to argue that we should always keep asking what we want radio to do for us—what its larger social and political purposes should be. We can certainly sense here the variety and vitality of radio. This is emphatically and brilliantly a book for allowing us to think of it afresh. But what should we take from this collection as a whole? Where is radio heading? Can we be sure that this wonderful medium, which did so much to shape the last century in quite profound ways, will continue to do the same in the present one? In the past it has helped connect us with the world at large—to lift our horizons beyond our own small corner of life. It has provided a space for contemplation and imagination, for evoking memories, for generating in its liveness and its reach a powerful sense of the collective. At best, it has offered a cluttered mosaic of sounds—factual, fictional, demotic and high-flown. How we shape the network society to our own human ends, so that it helps us to retain all this, even as radio opens up new and as yet unknown possibilities, is, I think, the most important question of all.

David Hendy
University of Sussex
May 2014

Introduction

The Listener as Producer: The Rise of the Networked Listener

Tiziano Bonini

"Audiences should be eliminated entirely."

(Kaprow 1996, 713)

"Every time a new consumer joins this media landscape, a new producer joins as well because the same equipment—phones, computers—lets you consume and produce. It is as if when you bought a book, they threw in the printing press for free."

(Shirky 2005)

"The people formerly known as the audience are those who were on the receiving end of a media system that run one way, in a broadcasting pattern, with high entry fees and a few firms competing to speak very loudly while the rest of the population listened in isolation from one another and who today are not in a situation like that at all."

(Rosen 2008, 163)

"We have three different ways of reaching our audience and interacting with our audience; that's broadcast, digital and social—and they are equally important."

(Martin Jönsson, deputy director of Swedish Radio, quoted in Marshall 2013)

This book is divided into two macro-sections: "Interactive Publics" and "Productive Publics." These two sections do not represent two different worlds of practices but, conversely, describe two different moments of the same process: audience participation mediated by radio. We conceive of audience participation in radio as a process that is articulated along a continuum, moving from interaction (with a low level of activity) to co-creation (Banks and Deuze 2009) and co-production (with a high level of participation). Here we will show and analyse different innovative practices of interaction and participation.

In this body of work, interactivity is intended in both its minimal technical meaning, as a sequence of action and reaction, as well as in the wider sense of a social-communicative relationship (listeners that reply to a call by a radio host by either phone, smartphone messaging systems, email or Facebook/Twitter texts; listeners that react to a call by a radio host by doing something, such as downloading content or liking/commenting/sharing social media posts; radio hosts and authors that reply to questions and content coming from listeners).

The boundary between interactive and productive publics is traced according to the ideal model of audience participation, the AIP model—access, interaction, participation (Carpentier 2007), where: "this difference between participation on the one hand, and access and interaction on the other, is located within the key role that is attributed to power, and to equal(ised) power relations in decision-making processes" (Carpentier 2011, 29). According to the AIP model, in the first section, contributors will analyse processes of participation that allow listeners to produce content (Short Message Service [SMS], phone calls, social media messages, etc.) but do not let them take part in the co-creation of radio programmes in any way.

The first section of this work will analyse contemporary forms of interaction between radio and its listeners, using specific case studies to examine all the technological means that are currently involved in these processes: the telephone, short text messages, social network sites (SNSs).

The second section will focus on examples in which the radio public not only reacts to the producers' requests using the technology at hand, but consciously participates in the production of radio content and has some voice in deciding the content being produced. Some examples in this section will look at the collective production of a playlist used by music programmes: a number of programmes have been built upon listeners' requests and music choices, by different means.

Further examples of co-creation refer to other genres, such as the documentary. In Sweden, Germany, Italy and Latin America, some radio producers seek to involve the public in one or more steps of the productive process of a radio documentary, by means of crowdfunding as well.

The title of the book, *Radio Audiences and Participation in the Age of Network Society*, highlights the paradigm shift that is transforming the nature of mass media audiences and publics. The rise of the network society (Castells 1996; van Dijck 1999; Wellman 2001), due to the diffusion of information and communication technologies, is also restructuring the topology, the properties and the very nature of media audiences, which have ceased to be understandable only as *diffused* in time and space (Abercrombie and Longhurst 1998). Audiences and publics attracted to media such as radio are no longer invisible, silent and disconnected. Listening habits are changing and listeners are increasingly used to both listen to radio and leave comments on social media, where their feelings and opinions are public, searchable, accessible and measurable. As Lacey (2013, 155) claims:

> Listeners are able to represent their listening to their social networks and track others' online listening in real or archived time. On the one hand, this means that listening is a practise that is increasingly surveilled and increasingly open to measurement and commodification. On the other hand, it is also a sign of persistent desire to create and partake in forms of collective listenings to mediated music, sound and speech, albeit in virtual space.

Radio audiences are a mix of traditional radio broadcasting audiences and networked publics (Boyd 2011; Varnelis 2008). This means not only that new media are changing the nature of listeners/viewers, transforming them into interactive users (Livingstone 2003), but also that radio publics, once organised into networks, now have different properties, different behaviours and different affordances. Networked publics are made up of listeners who are able to not only produce written and audio content for radio and co-create along with the radio producers (even definitively bypassing the central hub of the radio station), but that also produce social data, calling for an alternative rating system, which is less focused on attention and more on other sources, such as engagement, sentiment, affection, reputation and influence. What are the economic and political consequences of this paradigm shift? (see chapter 13). How are radio audiences perceived by radio producers in this new radioscape? (see chapter 2, 3, 4 and 6).What's the true value of radio audiences in this new frame? (see chapter 13). How do radio audiences take part in the radio flow in this age? (see chapters 6, 7, 8, 9, 11 and 12). Are audiences' interactions and co-creations overrated or underrated (see chapter 2) by radio producers? What's the role of community radio in this new context? (see chapter 10, 11 and 12). These are some of the many issues that this present book aims to explore.

FROM MASS AUDIENCES TO NETWORKED LISTENERS: THE FOUR AGES OF LISTENER PARTICIPATION

There have been several attempts to periodise the history of audiences. One of the best known analyses is Abercrombie and Longhurst's (1998). They identified three broad periods of audience history: the simple, co-located, face-to-face audience; the mass audience; and the diffused audience, which is "no longer contained in particular places and times, but rather part and parcel of all aspects of daily life" (Abercrombie and Longhurst 1998, in Livingstone 2005, 26). The diffused audience seems to be the most appropriate category for describing contemporary audiences, but Abercrombie and Longhurst published their work in 1998, at the beginning of the Web 1.0

era, and their periodisation now needs to be updated, given the great changes in the use of media content caused by the Internet and its further developments (Web 2.0, social media). For this reason, this work aims to propose a different historical periodisation of radio listening, one that is similar to Abercrombie and Longhurst's work, but more suitable to the comprehension of the properties of a media public in the age of the network society. The periodisation developed in the following pages identifies four historical ages corresponding to four different auditory regimes, the last of which is characterised by the hybridisation of broadcasting media with networked media. It remains clear that the emergence of a new regime and a new type of audience does not mean the disappearance of previous ones. As Lacey (2013, 22) maintains, "at any one time there are likely to be multiple 'auditory regimes'" that coexist.

The periodisation proposed here will attempt to portray how audience participation in radio has changed over time and investigate the causes that have determined the emergence of a new relationship between radio and its publics. This work does not want to focus on the progressive increase in the public's participation, corresponding to new technological integrations (telephones, mobile phones, the Internet, social media), but will instead highlight the different potentialities of the public's participation, inscribed in each auditory regime. Regardless of how the radio broadcasting public has often been described, as "disciplined and docile listeners in a space, drastically separate not only from that of the performer but from the fellow public as well" (Hilmes 1997, 186), the historical analysis proposed here shows us how interaction and participation have always been permanent features in the history of the radio audience. Listeners, as Lacey (2013, 113) claimed, "have always been active." Audiences have always longed to participate in radio, but over time this participation has taken on different forms and features.

The First Age (1920–1945): An Invisible Medium for an (Almost) Invisible Public

In this first historical period, radio, the new medium of the early twentieth century, is really, as Brecht maintained in 1934, an outdated device, used for political propaganda, educational purposes and the spread of consumer culture. The speakers are invisible (blindness represents the main feature of radio, according to Arnheim [1972]) and there is only one model: broadcasting, one-to-many communication.

The invention of focus groups (the 1937 Stanton-Lazarsfeld Program Analyzer, as reported by Douglas [2004]) and of the first audience surveys make listening habits measurable, but public sentiment remains undetected. The audience is invisible and inaudible. It is made up of individuals who are not linked to a network and who can only listen, without taking part in the conversation; they cannot publicly manifest their emotions or opinions to the host in real time. On this privatisation of the listening public, Sartre (1990, 271) wrote:

> When I listen to a broadcast, the relation between the broadcaster and myself is not a human one: in effect I am passive in relation to what is being said. . . . This passivity . . . can to some extent be resisted: I can write, protest, approve, congratulate, threaten, etc. But it must be noted that these activities will carry weight only if a majority of listeners who do not know me do likewise.

But we also have to remember that "falling silent to listen is not a sign of passivity, nor an act of submission, but is an active part of the communication process" (Lacey 2013, 47). But when listeners weren't satisfied with the "sit back and listen" model of communication (Gauntlett 2011), what could they do? If they didn't like a show, or, on the contrary, wanted to express their love for that show, they could do nothing but switch off the radio. Actually, listeners could do something more than switch off the radio: they could write a letter (Razlogova 2011).

Elihu Katz (1950) studied the letters received by the popular US radio host Ted Malone. During its first year on national US radio in 1935, his programme *Between the Bookends* generated between 4,000 and 20,000 fan letters a month, more than any other unsponsored programme at the time. The famous 1938 drama *The War of the Worlds* by Orson Welles received more than 1,400 letters in the days after the show (Cantril 1940), and the 1939 war drama *They Fly through the Air with the Greatest of Ease* by Norman Corwin received around 1,000 fan letters (Blue 2002). Writing letters to the radio was a widespread practice before the arrival of the telephone (and it has yet to completely disappear). However, as Sayre (1939, 272) claimed in his research on fan letters by the Office of Radio Research:

> Fan mail has been one of the curious facts concerning the radio industry. . . . In recent years fan letter writers have been thought to be among the neurotic, the deviates, the abnormal among the listeners. . . . As an answer to this, the theory has been proposed that fan-letter writers were not neurotic in what they thought, but in the fact that they wrote at all. They merely expressed attitudes held by other listeners, but differed from them in their ability to transgress the barrier between themselves and the impersonal broadcasting company.

As Sayre showed, the fans that wrote letters were considered misfits, weird people when compared with the normal and silent ones. If a minority of the public was inclined to dialogue and interaction, this participation was neither encouraged nor understood by radio producers in this first historical phase. Listeners were perceived by the American broadcasters as a mass of passive consumers, by the European public services as a mass of citizens to be culturally lifted up, and by the totalitarian regimes as a mass of opinions to be ideologically moulded. Nevertheless, writing letters to the radio has always been a (forgotten) tradition of audience participation. As

David Hendy (2013a, 122) remembers, "in 1970 BBC received 227,167 letters and phone calls about its programmes. This figure doesn't include the much larger number of fan-letters addressed directly to programme-presenters, just those written to the Corporation centrally."

Even though the dominant auditory regime was that of silent and private listening, Lacey reminds us that in the same period in the US and in Europe, many collective listening groups were created, an aspect that is easily forgotten by the history of broadcasting: "Radio was never only a solitary experience" (Lacey 2013, 135). In the UK at the end of the 1920s, approximately 20,000 listeners had organised listening groups. In the US, there were around 15,000 collective listening groups at the end of the 1930s.

Between 1924 and 1932 in the Weimar Republic, hundreds of collective listening groups were formed, the 'workers radio clubs.' One of their main objectives was to encourage a critical ear in their members by organising collective listening. Groups as large as 500 would gather in public halls to listen to the radio and to generate a critical public discussion of the output, not just in the hall but by sending reports of the proceedings to the party press and to the radio authorities (Lacey 2013, 150).

Even in an age characterised by the use of this means of communication by the strongly top-down radio institutions, there were clear attempts by the public to take part in the discussion and to meet in public spaces for collective and connected listening. Even in its first years of life, radio was ready to be used as a 'social medium,' able to interact and to connect people.

The first authors to understand the value of radio as a social medium, rather than as a distributor of content, were Brecht and Benjamin. But before Brecht, and even more remarkably, Walter Benjamin realised radio's radical potential as a 'social medium.' Benjamin, having produced ninety programmes for the public radio of the Weimar Republic between 1929 and 1933, had a deeper knowledge of this means of communication and maintained a positive outlook on radio, as it had the ability, in his view, to transform the public's relation to culture and politics (Baudouin 2009). In *Reflections on Radio* Benjamin (1999a, 543) expresses the most fruitful ideas for our own times:

> The crucial failing of [radio] has been to perpetuate the fundamental separation between producers and the public, a separation that is at odds with its technological basis. (. . .) The public has to be turned into the witnesses of interviews and conversations in which now this person and now that one has the opportunity to make himself heard.

The radio that Benjamin is advocating is a medium that closes the gap between broadcaster and receiver, allowing both the author/host and the listener to play the role of producer. The importance that Benjamin attributes to active reception is in stark contrast to the hypnotic effect of Nazi aesthetics (Baudouin 2009) and to the allure of a radio show seen as a product to be consumed. Benjamin juxtaposes the aestheticisation of politics and art embodied by Nazism (and more in general by propaganda and consumer culture) with the politicisation of art, something which requires, in his view, a more active and participant role for the listener.

Benjamin (1978) further developed this theme in *The Author as Producer*, a paper in which he pointed out the need for a new intellectual/ producer figure (writer, photographer, radio drama author, film director) and the end of the distance between writer and reader due to the advent of new mechanical and electrical reproduction technologies. Benjamin noticed that a growing number of people had started to become 'collaborators' in his own time through the rise of the newspaper, as editors created new columns according to the current tastes of their readers. These spaces were meant to make readers feel in touch with their culture, and in this sense the reader became a kind of author (Navas 2005). Benjamin (1999a, 771) saw the reader as redefining the literary text; his example was the Russian press:

> For as writing gains in breadth what it loses in depth, the conventional distinction between author and public, which is upheld by the bourgeois press, begins in the Soviet press to disappear. For the reader is at all times ready to become a writer, that is, a describer, but also a prescriber. As an expert even if not on a subject but only on the post he occupies he gains access to authorship.

Focus on the public's feedback can also be found in another short essay from 1932, *Two Types of Popularity* (Benjamin 1999b), in which he assesses the role of radio as a pedagogical tool. Benjamin is convinced that the public should be respected, rather than being given content in a top-down fashion; it should also perceive that its interests are 'real' and are being taken into account by the speaker. Benjamin puts the transmitter and the receiver on the same horizontal level.

Benjamin's ideas are especially relevant today for their focus on listener feedback. The German philosopher grasped the distinctive quality of a fledgling, electronically mediated society in its potential for public participation/ production.

The Second Age (1945–1994): An Invisible Medium for an Audible Public

This second stage is marked by: (1) the appearance of the transistor, which made radio listening mobile; (2) the birth of underground radio (pirate radio and free radio, according to the definitions given by Hendy [2000]); and (3) the introduction of the telephone into radio's productive practices, which made reaching people's voices outside the studio easier.

In Europe during the 1960s and 1970s, the transistor, underground radio and the telephone contributed significantly to blurring the lines between producers and listeners. In Paris, during the first days of May 1968, demonstrators tactically reclaimed radio thanks to transistors in order to communicate and organise protests in the streets (Bonini 2009; Sullerot 1968).

Between 1959 and 1964, the pirate radio stations of baby boomers (listeners who were tired of the public stations in their countries and decided to create their own means of communication) were born in international waters offshore from Holland, Denmark and the UK; independent local radio was established in the UK in 1973 and, as Guy Starkey reminds us in chapter 3, they relied a lot on call-in shows; between 1969 and 1980, thousands of free radio stations (*radio libere*)—unlicensed broadcasting stations—were created in Italy, shifting the balance of communication towards civil society (Downing 1984; Lewis and Booth 1990).

The free radio movement emerged in a social climate full of strong demands. People reclaimed the media for themselves. The monopoly on communication practised by public services could no longer adequately respond to the stimuli of society. The social and cultural climate of this age had a great influence on the public service, which was slowly attempting to self-regenerate and open itself up to the call for participation. All over Europe, public service radio was trying to cope with this demand. In Denmark, for example, public service radio tried to open its microphone to the listener's voice: Mette Simonsen Abildgaard (2014, forthcoming) investigated the radio listeners' and hosts' use of an answering machine in Danish public service radio's popular youth programme *P4 i P1*, which was created in the highly politicised climate of the 1970s. *P4 i P1* thus contained several experiments with emancipatory two-way radio for working-class youth, inspired by critical media theories such as Enzensberger's (1970) *Constituents for a Theory of the Media*.

In Italy, the work of Andrea Camilleri is well known; now a prominent Italian writer of bestsellers, he was once a radio producer for RAI, the Italian public service broadcaster. In 1974, along with Sergio Liberovici, he produced an inspiring and thought-provoking docu-drama, *Outis Topos*. The 50-minute radio show was the result of the editing of 200 hours of inhabitants' recordings in an outlying neighbourhood in Turin. The work is subtitled "Hypothesis of a Future Radio" and considers the issue of 'popular' radio created by citizens, not imposed from the top. Camilleri's description of this radio drama is revealing:

> The imbalance between the technical evolution of the means and the systems that manage it is increasingly clear. . . . Nevertheless, one of the possible answers may lie in the radical invention of its traditional functions: not only transmitting but receiving, not only allowing listeners to hear something but also allowing them to speak, not isolating them but connecting them with others, not only 'refueling' them but making

them become active, producers. . . . An experiment in citizens' self-management of radio, performed by the RAI in the first 25 days of July in a series of working-class neighbourhoods in Turin, provided a mass of information that was stimulating, though not always encouraging: beyond the unpredictability and authenticity of the speakers, what emerged was the conditioning deriving from the sometimes unconscious acquisition of certain expressive stereotypes, evoked by the great means of mass communication.

(Malatini 1981, 127)

But not only did listeners want to participate in communication through the mediation by public services: they wanted to bypass the institutions and take control of these means of communication.

"In 1977, Felix Guattari proudly announced that the Italian free radio stations had succeeded in creating the first electronic agora: the immense permanent meeting of the airwaves. The listeners were now broadcasters" (Barbrook 2007, 283). Guattari (1978, 1979) stressed the radically different function of free radio as opposed to conventional mass media. His notions of transmission, transversal and molecular revolution suggested that, unlike conventional radio, free radio would not impose programmes on a mass audience, but would come across freely to a molecular public, in a way that would change the nature of communication between those who speak and those who listen.

In 1983 in Japan, following the experience of the Italian free radio and autonomist movements, Tetsuo Kogawa founded the Mini-FM movement, a network of hundreds of low-power FM radios (with a radius of 100–500 meters) built up by very small communities of listeners/producers:

We tried to think about radio in a different way, as a means to link people together. To the extent that each community and individual has different thoughts and feelings, we believed there should be different kinds of radio—hundreds of mini-FM stations in a given area. (. . .) Radio could serve as a communication vehicle, not for broadcasting but for the individuals involved. (. . .) One must admit that mini-FM has a powerful therapeutic function: an isolated person who sought companionship through radio happened to hear us and visited the mini-FM station; a shy person started to speak into the microphone; people who never used to be able to share ideas and values found a place for dialogue; an intimate couple discovered otherwise unknown fundamental misunderstandings.

(Kogawa 1992)

The situationist dream of breaking down the boundary between media producers and consumers is (partly) coming true. Free radio stations, as well as giving voice to sectors of society that were previously ignored, introduced the significant use of the telephone to communicate with their public. Audience participation by telephone dates back to the mid-1940s for US commercial radio stations (the call-in radio format) and to the mid-1960s for European public radio. These are followed by free radios, which make the 'talk radio/open microphone' format the distinctive feature of their communication model, as the *Manifesto of Radio Popolare of Milan* (1975), written by its founder, journalist Piero Scaramucci, clearly highlighted:

> The telephone relationship with the public must be possible throughout the broadcasting day. The listener can intervene to give news, to pose a problem, to answer a question asked in the studio, to promote an initiative; the call can be an opportunity for a new, improvised broadcast, it can open up a case.
>
> (Ferrentino, Gattuso and Bonini 2006, 144)

Radio Popolare also used to select new contributors, producers and hosts from among the listeners who participated the most through phone calls: listeners became 'accomplices,' as Lewis and Booth (1990) brilliantly defined the audience of the European free radios.

Beyond the emergence of free radio, a great contribution to the diffusion of participatory practices was given by the *MacBride Commission Report* (MacBride 1984). Carpentier (2011, 90) emphasises how the *MacBride Commission Report* "took a strong position on audience participation." The fundamental features of this participation, according to the *MacBride Report*, were: (a) a broader popular access to the media, (b) the participation of nonprofessionals in producing and broadcasting programmes, and (c) the participation of the community and media users in management and decision making. This report served as a theoretical frame of reference for regulating nonprofit radio all over the world. Between the 1980s and 2000s, also thanks to the contribution of the World Association of Community Radio Broadcasters (founded in 1983), more and more nations have reformed their regulations in the field of communications and have introduced specific licences for community media (Canada and Australia in 1975, Sweden in 1979, Italy in 1990, the UK in 2002).

The public of free, underground and community radio stations is in part a productive one: it participates in a collective conversation, as Benjamin imagined in 1934, and as in community radio (see chapter 10), it even participates in the radio's management and decision making. Listeners begin to take part in radio production, both by using the telephone and by creating new radio stations. The public is still invisible, but it has become audible. Listeners' opinions and emotions are becoming increasingly public, but not measurable. The possibility of connecting more than one telephone line to the radio mixer allows the host to speak to several listeners simultaneously, or to make them interact with each other horizontally, so that more people are involved in the radio conversation (Pinseler 2008). However, a large part of the public—those not calling the radio, not building a station or not contributing to a pirate radio programme—remains passive, private and not linked together.

The Third Age (1994–2004): An Invisible Medium for a Readable Public

The technological innovations of this third phase are mobile telephones, text messaging, the World Wide Web, audio streaming, emails and, subsequently, blogs and podcasting. Mobile phones further facilitated radio reporting and producing from outside the studio, as well as listener participation in the radio conversation. The possibility of calling the radio station from a public place with a mobile phone transformed the role of the audience: from private citizens to potential reporters, or citizen journalists. The public's contribution to radio content production had a chance to evolve and strengthen. Listeners began producing information streams from the places they were calling from (traffic news, current affairs, local news, etc.). *Caterpillar* is a perfect example of this model: a radio programme born in 1997 and aired by Radio2 RAI—the Italian second national public service radio channel—it transformed listeners living abroad into foreign affairs correspondents.

This third auditory regime is also a readable one: radio producers not only listened to the voice of their public, but also read them through text messages; at the same time, listeners not only listened to the host's voice, but could read his blog and his replies to them by email.

Text messages and emails updated the private relationship between host and listener, which until then was only based on paper letters. The speed at which short digital texts could be transmitted thanks to mobile text messaging services and emails increased audience feedback to radio stations. This increase in textual flow became an invaluable source of information for producers; the information, filtered and re-elaborated, was then transformed into new content, ready to enter the radio flow. Software designed to manage emails and SMS enabled radio stations to organise content received by email or SMS in real time, to choose the most appropriate ones for the programme, and to broadcast them a few seconds or minutes after receiving them. Thus both the spatial and temporal distance between producer and listener were reduced. The readability and real-time access of SMS and email enhanced the publicness of the public's opinions and feelings. The public was not only audible, but easily readable as well (see chapter 3). Its emotions and opinions, however, still remained unmeasured.

The invention of streaming technology (1995) and subsequently of blogs (1999) and podcasting (2004) furthered the move towards public participation in audio communication introduced by free radio in the 1960s and 1970s. Free radio was the first to shift the balance of broadcasting from the institutions towards the individual. The encounter between radio and the

Internet was another step forward in this direction, bringing this process of the 'de-institutionalisation of communication' (Bonini 2006) a step forward: the costs of accessing communication tools lowered, as opening a Web radio cost less than an FM transmitter. The digitisation of cultural products (mp3 and other formats), the diffusion of simple free software for digital audio editing (Audacity) and the progressive increase in speed of Internet connections allowed for many more people to create radio content and broadcast it via streaming than in previous ages.

Streaming happenings were born, in which a number of musicians played together or shared show schedules with programs broadcast from different places in the world (Horizontal Radio in 1995; Net Aid in 1999). The first community of netcasters was composed of many different kinds of people: computer geeks, musicians, music lovers, open source software programmers, political activists and sound artists. Streaming happenings were a reinvention/remix of the pioneering spirit of the first amateur broadcasters, the free radio movement of the seventies and the first Californian phone phreakers of the 1970s (Johns 2009).

In 2004 another audio (and video) distribution technology was born: podcasting. Podcasting represented a step forward in the transformation of listeners into audio content makers. Streaming allowed listeners to find new ways of broadcasting audio content to be listened to in real time; podcasting, ten years later, allowed them to distribute audio content to be listened to on demand.

There is a thin red line that ties together the communities of amateur broadcasters of the 1920s, the radio pirates of the 1960s, free radio activists, the phone phreakers and computer hackers of the 1970s, the netcasters of the 1990s and the bloggers and podcasters of 2000s: they were all both producers and listeners and were all linked together in networks. Most of them could fit into the category of 'recursive publics' created by social anthropologist Christopher Kelty (2008, 27–28) for the more recent open source communities:

> A recursive public is constituted by a shared concern for maintaining the means of association through which they come together as a public. This kind of public includes the activities of making, maintaining and modifying software and networks and represents the subject of this making, maintaining and modifying.

Amateur broadcasters, radio pirates, free radio activists, phone phreakers, netcasters, podcasters and bloggers all demanded autonomy and free self-expression in media use and communication tools. Free software for streaming and blogging represented the opportunity for the revival of this spirit of creative conviviality (Illich 1973), as opposed to passive reception.

Today, netcasters, bloggers and podcasters do not limit themselves to participating in the radio flow produced by traditional broadcasters, but also create their own sound media. Web radio and podcasting are 'bypass technologies' (Dearman and Galloway 2005), allowing individuals to bypass the entire established radio industry. The radio studio has been outsourced: 'radio' is wherever I can stream or record a podcast. Listeners (at least a small part of them) have become producers of themselves, and online platforms such as Mixcloud, Soundcloud, Audioboo, Spreaker, Broadcast Yourself, Jelli Radio and others perfectly embody this principle. Spotify, Mixcloud, Audioboo and Spreaker are 'making and networking' tools, they enable people not only to discover and listen to new music and radio content but also to create new ones by themselves. The revival of DIY culture is visible also in the radio producing sector.

The Fourth Age (2004–?): A Visible Medium for a Networked Public

The rise of social networking sites (SNSs) is the milestone of this fourth age. SNSs have existed since 1997 (Boyd and Ellison 2007). The social network that has best integrated with radio has been Facebook, created in 2004, followed by Twitter. The fans/friends/followers of a radio station's or host's Facebook or Twitter profile are a public that is very different from the traditional one: this is due to the specific characteristics of the medium, as well as to changes in consumer culture brought about by the rise of the information economy. The traditional public of broadcasting media still fits the definition given by Gabriel Tarde in 1901, as Arvidsson (2013, 374) highlights: "A public is a mediated association amongst strangers who are united by a however momentary affective intensity that is directed towards a common thing." The new public emerging from the hybridisation of broadcasting and information/communication technologies is a networked one. Listeners are no longer just audiences (Rosen 2008). Of all the changes that network culture may bring us, the reconfiguration of the public sphere is likely to be the most significant.

The network society we live in today has produced a new configuration of mediated publics: the networked publics. Networked publics represent the missing link in Abercrombie and Longhurst's (1998) historical periodisation. Ito was the first to use the term, in a book published in 2008 and edited by Varnelis:

> The term *networked publics* references a linked set of social, cultural and technological developments that have accompanied the growing engagement with digitally networked media. The Internet has not completely changed the media's role in society: mass media, or one-to-many communications, continue to cater to a wide arena of cultural life. What has changed are the ways in which people are networked and mobilized with and through media. The term *networked publics* is an alternative to terms such as *audience* or *consumer*. Rather than assume that everyday media engagement is passive or consumptive, the term

publics foregrounds a more engaged stance. Networked publics take this further; now publics are communicating more and more through complex networks that are bottom-up, top-down, as well as side-to-side. Publics can be reactors, (re)makers and (re)distributors, engaging in shared culture and knowledge through discourse and social exchange as well as through acts of media reception.

(Ito 2008, 2)

This concept was further developed by Danah Boyd. Networked publics are "publics that are restructured by networked technologies" (Boyd 2011, 41). What distinguishes networked publics from other types of publics is their underlying structure: "Networked technologies reorganise how information flows and how people interact with information and each other. In essence, the architecture of networked publics differentiates them from more traditional notions of publics" (Boyd 2011, 41). These kinds of publics, according to Danah Boyd, all share four fundamental affordances that make them different from all the previous mediated publics: "Persistence, replicability, scalability and searchability" (Boyd 2011, 46). Persistence means that, on SNSs, the public's expressions are automatically recorded and archived. This means that feedback (opinions, feelings and comments) from each listener is public and, since this can remain online for a long time, it can also play a role in shaping the radio station's reputation. Replicability means that the content produced by networked publics is easily replicable. Scalability in networked publics refers to the possibility of tremendous—albeit not guaranteed—visibility. This means that, for example, individual listeners commenting and talking about a radio show on its social network profile can reach a wide audience. Searchability means that content produced by networked publics can be easily accessed.

Networked publics represent the type of public that has emerged from the network society and refer to any type of public that is organised in a network. Here, listeners from this age will be referred to as networked listeners. Networked listeners belong to the vast multitude of *produsers* (Bruns 2008). Produsage refers to the type of user-led content creation that takes place in a variety of online environments. This concept blurs the boundaries between passive consumption and active production. However, the term *produser* emphasises the productive aspect of the consumers/users, while the definition proposed here highlights the connections among listeners. Not all networked listeners are produsers, not all of them produce informational content; many listeners are still silent, but they are still visible nodes in an interconnected network (the network of a radio's digital community). The auditory regime found in this fourth phase is one of connected listening, listening that may also be defined as augmented listening, because, either simultaneously or at a later time, radio listening is overlapped with discussion, comments and the production of content on the social networks connected to the radio. Just as the mix of mobile devices and social network sites represent the second screen of television consumption, they may also represent the second screen of this new augmented radio listening experience.

As pointed out by the Head of the BBC Newsroom, Mary Hockaday, public service broadcasters are "shifting to a new formulation: Inform, Educate and Connect", which means that they are "no longer just trying to draw people in, but also more confidently reaching out on social networks, and a full range of distribution platforms that work for audiences, and that some of our journalism is done in partnership with the wider world" (Hockaday 2012, 7).

This new media ecosystem, created from a mix of broadcasting (radio) and networking (social media) cultures, has transformed how media content circulates. In this regard, Jenkins, Ford and Green (2013, 2) refer to *spreadable media* as all the media content that is put into circulation according to a hybrid model, which is a mix of top-down and bottom-up forces:

> This shift from diffusion to circulation signals a movement toward a more participatory model of culture, one which sees the public not as simply consumers of preconstituted messages, but as people who are shaping, reframing and remixing media content in ways which might not have been previously imagined. And they are doing so not as isolated individuals, but within larger communities and networks, which allow them to spread content well beyond their immediate geographic proximity.

Radio, and more generally, media audiences in the age of the network society are better understood as networks of listeners, rather than groups belonging to specific social and economic clusters. Listeners' actions (making comments, remixing media items, sharing media objects, producing user-generated or user-circulated content) all happen within networks.

As Rainie and Wellman (2012, 12) claimed, the "triple revolution of social networks, Internet and mobile communication" have made possible "the new social operating system we call 'networked individualism.' The hallmark of networked individualism is that people function more as connected individuals and less as embedded group members." Networked listeners have partial membership in multiple networks and rely less on permanent membership in settled groups. For this reason they should be investigated through the lens of network theory: "In network theory, a node's relationship to other networks is more important than its own uniqueness. Similarly, today we situate ourselves less as individuals and more as the product of multiple networks composed of both humans and things" (Varnelis 2008, 153).

Rainie and Wellman (2012, 55) believe that "each person has become a communication and information switchboard connecting persons, networks and institutions." Listeners are no longer alone and invisible, but connected with many others in a variety of social circles that provide them with diversified portfolios of social capital. The structure and the properties of the social networks of networked listeners associated with a radio or media company is the new frontier of media research. In network analysis, great importance is attributed to: (1) hubs and super connectors, highly connected nodes of the network able to shorten the distance that information must travel; (2) bridging or weak ties, connections between knots belonging to different social circles; weak ties are great for getting information in and out of a cluster of relationships; and (3) bonding or strong ties, connections within the same cluster that are necessary for internal trust, efficiency and solidarity. These three features could become important for radio (and media) audience research as well, as media companies could be progressively more interested in understanding the architecture and the properties of the networked public they have been able to gather around them. Some networks could prove to be made up of very strong community links, while others may be composed of people with many contacts with other social networks. These three characteristics of networks, and others that we still have to discover, could determine a new value of networked audiences, representing the new assets of new audience rating systems.

Some scholars have already tried to visualise the network structures of the social media crowds: Smith et al. (2014) demonstrated that in Twitter there are at least six distinctive structures of social media crowds which form depending on the subject being discussed, the information sources being cited, the social networks of the people talking about the subject, and the leaders of the conversation. Each has a different social structure and shape: divided, unified, fragmented, clustered and inward and outward hub and spokes.

We have shown how the participatory desire of radio listeners has been immanent throughout the history of radio. Listening to radio is different from hearing radio (Lacey 2013): while hearing "emphasizes *perception* and *sensation* of sound, listening emphasizes *attention* and *giving* to another" (Lacey 2013, 17). Listening to radio has always been a cultural activity, an aural experience augmented by side tools of interaction and participation: from letters to social media, people listening to radio have always tried to connect with the speaker and to each other. Letter writing and the collective public listening of the 1930s are the ancestors of phone calls, SMS, emails and social radio tools (SNSs used as second screens) of the contemporary age. The fourth phase, that of networked publics, is only the latest stage of a historical trajectory starting with the invention of electronic media.

Each of these four historical steps of the relationship between radio and its listeners produces a different kind of public, but at the same time these different publics are composed of the same people.

FIVE CHANGES IN THE RELATIONSHIP BETWEEN
RADIO PRODUCERS AND LISTENERS

The affordances of networked publics have given rise to a series of fundamental changes in how the relationship between radio and its public is conceived. Here, these changes will be identified as the Five Changes:

(1) Change in the Publicness of Publics (More Visible, More Audible, More Measurable)

The listeners connected to a social network site of a radio station have a face, a name, a personal space for discussion (the Facebook Wall, the Twitter Timeline) and a bio-cultural profile (the Info section). Being networked means potentially having more power. As Rainie and Wellman (2012, 13) put it: "Networked individuals have new powers to create media and project their voices to more extended audiences that become part of their social worlds." This is the end of the public as a mass that is invisible (it cannot be seen by the broadcaster), passive (it cannot take part in the conversation) and insensitive (it cannot express its emotions towards the speaker).

Networked listeners can potentially become extremely popular, through the exposure and the attention gained on digital platforms. According to Alice Marwick (2013), social media are technologies of subjectivity that teach users how to succeed and reach popularity in postmodern consumer societies. Marwick (2013, 16) critically claims that social media educate users to learn marketing techniques such as micro-celebrity, life streaming and self branding—"a strategy of success in which one thinks of oneself as a brand and uses social media to promote it, through creating, presenting and maintaining a strictly edited self." Borrowing from Foucault, Marwick (2013, 11) argues that "social media have become a way that people govern themselves."

Listeners take advantage of social media to better present themselves, manage their public image and build their online status, but their potentially increased publicity is often that which benefits technology companies: "A verifiable identity makes it possible to leverage status but it also makes it simple to track people as they move around the web" (Marwick 2013, 17).

The integration of SNSs in radio production routines makes the immaterial capital created by networked listeners become public and tangible. While until recently the audience was invisible to radio and confined to its private sphere, except in the case of phone calls during a programme, today listeners linked to the online profile of a radio programme are no longer invisible or private, and the same goes for their opinions and emotions. And if emotions and opinions are no longer invisible or private, they are measurable (see chapters 4 and 5). For the first time in the history of radio, listeners are not only numbers: their feelings, opinions and reputations are traceable and measurable through netnographic methods (Kozinets 2010) and social network analysis.

In the broadcasting age audience rating systems (diaries, telephone recalls, meters) measured 'eyeballs' and attention. In the age of social media, broadcasters can measure more than just attention. The rising importance of a revision of audience measurement was already underlined by Jenkins (2004, 38) at the dawn of the social media age:

> The American television industry is increasingly targeting consumers who have a prolonged relationship and active engagement with media content and who show a willingness to track down that content across the cable spectrum and across a range of other media platforms. This next generation audience research focusses attention on what consumers do with media content, seeing each subsequent interaction as valuable because it reinforces their relationship to the series and, potentially, its sponsors.

Affect is a new common good that media corporations are trying to commodify (see chapter 13). While the capitalists of the Industrial Revolution privatised and commodified common lands, social media capitalists like Zuckerberg fenced public conversations into private social media platforms and commodified them, giving rise to what van Dijck (2013) calls a 'platformed sociality': the novelty of social media platforms, according to van Dijck (2012, 168), is not that they allow for making connections but "lead to engineering connections." To this end, Arvidsson (2011, 41) claims that

> The remediation of social relations that has accompanied the rise of consumer culture has effectively managed to transform the nature of affect, from something private or at least located in small interaction systems, to something that acquires an objective existence as a value creating 'substance' in the public domain. Social media have taken this process one step further.

Networked platforms grant the private sphere civic and social legitimacy, as they effectively augment its connectivity potential. Online social networks, claims Papacharissi (2010, 139), "allow the individual to connect to local and remote spheres of family members, friends and acquaintances, and strong and weaker social ties." Online social networks publicise the listeners' private spheres. A person may post a Facebook comment or a tweet that expresses a personal opinion on public affairs being discussed on a talk radio show while on a short break from work. The private sphere of the networked listeners is, as Papacharissi (2010, 133) argued, a "networked private sphere," a private sphere augmented by online convergent technologies. In the case of Facebook and other commercial social networks, this augmented publicity of the listeners occurs within "commercially public spaces" (Papacharissi 2010, 129).

(2) Change in the Speaker-to-Listener Relationship

The new communication model deriving from the mix of radio and social media is a hybrid model, partly still broadcast, partly already networked. Radio is still a one-to-many means of communication. However, the telephone already partly made it a one-to-one (phone interview) and many-to-one medium (open mic, phone talk radio); to this we have to add SNSs, which are at the same time one-to-one (chat and Twitter mentions), one-to-many (tweets, Facebook notes or posts), many-to-many (Facebook Home, Twitter hashtags) and many-to-one (Facebook comments) kinds of media.

The mix between radio and the SNS considerably modifies both the hierarchical/vertical relationship between the speaker/host and the public, and the horizontal relationship between each listener. Both types of relationships are approaching a less hierarchical dynamic typical of peer-to-peer culture. Broadcasting logic—filter then publish—is replaced here by a networking logic, publish then filter: networked listeners do not have to wait to be selected to talk on air, they can publish a post on the Facebook page of the radio programme they like.

Networked listeners and radio hosts can become 'friends': when a programme's presenter and one of his or her listeners become friends on Facebook or follow each other on Twitter—even if their relationship is still asymmetric in terms of power—they establish a bi-directional tie: both can navigate on each other's profile, both can watch each other's online performance and, at the same time, be actors in it. Both can enact two types of performances, public and private: they can post comments on each other's walls or reply to each other's tweets, send each other private messages or communicate by chat or Skype in real time. For the first time in the history of radio, the speaker and the listener can easily communicate privately, far from the ears of other listeners, 'off air.' This gives rise to a 'backstage' behaviour (Goffman 1959) between host and listener that was previously unimaginable.

This change is a double-edged sword: it has an emancipatory side and a 'dark' side. The emancipatory side is that this change allows the listener and the speaker/producer/host of the radio to 'tune in' and listen to each other online, exchanging knowledge and ideas (see chapter 4). As Crawford (2009, 525) claimed, "The metaphor of listening can offer a productive way to analyse the forms of online engagement that have previously been overlooked, while also allowing a deeper consideration of the emerging disciplines of online attention."

On the other hand, the dark side allows radio producers to gather information about consumer habits, tastes and opinions. But this monitoring activity of how many people like/comment/talk of/share their content has more to do with surveillance than with paying real attention to listeners. Listeners don't want to be surveilled, they want to listen and to be listened to. Even if there is a very fine line between surveillance and listening—every listening activity is potentially a surveillance activity—there is a major difference between surveillance and listening: the aim of the first is to track listeners/consumers' behaviours in order to commodify them, while the aim of the latter is to tune in to listeners' thoughts/opinions/comments in order to serve them better quality content that is closer to their needs.

(3) Change in the Listener-to-Listener Relationship

At the same time, the relationship between listeners is similarly changing. Fans of a radio programme can establish links among each other online, exchange public comments on the programme's wall, express more or less appreciation for specific content, exchange content on their personal walls, write each other private messages or chat with each other. The radio's public has never been so visible. While before SNSs the concept of the radio public was a purely abstract entity, one that could be understood sociologically and analysed statistically, today this public is no longer only an imagined one (Anderson 1993): it is a visible network of listeners/producers.

For the first time, people who listen to a radio programme and are its fans on social network sites have the opportunity to see and recognise each other, to communicate, to recommend new contents and to create new links while bypassing the centre, this being the radio programme itself. "The gatekeeping function of mass media is challenged as individuals use digital media to spread messages much farther and more widely than was ever historically possible" (Gurak 2001, 13). While a radio public is an invisible group of people who are not linked together, the SNS audience of a radio programme is a visible group of people/nodes in a network, connected by links of varying intensity which, in some cases, can produce strong links that transcend the broadcaster. By exchanging and sharing content on the social network sites of a radio station, they establish new social ties or reinforce the existent ones. As Rushkoff (2000) put it in an article in *The Guardian*, "content is just a medium for interaction between people."

This change has a dark side as well. Listeners can network together and tune in to each other's social media profiles, exchanging content, opinions, ideas and making new valuable connections, while at the same time engaging in practices of 'coveillance' (Mann, Nolan and Wellman 2003), which means that people can observe and monitor each other as if they were in a collective digital panopticon.

(4) Change in the Value of Publics (SNS Public: Social Capital = Mass Media Public: Economic Capital)

This visible group of listeners/nodes/links is the most important new feature produced by the hybridisation between radio and SNSs. A radio programme's network of friends/fans on SNSs represent its specific social capital (Bourdieu and Wacquant 1992). While the wider (and invisible) radio public, as charted by audience rating companies, still constitutes the programme's economic capital, this work promotes the idea that the public of social media should be considered the real social capital of a programme, a tangible and visible capital, the meaning of which is well explained by Bourdieu and Wacquant when they define social capital as "the sum of the resources, actual or virtual, that accrue to an individual or a group by virtue of possessing a durable network of more or less institutionalized relationships of mutual acquaintance and recognition" (1992, 14).

However, there is an ongoing discussion on the strength of links within online social networks, as Ellison, Steinfield and Lampe (2007, 1146) noted:

> Researchers have emphasized the importance of Internet-based linkages for the formation of weak ties (Granovetter 1973), which serve as the foundation for *bridging* social capital (Putnam 2000). . . . It is possible that new forms of social capital and relationship building will occur on online social network sites.

Bridging social capital might be augmented by such sites, which support loose social ties, allowing users to create and maintain larger, diffuse networks of relationships from which they could potentially draw resources (Donath and Boyd 2004; Resnick 2001). Donath and Boyd (2004) hypothesise that SNSs could greatly increase the weak ties one could form and maintain, because the technology is well suited to maintaining such ties cheaply and easily. The definition of bridging social capital—a kind of capital better suited for information diffusion (Putnam 2000) and made of weak ties, which are loose connections between individuals who may provide useful information or new perspectives for one another, but typically not emotional support—seems to fit the kinds of ties normally found on SNSs. If we consider the networked public that forms around a radio programme as its bridging social capital, we can expect this listener-based network to produce, if not emotional and substantive support, then at least a certain amount of benefits in terms of news, tastes, information retrieval, cultural trends, comments and reviews. If we observe the SNS of the most popular radio programmes, we find that this is already taking place: on an SNS, listeners anticipate/continue discussions on the themes introduced by the radio show, adding comments, content, links, references, quotations and suggestions.

Moreover, the personal information and the public wall posts and tweets on the listeners' SNS profiles can help radio producers to better understand who is hiding behind a comment or link, allowing them to assess the reputation of the listeners/producers and consequently decide if they can trust them or not. The reputation (and trustworthiness) of each single listener belonging to the network of a radio programme contributes to the general reputation of that specific networked public and, due to the transitive property, constitutes the reputational capital of that radio programme. This reputational capital is of great value for radio producers, because, as Arvidsson (2013, 380) puts it: "Reputation is the form social capital takes among strangers. The higher a person's reputation, the easier for her to initiate processes, recruit talented co-workers, or start new projects. Finally reputation enhances the enjoyment of participation." On the public stage of the SNSs, reputation is conferred on an actor by the members of a public. Since, on this stage, radio producers and listeners can act both as actors and audience at the same time, their reputations (both the producer's and the listener's) are being continuously evaluated by the networked listeners. As Rainie and Wellman (2012, 19) claimed, "much of the activity by networked individuals is aimed at gaining and building trust, the primary currency of social networks." The social networks' economy is built on reputation.

It is therefore in the radio producer's interest to develop, nurture and care for this reputational capital and to manage the establishment of a high-quality and highly satisfied networked public. Ellison et al. (2011) showed a clear empirical relationship between a wealthy social network and the production of bonding and bridging social capital: the larger the network, the quicker the response from friends; the greater the network, the greater the social capital produced (in terms of benefits received by the network). Ellison et al. (2011, 138–139) clearly demonstrated that Facebook "enables individuals to: maintain a larger set of weak ties; make ephemeral connections persistent; lower the barriers to initial interaction; make it easier to seek information and support from one's social network and to provide these resources to others."

For radio makers, a wide network of friends/fans/followers is highly important for their future. Even if the fans' network does not generate tangible economic value, as the radio audience already does, it nevertheless generates great reputational capital. The message of the SNS public of a radio programme is the network itself, because this network is able to produce value. The value embedded in the networked public is not yet convertible into economic capital, but the crisis of traditional mass advertising will lead to a future increase in—and refining of—tools for the capitalisation of the wealth of networked publics linked to radio programmes and stations. Besides, building networked and productive publics for radio could be of strategic importance for public service media. Public service media are losing audiences and legitimacy, because they are forgoing serving listeners as citizens (Syvertsen 1999). Since making and participating mean 'connecting' and creating social relationships, as Gauntlett (2011) has shown, building and nurturing wealthy and productive networked publics for public service media could be an opportunity to legitimise their service as a real public one, a service that provides listeners with tools that let them participate and create new social relationships among each other.

The social capital embedded in the digital audiences of a media company has been well understood by Wolfgang Blau, digital strategist at *The Guardian*, when he claimed in an interview to the Italian magazine *L'Espresso*: "If we could visualize the social relations provided by a newspaper to its listeners, cultural associations, NGOs, clubs, companies, political subjects, cultural institutions, we would realize they look like a huge social network connecting thousands of nodes/people" (Rossano 2013).

In this kind of participatory media environment, the construction of the media company's reputation is less subject to corporate control and intervention, but it is co-created in a dynamic way along with the audience (Bunting and Lipski 2000; Kozinets 2010).

Although a system for the direct conversion of social capital into economic capital has not yet emerged, a good accumulation of social capital could prove to be fundamental for the success, for example, of a crowdfunding campaign (see chapter 8). The value of networked publics can be understood mostly as social capital, as we suggest here, but other scholars, like Eleanor Baird Stribling (2013), point out that the engagement of fans with a media company could also provide some kind of economic value. Stribling (2013) categorises the "broad spectrum of fan behaviours" into four categories of activity, two which provide direct economic value—"watching, listening or attending" and "purchasing primary or secondary products"—and two which provide indirect economic value, like "endorsing" and "sharing and commenting."

(5) The Change in the Role of the Radio Author (from Producer to Curator)

Radio is increasingly becoming an aggregator, a filter for the abundance of information, useful especially for the non-prosumer listeners, who do not publish videos and have no time to explore friends' profiles, which are a true goldmine for discovering new trends. The radio author's job thus increasingly resembles that of a translator, of someone who connects two worlds— niches and mass culture—by delving into niches and re-emerging with a little treasure trove that can then be used productively. The producer's function in the age of Facebook is thus to drag content emerging from small islands, small communities and to translate and adapt it to the public of large continents, transforming it into mass culture. Radio authors and producers are becoming more and more similar to the figure of the curator, a cultural shift in the role of all kinds of author's labour that was already noted by Brian Eno (1991), as Reynolds (2011, 130) reminds us: "Curatorship is arguably the big new job of our times: it is the task of re-evaluating, filtering, digesting and connecting together. In an age saturated with new artefacts and information, it is perhaps the curator, the connection maker, who is the new storyteller, the meta-author."

Today's radio producers do not look for content in the same way they did in the twentieth century. Their job is no longer to seek and create, but to select and co-create. During research for this book, I met and interviewed an Italian producer of a talk radio programme for a national radio broadcaster. He revealed that his work had completely changed with social media:

> Now I know the core of my audience, I talk with them, we exchange comments and thoughts via email, private messages on Facebook and mentions, replies and direct messages on Twitter. They spontaneously suggest to me new music songs, excerpts from novels, links to news and to YouTube videos. One of them spontaneously collects the podcasts of all my programmes on his blog, and he has become the most trustable sound archive of my entire radio work. Another keeps on sending me new music he thinks will fit with my playlist. I also play with them on Twitter: once a week we decide the playlist together, I have launched the hashtag #openplaylist. You might think I do this just to save time, or that it's audience exploitation. It is not, it's a lot of work for me, but it's a lot of fun for everyone, they all feel like part of a community and they have the opportunity to proudly share their expertise with a community of people that they trust. I call them the 'networked newsroom.'[1]

This is how the value production process in radio works in the era of SNSs: listeners enact their cultural tastes online, the radio author (increasingly a producer, as Benjamin predicted) re-interprets and re-elaborates them, providing the audience with a dramaturgically constructed listening experience in which it finds its contents mixed together. Listeners comment and supply new material to the community of listeners/producers so that the recursive process can start again. But what about this process? To what extent can we call it co-creation and to what extent must we call it exploitation? Andrejevic (2008) studied the productivity of the fan communities of TV shows and interpreted it as a double form of value-enhancing labour for television producers by allowing fans to take on part of the work of making a show interesting for themselves on the one hand, and by providing instant (if not necessarily statistically representative) feedback to producers on the other hand. But is he right?

As Australian scholar, Maura Edmond (2014), pointed out, "creating radio projects that are more social, immersive and engaging fosters a commercially valuable emotional attachment to a story, show, presenter, station and to a community of fellow listeners (what Jenkins 2006, 13) calls 'affective economics'." Audience engagement is being considered more and more commercially valuable, but can this engagement be understood under the frame of labour exploitation theories?

CO-CREATION OR EXPLOITATION?

> "We should thus describe this audience labor as engaged rather then exploited."
>
> (Jenkins et al. 2013, 60)

Radio makers (authors/presenters/producers) and radio listeners, once they are connected through SNSs, belong to the same horizontal and multipolar network. On the SNS stage everyone, radio makers and listeners alike, is able to perform, to take part, to alternatively play the role of the actor (contributing with content) and of the audience (contributing with comments and liking). As Benjamin hoped, the boundaries between authors and 'readers' have potentially been broken down.

The connection that has now been established between radio makers and listeners through social media also allows for new forms of content production to emerge, some of which will be analysed in this book (see chapters 6, 7 and 9).

The extent to which listeners take part in these production processes is still controlled by radio makers, who decide how to give value to user-generated content. Much has been written about the ambivalent status of this content as a source of both intrinsic reward and potential exploitation, as social media corporations' value, Andrejevic (2013, 162) argues, relies on the "private enclosure of productive resources." When can we still speak of co-creation, and when does cooperation become free-labour exploitation (Fuchs 2010, 2014; Terranova 2000)? Andrejevic (2013) claims that exploitation in social media not only occurs when audience labour (in terms of user-generated content) is not paid, but also when users lose control over their productive and creative activity. Ippolita, Lovink and Rossiter (2009) maintain that exploitation is embedded in SNSs: however radical they may be, they will always be data mined. They are designed to be exploited and to exploit.

The free labour exploitation theorists have built their propositions on a consolidated criticism of the economic policies of commercial media, which was very popular in the 1970s. To a certain extent, the attention of a passive public required by traditional media was already a form of exploitation and production of economic value: this was the late-1970s approach of Canadian media theorist Dallas Smythe (1978), who claimed that viewers were exploited as their viewing time was appropriated by media companies and sold as an 'audience commodity.'

From a Marxist perspective, audiences have always been put to work by media corporations, who have made a living on the backs of their audiences. From newspapers and radio to television, commercial media (Hearst's newspapers of the early twentieth century; NBC and ABC radio in the 1920s; today's commercial television networks like Fox News, just to name a few) have always sold the 'work' (attention paid to media content) of listeners to advertising.

Marxist researcher Christian Fuchs is one of the best known scholars to have contributed to the revival of Smythe's approach to the political economy of media. In Fuchs' (2010, 187) view, "citizens who engage in everyday politics" and those "radio listeners and television viewers who call in live" are somehow 'unpaid' knowledge workers being exploited by capital. For Fuchs, it seems, any participation by citizens in the public sphere itself is exploited labour, as opposed to the practical contributions to the democratic formation of public opinion that these citizens themselves clearly understand their actions to be. Fuchs goes even further in framing audience 'labour' as exploitation. He claims that digital users are also exploited: in the case of corporate social media, "the audience commodity is an Internet prosumer commodity" (Fuchs 2013, 217). Therefore, according to the free labour theories, the main reason for the exploitation of the audience's work is its appropriation and commodification, operated by both traditional and new commercial media. As Murdock (1978) already noted, Smythe's approach really only applies to advertiser-supported media. In the case of Facebook, it was Zuckerberg himself who, in 2010, publicly admitted the extraction of value from audience engagement in Facebook: "Our focus is just to help you share information and when you do that you are more engaged with our site and there are more ads on the side of the page and the more you do it the more the model works out."[2]

But even if we want to believe in the expropriation of value by commercial media, we would realise that yes, this value exists, but it is derisory. For example, let's take the three Italian public service radio channels (Rai Radio1, Radio2 and Radio3, which are also financed by advertising) and divide their total advertising revenue from 2012 (€35.3 million, according to Rai 2013[3]) by the grand total of their listeners on an average day (9.3 million, according to Eurisko 2012[4]). This gives us the alienated surplus of every single listener, which corresponds to €3.79 per person for an entire year of listening. If we apply the same theory to Facebook's earnings, we obtain similar results: if Facebook made a profit of $355 million in 2010 (according to its own figures[5]), when the active users were around 500 million, this would mean that each Facebook user was a 'victim of exploitation of surplus value' to the extent of $0.70 a year. Gauntlett (2011) has made the same calculation for YouTube videos, showing that each video uploaded by users is worth approximately $1.20.

Smythe's (1978) argument—that audience 'work' can be seen as being exploited in terms of the Marxian labour theory of value—was already controversial at the time of its publication (Hesmondhalgh 2010). This argument by Smythe and his 'sons,' such as Fuchs, has been criticised for two main reasons: (1) what they call audience 'work' cannot simply be called work, because it lacks coercion and (2) their approach doesn't take into account the pleasures of participation (Hesmondhalgh 2010).

Similarly, Arvidsson and Colleoni (2012) claimed that making the simple observation that just because media companies like Facebook or branded corporations like Apple live off audience and consumer co-production does not necessarily mean that the value of such co-production can be estimated in terms of the Marxian labour theory of value. They argue, in response to Fuchs (2010), that the labour theory of value does not apply to the activity of online prosumers, because "the value of online advertising is not primarily dependent on the number of users that a site can attract" or on the "time spent [in] online viewing or interacting with a particular site." Instead, "value is ever more defined according to the ability to mobilize affective attention and engagement" (Arvidsson and Colleoni 2012, 144; see also chapter 13). Jenkins et al. (2013, 116) claim that television (and radio too) is shifting from an attention economy that they call an "appointment based model" towards an "engagement based paradigm."

Banks and Humphreys (2008) and Banks and Deuze (2009) claimed that users clearly enjoy and benefit from online activities, even if they generate value for commercial media companies. They suggest that user-generated content should be understood in terms of mutual benefit (identity and reputational benefits) rather than of exploitation.

The idea that listener participation in radio's valuable production (in terms of both attention and actions performed on the social media linked to the radio) can be a source of exploitation is a useful point of view in order to defuse the rhetoric of participation and user-generated content, which new and old commercial media have appropriated. Even so, this work supports the view that the new wave of Marxist criticism of the exploitation of content generated by networked publics, in both traditional and digital media, is unable to comprehend the real value of this participation.

As Jenkins et al. (2013, 58) noted: "We feel it's crucial to acknowledge the concerns of corporate exploitation of fan labor while still believing that the emerging system places greater power in the hands of the audience when compared to the older broadcast paradigm."

We believe that many different distinctions can be found between these two extremes of exploitation and co-creation. The AIP model has been proposed by Carpentier (2007, 2011) for the analysis of the public's participation in the production of media (especially radio) content, which this work finds to be highly capable of considering such distinctions. Carpentier (2011, 24) claims that:

> The key defining element of participation is power. The debates on participation in institutionalized politics and in all other societal fields, including media participation, have a lot in common in that they all focus on the distribution of power within society at both the macro-and micro-level. The balance between people's inclusion in the implicit and explicit decision-making processes within these fields, and their exclusion through the delegation of power (again, implicit or explicit), is central to discussions on participation in all fields.

Participation is not the same as access or interaction: replying to a radio host's call for action with an SMS is a matter of interaction, not participation; liking, commenting, sharing or retweeting a message published by a radio host on his/her social network doesn't mean participating, but 'only' engaging with radio content. Participation, according to Carpentier (2011, 68), "deals with participation in the production of media output (content-related participation) and in media organisational decision-making (structural participation)." Carpentier asserts that we can only truly call it participation if the listeners are recognised as holding a certain amount of power in the decisions over what content should be broadcast, or even in the broadcaster's editorial and business choices. Even in this case, no single model for participation exists, but there are different forms and degrees. Audience participation is organised in many different forms by media institutions.

Carpentier's model is invaluable for clearly defining the theoretical differences between access, interaction and participation, but the complexity of the participative and cooperative processes generated by the compounding of old and new media in today's context requires a model that is even more complex. One model for the analysis of the forms of networked publics' participation, which complements Carpentier's considerations and goes into even greater detail, is that proposed by Hyde et al. (2010). According to the authors, in order to collaborate, participants must be aware of the fact that they are part of a collaborative project, and they must share its goals. If there is no intentionality, there is no collaboration. This first statement allows us to better respond to criticism coming from the free labour theorists. The aggregation of content produced by others (often unknown to them), which we may read as exploitation, is one thing; passionate and aware participation is another. There is a difference between the free appropriation of user-generated content performed by big newspaper editors (i.e., users' photographs of a particular news event taken from Instagram), which may even occur without the creator knowing anything about it, and the participation of passionate listeners in a radio programme by telephone and through social media.

Hyde et al. (2010) have proposed a series of eleven criteria in order to evaluate the quality of participation, which may be summarised as follows:

Questions of Intention

Must the participant actively intend to contribute?

Questions of Goals

Is participation motivated by the pursuit of goals shared with other participants or individual interests?

Questions of (Self) Governance

Are the structures and rules of engagement accessible? Can they be contested and renegotiated?

Questions of Property

How is control or ownership organised over the outputs? Who is included/excluded in the division of benefits?

Questions of Knowledge Transfer

Does the collaboration result in knowledge transfer between participants? Is it similar to a community of practice?

Questions of Identities

Does the collaboration process strengthen a more unified group identity?

Questions of Scale (size, duration, speed, space, scope)

How big or small is the number of participants? How long is the time frame of collaboration? Does the collaboration take place over a limited or extended geographic scale? How minimal or complex is the most basic contribution?

Questions of Network Topology

How are individuals connected to each other? Are contributions individually connected to each other or are they all coordinated through a unifying bottleneck mechanism? Is the participation-network model centralised or decentralised?

Questions of Accessibility

Can anyone join the collaboration? Is there a vetting process?

Questions of Equality

Are all contributions largely equal in scope? Does a small group of participants generate a far larger portion of the work?

This series of criteria provides a general guide for the qualitative assessment of the cooperative relationship. This work finds these to be excellent criteria for evaluating a co-creational or collaborative project, in either radio or online platforms such as BitTorrent, Slashdot, Wikipedia, Flickr, Vimeo, and open source operating systems, amongst others.

If we adopt the points of view presented by Carpentier (2011) and Hyde et al. (2010), the forms of participation utilised by both traditional and networked listeners can be seen under a new light, equidistant from both the democratising rhetoric of participation and user-generated content and that of the apocalypse of the exploitation of 'work' extracted from the public.

CONCLUSION: THE SOCIAL LIFE OF RADIO CONTENT

In their latest work, *Spreadable Media*, Jenkins et al. (2013) affirm that we are facing a paradigmatic change in the circulation of media texts. A hybrid model of circulation is emerging, a result of the combination of top-down institutional strategies (the media corporations that decide what to produce, when and how to launch a film/album/radio or TV series/bestseller book/event) and grassroots/bottom-up tactics. Control over media-produced content is no longer fully in the hands of the media themselves but is negotiated with the public, the latter being now connected into networks and capable of establishing the popularity or failure of a given content through sharing on its network.

Content produced by the media, and by the radio in particular, has never had such a rich social life. In the past, what one heard on a radio programme could only be discussed with a private circle of friends; today, the opinions of networked listeners generate more noise in the public space of (private) social networks. Audiences are making more 'noise' than ever. One can listen to content produced by radio again and again, with a podcast, by sharing it through Soundcloud, Mixcloud, Audioboo, on one's social network pages or one's own blog; it can circulate without broadcasters being able to control its movements.

In the ecosystem of spreadable media, content is both user generated and user circulated (Jenkins et al. 2013). Networked listeners are becoming more and more productive, and this productivity consists of both the generation of one's own content and the circulation of media content. The simple act of posting a link to a radio programme's podcast on one's personal Facebook page, along with adding a comment that provides a context for listening, is a highly productive act, which requires time, effort and intelligence.

Listeners have become producers on different levels: they produce comments/likes/retweets; they produce stories about radio content that they then share within their own social networks; they reproduce radio content, share podcasts and contribute to their circulation. Listeners produce content that is picked up by radio producers and included in the radio flow, such as SMS texts, posts and comments on Facebook, tweets, and phone calls, but also audio, photo, video and text contributions that allow them to co-produce radio programmes. They also become co-producers of radio programmes by financing their expenses (see chapter 9). Listeners produce feedback that influences the editorial decisions made by radio producers (as in the case of the co-creation of musical playlists; see chapter 10) and produce independent radio and sound content that bypasses radio (amateur podcasters, Spreaker webcasters, Mixcloud and Soundcloud audio content).

If the media companies do not get used to coexisting with this new ecosystem and do not allow it to grow, they risk losing the attention and affect of the networked publics because, as Jenkins et al. (2013) say, if content is not spreadable, it is dead. "Information wants to be free" was a famous slogan by American futurologist Stewart Brand. It is now time to say: "Media content wants to be free." Adaptation to the new media environment is fundamental. English scholar David Hendy (2013b) offers three examples of this adaptation: (1) the degree to which radio is enabling listeners to create their own schedule, (2) the degree to which it is abandoning a proprietorial attitude towards its own programme material and allowing it to be shared and manipulated in ways it doesn't control, and (3) the degree to which it 'crowdsources' by drawing on the creative efforts of 'ordinary' people.

The new intimacy between radio and its public that is emerging with SNSs is reshaping the notion of the public, as well as radio production practices. Whether this new intimacy is potentially liberating and democratic, in the direction indicated by Benjamin (2008) (the 'politicisation of art') or a means toward further exploitation is not only a question linked to the new social network platforms, but one that can also be moulded and managed by human factors. Radio producers and listeners can use radio and SNSs to engage in a fruitful exchange of content and build a more democratic and participative model of communication, or, on the contrary, reproduce the old, hypnotic, Pavlovian broadcast communication based on a master-slave (media/radio/SNS-audience/follower) relationship.

In this ecosystem, the traditional media, including radio, are no longer the sole guardians of knowledge and its circulation: they are immersed in a network and connected to each other and with the public, and they are only—for the moment—hubs for sorting larger quantities of information coming from the other nodes of the network that they belong to. But today's followers could be tomorrow's producers, and the relationships of power between those who produce and those who listen could be reversed, because, as David Gauntlett (2011, 223) asserts, the broadcasting culture of "sit back and be told" is hopefully, potentially, being replaced by a networking culture of "making and doing." Radio has always been a product of two players: the makers—who speak on the microphone—and the receivers—who listen and decode the message—but now listeners have more tools than ever before to act as makers too.

NOTES

1. Interview with Matteo Caccia, author, producer and host of the storytelling radio programme *Voi siete qui* [You Are Here], broadcast daily on Radio24, a national private news/talk Italian radio station. October 24, 2013.
2. Interview with Mark Zuckerberg, broadcast by CBS on May 27, 2010. Accessed March 14, 2014. http://audio.cbsnews.com/2010/05/27/audio6522748.mp3.
3. Rai (2013). *Relazioni e bilanci 2012.* Accessed January 18, 2014. http://www.rai.it/dl/bilancio2012/ita/dwl/pdf/Bilancio_Rai_2012.pdf.
4. Radio Monitor 2012. Accessed May 25, 2014. http://danielelepido.blog.ilsole24ore.com/i-bastioni-di-orione/files/radiomonitor2012.pdf.
5. For data on Facebook's economic performance in 2010, see Guerrera, F. "Facebook Raises Investor Hopes with IPO Hint." *Financial Times,* January 6, 2011. Accessed February 12, 2014.http://www.ft.com/cms/s/2/a2935290–19dc-11e0-b921–00144feab49a.html#azz1ALd5SuI9. Data on Facebook's economic performance varies significantly (not being a publicly traded company, Facebook has no obligation to publicise details of its accounts). Profit estimates for 2009 have varied between tens of millions and $200 million. The figure of $355 million comes from Facebook's own promotional documentation supporting its $2 billion investment round, so it is likely to be exaggerated.

REFERENCES

Abercrombie, N. and Longhurst, B. (1998). *Audiences: A Sociological Theory of Performance and Imagination.* London: Sage.
Abildgaard, M. S. (2014, forthcoming). "Sometimes I Think It Is Hell to Be a Girl: A Longitudinal Study of the Rise of Confessional Radio." *Media, Culture & Society.*
Anderson, B. (1993). *Imagined Communities.* London: Verso.
Andrejevic, M. (2008). "Watching Television without Pity. The Productivity of Online Fans." *Television & New Media,* 9(1), 24–46.
———. (2013). "Estranged Free Labor." In Scholz, T. (ed.), *Digital Labor. The Internet as Playground and Factory.* New York: Routledge, 149–164.
Arnheim, R. (1972). *Radio: An Art of Sound.* New York: Da Capo Press.
Arvidsson, A. (2011). "General Sentiment: How Value and Affect Converge in the Information Economy." *The Sociological Review,* 59(2), 39–59.
———. (2013). "The Potential of Consumer Publics." *Ephemera: Theory & Politics in Organization,* 13(2), 367–391.
Arvidsson, A. and Colleoni, E. (2012). "Value in Informational Capitalism and on the Internet." *The Information Society,* 28(3), 135–150.
Banks, J. and Humphreys, S. (2008). "The Labour of User Co-Creators Emergent Social Network Markets?" *Convergence: The International Journal of Research into New Media Technologies,* 14(4), 401–418.
Banks, J. and Deuze, M. (2009). "Co-creative Labour." *International Journal of Cultural Studies,* 12(5), 419–431.
Barbrook, R. (2007). *Imaginary Futures.* London: Pluto Press.
Baudouin, P. (2009). *Au microphone: Dr. Walter Benjamin. Walter Benjamin et la création radiophonique 1929–1933.* Paris: Editions de la Maison des sciences de l'homme.
Benjamin, W. (1978). *The Author as Producer.* New York: Schocken.
———. (1999a). "Reflections on Radio." In Jennings, M. W., Eiland, H. and Smith, G. (eds.), *Walter Benjamin: Selected Writings,* 2 (Part 2). Cambridge, MA: Harvard University Press, 543–544.

———. (1999b). "Two Types of Popularity." In Jennings, M. W., Eiland, H. and Smith, G. (eds.), *Walter Benjamin: Selected Writings*, 2 (Part 2). Cambridge, MA: Harvard University Press, 768–782.

———. (2008). *The Work of Art in the Age of Mechanical Reproduction*. London: Penguin.

Blue, H. (2002). *Words at War: World War II Era Radio Drama and the Postwar Broadcasting Industry Blacklist*. Lanham: Scarecrow Press.

Bonini, T. (2006). *La Radio nella rete. Storia, estetica, usi sociali*. Milan: Costa & Nolan.

———. (2009). "Revolution Will Not Be Televised. Il 68 in radio da Parigi a Città del Messico." In Casilio, S. and Guerrieri, L. (eds.), *Il '68 diffuso*. Bologna: Clueb, 51–72.

Bourdieu, P. and Wacquant, L. (1992). *An Invitation to Reflexive Sociology*. Chicago: University of Chicago Press.

Boyd, D. (2011). "Social Network Sites as Networked Publics: Affordances, Dynamics, and Implications." In Papacharissi, Z. (ed.), *A Networked Self. Identity, Community, and Culture on Social Network Sites*. London: Routledge, 39–58.

Boyd, D. and Ellison, N. (2007). "Social Network Sites: Definition, History, and Scholarship." *Journal of Computer-Mediated Communication*, 13(11), 210–230.

Bruns, A. (2008). *Blogs, Wikipedia, Second Life and Beyond: From Production to Produsage*. New York: Peter Lang.

Bunting, M. and Lipski, R. (2000). "Drowned Out? Rethinking Corporate Reputation Management for the Internet." *Journal of Communication Management*, 5(2), 170–178.

Cantril, H. (1940). *The Invasion from Mars*. Princeton: Princeton University Press.

Carpentier, N. (2007). "Participation and Interactivity: Changing Perspectives. The Construction of an Integrated Model on Access, Interaction and Participation." In Nightingale, V. and Dwyer, T. (eds.), *New Media Worlds. Challenges for Convergence*. Melbourne: Oxford University Press, 214–230.

———. (2011). *Media and Participation. A Site of Ideological-Democratic Struggle*. Bristol: Intellect.

Castells, M. (1996). *The Rise of the Network Society, the Information Age: Economy, Society and Culture*, Vol. I. Malden: Blackwell Publishers.

Crawford, K. (2009). "Following You: Disciplines of Listening in Social Media." *Continuum: Journal of Media & Cultural Studies*, 23(4), 525–535.

Dearman, P. and Galloway, C. (2005). "Putting Podcasting into Perspective." In Healy, S., Berryman, B. and Goodman, D. (eds.), *Radio in the World: 2005 Melbourne Radio Conference*. Melbourne: RMIT University Press, 535–546.

Donath, J. and Boyd, D. (2004). "Public Displays of Connection." *BT Technology Journal*, 22(4), 71–82.

Douglas, S. J. (2004). *Listening In. Radio and the American Imagination*. Minneapolis: University of Minnesota Press.

Downing, J. (1984). *Radical Media: The Political Experience of Alternative Communications*. Boston: South End Press.

Edmond, M. (2014). "All Platforms Considered: Contemporary Radio and Transmedia Engagement." *New Media & Society*. Accessed October 6, 2014. http://nms.sagepub.com/content/early/2014/04/06/1461444814530245.abstract.

Ellison, N., Lampe, C., Steinfield, C. and Vitak, J. (2011). "With a Little Help from My Friends: How Social Network Sites Affect Social Capital Processes." In Papacharissi, Z. (ed.), *A Networked Self. Identity, Community, and Culture on Social Network Sites*. London: Routledge, 124–145.

Ellison, N., Steinfield, C. and Lampe, C. (2007). "The Benefits of Facebook 'Friends': Social Capital and College Students' Use of Online Social Network Sites." *Journal of Computer-Mediated Communication*, 12(4), 1143–1168.

———. (2011). "Connection Strategies: Social Capital Implications of Facebook-Enabled Communication Practices." *New Media & Society*, 13(6), 873–892.

Eno, B. (1991). "Review of Jay David Bolter's Writing Space." *Artforum International*, 30(11), 13–14.

Enzensberger, H. M. (1970). "Constituents of a Theory of the Media." *New Left Review*, 64, 13–36.

Ferrentino, G., Gattuso, L. and Bonini, T. (eds.). (2006). *Vedi alla voce Radio Popolare*. Milan: Garzanti.

Fuchs, C. (2010). "Labor in Informational Capitalism and on the Internet." *The Information Society*, 26(3), 179–196.

———. (2013). "Class and Exploitation on the Internet." In Scholz, T. (ed.), *Digital Labor. The Internet as Playground and Factory*. New York: Routledge, 211–224.

———. (2014). *Social Media. A Critical Introduction*. London: Sage.

Gauntlett, D. (2011). *Making Is Connecting*. Cambridge: Polity Press.

Goffman, E. (1959). *The Presentation of Self in Everyday Life*. New York: Anchor.

Granovetter, M. (1973). "The Strength of Weak Ties." *American Journal of Sociology*, 78(6), 1360–1380.

Guattari, F. (1978). "Les radios libres populaires." *La Nouvelle Critique*, 115(296), 77–79.

———. (1979). *La revolution moleculaire*. Paris: Editions Recherches.

Gurak, L. J. (2001). *Cyberliteracy: Navigating the Internet with Awareness*. New Haven: Yale University Press.

Hendy, D. (2000). *Radio in the Global Age*. Cambridge: Polity Press.

———. (2013a). "The Undercoat of Life—Listening to Radio." In Carlyle, A. and Lane, C. (eds.), *On Listening*. Devon: Uniformbooks, 122–124.

———. (2013b). *Public Service Broadcasting*. Houndmills: Palgrave Macmillan.

Hesmondhalgh, D. (2010). "User-Generated Content, Free Labor and the Cultural Industries." *Ephemera: Theory & Politics in Organization*, 10(3–4), 267–284.

Hilmes, M. (1997). *Radio Voices: American Broadcasting 1922–1952*. Minneapolis: University of Minnesota Press.

Hockaday, M. (2012). "BBC News: Why Good Journalism Matters in the Digital Age." Talk at the London School of Economics, London, October 9.

Hyde, A., Kanarinka, Linksvayer, M., Mandiberg, M., Peirano, M., Tarka, S., Taylor, A., Toner, A. and Zer-Aviv, M. (2010). *Collaborative Futures*. New York: Lowercase Press.

Jenkins, H. (2004). "The Cultural Logic of Media Convergence." *International Journal of Cultural Studies*, 7(1), 33–43.

———. (2006). *Convergence Culture: Where Old and New Media Collide*. New York: New York University Press.

Jenkins, H., Ford, S. and Green, J. (2013). *Spreadable Media. Creating Value and Meaning in a Networked Culture*. New York: New York University Press.

Johns, A. (2009). *Piracy: The Intellectual Property Wars from Gutenberg to Gates*. Chicago: University of Chicago Press.

Kaprow, A. (1996)."Untitled Guidelines for Happenings." In Stiles, K. and Selz, P. (eds.), *Theories and Documents of Contemporary Art. A Sourcebook of Artists' Writings*. Berkeley: University of California Press, 709–714.

Katz, E. (1950). "The Happiness Game: A Content Analysis of Radio Fan Mail." Master's thesis, Columbia University, New York, NY.

Kelty, C. (2008). *Two Bits: The Cultural Significance of Free Software*. Durham: Duke University Press.

Kogawa, T. (1992). "Toward Polymorphous Radio." *Translocal.jp*. Accessed January 27, 2014. http://anarchy.translocal.jp/non-japanese/radiorethink.html.

Kozinets, R. (2010). *Netnography. Doing Etnographic Research Online*. London: Sage.

Illich, I. (1973). *Tools for Conviviality*. London: Calder and Boyars.

Ippolita, Lovink, G. and Rossiter, N. (2009). "The Digital Given: 10 Web 2.0 Theses." *Fibre-culture*, 14. Accessed December 14, 2013. http://fourteen.fibreculture-journal.org/fcj-096-the-digital-given-10-web-2-0-theses/.

Ito, M. (2008). "Introduction." In Varnelis, K. (ed.), *Networked Publics*. Cambridge, MA: MIT Press, 1–14.

Lacey, K. (2013). *Listening Publics: The Politics and Experience of Listening in the Media Age*. Cambridge: Polity Press.

Lewis, P. M. and Booth, J. (1990). *The Invisible Medium: Public, Commercial and Community Radio*. Washington DC: Howard University Press.

Livingstone, S. (2003). "The Changing Nature of Audiences: From the Mass Audience to the Interactive Media User." In Valdivia, A. (ed.), *The Blackwell Companion to Media Research*. Oxford: Blackwell, 337–359.

———. (2005). "On the Relation between Audiences and Publics." In Livingstone, S. (ed.), *Audiences and Publics: When Cultural Engagement Matters for the Public Sphere*. London: Intellect, 17–43.

MacBride, S. (1984). *Many Voices, One World: Communication and Society, Today and Tomorrow: The MacBride Report*. New York: Unesco.

Malatini, G. (1981). *Cinquant'anni di teatro radiofonico in Italia. 1929–1979*. Turin: RAI-ERI.

Mann, S., Nolan, J. and Wellman, B. (2003). "Sousveillance." *Surveillance and Society*, 1(3), 331–355.

Marshall, S. (2013). "Ten Social Media Lessons from Swedish Radio." *BBC Journalism College*. December 4. Accessed March 4, 2014. http://www.journalism.co.uk/news/10-social-media-lessons-from-swedish-radio/s2/a555306/.

Marwick, A. (2013). *Status Update: Celebrity, Publicity and Branding in the Social Media Age*. New Haven: Yale University Press.

Murdock, G. (1978). "Blindspots about Western Marxism: A Reply to Dallas Smythe." *Canadian Journal of Political and Social Theory/Revue Canadienne de Theorie Politique et Sociale*, 2(2), 109–119.

Navas, E. (2005). "The Blogger as Producer." *Netart Review*. Accessed November 14, 2013. http://www.netartreview.net/monthly/0305.3.html.

Papacharissi, Z. (2010). *A Private Sphere: Democracy in a Digital Age*. Cambridge: Polity Press.

Pinseler, J. (2008). "The Politics of Talk on German Free Radio Stations." *Westminster Papers in Communication and Culture*, 5(1), 67–85.

Putnam, R. (2000). *Bowling Alone*. New York: Simon & Schuster.

Rainie, L. and Wellman, B. (2012). *Networked: The New Social Operating System*. Cambridge, MA: MIT Press.

Razlogova, E. (2011). *The Listener's Voice. Early Radio and the American Public*. Philadelphia: University of Pennsylvania Press.

Resnick, P. (2001). "Beyond Bowling Together: Sociotechnical Capital." In Carrol, J. (ed.), *Human-Computer Interaction in the New Millennium*. Boston: Addison-Wesley, 247–272.

Reynolds, S. (2011). *Retromania: Pop Culture's Addiction to Its Own Past*. New York: Faber.

Rosen, J. (2008). "Afterword: The People Formerly Known as the Audience." In Carpentier, N. and De Cleen, B. (eds.), *Participation and Media Production. Critical Reflections on Content Creation*. Cambridge: Cambridge Scholars Publishing, 163–165.

Rossano, A. (2013). "Wolfgang Blau: 'Il giornalismo sarà dominato da poche testate globali.'" *L'Espresso*, November 11, 67.

Rushkoff, D. (2000). "Second Sight. The Internet Is Not Killing Off Conversation but Actively Encouraging It." *The Guardian*, June 28. Accessed January 22, 2014. http://www.theguardian.com/technology/2000/jun/29/onlinesupplement13.

Sartre, J-P. (1990). *Critique of Dialetical Reason*. London: Verso.

Sayre, J. (1939). "Progress in Radio Fan-Mail Analysis." *Public Opinion Quarterly*, 3(2), 272–278.

Shirky, C. (2005). "Institutions vs. Collaboration." Talk at TED Global 2005, Oxford, July 14. Accessed February 17, 2014. http://www.ted.com/talks/clay_shirky_on_institutions_versus_collaboration.html.

Smith, M., Rainie, L., Shneiderman, B. and Himelboim, I. (2014). "Mapping Twitter Topic Networks: From Polarized Crowds to Community Clusters." *Pew Research Internet Project*, February 20. Accessed March 26, 2014. http://www.pewinternet.org/2014/02/20/mapping-twitter-topic-networks-from-polarized-crowds-to-community-clusters/.

Smythe, D. (1978). "On the Audience Commodity and Its Work." In Duham, M. G. and Kellner, D. (eds.), *Media and Cultural Studies: Key Works*. Oxford: Blackwell, 253–279.

Stribling, E. B. (2013). "Valuing Fans." In Jenkins, H., Ford, S. and Green, J. (eds.), *Spreadablemedia.org*. Accessed April 14, 2014. http://spreadablemedia.org/essays/stribling/#.UpuFPo0WlP4.

Sullerot, E. (1968). "Transistors et barricade." In Labro, P. and Manceaux, M. (eds.), *Ce n'est qu'un debut*. Paris: Maspero, 124–139.

Syvertsen, T. (1999). "The Many Uses of the 'Public Service' Concept." *Nordicom Review*, 1(99), 5–12.

Terranova, T. (2000). "Free Labor: Producing Culture for the Digital Economy." *Social Text*, 63(18), 33–57.

van Dijck, J. (1999). *Network Society: Social Aspects of New Media*. London: Sage.

———. (2012). "Facebook as a Tool for Producing Sociality and Connectivity." *Television & New Media*, 13(2), 160–176.

———. (2013). *The Culture of Connectivity. A Critical History of Social Media*. Oxford: Oxford University Press.

Varnelis, K. (ed.). (2008). *Networked Publics*. Cambridge, MA: MIT Press.

Wellman, B. (2001). "Physical Place and Cyber-Place: Changing Portals and the Rise of Networked Individualism." *International Journal for Urban and Regional Research* 25(2), 227–252.

Part I

Interactive Publics (Telephone, Short Message Service, Social Networks)

1   When Speech Was 'Meaningful' and Presenters Were Just a Phone Call Away

The Development of Popular Radio Talk Formats in Early UK Commercial Radio

Guy Starkey

INTRODUCTION: FROM BRECHTIAN 'PIPES' TO TELEPHONE LINES

> . . . radio is one-sided when it should be two. It is purely an apparatus for distribution, for mere sharing out. So here is a positive suggestion: change this apparatus over from distribution to communication. The radio would be the finest possible communication apparatus in public life, a vast network of pipes. That is to say, it would be if it knew how to receive as well as to transmit, how to let the listener speak as well as hear, how to bring him into a relationship instead of isolating him. On this principle the radio should step out of the supply business and organise its listeners as suppliers.
>
> (Bertolt Brecht 1932, reprinted in Brecht 1967, 129–130)

The understandable preoccupation today, of media academics and practitioners alike, with relatively recent developments in social media provision and use, is based not only on the steadily increasing popularity of such platforms, but also on their implications for democratic and constrained societies across the developed and developing world. It is entirely reasonable to focus attention on such elements of the social networking phenomenon as Facebook and Twitter because they have, through the levels of public participation in them, demonstrated considerable impact as artefacts implicated in the associated processes of mediatisation and communication, just as much as once did the older media of print, film, radio and television when they were new. However, some academic discourse is so preoccupied with new phenomena that it tends to discount—or at least to ignore—older media, as if they were no longer relevant. Neither this book in general, nor this chapter in particular would wish to intentionally or inadvertently do the opposite. That is, to discount the still relatively 'new' in favour of an unfashionable preoccupation with the 'old'—or, perhaps more appropriately, 'established'—media. Nonetheless, there is considerable merit in academic study in a less myopic approach than one which recognises only innovation while paying scant regard to its precursors and competitors. So, we propose here to provide some greater depth of perspective in considering some origins of contemporary social networking which are to be found in historical accounts of popular talk radio formats in a particular national context.

The early Brechtian perspective above on what today might be labelled 'user-generated content' reveals considerable foresight on the part of the influential German playwright in suggesting in the 1930s that what was missing from broadcast—as opposed to 'two-way'—radio was an ability to be a medium of interactive and even peer-to-peer communication. Brecht could hardly have known that, decades later, his partially formed vision would be realised and that far from remaining merely a medium of 'distribution,' radio would become a medium of what he perceived to be a more desirable form of 'communication.' That would require listeners to become 'suppliers'—or contributors—and thus find a voice that could be heard as well as those of the broadcasters. In essence, such notions of progress in communication technology over time as were articulated by McLuhan (2001) identified the potential for individual voices to be heard around a shrinking 'global village.' Nonetheless, that newfound voice brought with it some potential for a form of participation in the wider discourse often characterised, in the term used by Habermas (1989), as taking place in the 'public sphere.' That participation bore all the characteristics of the much newer model of collaborative media production identified by Carpentier (2011) as AIP—access, interaction, participation—because of the synergies present during the period among the technology, content, people and organisations involved. However, this transformation was not immediate. It happened at different times in different countries and, inevitably, in different ways. Nevertheless, although Brecht was writing specifically about radio, his notion of listeners—that is, audiences—as being able to express themselves in a connected media environment was not far removed from some of the new platforms upon which user-generated content is communicated today, and upon which is now focused so much contemporary academic attention. For a 'network of pipes,' we can easily substitute the network of cables and interconnections that now constitutes the Internet.

THE PRECURSOR ROLE OF UK INTERACTIVE SPEECH RADIO

This chapter sets out to examine, by way of example, the development of local talk radio broadcasting in one particular national context, the commercially funded private sector in the United Kingdom. Here, the catalyst for this transformation of an otherwise distributive medium was very heavy-handed content regulation, in an age when commercial radio was relatively new in the UK and presented a significant challenge to the established media, including local newspapers and even the BBC. Interestingly, the role of interactive speech radio as a precursor to some of the newer media platforms of today is even recognised by some practitioners. In October 2013, at the annual gathering of mainly radio professionals at Salford Quays in Greater Manchester for the event organised by the Radio Academy and known as the Radio Festival, a constant refrain was the notion that radio might have been the earliest electronic form of social networking. This assertion was not made and repeated several times frivolously. Even among those present in order to engage in forms of necessarily intermittent contemplation of the current state of their industry and its prospects for the future, the idea was one that rapidly gained currency. In comparing widespread use of the phone-in in radio broadcasting in the 1970s to modern-day social networking, several speakers unwittingly related the phone-in to the 1930s Brechtian vision of radio for communication rather than just distribution.

Just as media develop over time, so does academic theory, and we can also observe in radio phone-ins some characteristics of Carpentier's model of participation (2011) they share with some of the popular new media interactivity of today. If, momentarily freed from the time constraints of daily industrial routine to reflect in quasi-academic ways on their own practices, both past and present, our practitioner colleagues are able to draw comparisons between these two superficially radically diverse paradigms, then surely we in academia should also be able to explore such a discourse, however tentative. Therefore, we intend to explore here this example of a radio market upon which tight content regulation and draconian copyright agreements imposed on broadcasters an urgent need to develop popular radio speech formats that worked in commercial terms, drawing large audiences to new radio services and enhancing the potential for commercial revenues they brought with them.

THE ARRIVAL OF COMMERCIAL RADIO IN THE UK

Privately owned commercial radio finally arrived on the UK mainland in 1973—as is documented in detail elsewhere, such as by Crisell (1994, 1997), Stoller (2010), and Street (2002). We must immediately draw a distinction between this sector, which was then called Independent Local Radio (ILR), and its predecessors on the European continent (including the English-language service of Radio Luxembourg, which began in 1933), on the high seas outside British territorial waters (including Radio Caroline from 1964) and on the Isle of Man (Manx Radio, also from 1964). The monopoly of licensed, mainland wireless broadcasting which the BBC had enjoyed from its incorporation in 1927 only began to widely appear anachronistic in the 1960s, with the arrival of up to a dozen radio stations on ships at anchor and on abandoned military forts around the coastline of the British Isles (Skues 2009). Legislation which in 1967 all but outlawed those stations and made broadcasting from ships and fixed structures offshore very difficult was accompanied by a commitment to introduce local radio run by the BBC. Then, a change of government and an election manifesto promise (Conservative Party 1970) led to the introduction of advertising-funded, privately owned local radio in 1973 (Starkey 2011). Much of the chequered history of ILR is chronicled in detail by Stoller (2010), who became a regulator of the commercial sector, but our interest focuses upon its early years, when it had been conceived on the one hand as an opportunity for private capital to make profits from radio broadcasting, but also as a second provider of public service broadcasting (PSB). This initial split personality of a radio station with a commercial resource base and a public service imperative, although now almost entirely abandoned, was imposed upon the sector in the 1970s for largely political reasons (Stoller 2010).

The worst fears of those who opposed the initiative on political or cultural grounds were that the new stations would broadcast little other than popular music in order to maximise their listening figures and, hence, profits, while denying the BBC's more expensively produced programming of large enough audiences to justify the continuation of its public funding, a concern which persists today (O'Malley 1983). A strong licensing and regulatory burden upon the new ILR companies to include substantial amounts of content that might reasonably be deemed as providing a *public service* not unlike that offered by the BBC, it was argued, was a compromise that should meet the concerns of the sceptics that the introduction of ILR might become a 'licence to print money.'

Also present at this difficult birth, and similarly not without hostile intent, was a coalition of interests in the music industry, among them copyright bodies and the musicians' union, which quite reasonably feared that more—and more popular—music radio might adversely affect the income of songwriters, performers and record labels. The result was that stations were allowed to broadcast only a maximum of nine hours of commercially available recorded music in a nineteen-hour broadcasting day (Stoller 2010). Some of them, such as 194 Radio City in Liverpool, began broadcasting 24 hours a day, stretching the same allocation of 'needletime' even farther (Barham 2006). The rest of the time would have to be filled with other forms of content, including news, interviews, commercials, competitions, drama and 'non-needletime' specially recorded music that would generate employment for musicians. While certain specified levels of news output were a regulatory requirement, both drama and bespoke music were relatively expensive forms to produce and so there was little appetite among programme controllers for spending initially scarce advertising revenue on them in the challenging economic climate of the mid-1970s. This was a period in which several stations had struggled even to raise the initial capital to finance their launch (Baron 1975).

As a further compromise to the sceptics, another early regulatory requirement was that each station should broadcast at least minimum amounts of 'meaningful' speech, as opposed to what was at the time often pejoratively labelled 'prattle.' So, initially one frequent outcome of the awarding of an ILR licence to an applicant competing in a 'beauty contest'-style selection process was a programme schedule offering to produce the most appropriate and appealing speech that could essentially be described as meaningful while remaining attractive enough to large numbers of listeners for the station to be commercially viable. Once on air, most radio stations in the fledgling network were committed—initially, at least—to honouring the promises made in their licence applications. At that time even minor changes to the schedules, such as reshuffling presenters around the various programmes, had to be approved by the regulator, the Independent Broadcasting Authority (IBA), so a weakening of the commitment to public service content in general and meaningful speech in particular was out of the question. This, and the scarcity of needletime, meant long broadcasting hours had to be filled with speech—but cheaply and without scaring away audiences through being too worthy. In essence, during this period both the right people and the right organisational structures were in place to promote unknowing early conformity with the AIP model of collaborative media content production latterly identified by Carpentier (2011).

LISTEN TO WHO'S TALKING: THE PHONE-IN AND THE OUTSIDE BROADCAST

The public service imperative placed upon the stations by the initial political wrangling and the compromise of tight content regulation meant that a certain piece of technology—the phone—was to be central to early ILR programme schedules at certain times of the day and night. The role of the IBA included approving studio equipment before it could be used on air, and because their technical provision had to meet very high standards in order for them to be allowed by the IBA to begin broadcasting, most of the new ILR stations had telephone-balancing units (TBUs) already installed before they launched, enabling the easy use of the telephone in programming. One use for this equipment was for phoning out from the studio, to conduct an interview for example, but because it was common to have as many as ten lines or more, the primary purpose of the TBU was to allow listeners to phone *in*. In practice, the sound quality would be only as good as the ordinary telephone line and the caller's telephone handset allowed—that is, seldom as good as that from a studio microphone, but usually tolerable, at least for limited periods (Starkey 2013). In Brechtian terms, this interface between the studio sound mixing desk and a number of lines on the public telephone system was the very 'network of pipes' that would empower listeners by letting them 'speak as well as hear,' enter into a relationship with the radio station instead of remaining isolated and become organised as 'suppliers' of radio content (Brecht 1932).

Most early ILR stations embraced the technology enthusiastically, and even though the phone-in was already an established format in several other countries, because the BBC had used it only very rarely, to UK commercial radio's new and growing audiences it had considerable "novelty value" (Fleming 2002, 137). Using the academic discourse of today, as a media platform, radio suddenly became more interactive than had been allowed by the traditional means of inviting listener contributions to programming, via the overland postal service, the Royal Mail. Consequently, this relatively innovative technology can now be identified as having then had the potential to be firmly situated within Carpentier's (2011) AIP model as the technology to which he was referring as a necessary component for user participation, just as there are similarities and differences between the broadcast radio content we are about to discuss and the online 'user-generated content' of today which forms the focus of so much contemporary academic analysis. The content that was thus user-generated also bore considerable similarity to that which can dominate social networking today, because in the 1970s the inevitable commercial requirement to make money meant that phone-ins on ILR stations were rarely highbrow in nature, and they were often preoccupied with trivia.

Phone-in Genre: Calls between Music

Often the phone would be used as a form of padding between songs in a music sequence, perhaps for a competition in which listeners had to identify a mystery noise or a record played backwards, or simply to exchange greetings or request a particular song. The simple act of talking to a listener between songs enabled the presenter—and so, the radio station—to be heard connecting with a near neighbour, who in some ways was a representative by proxy of many others hearing the conversation. The phenomenon of local radio was so new to many people—the first wave of BBC local radio stations having made relatively little impact on the listening figures for the national networks operated by the corporation, which compared to the remoteness of national network radio to most communities—that the new ILR stations seemed to connect in almost astonishing ways with local people. Merely naming the town or locality from where the caller was speaking to the presenter, then, was a form of identification with audiences in that place or nearby. When the caller had a local or regional accent or used local idiosyncrasies of expression, such as traditional words or phrases from the area, the act of identification was reinforced.

The dialogue was also interactive, in that the conversation was real and happening in real time (unless a profanity delay system meant that, imperceptibly, a few seconds separated the studio output from the transmitted signal) but it was normally limited in scale to two people. This does of course contrast very noticeably with the multiple conversations that occur through social media today, in which the number of contributors is potentially unlimited, and we shall enter a number of other caveats to the premise later. However, it is worth noting at this point that the mainly text-based forms of social interaction offered by such platforms as Facebook and Twitter today clearly lack the real-time interaction of a telephone conversation heard by many, the paralinguistic potential of the spoken word to convey additional meaning which cannot even be rendered faithfully by skilful use of a bank of emoticons and the spontaneity of a discourse which is unfiltered by the dependence of most social media upon keyboard usage for it to be articulated.

In this way, a competition conducted over the phone during a music sequence programme provided the radio station with a number of benefits. The speech was, in the regulator's terms, undeniably meaningful—it was not mere chatter because it was a discourse with a purpose, be it to pose and later reveal the answer to a question or to allow a 'win or lose' narrative to unfold for listeners' entertainment. The conversation allowed listeners to hear other people from an identified neighbouring locality—that is, to hear someone arguably not dissimilar to themselves—and to relate to that person. Furthermore, the time spent on the conversation delayed the playing of the next song, and so saved some needletime for later in the programme, thus spreading its sparse allocation more thinly over the hours of broadcasting.

Callers, especially when call-screening before going live identified those with the greatest potential for this, often provided presenters with opportunities to reinforce and extend their on-air personalities, providing source material—that is, user-generated content—to exploit through an exchange with the caller of witty banter. An example of this was on Piccadilly Radio in Manchester, where one presenter, Phil Wood, would ask female competition winners for the size of their 'bumps,' instead of asking what size T-shirt they wanted as their prize. Furthermore, the element of interactivity inherent in the two-way discourse between presenter and listener (albeit enjoyed at any one time by only one member of the audience) could at that time be characterised as an act of enfranchisement or empowerment of the audience as part of a local community being supported by an ILR station which is firmly rooted in that community (Stoller 2010). Inevitably, though, this was normally an interaction which was light and entertaining and more likely to engage listeners than to cause them to turn off or tune away. There was of course then, as now, considerable focus on audience ratings as a measure of listenership (Starkey 2004).

Phone-in Genre: 'Ask the Expert'

Similarly, in a different subgenre of the phone-in which we might term 'ask the expert,' stations would often programme features in which a studio guest would take comments or questions from callers. In this format, at the instigation of the presenter or the programme producer, listeners shared with each other problems in the garden, the kitchen or even the bedroom, and also benefited from the expert advice of the studio guest. This, and the caller-presenter relationship described above, does position the caller in an inferior position in the dialogue, in stark contrast to the peer-to-peer relationships often found in the discourse of social media today, where quite commonly there is no expert involved in the discourse. By calling in to ask for the solution to a problem, callers to early ILR phone-ins on gardening, for example, were by definition people with problems seeking solutions, and they were put in touch with a studio guest defined as an expert.

This representational divide between participants in the resultant dialogue and the almost inevitably unequal relationship between them created by the practice became more acute when the subject of the phone-in was emotional, health or even sexual problems. For example, in the 1970s agony aunt Anna Raeburn pioneered the late-night relationship and sexual health phone-in on Capital Radio in London. Not only was this considered compelling listening by many, by virtue of the previously taboo subjects it covered, but many listeners felt they could raise with Anna and her studio experts issues that could not be broached with their families, peers or doctors. The programmes also met the other desirable criteria listed above, of being meaningful, entertaining and amply substituting for scarce needletime on an otherwise music-orientated radio station.

Phone-in Genre: Early Form of eBay

Another popular phone-in format was transactional—on several stations it was identified using the name *Tradio*—in which callers would speak to the studio presenter about goods they wished to sell or alternatively wished to acquire. Table 1.1 shows the widespread distribution of this format across different stations in the early ILR network, and the different branding applied to it. The conversation would conclude with the phone number of the caller being given on air, so interested listeners could then call that number to complete the physical transaction verbally, rather like an early form of the auction website eBay.

The kind of item offered for sale varied considerably, but when *Tradio* was scheduled in the daytime, the presence of relatively large numbers of young mothers in the audience, particularly from low-income families, could lead to a predominance of baby and toddler items, such as buggies and toys. Of course, despite the obvious popularity of the transactional phone-in, it also had considerable potential to alienate listeners. Because the items for sale and, often, being sought were necessarily discussed one-by-one, the genre relied upon listeners who were not in need of such an item being sufficiently entertained by the conversation to remain tuned in, rather than tuning to another radio station to find music or speech

Table 1.1 Early ILR stations using the transactional format of phone-in programming in the 1970s and the branding applied

ILR station	Location	Branding
BRMB	Birmingham	*Tradio*
Downtown Radio	Belfast	*Swap Shop*
Plymouth Sound	Plymouth	*Tradio*
Radio City	Liverpool	*Trading Post*
Radio Forth	Edinburgh	*Swap Shop*
Radio Tees	Teesside	*Tradio*
Swansea Sound	Swansea	*Take It Away*

Source: Radio Guide programme listings, 1975.

that was potentially of greater relevance or interest to them. This is quite unlike the modern searchable database that is eBay and its imitators, because they allow individuals to customise their searches without having to trawl through large numbers of items for sale in which they have no interest.

Phone-in Genres: Comments and Opinions. Call the 'Rudest Man on the Radio'

An analysis of early ILR programme schedules reveals widespread programming of phone-in content *between* music sequences (Starkey 2011). Typically, these were opinion programmes, in which listeners' opinions were sought in order to generate meaningful speech on matters of local or national controversy. Often, producers thought that the more controversial the speech was, the better, because—then as now—a good argument on the radio could generate increased listening as listeners told other people in their informal social networks what they had heard, with a recommendation to listen the next day. In order to promote this effect of the audience snowballing in size—one which today would be termed 'going viral'—presenters of such programmes would often use rhetoric and devil's advocacy to provoke callers into more and more heated responses.

On Manchester's Piccadilly Radio, a presenter named James Stannage imported some of the approaches of the 'shock jocks' in the United States, so listeners were invited to tune in to and call 'The rudest man on the radio.' The aim for many such listeners was not only to talk 'on air' with James, but for him to insult them and rudely cut them off without their having been able to have the last word in an argument that was being broadcast almost live to a large audience of listeners in the Greater Manchester area. This went 'viral' as well, as might have been possible in that era when a nationally famous comedian, Jasper Carrott, incorporated into his stand-up routine the anecdote of his having been driving through the area listening to the programme on the car radio and having to stop the car to avoid losing the signal before Stannage's phone-in was finished. Carrott's routine was pressed on vinyl record and played back by his many fans—most of whom would naturally have been outside Greater Manchester—and so Stannage's own fame spread nationally through Carrott's intervention.

This led to a number of imitators, or at least presenters adopting a similar approach to phone-in callers, on other ILR stations in other locations around the UK (Starkey 2013). Many of these discussions concerned celebrities or trivia, which meant they bore even more resemblance to the popular online networking of user-generated content of today. When the subject matter was news and current affairs, or such locally important issues as household refuse collection and the maintenance of municipal graveyards, such programming could be said to more closely resemble the kind of public-sphere discourse envisaged by Habermas. Table 1.2 lists examples of 'built' programmes featuring opinion-based phone-in comment on a number of the first ILR stations to broadcast in the mid-1970s. Inevitably, the representation of matters of

Table 1.2 Examples of early ILR stations featuring built programmes based on comment and opinion, including about current affairs

ILR station	Location	Programme title and scheduling
LBC	London	*Open Line* Monday to Friday 10.00–12.00
LBC	London	*Jellybone* Saturday & Sunday 10.00–12.00 (for children)
Capital Radio	London	*Open Line* Monday to Friday 19.30–21.00
BRMB	Birmingham	*Sunday Edition* Sunday 13.00–14.30
Piccadilly Radio	Manchester	*Piccadilly Line* Monday to Friday 18.00–19.00
Downtown Radio	Belfast	*Dial Downtown* Monday & Thursday 19.00–20.00
Metro Radio	Newcastle	in *The James Whale Show* Monday to Friday 00.00–02.00
Plymouth Sound	Plymouth	*Phone Forum* Monday to Friday 10.00–12.00
Radio City	Liverpool	*Hotline* Monday & Friday 21.00–22.00
Radio Forth	Edinburgh	*Dial Webster* Sundays 11.00–11.30
Radio Trent	Nottingham	*Open Line* Monday-Friday 18.30–19.30
Radio Hallam	Sheffield	*Call-in* Monday-Friday 19.30–20.30
Swansea Sound	Swansea	*Gorseinon 893031* Tuesday to Friday 12–13
Pennine Radio	Bradford	*Phone-in* Monday to Friday 19.00–20.00

Source: *Script* and *Radio Guide* programme listings.

controversy, with all its potential for bias in an environment which was, and remains, regulated over its 'impartiality,' was problematic (Starkey 2007). Other, less trivial subjects included sport, of course, and the football phone-in on radio continues to be popular even now that an ever-lighter regulatory regime since the 1980s, successive changes in broadcasting legislation and far more generous copyright settlements with the UK radio industry by the music licensing bodies have long ceased to favour filling transmission hours with 'meaningful speech.'

To a far lesser extent, during the period some ILR stations combined the need to programme meaningful speech and spread needletime thinly with the marketing and awareness-raising potential of the outside broadcast (OB). Taking a radio programme out of the studio on whatever scale normally involves greater effort and has more demanding resource requirements than broadcasting from the usual studio back at base. The tight budgets of early ILR meant that few stations did this regularly, but one, 194 Radio City in Liverpool, launched with a daily lunchtime OB that took the station to a different location in the editorial area each day (Barham 2006). The technology would have allowed this to be done live, but at far greater expense than the solution adopted by the station. Getting music-quality audio from the location could have been achieved by booking and connecting to bundled telephone lines, but at considerable expense. Instead, the station would record a programme as if it were live and broadcast the recording the next day. This subterfuge remained largely undetected by the radio audience, although it would have been more apparent to anyone present at the recording. Although lacking the liveness of the phone-in, the outside broadcast did nonetheless achieve some of the spontaneity and excitement of the rival OBs mounted by the BBC's national popular music network, Radio 1, which the corporation regularly used as a 'spoiler' to distract local audiences around the country from paying too much attention to their new ILR service as it launched.

Generally, the OB involved frequently allowing members of the audience *in situ* to speak via the presenter's microphone when invited to, again giving a voice through a different kind of Brechtian 'pipe' to individuals who would otherwise lack such a voice in the public sphere. Even some of the smaller ILR stations that launched in the 1980s ran limited series of OBs, often when there was some synergy to exploit with an advertiser or a public event, and often using the cheaper pre-recorded approach to broadcasting on location on a tight budget. Not every OB was done cheaply, though. The launch of a speech-based alternative to the mainstream output of Radio City, City Talk 1548 AM in 1990 led to extensive use of music lines for a series of OBs in locations as varied as Aintree Racecourse and the site of the former Cavern Club, where the Beatles had once performed live (Starkey 2011). Although far less common than the phone-in, this form of broadcasting did conform in many ways to the AIP model of collaborative media production later identified by Carpentier (2011).

CAVEATS: IDENTITY, LINEARITY AND POWER

The premise that some radio programming might effectively have been the earliest electronic form of social networking does require some further critical scrutiny. In claiming that participants in a radio phone-in of the last century of whatever duration were using Brechtian principles to participate in a wide Habermasian-style public-sphere discourse with similarities to modern-day social networking, we must recognise the existence of some potential caveats to that premise.

One of them lies in the nature of identity and, conversely, of anonymity as expressed in the two paradigms. In constructing and moderating phone-in programming, for a variety of reasons it has often been considered prudent to offer callers some element of anonymity. It is not just that the confessional style of Anna Raeburn's emotional and sexual counselling programmes favoured some concealment of a caller's identity for fear of recognition by neighbours, colleagues, family or friends, but in identifying a caller by only a first name, radio stations insulate themselves quite effectively against legal action for defamation. That is, if a caller speaking on air on whatever subject identifies a third party in a pejorative way, it could expose the station to potential legal action. Leaving out the caller's surname effectively blurs the identity of others they might suddenly refer to by association or through a relationship, and the practice can therefore reduce the potential for legal action by someone who feels that he or she has thus been defamed on air.

The citizen with the newfound voice in the public sphere was, then, partially emasculated by this professional practice, whereas in framing their own profiles on a social media platform today, people are free to decide the extent to which they disclose their identity to others, and any legal risks are, apparently, borne by them alone. In addition to the practice of imposing on phone-in callers vague lexical identities such as 'June from Croydon,' radio is of course also constrained in its use of images. In all but the rarest of exceptional circumstances, in the 1970s phone-in just as today, the caller was just a voice, stripped of physical appearance because no pictures were available to the listener. The social networker of today, by contrast, is able to either disclose identity with a clear profile picture or obscure it with an alternative, more anonymous image.

Secondly, it is worth considering the linearity of the use of the phone-in or outside broadcast in putting listeners on air only one-by-one, as opposed to simultaneously in the manner that social media platforms today suggest many-to-many communication. Radio, being a medium that relies on its audiences hearing sound without the simultaneously evolving visual discourse of some screen-based media, can easily become cluttered. That is, without the visual clues of a televised debate, in which multiple cameras at the disposal of the director can *show* its audiences who is speaking, a radio programme can quickly become confusing to listeners if more than one person speaks at a time.

Perhaps a male and a female voice, each with its contrasting pitch, can still be discernible if speaking at the same time on radio, but one or two more voices speaking at the same time quickly become a cacophony, in which nobody's discourse is clear to the listener. For this reason, radio production practice dictates that different contributors' voices are heard in a sequence, in which they take turns in order to be understood (Starkey 2011). Callers taking part in a discussion programme, or individuals clustered around the broadcaster's microphone at an outside broadcast are managed or organised into speaking one at a time, just as those taking part in an on-air competition take turns one after another.

This may on first inspection seem to lack the immediacy and the multiple-user element of interactive social media, engagement with which does not require users to wait for a 'turn.' Instead, they may submit their contributions at will, without there being any moderation from a presenter, producer or call-taker. However, this distinction is largely illusory, because in the way they are perceived by their audiences, the mainly text-based social media platforms do also operate in a linear fashion. Irrespective of the time a message is sent, it will appear on an indisputably linear timeline of responses to an initial post, organised by the software into a sequence of contributions.

This apparently linear conversation often defies a logic of discourse that would normally result from a two-way conversation in real time because it can become corrupted even when there are only two participants because of the time lag imposed by the use of the keyboard to respond to a previous post and delays in data transmission and processing. That is, if a response is still being typed, the original message might change the subject of the conversation before a reply becomes apparent, and a further digression then becomes likely. Twitter presents its users with a constant feed of tweets, giving a similar—often even faster—impression of connectedness, but it, too, organises the user-generated content originated by its many contributors into a rigidly presented linear discourse.

A further caveat to our premise lies within the issue of power, or at least *control* of such discursive content as we have explored in this chapter. Much social networking today, particularly with the development of Web 2.0 platforms that put content creation and aggregation tools at the disposal of the contributor, positions users in a peer-to-peer relationship with others, rather than in the contributor-moderator relationship which characterises most forms of radio phone-ins and outside broadcasting, as we have seen. A social networking platform such as Facebook or Twitter typically intervenes very little in the generation and distribution of content, as the site owners mainly limit themselves to defining the available tools and applying their design and marketing expertise to framing the tools and the content in terms of appearance, style and branding.

It is relatively rare that moderators edit or remove content, or block individual contributors from distributing content. This even means that large amounts of material, including commercially made music, film and video content is placed online by users of a platform without any permission or royalty issues having been settled with the rights holders, as would *bona fide* broadcasters. This is particularly prevalent on YouTube, which provocatively encourages each user to 'broadcast yourself.' Homemade videos and opportunistic mobile-phone grabs aside, many users interpret this as 'broadcasting' their own edits of found material created by others, such as clips from films and television programmes or music videos that they like. Ironically, with the advances in technology that have taken place over forty years, the element of control exercised in the 1970s by the music copyright bodies over the use of found copyright material produced by others has been significantly eroded by custom and practice in the domain of online activity. This has occurred to such an extent that enforcement activity by rights holders or their representatives is limited by the extent of their resources to sporadic firefighting, as breaches of copyright are tackled individually and platforms are forced to block or restrict access to particular content items, rather than having to ensure that their output does not abuse the technology to infringe the rights of others, as the real broadcasters are still obliged to.

More sinister is the ability of contemporary social networking and other peer-to-peer content distribution platforms to harbour malicious users, often anonymously, or simply to unwittingly distribute potentially harmful content that can damage the reputations of individuals, groups and organisations, upset people or even create fear in them of being shunned, harmed or killed. To the often unseen, yet sometimes tragic, instances of children being bullied online must be added from the UK context the higher-profile cases of two members of Parliament and a feminist campaigner receiving anonymous rape threats through Twitter (Morrison 2013). The existence of the Internet 'troll'—partly for the legal and practical reasons of identity discussed above, but also because of commercial considerations and the remaining regulatory requirements on broadcasters—is virtually without parallel in mainstream radio. Content that would arguably be offensive either generally or only to individuals, apart from the self-inflicted verbal rebuke of the shock jocks, had no place on ILR in the 1970s and would be equally incongruous on radio in most territories today. In practical terms, this is because in the radio phone-in, as in the OB, the presenter remains in apparent control by performing a role of effective, real-time moderation over the rest of the content producers, be they telephone callers or interviewees on location. In fact, in the production of a relatively generously resourced radio programme, there might be an unseen producer giving instructions to the presenter over the direction or duration of an on-air conversation and deciding which callers are put through to the presenter—but in organisational terms it remains the broadcaster who is in control at all times, and not the contributor (Starkey 2013).

This dichotomy is of course mainly symptomatic of the different technologies involved, as well as a matter of the kind of organisations involved, both distributive and regulatory. Today's social media platforms deploy information technology hardware that is capable of interacting virtually simultaneously with very large numbers of users at the same time. The radio studio TBU, by contrast, rarely connects with more than a dozen lines at a time, and for the practical and aesthetic reasons identified in our earlier discussion of linearity, it is uncommon for the TBU to be used to enable more than two or three callers to speak at the same time.

It is the sheer volume of users and posts that effectively overwhelms any serious attempt by social networking operators to moderate with any agility of response their online platforms. Furthermore, a profanity delay in the radio studio, if used well, provides a proactive opportunity for the broadcaster to prevent the broadcasting of content it wishes to block, whereas the reporting to a moderator of potentially offensive material on an online platform can by definition only result in a reactive response, often after weeks have elapsed and serious harm has been done.

The power relationship between broadcaster and caller or participant in an OB is also one that in terms of ease of access is signally *not* replicated between social-media platform and user. Once a subscriber to such a platform, one may post seemingly at will, making the content almost immediately available to other subscribers—or at least a subset of them if peer-to-peer access is enabled through the granting of permissions, such as 'friendships' or follower status. Broadcasting time is, however, a finite resource, and a phone-in cannot necessarily accommodate everyone who might wish to participate. Once on air, a caller cannot expect to be given unlimited time to articulate a discursive point, so this form of access to the public sphere is significantly time-constrained. Presenters and producers may also consciously or unconsciously 'ration'exposure time for individual callers, perhaps discouraging, cutting short or excluding repeat callers who might for various reasons be considered to have a greater potential than others to bore the audience or for whatever reason even disadvantaging members of minority groups of all kinds—whereas such considerations would appear not to restrict access to social media.

CONCLUSION

What, then, does this mainly historical study of a significant period in the development of the radio industry in a single European country add to this wider volume of texts focusing mainly on more contemporary issues, especially with its frequent referencing of a German playwright's earlier musings on the nature of a medium which was in the 1930s still in its infancy? The conclusions we can reasonably draw are, in fact, qualified to a significant extent, but that should not detract from their validity in theorising the present and the future of radio as contextualised and to a certain extent influenced by the past. Notwithstanding the significant caveats noted in the section above, we can, based upon the evidence preceding them, draw the reasonable conclusion that there is some validity in the claims made at the 2013 Radio Festival for early UK commercial radio having been a precursor to social networking, and that it bore many of the characteristics of the phenomenon as represented more recently by Carpentier's AIP model of access, interaction, participation. Although mainly for reasons of economics, regulation and rights management, as opposed to any altruistic purpose, the phone-in and, to a lesser extent, the public outside broadcast, which were common in the programming of ILR stations in the UK in the 1970s, did provide individual listeners within these stations' audiences with real possibilities to communicate back to the broadcaster in the sense previously imagined by Bertolt Brecht with his 'series of pipes' metaphor.

It would be reasonable to consider, though, whether Brecht was really imagining a better future for radio at all, or instead foreseeing a future connected world of digitally enabled interaction in the sense that we are all now connected by the Internet, with the myriad communicative potential that entails, but without the characteristics of genre and formatting that defines what was then, just as now, considered to define the medium of radio. He could not, of course, have imagined in detail the technical characteristics of the Internet which today make it possible but were then many years away from their eventual discovery and exploitation. His theorising was naturally more one of principles than of actual technology. However, to pretend he was predicting the invention of the Internet would be to ignore the evolutionary nature of technological development, as well as the role of the playwright as a content creator as opposed to a mere contributor to an essentially democratic but overwhelmingly mutual content exchange, as the Internet has become. The radio with which he was expressing some frustration in 1932 was nonetheless a performance medium, just like the theatre. Brecht himself spoke to his audiences far more than they contributed to his works.

During the period upon which we have focused, then, at a particular stage in the evolution of a medium, listeners could generate content which involved some level of interaction with the radio station as a media platform as well as with unknown other 'users' within a limited peer-to-peer paradigm. Nevertheless, there were significant limitations to this interaction. They constrained frequency and duration of engagement and ease of access through gatekeepers because of concerns over content and the status of the caller in the power relationship with the broadcaster—who in turn would be mindful of the effect on audience ratings of poor quality callers to phone-ins and, unlike social media platforms, of their own capacity for user-generated content that was of necessity distributed entirely in a linear fashion. As suggested by Brecht might be the case, listeners were thus enabled, at least in limited ways that do share characteristics with Carpentier's AIP model of collaborative media content creation, to engage in the wider discourse Habermas called the 'public sphere.'

REFERENCES

Barham, K. (2006). *Radio City: The Heart of Liverpool*. Raleigh: Lulu.com.

Baron, M. (1975). *Independent Radio*. Lavenham: The Lavenham Press.

Brecht, B. (1932). "Radio as an Apparatus of Communication." *Bjitter des Hessischen Landestheaters*, Darmstadt, July 16, reprinted in Brecht, B. (1967), *Gesammelte Werke*, Frankfurt am Main: Suhrkamp Verlag, 129–130.

Carpentier, N. (2011). "The Concept of Participation. If They Have Access and Interact, Do They Really Participate?" *CM: Communication Management Quarterly/Casopis za upravljanje komuniciranjem*, 21, 13–36.

Conservative Party. (1970). *1970 Conservative Party General Election Manifesto: A Better Tomorrow*. London: Conservative Party.

Crisell, A. (1994). *Understanding Radio*, 2nd edn. London: Routledge.

———. (1997). *An Introductory History of British Broadcasting*. London: Routledge.

Fleming, C. (2002). *The Radio Handbook*, 2nd edn. London: Routledge.

Habermas, J. (1989). *The Structural Transformation of the Public Sphere*. Cambridge: Polity Press.

McLuhan, M. (2001). *Understanding Media: The Extensions of Man*. London: Routledge.

Morrison, S. (2013). "Twitter Faces Inquiry over Internet Trolls' Rape Threats Against MPs and Activist, as Man Is Arrested." *The Independent*, July 30. Accessed January 20, 2014. http://www.independent.co.uk/news/uk/home-news/twitter-faces-inquiry-over-internet-trolls-rape-threats-against-mps-and-activist-as-man-is-arrested-8738379.html.

O'Malley, T. (1983). "Radio Franchises." *Marxism Today*, November, 35–36.

Skues, K. (2009). *Pop Went the Pirates II*. Horning: Lamb's Meadow Publications.

Starkey, G. (2004). "Estimating Audiences: Sampling in Television and Radio Audience Research." *Cultural Trends*, 49, 3–25.

———. (2007). *Balance and Bias in Journalism: Representation, Regulation and Democracy*. Basingstoke: Palgrave Macmillan.

———. (2011). *Local Radio, Going Global*. Basingstoke: Palgrave Macmillan.

———. (2013). *Radio in Context*. Basingstoke: Palgrave Macmillan.

Stoller, T. (2010). *Sounds of Your Life: A History of Independent Radio in the UK*. New Barnet: John Libbey Publishing.

Street, S. (2002). *A Concise History of British Radio*. Tiverton: Kelly.

2 Domesticated Voices
Listener 'Participation' in Everyday Radio Shows

Jan Pinseler

INTRODUCTION

If you listen to any morning show on radio, very probably the presenter will wish you a good morning, s/he will make assumptions about what you did or do, what you like and do not like, s/he will ask you to call in with information, most likely about traffic jams or speed cameras, or to join a debate on some topic and to do so not only via phone but also using a social media website like Facebook or Twitter. And in all likelihood you will ignore these requests and just go on with whatever you usually do in the morning. So why do radio programmes permanently try to get their listeners to respond and what does this mean for the role of listeners within these programmes? Obviously, explicitly or implicitly, listeners are the focus point of all types of radio programmes. While they are always present as an idea of who the audience of a radio programme may actually consist of, they can also literally be present in programmes. This chapter analyses the ways in which listeners' presence in actual radio programmes can be traced. And it asks whether and to what degree listener presence can be understood as participation in these programmes.

To do this, I will look at morning shows of several radio stations. Since morning and afternoon are the times of day when radio is listened to most, and radio stations put the most effort into producing these shows, analysing radio stations' morning shows constitutes a pragmatic approach to answering these questions with limited research resources. I will start by briefly sketching the debate on listener 'participation' on radio, a debate that is as old as radio itself and overlaps into a debate of audience participation in media in general. It is not only a scientific debate but also one of radio practitioners reflecting on their use of the audience within their programmes.

Since research on radio is not as common as research on television, print media or the Internet, there is not much work devoted to methods of radio analysis. But there are some approaches to analysing media talk that will be discussed here. Especially, the element of conversation analysis that deals with media talk is very useful for the analysis presented here, and its combination with other methods, particularly Grounded Theory, is discussed here to introduce the method used to answer the questions posed above. The primary focus of this chapter will be on analysing listener participation on morning shows by using a few extracts from these shows to demonstrate that this, in fact, can hardly be called participation.

LISTENERS' VOICES—ASPIRATIONS AND APPROACHES

The role of listeners talking back on radio programmes has been discussed since radio broadcasting was invented. There are several elements in this discussion. Most notedly, in the early days of radio—and the last days of the Weimar Republic—the German poet and playwright Bertolt Brecht put his ideas about what radio could be into words, a speech that became known as his 'radio theory.' Brecht envisioned a change of radio from a one-sided distribution apparatus to a means of communication by "organizing its listeners as suppliers" (1993, 15; orig. 1932). Although this was more a sketch of ideas than a full-fledged theory, to this day these short paragraphs are a reference point for discussions of listener participation in radio and audience participation in media in general, most recently in early discussions of the Internet that argued that finally, Brecht's vision had come true. But one point which is overlooked regularly, possibly due to its not being included in the most cited English translation of this text, is Brecht's insistence that this aim could not be accomplished in a capitalist society but is meant to help bring about a different social order (Brecht 1992). Around the same time but from a different angle, Walter Benjamin (1978; orig. 1934) also concluded that social change can be achieved not by a change in media content but only by socialising the means of media production. In discussions of participation in the media in the second half of the twentieth century these arguments were mostly reduced to an optimistic view on the promises of participation (e.g., Enzensberger 1997; orig. 1970). All this can be understood as normative approaches to listener participation on radio programmes, since it is built on principal considerations on the role of radio in society. Brecht, Benjamin and, to a lesser degree, Enzensberger envision a different form of radio programming that can bring about a new social order and can be instrumental in this new social order—although they differ on what this social order should be.

Recently, Carpentier (2011) undertook the task of systematically differentiating between participation on the one hand and interaction and access on the other hand, concepts that in debates on participation usually are mixed up. While access (to media technologies or media organisations) and interaction are preconditions of participation, he argues that there is a fundamental difference, with the latter necessarily including involvement in decision making. This differentiation may help us to understand why so many books and articles struggle with analysing listeners talking on radio and grapple with how to describe this. Obviously, callers who are put on air on radio programmes are not participating in the sense of Carpentier's definition. But it is less obvious what role it is that listeners are playing when talking on air.

There are quite a few studies taking an analytical approach to the study of listener participation on radio programmes, as opposed to the normative approach described above. Most of these studies struggle with the contradiction that individual listeners can regularly be heard on radio programmes but that the listener as such has almost no influence on which arguments are discussed on the air. Some conclude that radio always reinforces mainstream arguments (e.g., Higgins and Moss 1982), some see this as a potential that should and can be realised (e.g., Shingler and Wieringa 1998). Most researchers agree that the listener on air stands in for listeners in general. Research on how talks on air are actually organised shows that they systematically diverge from everyday talk and that there are underlying power structures in radio talks that are realised here. Even on community radio stations, with its much less restraints on programming, most listener 'participation' other than listeners coming to the station and producing their own programme, has restraints on listener participation (Pinseler 2008).

As early as 1982 Higgins and Moss describe call-ins on Australian radio morning shows as not only not increasing possibilities of expression for listeners but even as inhibiting listeners expressing themselves. To this extent, the authors argue that "not only has radio not helped democratize culture, despite its potential, but that even in talk back radio programs the ability of people to make their own culture is inhibited rather than enhanced" (1982, 32). The reason for this, they argue, is that comments of callers are always framed by the programme and by contextualisations of presenters so that views differing from the mainstream are constantly "overpowered by the accepted, authoritative messages" (Higgins and Moss 1982, 33).

In a less critical approach, Orians (1991) also concludes—from the analysis of call-ins, this time on German radio—that producers and presenters always have more power than callers. Presenters and producers, Orians argues, see phone-ins as a democratic element within radio programmes. Furthermore, voices of specific listeners on the programme are seen as substitutes for listeners in general and opinions listeners can identify with (Burger 1990, 1991). They stand for the world outside the media, for those actually affected by something the media report on (Burger 1996). Shingler and Wieringa (1998) see radio as a medium that constantly creates the impression of being bidirectional communication, without really being bidirectional. Since only a few listeners actually call in to a radio programme, they refer to this participation as taking place "by proxy" (Shingler and Wieringa 1998, 114). Although Shingler and Wieringa argue that phone-ins give the audience an opportunity "to have their say" (1998, 118), they also stress the controlling power of presenters and producers: ". . . radio stations have recognised only the need to appear more accessible and reciprocal," while "the power within radio broadcasting surely remains one-sided" (1998, 124).

This is a point also demonstrated by research applying conversation analysis to news interviews (Heritage 1985; Heritage, Clayman and Zimmerman 1988; Heritage and Greatbatch 1991). News interviews only allow questions and answers, determining in advance that the interviewer asks questions and the interviewee answers them. Interviewers might utter preliminary statements that lead to a question or substantiate a question, but this always leads to some form of question being asked. Therefore, interviewer and interviewee jointly produce the interactive form called the news interview.

In contrast to ordinary conversations, participants in news interviews avoid continuers, those small utterance like 'yes' or 'hm,' which in ordinary conversation signal attention. Interviewers systematically avoid taking a stand on anything the interviewee says. Individual turns in news interviews are often longer than those in ordinary talk. They consist of several turn-constructing units which follow each other without interruption. Interviewers expect this from interviewees. This becomes obvious when interviewees give exceptionally short answers that usually lead to a short silence.

In news interviews the right to select the next speaker is distributed asymmetrically. Interviewees can neither open or close a conversation nor select themselves as the next speaker (except if several people are interviewed at the same time). Interviewers have the right to choose the topic of the interview, and interviewees have to go to great lengths not to break this question-answer pattern if they wish to avoid answering a question. Applying this research to the analysis of radio talk, one can show that it is possible to have conversations on radio between listeners and presenters that, up to a point, are free of most of these constraints of news interviews. This can only be achieved by changing the modes of media production, as tried, for instance, by some community radio stations. But even those that try rarely succeed. Obviously, a certain imbalance of power between listeners and producers can hardly be eliminated (Pinseler 2001, 2008). Therefore, although the listeners can be heard on radio programmes, there is always an imbalance between listeners and presenters. Basically, this is an imbalance of power that stems from presenters allowing or denying someone the opportunity to speak on air, deciding the topic of the conversation, framing the statements of listeners and being able to edit listeners.

If this is the case, it must be possible to find evidence of this not only in the content of conversations between presenters and listeners but also in how these conversations are shaped and conducted. There are several ways to analyse form and content of conversations. How conversations are organised can best be understood by applying conversation analysis to radio talk, as has been done repeatedly. Having been developed mainly by Sacks and Schegloff in the 1960s for examining everyday talk (Sacks, Schegloff and Jefferson 1974), conversation analysis aims at reconstructing how reality is produced in ordinary conversations. Since the techniques to conduct conversations are basic techniques of interaction, showing how institutionalised forms of interaction differ from ordinary everyday conversations reveals the social order within these organisations (Drew and Heritage 1992; Heritage and Great-batch 1991). Therefore, conversation analysis gives us a useful tool to look at how talk on radio is organised, and by comparing this with rules applying to the organisation of everyday talk, we can deduce power structures within radio talk from this comparison (Pinseler 2008).

This kind of analysis does not primarily look at what is said but how the talking is organised, or, as Tolson (2006, 6) puts it, at "the doing of the talk-ing." Yet, to construct an antagonism between interpretative approaches and conversation analysis, as Tolson does, is rather misleading. First, conversa-tion analysis, as every form of research, depends on interpretative acts by researchers, the difference being that interpretations in conversation analysis stem from the organisation of talk rather than interpreting its content. More importantly, analysing talk on radio programmes should be concerned with form and content, i.e., with what is said, which ideas are framed as ordinary and unquestionable and which are problematised as deviating from common knowledge, and how talking is organised in a way to allow some people to talk on air while others do not get that chance or are discouraged from talk-ing and for some arguments to be made while others are excluded from being aired or put in a context that invalidates them. Therefore, to understand radio talk in addition to analysing its form, it is also useful to look at its content.

It is useful to bring these elements—content and form—of radio talk together analytically, using Grounded Theory as a methodological frame-work (Glaser and Strauss 1967; Strauss and Corbin 1990). This approach aims at developing a theory from data. It uses coding to build concepts and categories to describe phenomena in the material analysed and the constant creation and revision of hypotheses to develop these categories and their relations by constant re-evaluation of the evolving theory by analysing new material. According to Grounded Theory, there are latent patterns within the data analysed that have to be discovered by researchers to develop a theory. For the analysis of radio programmes, this means to analyse pro-gramme by programme by coding the recording and its transcript. Thereby categories are developed into concepts. While doing this, assumptions about connections between concepts are developed and constantly revised. With these preliminary theories in mind, other programmes are analysed and re-analysed, and by so doing these preliminary theories are constantly revised. The evolving theory is finally tested by applying it to the original data. This approach is especially useful, since it allows for combining the analysis of diverse forms of data, like sound and talk.

The findings discussed here are part of a larger ongoing research project on representation of the political on German radio. To look at listener par-ticipation specifically, I will focus here on the analysis of morning shows of four radio stations, namely MDR Sachsen-Anhalt, Radio SAW, Radio Eins and Radio Corax. These stations have been chosen to reflect a variety of morning shows. At the core of the analysis here are one commercial (Radio SAW) and one public service broadcaster (MDR Sachsen-Anhalt), both aimed mainly at the German state of Saxony-Anhalt and at differing but overlapping age groups. In addition, the morning show of a public service broadcaster for the neighbouring states of Brandenburg and Berlin (Radio Eins) was included in the analysis to look at a station that is also aimed at a mass audience but is more information oriented. Finally, a community radio station (Radio Corax) was analysed to see whether there was any difference in listener participation in this programme.

MDR Sachsen-Anhalt is a regional station of Mitteldeutscher Rundfunk (MDR), the public service broadcaster for the German states of Saxony, Thuringia and Saxony-Anhalt. While all the other radio and television programmes of MDR are transmitted in all three states, there is one programme specifically aimed at each of these states, *MDR Sachsen-Anhalt* being one of these. The station describes itself as a 'Heimatsender' ('home radio'), using the German concept of *Heimat*, which refers to a regional as well as social identity and is associated with light pop and a commercialised version of folk music and therefore with an older generation. *Guten Morgen Sachsen-Anhalt* (Good Morning, Saxony-Anhalt) is the name of the morning show of MDR Sachsen-Anhalt and is transmitted from 5 to 9 a.m. every weekday with a female and a male presenter taking weekly turns in presenting the show.

Radio SAW, a commercial broadcaster also based in Magdeburg, the capital of Saxony-Anhalt, uses the claim 'Superhits fürs SAW-Land' and aims at a broader but slightly lower age group than MDR Sachsen-Anhalt. It tries to use its powerful FM transmitters to attract listeners not only in Saxony-Anhalt, where the station holds its licence, but also in neighbouring states and therefore no longer uses the name *Sachsen-Anhalt-Welle* that refers to the state but only the acronym SAW. The morning programme of Radio SAW is called *Muckefuck*, referring to a colloquial term for famous ersatz coffee that was also once produced in Magdeburg for all of East Germany. This morning show is transmitted every weekday from 4.51 to 10 a.m. and is jointly presented by one female and two male presenters.

Radio Eins claims to be a programme "Nur für Erwachsene" ("for adults only"), positioning itself as aimed at a certain age group but also using this slogan to underline the programme's format of playing a wider range of music and including more non-musical content and in-depth information than other radio programmes aimed at a mass audience. This programme is produced by Rundfunk Berlin Brandenburg (RBB), the public service broadcaster of these two German states. It is presented by two pairs of male presenters each, taking turns weekly. The programme is called *Der schöne Morgen* (The Nice Morning) and is transmitted daily throughout the week from 5 to 10 a.m.

The morning programme of Radio Corax, *Morgenmagazin*, is likewise transmitted daily throughout the week from 7 to 10.10 a.m. and is presented by changing presenters. Radio Corax is a community radio station based in Halle (Saale), one of the two big cities in Saxony-Anhalt.

For the purpose of this paper, five shows of each station transmitted in November 2013 have been analysed. Using conversation analysis and

Grounded Theory as outlined above, these shows were transcribed using a word-by-word transcription. A more detailed transcript using transcription rules usually used for conversation analysis (Sacks et al. 1974) was produced only where necessary. The shows were then analysed using conversation analysis and the coding paradigm of Grounded Theory.

IMAGINED LISTENERS

The most common form of listeners' appearances on radio programmes is not being heard but being referred to. This can be done directly or indirectly. Listeners are present within radio programmes indirectly all the time, especially in the ideas of station managers, editors and presenters, who produce these programmes. We can call this the imagined listener.[1] Listening to the programmes discussed here, this presence is actually audible, as can be seen in transcription extracts 1 and 2:

Transcription Extract 1: MDR Sachsen-Anhalt, November 26, 2013, 8:15 a.m.[2]

Presenter: How do you get on with the elk now? So people know how this works. So, which ingredients do you still need now?

Imagined listeners are audible when a presenter asks interviewees questions that are justified by claiming that the programme's audience might be interested in the answer; in this particular situation, the issue concerns how to make an elk puppet to put in the window, a topic that is discussed in a studio interview with a woman who owns a haberdashery that offers sewing courses. Less often, questions are justified directly by attributing them to listeners without these listeners actually being heard or quoted, as seen in extract 2:

Transcription Extract 2: MDR Sachsen-Anhalt, November 26, 2013, 8:44 a.m.

Pres: We obviously also have to settle something. How many men take part in your sewing courses in your shop? This also was a question from one of the many fans of MDR Sachsen-Anhalt.

Not only does the presenter justify his question with questions from the audience, he also uses this to claim—in a none too subtle way—that the radio station has a wide and dedicated audience. Generalised listeners are also talked to constantly, from greeting them to talking to them one-sidedly. This can be heard on all programmes analysed here. For instance, the presenter of Radio Corax's *Morgenmagazin* introduces a segment as follows:

Transcript Extract 3: Radio Corax, November 26, 2013, 7:38 a.m.

> Pres: I don't know. Do you still remember? *10th grade lessons in poetry.*
> I don't really remember hearing about the poet Joseph Eichendorff at
> school.

In this extract, two things happen that can be seen in all the other morning shows analysed here. The presenter first asks his listeners, or rather one
imagined listener, a rhetorical question and directly addresses this imagined
listener as if he knew him or her well. Especially the latter form of addressing listeners is a very common one in the programmes analysed here. As in
many other instances, the listener is very present as an imagined individual
addressed by the presenter. This can be also done more indirectly, as in the
following extract from the Radio Eins programme *Der schöne Morgen*:

Transcript Extract 4: Radio Eins, November 26, 2013, 9:47 a.m.

> Pres: If I asked the listeners of Radio Eins, I guess at least 80 per cent
> would say yes.

In a more direct way, listeners are present in what might be called
alleged interaction between radio station and audience. Presenters repeatedly talk about listeners' feedback on social media platforms or—more
rarely nowadays—about listeners calling the station without actually talking about what they are saying. Just mentioning the fact that listeners call,
tweet or post something seems to be enough. In other instances interactions
with listeners are talked about without listeners being heard. This is done
for instance by mentioning listeners' preferences for justifying the music
that is played or by talking about how happy a listener was after winning
something in a previous programme. Listeners are also regularly asked to
do something. And listeners are present when programmes talk in general
about getting feedback from listeners. Hence, radio programmes refer to
listeners all the time. They use several devices to do this, starting with their
being present as imagined listeners in presenters' ideas about whom they are
talking to. They are also present as directly addressed imagined listeners,
who are asked to agree with the presenter, to imagine something or to do
something. All these forms produce a communality between radio station
and listeners in which all of them can feel part of a shared project.

LISTENERS' VOICES

Listeners are not only present as imagined listeners or without having a voice
on the programmes. They can also be heard. The following is an extract from
the morning programme of the commercial regional broadcaster Radio SAW:

Transcript Extract 5: Radio SAW, November 19, 2013, 9:30 a.m.

> Announcer male (Am): Autumn in SAW-land. The nice thing about it is:
> Sound bite female 1 (Sbf1): When the sun is shining, the foliage turns golden and the leaves rustle.
> Am: This is what is done in autumn.
> Sbf2: You can have a nice walk through autumn forests.
> Am: And this is what is listened to.
> Sbm: Hi, this is Karsten from Biere and in autumn I really like to listen to Adele singing her song *Set Fire to the Rain*.
> Am: This is what autumn sounds like on your radio. Radio SAW.

This jingle starts with an announcer talking about a fictional region, 'SAW-Land,' and the time of year. While nominally being a broadcast for the—rather small—German state of Saxony-Anhalt, it can be and is listened to in several neighbouring states, or part of these states. 'SAW-Land,' therefore, mainly seems to refer to the region where the radio station can be listened to via FM. In other parts of the programme, what this means is actually defined in more detail. Especially, the traffic service asks listeners to call in with information about traffic problems not only in Saxony-Anhalt but also the neighbouring states of Saxony, Thuringia and Lower Saxony. But this definition is ambiguous and by using the designation 'SAW-Land' the radio station invites every listener to feel included, regardless of where s/he is situated physically. In addition, this 'SAW-Land' identifies the radio station with a region and at the same time makes itself a voice of this region.

The announcer then starts a sentence which is completed by a female voice talking about what is nice about autumn, the current season at the time of this transmission. By starting the sentence, the announcer sets the topic the female voice then talks about. This is followed again by the announcer introducing a statement followed by a different female member of the audience, this time talking about nice things one can do in autumn. This again is followed by the announcer introducing a statement about music appropriate for the time of year. A male speaker then introduces himself by saying his name and where he is from and goes on to mention a specific song he likes to listen to in autumn. All voices, except for the announcer, are obviously not voices of trained or practised speakers. They have a slight accent typical for the northern part of Saxony-Anhalt, where the station is based, the statements sound slightly unnatural, neither like what you would expect in everyday statements nor like the cleverly designed statements of the announcer. Thus, they stand for the audience talking back to the station. The announcer finally winds up this jingle by making a claim and mentioning the name of the radio station again, and the song that was mentioned by the male voice is played.

This jingle uses a classical rhetorical device, a list of three (Atkinson 1984), to make its point: Autumn is nice; nice things can be done in autumn and there is music that is suitable to listen to during that season. This is also used to make authoritative statements by not using the personal pronoun but impersonal passive constructions (announcer), or the impersonal German *man* ('you' in the sense of anyone, second female voice). Only the male voice uses the personal pronoun, talking about what kind of music *he* likes to listen to. In effect, listeners' voices together with the text spoken by the announcer and the fact that the song mentioned in the jingle is played directly after the jingle again create an impression of communality between radio station and listeners.

First, this is done by creating geographical communality. Both radio station and listeners exist in a shared universe that is regularly referred to. To exclude no one, the fictional universe of 'SAW-Land' is created. Second, social communality is produced by referring to shared everyday experiences from the world both live in, here by talking about autumn, the time of year of the transmission, and by framing statements by individuals in a way that makes the statements stand for the shared experience of all listeners. Third, the jingle produces a communality of tastes and interests, here related specifically to musical tastes. A declaration of the musical taste of one individual is converted into a declaration of musical taste of all those listening to this station. In addition, this is linked to the shared seasonal experience of listeners of this radio station, thereby strengthening the produced communality.

One more thing is worth listening to in this extract: The jingle links the season and the music with only good feelings. Autumn is associated with only good things: autumn foliage, sun. Other possible associations with this season, especially rain, are only referred to in a way that can be understood as ironic, that is, the listener saying that he particularly enjoys listening to a song called *Set Fire to the Rain* in autumn. Thus, the programme links the communality of listeners and radio station to these good feelings and pokes fun at the mainly unmentioned downsides of this time of year.

As has been shown so far, listeners are constantly present in radio programmes, but in the role of being talked 'to' rather than being talked 'with.' They are present as imagined listeners and they are present with pre-recorded, edited and framed utterances that are used in the programme. The communality produced here is even emphasised by the programmes' use of the personal pronoun *wir* ('we') in a way that refers to the community of presenters and listeners. Especially, the public service broadcaster MDR Sachsen-Anhalt repeats this frequently, starting with the slogan 'Das Radio wie wir' ('The radio like us'), which is used in on- and off-air promotions of the station. It also uses the first person plural pronoun to talk about either presumably shared experience, as in the example discussed above, or future events. But what about actual verbal interaction between listeners and presenters in the programme?

CONVERSATIONS WITH LISTENERS

Let us have a look at a somewhat longer exchange on Radio SAW about Christmas, and whether it is too early to get into a festive mood and play Wham's *Last Christmas* on radio in November.

Transcript Extract 6: Radio SAW, November 19, 2013, 7:43 a.m.

> Presenter male (Presm): [. . .] For me it's much too early and all this hype really gets on my nerves, if I'm honest. What about you?
>
> Female voice 1 (Sf1): Yes, hallo, this is Anja. I wanted to tell you something about Christmas.
>
> Presm: Yes Anja, tell us.
>
> Sf1: Christmas isn't a holiday for me anyway and obviously it's definitely much too early and all the ballyhoo about it. I even can't look right or left in shops anymore.
>
> Presm: But the interesting thing about that is why Christmas is not your thing at all.
>
> Sf1: I don't know. Probably it's a holiday that just lasts too long for me.
>
> Presm: Yes, I realise that. Your way of talking, faster, faster, faster and to the point.
>
> Sf1: Yes. Exactly. I already slowed down.
>
> Presm: All right. Thanks for your call. Nice day, yes.
>
> Sf1: Nice day. Bye.

This segment starts with one of the presenters reintroducing that day's topic, a discussion on whether it is too early to get into the Christmas mood in November. This is repeatedly introduced by the female presenter trying to play *Last Christmas*, which, after the first words can be heard, is immediately drowned out by the sound of a horn and by one of the male presenters acting annoyed. The presenter asks listeners for their views on the topic. First a caller named Anja introduces herself. After being prompted to do so, she says that she is no fan of Christmas and that she doesn't like the fuss about it. The presenter chimes in, saying that there was something more interesting she wanted to say. And Anja explains that for her, Christmas lasts much too long and therefore she does not like it. After a short exchange with the caller talking rather fast and preferring things done quickly, this call is ended.

Not really surprisingly, the talk is driven by the presenter who initiates the talk, sets its topic and tone, assigns turns and finishes the talk. But the most interesting part here is the presenter prompting the caller to tell a specific story. He does not simply ask her why she does not like Christmas but does so in a way that makes obvious that he already knows the answer to this question by using the past tense ("the interesting thing was"), thereby indicating that he or one of the editors or producers of the show and the caller have talked about this before. Anja, therefore, clearly is not someone who just happens to be on the line when the presenter asks his question, but her getting to speak is the result of an editorial process that screens calls before putting them on the air and informs presenters of the points the callers want to make so that they can organise the on-air talk. While this sounds like live broadcasting—e.g., because of the repetitions of greetings or of exchanges that would have been cut out due to its redundant nature had this segment been edited beforehand—it actually might have been taped shortly before the transmission, i.e., recorded 'live on tape,' to allow for editing in case of something unexpected being said by the listener. Whatever the case is here, the fact is that the callers are obviously asked before getting on air (or tape) about what they are going to say. This knowledge is used by the presenters to control the flow and content of the talk that is transmitted. And the callers are obviously instructed at least on how to introduce themselves and what to say first. Mostly callers identify themselves by giving their name and saying where they live without being asked to do this. So does the second caller in the segment printed below, Sabine.

Transcript Extract 7: Radio SAW, November 19, 2013, 7:43 a.m., continued

Presenter male (Presm): Hallo, good morning. Radio SAW. Muckefuck.

Female voice 2 (Sf2): Hallo you Muckefucks. This is Sabine from Schönebeck.

Presm: Sabine, today we are talking about Christmas spirit in department stores and Christmas music everywhere, yes or no. What do you say?

Sf2: Well, I say a clear yes. Christmas is so beautiful, it has to be rung in now.

Presm: It's not too early for you?

Sf2: No. Christmas is only once a year and you have to celebrate it as it is. And if that's six weeks before. My God.

Presm: Okay, all right. Thanks.

Sf2: Thank you too. Have a nice day. Bye.

Sabine answers the clear alternative she is given—Christmas: yes or no—by saying yes. The presenter then offers her the chance to expand on this, something well known in research of news interviews as a cooperative recycle (Heritage 1985). The caller takes this chance and elaborates on her views on Christmas. After that the interview ends. The listeners who take part in this conversation are clearly managed by presenters, producers and editors. What sounds like a conversation is actually at least partly a staged conversation, in which those who get on air are screened beforehand, chosen for what they want to say and organised by the editors to fit a pre-planned framework. We have two listeners put on air, each supporting one side of an argument that is framed as a yes-or-no question. They are asked to illustrate their point in a way that reveals the editorial process behind the calls, being put on air. This process consists of at least figuring out the point the callers want to make and giving them instructions on how to make this point once they are on air. These listeners are then helped by the presenters to follow this script by prompting them to give the pre-arranged statements. This does not mean that callers do not say what they want to say, but rather that the editorial process of the programme ensures that callers are managed in a way that fits the editorial aim.

The presenters immediately follow this by reading comments on the topic that listeners left on Facebook.

Transcript Extract 8: Radio SAW, November 19, 2013, 7:43 a.m., continued

Presenter male (Presm): Bye. And also many thanks for your comments on Facebook via radiosaw.de. There Astrid Krause writes: "My ears hurt already. Soon music's everywhere again. I hate it, I can't even escape." I suppose she might be a shop assistant, too and I'm afraid she will have to face this.

Presenter female (Presf): Ronny, he is on my side, since he writes: "Come on, put it on the turntable, with *Last Christmas*. I already look forward to it."

The male presenter is reading a post from someone who hates Christmas, and the female presenter is reading one from someone who cannot wait for it. The time devoted to each listener here is much shorter than that given to the callers talking in the show. The presenters apparently quote what listeners posted on Facebook. The quotes chosen are succinct and to the point and are read so that each agrees with one side of the 'argument' here. Since the listeners quoted cannot talk back, it is even easier to use listeners' statements in a way that serves the purpose of the programme: to have a debate with listeners without giving away the power of presenters to control this debate.

While users—on some programmes, like in this example Radio SAW's *Muckefuck*—are regularly encouraged to comment on Facebook and these comments are sometimes read on the programmes, other social media services are very rarely actively used on the programmes analysed. While messages from Twitter are sometimes used when presenters comment on something, this is rarely related specifically to the programme or the station, and listeners are never actually encouraged to post on Twitter, as they are to make a comment on Facebook. Text messages were not used at all in the programmes analysed; indeed, text messages were not read on the shows, nor were listeners asked to send text messages.

CONCLUSION: DOMESTICATED VOICES

Listeners can be heard on radio morning shows all the time and in different ways, but mostly they are simply present without having a voice. They are present as the imagined listener that is implied in the programme itself, or they are present when they are talked to directly, for instance in greetings. And they are present as explicitly mentioned motivation for presenters to do or ask something. When voices of listeners are actually put on the air, this is often done by including pre-recorded and edited statements of listeners, sometimes as sound bites, sometimes being read as quotes from social media websites. There are also conversations between presenters and callers on air.

But these conversations are highly managed. Not only do the presenters and editors define what is talked about, when something is talked about and how this talk is framed, but they also organise the talk in a way that uses these conversations with listeners to realise the editorial plan for the show. The result sounds like listeners having their say on the air, but in fact it consists rather of a highly organised and orchestrated impression of listeners speaking their mind on the programme. The use of social media makes this even easier, since posts from Facebook or Twitter can be selectively quoted as to organise them in a way that fits the editorial plan.

Surprisingly, while in matters of content, tone, music and editorial concept the radio stations analysed here differ greatly, how they refer to listeners is—at least on an analytical level—rather similar. What is different is the balance between these forms of listeners being heard on radio. MDR Sachsen-Anhalt uses only very few conversations with listeners on air, something more common with Radio SAW and Radio Eins. Radio Eins especially transmits quite a lot of short conversations with listeners, mostly in connection with small competitions. When it comes to expressing opinions, something also done regularly, the station asks listeners to call an answering machine and uses these messages to produce an edited item later in the programme. Radio SAW actually puts listeners on air and talks to them but manages these conversations to ensure that they fit the editorial aim. Surprisingly, the morning programme of community radio station Radio Corax did not feature any voices of listeners in the shows analysed here.

While past studies have previously indicated that listeners are not really participating in the programmes, here it is systematically shown how listeners' voices are used to create an *impression* of listener participation. All of the programmes analysed here constantly create an impression of a community of all those listening to the station and those presenting the programme. What characterises this community might be different in these programmes, but they all refer to this community of listeners and presenters again and again. Sound bites and quotations of and conversations with listeners also take part in producing this communality. They refer to a shared social history, shared experiences and a shared geographical space. Voices of listeners heard are not so much expressions of opinions, ideas or beliefs of individuals but domesticated voices, i.e., voices of individuals used as material in an editorial process. They stand for listeners being heard, but they are not listeners freely expressing themselves. Arguably, this does not even constitute access or interaction in the definition of Carpentier (2011), since it is mainly the voices as such that the radio programmes are interested in. The opinions expressed might be important to the listeners calling in, but to the radio programme this mostly is raw material to fill pre-defined concepts with. Only rarely does the content of what the voice actually says really count and then this can only, if at all, be understood as interaction, not participation. What looks like listener participation mostly is a product of radio practitioners using listeners' voices to produce the appearance of an audience actively involving itself in the programme.

NOTES

1. For a current account of presenters' concepts of their listeners, see Wolfenden (2012).
2. Please note that the translation of these transcript extracts aims to be as true to the original as possible, and, therefore, not necessarily correct English, as spoken German does not always follow the rules for written German.

REFERENCES

Atkinson, M. (1984). *Our Master's Voices. The Language and Body Language of Politics*. London, New York: Routledge.

Benjamin, W. (1978). "The Author as Producer." In Arato, A. and Gebhardt, E. (eds.), *The Essential Frankfurt School Reader*. New York: Urizen Books, 254–269.

Brecht, B. (1992). "Der Rundfunk als Kommunikationsapparat." In *Schriften 1: Texte zu Stücken* (Bertolt Brecht, Werke, Große kommentierte Berliner und Frankfurter Ausgabe, Band 21). Berlin & Frankfurt am Main: Aufbau & Suhrkamp, 552–557.

———. (1993). "The Radio as an Apparatus of Communication." In Strauss, N. (ed.), *Radiotext(e)*. New York: Semiotext(e), 15–17.

Burger, H. (1990). *Sprache der Massenmedien*. Berlin: de Gruyter.

———. (1991). *Das Gespräch in den Massenmedien*. Berlin: de Gruyter.

———. (1996). "Laien im Fernsehen. Was sie leisten—wie sie sprechen—wie man mit ihnen spricht." In Biere, U. and Hoberg, R. (eds.), *Mündlichkeit und Schriftlichkeit im Fernsehen*. Tübingen: Gunter Narr, 41–80.

Carpentier, N. (2011). "The Concept of Participation. If They Have Access and Interact, Do They Really Participate?" *CM: Communication Management Quarterly/Casopis za upravljanje komuniciranjem*, 21, 13–36.

Drew, P. and Heritage, J. (1992). "Analyzing Talk at Work. An Introduction." In Drew, P. and Heritage, J. (eds.), *Talk at Work. Interaction in Institutional Settings*. Cambridge: Cambridge University Press, 3–65.

Enzensberger, H. M. (1997). *Baukasten zu einer Theorie der Medien*. München: Fischer.

Glaser, B. G. and Strauss, A. (1967). *The Discovery of Grounded Theory. Strategies for Qualitative Research*. New York: de Gruyter.

Heritage, J. (1985). "Analyzing News Interviews. Aspects of the Production of Talk for an Overhearing Audience." In van Dijk, T. A. (ed.), *Handbook of Discourse Analysis*. Amsterdam: Academic Press, 95–117.

Heritage, J., Clayman, S. and Zimmerman, D.H. (1988). "Discourse and Message Analysis. The Micro-Structure of Mass Media Messages." In Hawkins, R. P., Wiemann, J. M. and Pingree, S. (eds.), *Advancing Communication Science. Merging Mass and Interpersonal Processes*. Newbury Park: Sage, 77–109.

Heritage, J. and Greatbatch, D. (1991). "On the Institutional Character of Institutional Talk. The Case of News Interviews." In Boden, D. and Zimmerman, D. H. (eds.), *Talk and Social Structure. Studies in Ethnomethodology and Conversation Analysis*. Cambridge: Polity Press, 93–137.

Higgins, C.S.C. and Moss, P. D. (1982). *Sounds Real. Radio in Everyday Life*. St. Lucia: University of Queensland Press.

Orians, W. (1991). *Hörerbeteiligung im Radio. Eine Fallstudie zu Motivation, Erwartung und Zufriedenheit von Anrufern*. München: R. Fischer.

Pinseler, J. (2001). "Sprechen im freien Radio. Eine Fallanalyse zu Möglichkeiten alternativen Hörfunks." *Medien & Kommunikationswissenschaft*, 49(3), 369–383.

———. (2008). "The Politics of Talk on German Free Radio Stations." *Westminster Papers in Communication and Culture (WPCC)*, 5(1), 67–85.

Sacks, H., Schegloff, E. A. and Jefferson, G. (1974). "A Simplest Systematics for the Organization of Turn-Taking for Conversation." *Language*, 50, 696–735.

Shingler, M. and Wieringa, C. (1998). *On Air. Methods and Meanings of Radio.* London: Arnold.

Strauss, A. and Corbin, J. (1990). *Basics of Qualitative Research. Grounded Theory. Procedures and Techniques.* Newbury Park, London, New Delhi: Sage.

Tolson, A. (2006). *Media Talk. Spoken Discourse on TV and Radio.* Edinburgh: Edinburgh University Press.

Wolfenden, H. (2012). "'I Know Exactly Who They Are': Radio Presenters' Conceptions of Audience." In Oliveira, M., Portela, P. and Santos, L. A. (eds.), *Radio Evolution: Conference Proceedings, September, 14-16, 2011.* Braga, University of Minho: Communication and Society Research Centre, 379–390.

3 Radio Audience Interaction
SMS Mobile Texting vs. Facebook

Asta Zelenkauskaite

INTRODUCTION

With the rise of social media such as Facebook, Twitter and texting via mobile phones (such as the Short Message Service, or SMS), radio continues to reconfigure itself by placing emphasis on its interactive potentials. Radio, historically renowned for its flexible adaptability to new technological developments and changing social practices, has been a pioneer in embracing new ways of connecting with its audiences (Hendy 2000; Rhoads 1993) despite lingering uncertainty regarding its future (Ala-Fossi et al. 2008). Current research focuses on how social media are used for the interaction between listeners and radio, considering how social media have become an inseparable part of media life (Deuze 2010). This study analyses established and emergent user interaction practices in radio by comparing Facebook and mobile texting.

Social media–based radio is conceptualised as a sociotechnical system that includes technological affordances, constraints and social practices that users engage in (Niederer and van Dijck 2010). Given that radio has incorporated multiple social media outlets over time by adopting the Latourian notion of 'sociotechnical ensembles' (Latour 1991), it is perceived as a space where social media–based radio is embedded in a multiplatform content of production, consumption and integration. The technical side of this phenomenon is foregrounded in a process of digitisation, which in turn has increased the number of its services and immersed radio in a multimedia world (Hendy 2000). Through the process of digitisation, multiplatform media have aimed to fulfil the promise of an enhanced listener experience. Multiplatform interactivity has created new spaces for user engagement with radio content. The Italian radio RTL 102.5, serving as a case study, is currently available on several platforms, ranging from traditional mass media platforms such as radio and TV to social media and its applications designed specifically for portable devices. Regardless of technological integration in programming, user practices on these platforms are not clear. Moreover, each platform differs based on its technological affordances, which predict differences in adoption and social practices.

The need to analyse multiplatform user interaction is driven by the fact that while two-way interactivity occurs between radio listeners, user participation is placed at its core. Thus, interactivity has been reflected through the development of the talk radio genre during the process of digitisation (Hendy 2000). The talk radio genre implies talking not only *to* audiences, but also *with* audiences. In spoken communication, the term "interactivity" is used by Yngve (1975) to describe listeners' behaviours during verbal communication. It is through talk radio that audiences have been historically involved in programme content production.

Due to radio's technological constraints, audiences have not been able to use the same radio device to provide their feedback through two-way interaction, causing backchannels to emerge in the mass media landscape. The term 'backchannel' refers to the ways in which messages can be returned to the sender. A backchannel thus functions as a discourse that underlies public conversations in either synchronous or asynchronous communication environments and can relate to the main content or be independent from it (Cogdill et al. 2001). Such backchannels have been predominantly implemented through external sources: fax messages, postcards, letters, phone calls and even direct conversation in the studio, where audience members can visit radio personalities. Digital media open up spaces for audience involvement through social and mobile media. In the era of digital media, backchannels have emerged as supplementary communication channels for users, mainly to enhance communicative exchanges with radio.

As more technological affordances are included in mass media contexts, the sociotechnical outcomes of interactive components have been positioned in ambivalent ways. Media-centric evaluations have considered the commercial and monetary value of radios that can be extracted from interaction, in addition to listener experience (Resmann 2009). User-centric approaches postulate how two-way communication streams may fulfil the positive outcomes of interactivity, such as community formation, exchange and constant feedback (Sundar 2004). Two-way communication via digital media establishes an intricate relationship with the concepts of access and interaction (Carpentier 2007). Interaction facilitates co-creation (e.g., Cha et al. 2007) or prosumer culture (Jenkins 2006; Toffler 1980).

Two-way communicative affordances have been introduced into mass media contexts in Italy, pioneering with SMS messages serving as interactive backchannels. In TV settings, interactivity was found to be a vehicle not only for interaction with the TV programme, but also for interpersonal dyadic conversation exchanges (Zelenkauskaite and Herring 2008).

Two-way interaction is theoretically positioned within the concept of interactivity, comprising its technological and communicative dimensions (Jensen 2008; Kiousis 2002; McMillan 2002; Sundar 2004). Interactivity highlights instant feedback, which has been defined as a key aspect of real-time audience participation (Tuomi and Bachmayer 2011). Communication via digital radios can also be viewed pessimistically, as the outsourcing of the production of self-gratifying content (Resmann 2009).

Given that interactivity is positioned within the remit of technological affordances, this study considers each social media platform as fulfilling the different needs of different users (Zelenkauskaite and Simões 2013). Also, user behaviours are expected to differ according to the social media platforms utilised, which vary in their sociotechnical affordances and purposes, as well as the culture that has formed over the course of their existence (Baym, Zhang and Lin 2004). Even if user content has mostly been analysed within a single platform, it has been found that user content posting behaviours vary across multiple platforms according to individual psychological traits (Panek, Nardis and Konrath 2013). The user interaction analysis of radio stations across three social media platforms, Facebook, Twitter and Google+, revealed preferences for Facebook, with other platforms being less popular, indicating sociotechnical differences in their adoption by radios and users on one hand, and technological constraints of content access on the other (Zelenkauskaite and Simões 2014).

In order to compare two platforms, Facebook and mobile texting, this study focuses on the deictic dimensions of interactivity. The temporal aspect includes interactivity and the real-time interaction of users. Real-time interactivity here refers to asynchronous interaction on Facebook, where messages can be retrieved at any given moment, as well as quasi-synchronous interaction via mobile texting, where messages offer potential for immediate interaction, even if this is not exploited.

The spatial aspect refers to a cross-platform content distribution and its implications for meaningful user content integration. Specifically, the cross-platform analysis performed included the degree to which Facebook and mobile texting are used differently or similarly in terms of content distribution over time, the frequency of content posting to RTL 102.5, and content structure. The assumption is that each of these platforms provides different temporal dimensions associated with the immediacy of exchange by extending this immediacy via traditional backchannels such as phone calls and fax, allowing for the fastest content reception by the radio station, with snail-mail letters and postcards representing the slowest mode of content reception.

This research is based on the following questions: Given that audiences can interact at any time, is interaction regularly distributed over time? Are there differences between message types across the platforms? Does user interaction differ in cross-modal contexts? Due to sociotechnical differences between Facebook and mobile texting, would it be possible to predict different user behaviours associated with content posting, even if the target addressee is the radio station? Given the diversity in scope, history and technologies, this study focuses on audience interaction via various social media outlets. By doing so, we have focused on the unexpected consequences of social media outlets as spaces through which media companies have built up participation-based interactivity.

This research project is based on a case study of a commercial Italian radio station, RTL 102.5, which pioneered in integrating social media outlets in its programming. Comparisons have been made between Facebook audience interaction patterns over time, considering both addressee types and content structure.

THEORETICAL PREMISES

The Notion of the Active Audience

Despite recent attempts to enhance audience activity, audiences have traditionally been perceived as an important but passive component of mass media. Despite the dominant assumption that classic media outlets have low levels of audience participation, audiences have always shaped classic mass media products through the process of interaction (van Dijck 2009). A broader definition of audience interaction is "any activity that involves individuals in any form of communication with media, including playful activities with no clear societal purpose" (Enli and Syvertsen 2007, 154).

The notion of active audiences resides in multiple audience analysis traditions. Imaginative and interpretative communities have been proposed to illustrate audience activity (Abercrombie and Longhurst 1998) and fandom, viewed as emotional involvement (Siapera 2004). A continuum-based approach was also theorised by Moorhouse (1991). He positioned audience participation along an enthusiasm-based continuum that comprised the general public, the interested public (i.e., subcultural audiences) and leisure practitioners. The general public is defined as mass society, with individuals who are persuaded to be active or consume mass products. Subcultures constitute subgroups of individuals within the general public. Moorhouse (1991) argues that it is the subcultural groups that become the creators of related goods; they create slang, magazines, stickers and styles. In these ways, they enter into competition with professionals who have traditionally constituted the core of the production of goods.

Another model of audience continuum positions enthusiasts closer to producers (Abercrombie and Longhurst 1998) by identifying audiences as consumers, then going on to include fans, enthusiasts and petty producers. Thus, in addition to professional production, the ultimate level of audience engagement embodies the idea of audiences being actively involved in the process of product realisation. However, for Abercrombie and Longhurst (1998), audience members do not need to produce actual products to be active. Audience activity is also part of the imaginative and interpretative communities that were proposed as a concept to draw attention to specific spaces dedicated to participation (Abercrombie and Longhurst 1998).

The idea of active audience members resonates with participatory and fan culture. By virtue of being more active than regular audience members, active audience members resemble mass media fans, who are described by Jenkins (2009) as being engaged in the following ways: (1) they have a particular mode of content reception (with close and undivided attention); (2) they have a particular set of interpretative practices that involve converging their own lives with media life; (3) fandom constitutes a base for consumer activism, as fans are the ones who speak back to networks by expressing their views regarding programming; (4) fandom generates its own genres with no clear-cut distinction between artists and consumers; (5) the functions of fandom include the creation of an alternative social community that spends a lot of time with other fans.

This study treats audience interactivity as a continuum in terms of the level of engagement with media content through backchannels. Thus, in contrast to a dichotomous, passive audience, audience interaction is considered as a continuum, visible in the varying degrees of its involvement in programming in a changing media landscape (Jones 2009; Lotz 2007; Napoli 2011).

Interactivity

In media's changing landscape, user experience has been reconceptualised with the emergence of the concept of interactivity, a central characteristic of digital technologies (Bucy 2004; McMillan 2002). Vorderer (2000) has declared that the term 'interactive media' is to be used synonymously with new media. Interactivity is discussed in a context of cross-platform user content exchange and its implications for content integration in radio programming.

Interactive applications have developed due to technological developments, in line with a trend towards technological convergence, though they have also been shaped by user practices. Convergence, in turn, has resulted in the reconfiguration of classic mass media products (Van der Wurff et al. 2008). The reconfiguration of classic mass media into converged media and multimedia distribution has involved interactive applications that foster two-way communication, synchronicity and exchange. It has been argued that multiplatform convergence has transformed the concept of mass media into a hybrid type of interaction that includes both interpersonal communication and mass media (Walther et al. 2010).

Carpentier (2007) positions 'interactivity' as a term deriving from 'interaction,' with reference to Rheingold (1993), who proposed that online media increase opportunities for interacting with diverse users and engaging in new forms of communication. However, the term 'interactivity' as related to audience activity has been described in various facets. Facets of interactivity include participation in classic mass media, participation in digital media and concepts such as co-creation and prosumer culture (Jenkins 2006). Interactivity in this study is viewed as a multifaceted construct that varies across media platforms due to its technological affordances, user perception and diversified user practices.

Interactive applications that have emerged in online contexts have primarily been debated for how they address the properties of interactivity. Interactivity has been viewed from the perspective of technological properties that enable interactive contexts, perceived communication and user perceptions (Kiousis 2002; McMillan 2002). McMillan (2002) synthesised various approaches into a mixed human and technology approach. She outlines three traditions of interactivity research: human-to-human interaction, human-to-document interaction and human-to-system interaction (McMillan 2002). A typology-based approach of interactive applications has been proposed based on the framework of idealised information traffic patterns (Jensen 2008). The elements that constitute these traffic patterns are transmission, registration, consultation and conversation. Content-based exchange as conversation has been proposed by Rafaeli (1988). His conversational approach explicates interactivity as a property of message exchange. In this kind of exchange, the ideal three-way message exchange occurs when two messages are synthesised by a third message. Interactivity has been analysed as a technological attribute (Sundar 2004), favouring the argument that interactivity actually resides within the technological affordances of the system. Interactivity has also been described in terms of control (Sundar and Marathe 2010). The level of control within the interactive systems has been attributed to the differentiation of power and levels of control (van Dijk 2004).

Van Dijk (2000) referred to four broad conceptualisations of interactivity with regard to space and time. First, the spatial dimension considers the mere availability of interactive applications, thus allowing for a reaction. Second, the temporal dimension analyses aspects that are embedded into synchronicity, where the time lag has damaging consequences for communication. The third dimension is described as the level of control that communicative actors exercise in order to choose the types and amount of content to be exchanged. The fourth, the mental dimension, comprises the highest abstract dimension that deals with the understanding of contexts.

In addition to levels of control and the complexity of spatial and temporal dimensions of interactivity, van Dijk (2004) criticises the interactive potential of users, arguing that media are stuck on the second or third levels, being guided by perceived choice rather than actual change. Similarly, attempts were made to integrate interactivity as a vehicle of user empowerment with the notion of participation and access (Carpentier 2007). Carpentier (2007) has proposed an integrative model that embraces different theoretical positions on access, interaction and participation. The scholar makes a clear-cut distinction between production and reception, describing it in four progressing levels, where level 1 represents access; level 2 deals with access and ability to receive content; level 3 incorporates interaction; and level 4 accumulatively leads to participation (Carpentier 2007).

Carpentier's (2007) content production and evaluation scheme integrates aspects of the decision-making process in relation to content. In this model, levels 1–3 emphasise the power relationship and the process of co-deciding at the level of the organised production of content and technology. Moreover, Carpentier sheds light on a critical aspect of participation. His fourth level of participation speaks to the limitations of levelled-out judgment with regard to the value of user-produced content. Even if users are given the right to engage in the content production process, they are still excluded from opportunities to make these choices together with the companies and media organisations (Carpentier 2007).

Regardless of the limitations of user participation, interactive applications involving text messaging and broadcasting have been widely implemented in SMS-based mass media. With the rise of new media, participation became central to the idea of being fans (Roscoe 2004). The notion of the active audience does not only reside in the idea of real action. In fact, it has been argued that the audience interacts with programming on different levels, from viewing and interpreting content to reflection regarding content.

Viewers can engage in various levels of interactivity (Menduni 2007). The degree of interactivity differed based on the interactivity zones in an SMS television interactive model (Beyer et al. 2007). In this model, there was a moderator who managed content flows and served as a connecting point among audience members, individual users and hosts. The highest degree of interactivity is conceptualised to occur in a user-to-user, user-to-moderator and user-to-host interaction, while the lowest degree of interaction occurred in audience-to-host and audience-to-moderator interaction. This analysis indicated that interactivity was placed on an interpersonal level between individuals, rather than between the host and the audience as a whole.

Audience Interaction with Programming

In the Norwegian context, levels of interactivity have been documented based on empirical analyses of various programme formats, such as differentiating degrees of interactivity. Audiences were integrated into programming from the inception of mass media (Karlsen et al. 2009). Audience interaction can be traced to its historical roots: it is argued that these emerged with the rise of the cultural movements of the 1960s and 1970s, with an upsurge of participation in the 1990s (Carpentier 2011; Comor 2010). Audience members were increasingly given a more diversified programming choice, which was geared towards audiences.

Interactivity has influenced a two-way communication between audiences and radio by establishing standardised procedures related to programming since the 1930s, when audience participation in call-in talk shows started to be aired (Chase 1942). It was in the 1970s that broadcasting changed drastically: because of a clearer signal, talk radio shows took off in popularity (Marr 1985). Talk shows may have reached their zenith of popularity as a genre in the 1990s, especially with politically oriented call-in shows during election campaigns (Herbst 1995). Talk show popularity was reinforced by the call-in shows, which became a cornerstone of the 1992 USA presidential elections (Newhagen 1994), serving as a genre of radio talk shows that pioneered democratic audience participation (Carpentier 2011).

The classic talk show format involves two to five hours a day of time dedicated to audience participation (Marr 1985). Thus, the talk show format involves three main factors: the radio personality (the show host), the events of the moment that serve as fodder for discussion and the caller (Turow 1973). The audience constitutes the spontaneous part of the programming.

Content Management

Temporal and spatial dimensions were found to contribute to content production by users. With regard to content production, deictic components such as time and space have to be controlled in a very precise manner. In the context of the emergence of traditional call-in participation via telephone, content production with live audience participation was found to pose multiple challenges to content control. In order to reduce unpredictability, audience members are pre-selected before receiving air time. In this way, the programme strives to maintain control over incoming content. Control of the programme is exercised and can be described in four ways: (1) preview of the content, (2) content delay, (3) development of work ethics, and (4) implementation of the journalistic practice in content selection (Marr 1985). Telephone screeners (or producers), who directly interact with callers and pre-select participants, become a vital part of the talk show staff, since these staff members are responsible for delivering content to the show (Marr 1985). In order to implement control over content flow, radio stations in the USA also use a 4- to 7-second delay strategy to filter out profanity or other content that must be avoided on air (Marr 1985).

With the rise of digital backchannels, timing in real-time production still remains a crucial issue, since media production is all about staying on time. Thus, control over time is highly valued in the production process, and the timetable is a crucial part of media production (Ytreberg 2006). Managing live performance requires levelling out differences in content types, flows and structure that may increase in complexity. Media producers need to adopt a series of practices that help to maintain the format of the programme (Ytreberg 2006). Real-time programming places constraints on the content itself. Because mass media products are still highly dependent on a rigid programming schedule, content is prepared before the broadcasting. However, audience-based content cannot be prepared in advance, since such content is usually received as the programme proceeds. Therefore, even though rigorous scripting is performed, audience-based participation in traditional mass media is unpredictable. Given this tension between rigid structure and associated degrees of unpredictability, television production uses strategies to cope with this uncertainty. These strategies include probabilistic scripting, last-minute production and cueing (Ytreberg 2006). Probabilistic scripting allows producers to pre-define the themes that the programme would like to cover by including only relevant audience posts, due to their relatedness to the programme.

Real-time programming leaves little time to incorporate the content that is submitted in real time by audience members. Such time constraints have to be overcome by implementing certain rules by which content gets integrated. Beyer et al. (2007) described cheating strategies by the interactive television host, who posted a message himself in order to get the conversation going, thus acting as another audience member rather than exclusively as a host. Based on research performed, our study has analysed the temporal dimension of user interaction.

Social Media–Based Interactivity: The Case of RTL 102.5

This chapter is based on RTL 102.5, an interactive Italian contemporary hit radio-TV station, which distributes its content on several platforms, where users can interact with the programming via social media outlets such as Facebook, Twitter and more recently Whatsapp. Conceptually, RTL 102.5 is a sociotechnical system that has social and technological constraints while providing interactivity and challenging meaningful content integration. Established in 1975, RTL 102.5 transmits its programming via radiovision—radio programming that is not only listened to but also visible on television or the Web.[1] Currently, RTL 102.5's programming is transmitted simultaneously in real time via radio, through radiovision, which represents radio in its audio and video formats via digital terrestrial and satellite television, as well as through online streaming of the programmes in radio and radiovision formats.

It is also possible to download applications that allow people to connect to radio via portable mobile devices. SMS messages were first used by RTL 102.5 around 2001 via a software platform known as Media Platform, which was integrated into the programmes' systems of organisation and production. Media Platform activates the backchannels of communication, creating new formats and services based on interactivity, which integrate users into the programming (Acotel 2012). Facebook messages were first incorporated into the station's programming in 2009. In 2012, only two listeners' calls were included in an hour-long programme of RTL 102.5, while the incorporation of SMS and Facebook messages has been much higher, especially in the programme's audiovisual format, where messages are displayed on TV screens.

Regarding online presence, RTL 102.5 created a YouTube channel[2] on November 7, 2006, which remains active. It also has a Twitter channel,[3] where it tweets the question of the day to its audience members and informs them about any important news. RTL 102.5 broadcasts have specialised in content on Google+. It is also possible to download applications that allow for connection to the radio station via cell phones (smartphones).

METHODOLOGICAL APPROACHES

A quantitative analysis was performed of user frequency interaction by platform, types of content and interaction frequency over time. The samples were collected from January 1, 2011 to April 30, 2011: the complete sample of SMS messages was $N = 308,339$; the complete sample of Facebook messages was $N = 62,152$. Data were gathered from RTL 102.5 contributions to Facebook and user messages sent to RTL 102.5 programmes.

The underlying questions of this study refer to the social practices of users via Facebook and SMS. User content contribution patterns and user interaction frequency over time were analysed from the data collected over the 4-month period. In addition, the user practices were operationalised in terms of the interaction's addressee—the person whom content is addressed to—and types of content. Content addressees were based on the subset of 2,000 messages, half of which consisted of SMS data and the other half of Facebook data. Each message could have more than one utterance, and each utterance was coded separately. A total of 2,635 utterances were identified in the sample. Intercoder reliability reached an acceptable 80% of agreement based on Krippendorff's (2004) alpha coefficient (Lombard, Snyder-Duch and Bracken 2002). The types of addressees included content addressed to one person (see the SMS message in Example 1), to all listeners (as featured in Example 2, taken from a Facebook message), to a programme (Example 3), with no addressee (Example 4 taken from SMS,), to others (as in Example 5 from Facebook) and to *non sequiturs* (Example 6 from SMS).

Example 1   "Stefano sei la mia vita!!! Ti amo by Bruno"
"Stefano you are my life!!! I love you by Bruno"
Example 2   "Ciao a tutti e buon carnevale vvb"
"Hello to everyone and enjoy the carnival. I love you"
Example 3   "un saluto a RTL . . . spero finisca d piovere . . . :(. . . ciao pap?†"
"Greetings to RTL . . . I hope it will stop raining. . . :(. . .hi pap?†"
Example 4   "La paura detta visiva scatena reazioni quasi immediate di protezione prima percepisce lokkio poi paura e quindi ti difendi nei modi piu di protezione ke"
"Visual fear triggers almost immediate reactions of protection first the eye perceives it then fear and so you defend yourself in the most protecting ways"
Example 5   FORZA MILAN...............STASERA 11 LEONI!!!!!!!"
"Go Milan............... Tonight you will be 11 lions!!!!!!!"
Example 6   "AUGH AUGH . . . . INDIANI."
"Augh Augh . . . . Indians."

Given that SMS has a length constraint of 160 characters, which has influenced writing strategies (Herring and Zelenkauskaite 2009), including the use of spaces, the length of messages was analysed as a structural feature calculated by number of words and number of characters.

RESULTS

In order to assess the similar or diverging interaction practices via SMS and Facebook, the overall user content traffic on two analysed platforms and the message posting frequency per platform were compared. The overall sample

Table 3.1   Frequency of message distribution by user in SMS

Users	N of messages	% of users
59,398	1	57.3
21,495	2	20.7
8450	3	8.1
6781	5	6.5
4566	10	4.4
1778	20	1.7
782	50	0.7
197	100	0.2
86	200	0.08
43	500	0.04
22	6,000	0.02

Source: Author's own elaboration.

indicated that mobile texting and Facebook content frequency differed: there were 308,399 SMS messages comprising 83.2% of overall messages, with 62,152 Facebook messages constituting 16.7% of the total messages, showing that Facebook was more often utilised for user interaction with radio.

Frequency of User Interaction

In order to measure the frequency of user interaction, a specific number of users were plotted by the frequency of their content over time, for SMS and Facebook separately. Over the 4-month period, the total number of users who sent at least one message was equal to $N = 103,598$ (users), for a total of $N = 308,398$ sent messages. The mean (ratio) number of sent messages per person was 2.97.

However, the highest number of sent messages by a single person was 5,094 (averaging 50 messages per day). Table 3.1 shows the number of messages in relation to the number of contributors of SMS for a total of 103,598 users.

RADIO AUDIENCE INTERACTION: MOBILE TEXTING SMS VS. FACEBOOK

Results show a power-law distribution, where a vast majority of users contributed few messages, while a few audience members ($N = 65$) contributed from 500 to 6,000 messages during the 4-month period. This suggests that these users served as the core of the audience community, while the majority of users were occasional writers.

Table 3.2 Frequency of message distribution by user in Facebook

Users	N of messages	% of users
7409	1	64.6
2232	2	19.5
816	3	7.1
453	4	3.9
226	5	2.0
244	6 to 9	2.1
76	10 to 19	0.7
11	20 to 49	0.1
2	50 to 99	0.02
1	100 to 105	0.01

Source: Author's own elaboration.

For Facebook message senders, the following was observed: a total of 20,498 messages were analysed, and the total number of single users was 11,470. Thus there were 1.78 messages sent per user. In comparison with SMS users, Facebook users are less likely to send multiple messages.

As for Facebook user activities, the following user contribution graph was constructed based on the frequency of selected message distribution:

Tables 3.1 and 3.2 show that Facebook messages were predominantly sent through a power-law distribution, where many users wrote only 1 message, but several users wrote up to 100 messages. This finding indicates that listeners, through their commenting interaction, can be categorised as core users who constantly and actively engage with radio, having been called 'regulars' in traditional call-in radio (Marr 1985), while the rest of the audience members occasionally engage in interaction with radio by sending one or two messages. This finding shows continuity in listenership practices with call-in interaction through telephones. Even if users can currently interact through social media outlets, practices are similar.

The Spatio-temporal Dimension

In order to account for message flows from the two social media platforms, messages were plotted over a random day. Figure 3.1 shows the total SMS versus Facebook messages received on a random day.

In the previous analysis of the total of SMS versus Facebook messages received, it is possible to see clear-cut differences in message-posting activity.

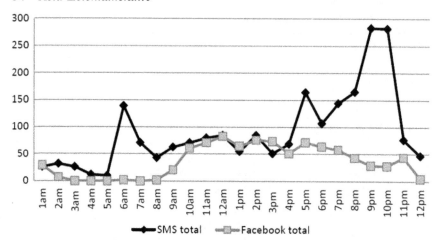

Figure 3.1   The total number of SMS vs. Facebook messages received on a random day, April 26, 2011

Source: Author's own elaboration.

On one hand, Facebook messages are almost zero from 1 a.m. to 10 a.m., while from 10 a.m. to 11 p.m. they are sent in equally distributed proportions. SMS messages, on the other hand, show peaks at 6 a.m., 5 p.m., and 10–11 p.m.

These results highlight the role of technologies as being part of our lifestyles, based on their accessibility and portability, as 64% of Italian listeners access radio through their cars, 41% use traditional radios and the remaining 3% access radio through the Internet (Eurisko 2012). The radio listening experience during travelling time gets accompanied by text messaging, being a useful portable device for interaction with radio. The use of SMS during rush hours may serve as an activity that fills waiting time in a traffic jam, or in the evening when listeners are relaxed and thus willing to engage in interaction with their favourite programme. However, Facebook messages are used less frequently, with spikes during the daytime, probably during work time when listeners check their Facebook profiles during work or study breaks.

The Content Addressee

Given the differences found in the overall number of messages sent via the two platforms, further analysis explored to whom messages were sent on the two platforms. The overall breakdown of the addressee categories shows that most messages were sent to the programme ($n = 901$) by one person ($n = 552$), while the rest of the categories comprised $n = 676$. By comparing the categories between the two platforms, the pattern in Figure 3.2 emerged:

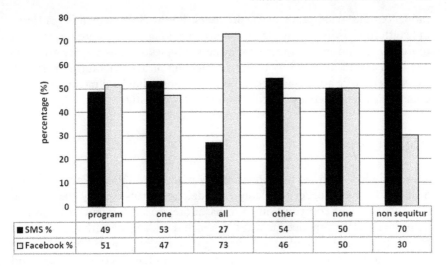

	program	one	all	other	none	non sequitur
■ SMS %	49	53	27	54	50	70
□ Facebook %	51	47	73	46	50	30

Figure 3.2   Facebook and SMS addressee analysis

Source: Author's own elaboration.

Messages addressed to all audience members were more likely to be sent via Facebook, yet *non sequiturs* were dominant for SMS. This finding could be interpreted as a perceived anonymity via SMS messages, since none of the author authentications are visible to the audience, compared with Facebook, where the user's name and a profile photo are available to all the radiovision spectators. In other words, users would avoid engaging in the posting of *non sequitur* content, since they are easily identifiable on RTL 102.5's Facebook wall.

Regarding the remaining categories, messages from one person to another were more common with SMS as compared with Facebook. SMS messages have historically been designed for interpersonal interaction; this result shows the continuity of such practices. In contrast, on Facebook, where wall messages are accessed mostly by multiple people, more messages were directed to everyone.

Content Structure

The length of all SMS and Facebook messages received (the total sample) were compared. Results show that there were more words used in SMS (M = 14.66, sd = 8.762) overall than in Facebook (M = 14.25, sd = 12.756), and this result is statistically significant, $F(1, 308399) = 92.932$, $p < .001$. However, when comparing the number of characters with spaces, Facebook messages were found to be longer (M = 86.93, sd = 72.915) than SMS (M = 82.84, sd = 46.766), and this difference is statistically significant, $F(1, 370551) = 318.025$, $p < .001$. These results indicate how technology influences the social practices of the users. For an SMS, which is restricted in length (one SMS message is 160 characters long), users were trying to fit more words and more content by using strategies such as abbreviation, as has been found in previous research (Herring and Zelenkauskaite 2009). Thus, users were adapting to technological constraints and navigating their communicative practices in order to interact with radio.

CONCLUSION

This study has analysed how interactivity practices differ via Facebook and SMS platforms, in order to account for deictic dimensions, by focusing on three aspects: user contribution patterns, addressee and content structure. By analysing specific practices as ways in which users engage with radio, it was found that Facebook and mobile texting function as sociotechnical systems with different technological affordances, which influence content length and associated user practices, such as the use of SMS during rush hour and its implications for the prevalence of radio listenership in cars. Platforms were found to be similar in terms of the presence of the same content addressee categories and a power-law user level of interaction, where the majority of users contributed one or two messages and a few users contributed large amounts of content. Differences were also found in terms of the addressee of the interaction, flow of messages and message length.

Regarding addressee categories, given that SMS has traditionally been used for interpersonal one-to-one communication, when considering interaction with RTL 102.5 it was used more frequently to address a single person. Facebook, on the other hand, reflected ways of addressing content to all listeners, which happens mostly on the Facebook wall. Differences in structure—specifically, length—could be attributed to the technological constraints imposed by the platform, e.g., SMS messages are 160 characters long. This also speaks to the social practices associated with them: SMS messages have more words but are shorter in length. Previous studies have found abbreviation strategies associated with SMS which could explain these differences (Bieswanger 2008; Herring and Zelenkauskaite 2009).

Cross-platform differences between Facebook and SMS can be attributed to the adoption of these two modes. SMS was introduced in RTL 102.5 in 2001, while Facebook was introduced in RTL 102.5 in 2009, which could explain the difference in use of these modes for interaction with the radio station. Also, SMS was initially designed for interpersonal exchanges. The prevalence of interpersonal user-to-user exchange is evident from this analysis. User-to-user exchanges have spilled over to radio-mediated contexts: on radio platforms, users were more likely to address content to other users via SMS than Facebook.

Considering diversity in terms of user participation, user content and user contribution patterns over time, on one hand it seems that interactivity provides this promise of 'utopian' discussion in relation to content production, where users add more diverse content through different platforms. On the other hand, from the perspective of content integration, there can be problematic issues in providing a meaningful and coherent picture of content. Multiplatform audience-based programming thus resembles last-minute production, which requires the flexibility to accommodate the flow of incoming content (Ytreberg 2006). Regardless of the fact that social media increasingly constitute larger data pools for media companies, so far there are limits to the ways that radio capitalises on the value of user content (Zelenkauskaite and Simões 2013). This study sheds new light on the diversity and similarity of listenership, and on the diverse needs that listeners have across platforms.

In relation to deictic dimensions, the platforms offered varying degrees of temporality, indicating different temporal layers that social media bring to radio. These layers include temporality relative to programmes, where users participate by reacting to programme events. It was found that users interact with other users, and such interaction might be independent from the programme time. As for space, multiple platforms theoretically provide more of it, yet offer a limited temporal window of content visibility, since new messages hide the older ones. An absence of unified access to all platforms as a way to interact with radio content results in isolated islands of space, which potentially segregate users rather than uniting them in a community. Value creation for the users was proposed by unified access to the users to foster a user-centric approach to interactive contexts (Zelenkauskaite and Simões 2013).

The theoretical implications of this study are that interactivity is relative and ranges among technological affordances, content management, user engagement level and backchannels, the properties of which evolve over time. This chapter shows that text-based interactivity allows for more content to be collected by the audiences. Additionally, text provides a co-occurrence of multiple content access and archiving spaces, ranging from social media spaces such as Facebook and Twitter to Web-based SMS depositories and real-time display via TV screens. Multiplatform media analysis also calls for new ways of conceptualising audience analysis in cross-platform contexts.

The question of the anonymity of social media content calls for the reconsideration of the notion of invisible audiences. Currently, with social media identifiers, both audiences and individual members are visible through their photos, and names are verifiable and recognisable to the other audience members. Future studies should address questions regarding user interaction with multiple social media platforms.

NOTES

1. http://www.rtl.it.
2. http://www.youtube.com/user/rtl1025.
3. http://twitter.com/rtl1025.

REFERENCES

Abercrombie, N. and Longhurst, B. (1998). *Audiences: A Sociological Theory of Performance and Imagination.* London: Sage.

Acotel. (2012). *Acotel Interactive.* Accessed March 3, 2014. http://www.acotel.com/aree_business.php?lingua=en&pag=13.

Ala-Fossi, M., Lax, S., O'Neill, B., Jauert, P. and Shaw, H. (2008). "The Future of Radio Is Still Digital—but Which One? Expert Perspectives and Future Scenarios for Radio Media in 2015." *Journal of Radio & Audio Media,* 15(1), 4–25.

Baym, N. K., Zhang, Y. B. and Lin, M. (2004). "Social Interactions Across Media: Interpersonal Communication on the Internet, Telephone and Face-to-Face." *New Media & Society,* 6, 299–318.

Beyer, Y., Enli, G. S., Maasø, A. J. and Ytreberg, E. (2007). "Small Talk Makes a Big Difference: Recent Developments in Interactive, SMS-Based Television." *Television & New Media,* 8(3), 213–234.

Bieswanger, M. (2008). "2 abbrevi8 or Not 2 abbrevi8: A Contrastive Analysis of Different Shortening Strategies in English and German Text Messages." *SALSA.* Accessed January 24, 2014. http://studentorgs.utexas.edu/salsa/proceedings/2006/Bieswanger.pdf.

Bucy, E. P. (2004). "Interactivity and Society: Locating an Elusive Concept." *The Information Society,* 20(5), 275–385.

Carpentier, N. (2007). "Participation, Access, and Interaction: Changing Perspectives." In Nightingale, V. and Dwyer, T. (eds.), *New Media Worlds: Challenges for Convergence.* New York: Oxford, 214–231.

———. (2011). *Media and Participation. A Site of Ideological-Democratic Struggle.* Bristol: Intellect.

Cha, M., Kwak, H., Rodriguez, P., Ahn, Y.-Y. and Moon, S. (2007). "I Tube, You Tube, Everybody Tubes: Analyzing the World's Largest User Generated Content Video System." Paper presented at ACM Internet Measurement Conference, San Diego, CA, October 24–26.

Chase, F. (1942). *Sound and Fury: An Informal History of Broadcasting.* New York: Harper.

Cogdill, S., Fanderclai, T. L., Kilborn, J. and Williams, M. G. (2001). "Backchannel: Whispering in Digital Conversation." Paper presented at the 34th Annual Hawaii International Conference, Kihei, Maui, Hawaii, January 3–6, 1–8.

Comor, E. (2010). "Contextualizing and Critiquing the Fantastic Prosumer: Power, Alienation and Hegemony." *Critical Sociology,* 37(3), 309–327.

Deuze, M. (2010). *Media Life.* Oxford: Polity Press.

Enli, G. S. and Syvertsen, T. (2007). "Participation, Play and Socializing in New Media Environments." In Nightingale, V. and Dwyer, T. (eds.), *New Media Worlds: Challenges for Convergence.* South Melbourne: Oxford University Press, 147–162.

Eurisko. (2012). *Radio Monitor 2012.* Accessed March 3, 2014. http://danielelpido.blog.ilsole24ore.com/i-bastioni-di-orione/files/radiomonitor2012.pdf.

Hendy, D. (2000). *Radio in the Global Age.* Cambridge: Polity Press.

Herbst, S. (1995). "On Electronic Public Space: Talk Shows in Theoretical Perspective." *Political Communication,* 12, 263–274.

Herring, S. C. and Zelenkauskaite, A. (2009). "Symbolic Capital in a Virtual Heterosexual Market: Abbreviation and Insertion in Italian iTV SMS." *Written Communication,* 26(1), 5–31.

Jenkins, H. (2006). *Convergence Culture: Where Old and New Media Collide.* New York: NYU Press.

———. (2009). *Textual Poachers: Television Fans and Participatory Culture.* New York and London: Routledge.

Jensen, J. F. (2008). "The Concept of Interactivity—Revised. Four New Typologies for a New Media Landscape." Paper presented at the Conference on Designing Interactive User Experiences for TV and Video, San Francisco, CA, October 22–24.

Jones, J. P. (2009). "I Want My Talk TV." In Lotz, A. D. (ed.), *Beyond Prime Time: Television Programming in the Post-Network Era*. New York and London: Routledge, 14–35.

Karlsen, F., Sundet, V. S., Syvertsen, T. and Ytreberg, E. (2009). "Non-professional Activity on Television in a Time of Digitalization: More Fun for Elite or New Opportunities for Ordinary People." *Nordicom Review*, 30(1), 19–36.

Kiousis, S. (2002). "Interactivity: A Concept Explication." *New Media & Society*, 4(3), 355–383.

Krippendorff, K. (2004). *Content Analysis: An Introduction to Its Methodology*. Thousand Oaks: Sage.

Latour, B. (1991). "Technology Is Society Made Durable." In Law, J. (ed.), *A Sociology of Monsters: Essays on Power, Technology and Domination*. London: Routledge, 103–132.

Lombard, M., Snyder-Duch, J. and Bracken, C. C. (2002). "Content Analysis in Mass Communication: Assessment and Reporting of Intercoder Reliability." *Human Communication Research*, 28(4), 587–604.

Lotz, A. D. (2007). *The Television Will Be Revolutionalized*. New York, London: New York University Press.

Marr, B. W. (1985). "Talk Radio Programming." In Eastman S. T., Head, S. W. and Klein, L. (eds.), *Broadcast Programming: Strategies for Winning Television and Radio Audiences*. Belmont: Wadsworth, 311–323.

McMillan, S. J. (2002). "Exploring Models of Interactivity." In Lievrouw, L. A. and Livingstone, S. (eds.), *Handbook of New Media. Social Shaping and Consequences of ICTs*. London, Thousand Oaks, New Delhi: Sage, 163–182.

Menduni, E. (2007). *Fine delle trasmissioni: Da Pippo Baudo a Youtube*. Bologna: Il Mulino.

Moorhouse, H. F. (1991). *Driving Ambitions: An Analysis of the American Hot Rod Enthusiasm*. Manchester, New York: Manchester University Press.

Napoli, P. M. (2011). *Audience Evolution: New Technologies and the Transformation of Media Audiences*. New York: Columbia University Press.

Newhagen, J. E. (1994). "Self-efficacy and Call-in Political Television Show Use." *Communication Research*, 21, 366–379.

Niederer, S. and van Dijck, J. (2010). "Wisdom of the Crowd or Technicity of Content? Wikipedia as a Socio-technical System." *New Media & Society*, 12(8), 1368–1387.

Panek, E. T., Nardis, Y. and Konrath, S. (2013). "Mirror or Megaphone?: How Relationships Between Narcissism and Social Networking Site Use Differ on Facebook and Twitter." *Computers in Human Behavior*, 29, 2004–2012.

Rafaeli, S. (1988). "Interactivity: From New Media to Communication." In Hawkins, R. P., Wiemann, J. M. and Pingree, S. (eds.), *Advancing Communication Science: Merging Mass and Interpersonal Processes. Sage Annual Review of Communication Research, Volume 16*. Newbury Park, Beverly Hills, London, New Delhi: Sage, 110–134.

Resmann, N. (2009). *Mapping North Belgian Participatory Television Programmes 1989–2008*. Centre for Studies on Media and Culture (Cemeso). Accessed January 25, 2012. http://www.vub.ac.be/SCOM/cemeso/wpapers.htm.

Rheingold, H. (1993). *The Virtual Community: Finding Connection in a Computerized World*. Boston: Addison-Wesley Longman.

Rhoads, B. E. (1993). "Looking Back at Radio's Future." In Pease, E. C. and Dennis, E. E. (eds.), *Radio. The Forgotten Medium*. New Brunswick: Transaction, 15–21.

Roscoe, J. (2004). "Multi-plaform Event Television: Reconceptualising Our Relationship with Television." *The Communication Review*, 7, 363–369.

Siapera, E. (2004). "From Couch Potatoes to Cybernauts? The Expanding Notion of the Audience on TV Channels' Websites." *New Media & Society*, 6, 155–172.

Sundar, S. S. (2004). "Theorizing Interactivity's Effects." *Information Society*, 20(5), 385–389.

Sundar, S. S. and Marathe, S. S. (2010). "Personalization versus Customization: The Importance of Agency, Privacy, and Power Usage." *Human Communication Research*, 36, 298–322.

Toffler, A. (1980). *The Third Wave*. London: Collins.

Tuomi, P. and Bachmayer, S. (2011). "The Convergence of TV and Web (2.0) in Austria and Finland." Paper presented at Euro ITV'11, Lisbon, Portugal, June 29–July 1.

Turow, J. (1973). "Talk Show Radio as Interpersonal Communication." *Journal of Broadcasting & Electronic Media*, 18(2), 171–179.

Van der Wurff, R., Lauf, E., Balčytienė, A., Fortunati, L., Holmberg, S. L., Paulussen, S. and Salaverría, R. (2008). "Online and Print Newspapers in Europe in 2003. Evolving towards Complementarity." *Communications*, 33(4), 403–430.

van Dijck, J. (2000) "Models of Democracy and Concepts of Communication." In Hacker, K. L. and van Dijk, J. (eds.), *Digital Democracy: Issues of Theory and Practice*. Thousand Oaks: Sage, 30–54.

———. (2004). "Digital Media." In Downing, J.D.H., McQuail, D., Schlesinger, P. and Wartella, E. (eds.), *The Sage Handbook of Media Studies*. Thousand Oaks: Sage, 145–164.

———. (2009). "Users Like You? Theorizing Agency in User-Generated Content." *Media, Culture & Society*, 31(1), 41–58.

Vorderer, P. (2000). "Interactive Entertainment and Beyond." In Vorderer, P. (ed.), *Media Entertainment: The Psychology of Its Appeal*. Mahwah: Lawrence Erlbaum Associates, 21–36.

Walther, J. B., Carr, C. T., Choi, S.S.W, DeAndrea, D. C., Kim, J., Tom, S. and Van Der Heide, B. (2010). "Interaction of Interpersonal, Peer, and Media Influence Sources Online: A Research Agenda for Technology Convergence." In Papacharissi, Z. (ed.), *Networked Self: Identity, Community, and Culture on Social Network Sites*. New York and London: Routledge, 17–38.

Yngve, V. H. (1975). "Human Linguistics and Face-to-Face Interaction." In Kendon, A., Harris, R. M. and Key, M. R. (eds.), *Organization of Behavior in Face-to-Face Interaction*. Chicago: Mouton, 47–63.

Ytreberg, E. (2006). "Premediations of Performance in Recent Live Television: A Scripting Approach to Media Production Studies." *European Journal of Cultural Studies*, 9(4), 421–440.

Zelenkauskaite, A. and Herring, S. C. (2008). "Television-Mediated Conversation: Coherence in Italian Itv SMSChat." *Proceedings of the Forty-First Hawaii International Conference on System Sciences (HICSS-41)*. Los Alamitos, CA: IEEE Press, 145–146.

Zelenkauskaite, A. and Simões, B. (2013). "The Big Data User-Centric Model." Paper presented at the World Congress in Computer Science, Computer Engineering, and Applied Computing, Las Vegas, NV, July 22–25.

———. (2014). "Big Data through Interest-Based Cross-Platform Interactivity." Paper presented at the International Conference on Big Data and Smart Computing (BigComp 2014), IEEE Computer Society, Bangkok, Thailand, January 15–17.

4 Listeners, Social Networks and the Construction of Talk Radio Information's Discourse in the 2.0 Age

Belén Monclús, Maria Gutiérrez, Xavier Ribes, Iliana Ferrer and Josep Maria Martí

THE POTENTIAL OF WEB 2.0 AND SOCIAL NETWORKING FOR LISTENERS

Using the Internet and social media has become an everyday activity in developed societies, changing users' cultural and media practices, but also the activity of the media and the relationship between the two. The development and implementation of Web 2.0 has enabled the audience to access and participate in media discourse more easily. As Napoli (2010, 509) argues:

> The communication dynamics reflected in Web 2.0 . . . applications such as YouTube, Facebook, MySpace and Twitter increasingly foreground an approach to mass communication in which the individual audience member operates on nearly an equal footing with traditional institutional communicators.

In this environment of new media technologies, a new audience of active users is being established (Livingstone 2003), capable of becoming prosumers (Toffler 1980), produsers (Bruns 2005) or co-creators (Banks and Deuze 2009) by being able to produce their own content (User Generated Content [UGC]) and distribute/share it with other users (Beer and Burrows 2007; Napoli 2010), including the media. As Cohen (2008, 7) notes:

> Web 2.0 has altered the terrain of the media business, notably by adjusting consumers' roles in the production process. (. . .) In mass media models, the role of consumers has been just that, to consume, or to watch and read the product. Web 2.0 consumers, however, have become producers who fulfil a critical role.

Social network sites (SNS) such as Facebook and Twitter have become excellent platforms for the audience to co-create content (Boyd and Ellison 2008). But social media also make it easier for listeners to communicate with each other and for communities of listeners who share views or ideals to form (Castells 2001). These spaces have become central to young people:

> The popularity of social networking among the young in particular testifies to the importance they attach to the options the Internet provides for content creation, for meeting and 'socialising' with people beyond their local environments, and for the satisfaction of their curiosity about global issues.
>
> (Nightingale 2007, 32)

Thus, these new virtual social spaces provide radio, for example, with the ideal scenario in which to interact and generate new dynamics with its audience, especially with a young generation that prefers computers to transistor radios (Gutiérrez, Ribes and Monclús 2011).

Against this background, the old media have been forced to react to the challenges that technological changes have imposed on them regarding their business activity and therefore their business model, but also to the new role that audiences are adopting in this digital environment, particularly in the social networking age. In this sense, Jenkins (2006, 24) notes that "Audiences, empowered by these new technologies, occupying a space at the intersection between old and new media, are demanding the right to participate within the culture." The emergence of this 'convergence culture,' defined by Jenkins, creates new forms of participation and collaboration that force the old media—such as radio—to renegotiate their relationship with their listeners. And this process is not without complexity, as Nightingale (2007, 27) indicates, "There is ongoing tension between traditional (or 'old') media and the emerging entrepreneurial culture of the World Wide Web."

Like all old media, radio has been forced to have an online presence and, specifically, to be present in social networks, but without knowing how to manage these new virtual spaces on a business level nor the relationship established in them with their users (Martí et al. 2013). Thus, radio has also developed its own virtual space:

> Radio is now a virtual space, network space, mobile space while at the same time remaining a physical space when conceptualized in its studio format where citizens can participate in public debate. This pluralisation of spaces by new media technologies is subverting the old notion of radio as a unified and bounded medium—hence its greater accessibility through newer means that traverse the traditional methods of radio consumption. Radio as a space is now much more open, dispersed, through informal spaces of content production. Greater accessibility of radio to audiences therefore means that digitization and convergence can potentially make radio more participative within and across social divides. The multiple platforms of websites, Social Media, podcasts, online and

mobile streaming should, in principle, make radio vertically and horizontally accessible within and across social classes.

(Moyo 2012, 214–215)

This approach by Moyo (2012) brings together the possibilities and, at the same time, the most important challenges of this new virtual radio space in the hands of both broadcasters and receivers/listeners/users. Foremost among the challenges is the creation of a new participatory environment with multiple opportunities for both actors.

The Configuration of a New Participatory Space: Reality or Mirage?

The Internet has become a new leader within the digital media ecosystem because it is more and more accessible to more people and is increasingly used as a legitimate source of information, partly replacing the old media (Gherhards and Schäfer 2010, citing a 2004 study by Brigit Von Eimeren et al.). In this sense, Gherhards and Schäfer point out that

> Many political scientists, media researchers and other scholars, as well as political activists, believe that this new medium has the potential to fundamentally change societal communication and that, in a nutshell, Internet communication makes for a better public sphere than have the old mass media. . . .

(2010, 145)

These expectations are based on the fact that the structure of communication on the Internet is completely different from that of the old media.

In the online scenario, the user acquires greater power and the media seem to play a less important role (see Carpentier 2011a; Jenkins 2006; Willens 2013), encouraging hopes of an idealised participatory model of the public sphere. The role that the audience can play on Web 2.0 and on SNS recovers and updates the concept of public sphere defined by Habermas (1974, 1996), understood to be a network for communicating information and points of view. For other authors, these spaces do not correspond to Habermas' concept because, as Papacharissi (2010, 129) argues, SNSs are "commercially public spaces that connect networked individual private spheres." Without entering into this debate, the new online media sphere is becoming a space where citizens can easily make their voices heard, express their opinions, disseminate them and interact with other stakeholders.

However, achieving this ideal participatory model is not so easy. As Carpentier (2011a, 68) indicates:

> Participation in the media deals with participation in the production of media output (content-related participation) and in media organisational

decision-making (structural participation). These forms of media participation allow citizens to be active in one of the many (micro-)spheres relevant to daily life, and to put into practice their right to communicate.

Furthermore, as the author argues in his AIP (access, interaction, participation) model (Carpentier 2011b), the access of the audience to the media sphere and its interaction by providing UGC or establishing socio-communicative relations with media—whilst being important conditions for the possibility of participation—cannot be equated with participation itself. In Carpentier's words: "This difference between participation on the one hand, and access and interaction on the other is located within the key role that is attributed to power, and to equal(ized) power relations in decision-making processes" (2011b, 29).

From this perspective, listeners participate in the construction of radio news discourse inasmuch as they are on an equal footing in making the decisions that determine this discourse. In this context, a participatory journalism is developed: ". . . An embrace of this networked environment by journalism challenges news organisations to extend the level of their direct engagement with audiences as participants in the processes of gathering, selecting, editing, producing and communicating news" (Deuze, Bruns and Neuberger 2007, 323).

Recent studies focusing on the medium of radio, such as those by Moyo (2012) and Willens (2013), present disappointing scenarios in relation to the possibilities of achieving this ideal model of participation. In this sense, Moyo shows that increased access to radio through new digital technologies has not resulted in a more significant level of audience participation despite the existence of a greater predisposition on the part of professional journalists to incorporate content produced by the audience. For her part, Willens (2013, 230–231) demonstrates the ease of 'silencing' new media participation by confirming:

> There is nothing inherently participatory in the use of Internet and mobile phones by radio stations because audience input channelled via these media can be as effortlessly censored as were old-fashioned letters from listeners. The immediacy and spontaneity of mobile phone calls has arguably empowered listeners more as their contribution to live phone-in programmes cannot be as easily managed by radio producers as SMS messages, email or Facebook posts. New media therefore offer both opportunities and limits to the involvement of audiences in content production.

To achieve this ideal stage of participation, two elements become indispensable: first, the willingness of listeners to act as produsers or co-creators; and second, the willingness of radio stations to incorporate this new audience role by building a truly participatory online media sphere. This study sketches out a 'participatory scenario' that is, more than anything, a mirage: a vision of what could be.

Research Design and Method

The results presented here form part of a research project conducted by the Observatori de la Ràdio a Catalunya[1] (Catalonia Radio Observatory, GRISS-UAB), studying the broadcaster, the message and the receiver both in social networks and on air (conventional/analogue broadcasting), in order to understand the synergies that exist between broadcaster and listener on different radio broadcasting platforms, the continuity between conventional scheduling and online radio, and how audience participation and interaction is managed, among other areas. However, this chapter focuses exclusively on the activity and role of the audience in the construction of online radio discourse through the social networks Facebook and Twitter in prime-time talk-radio magazine programmes (broadcast between 6 a.m. and 12:20 p.m.), since these programmes play a key role in shaping the news agenda, the editorial line and the brand image of radio stations.

To analyse the contribution of listeners to the construction of online radio information discourse by means of the SNS, we started with the following research questions:

RQ1: How exactly does the audience use social media to participate in on-air broadcasting discourse?

RQ2: What kind of participation and content do listeners and Internet users generate?

RQ3: Do the social media selected and the gender of the audience determine the nature of their participation?

RQ4: To what extent do they affect radio stations' broadcasting discourse?

To answer these questions, an analysis was made of a composite week's sample (Riffe et al. 1993) of activity and content generated from Monday to Friday in March 2012, both on air and in Facebook and Twitter profiles, on the morning news magazine programmes *En días como hoy*, produced by Radio 1 of Spain's national public broadcaster Radio Nacional de España (RNE), *Hoy por hoy*, by commercial Spanish broadcaster Cadena SER, *El matí de Catalunya Ràdio*, by the Catalan regional public broadcaster Catalunya Ràdio, and *El món a RAC1* by the Catalan regional commercial station RAC1. The selection of radio stations was based on the fact that they are the public and commercial broadcasters with the largest audiences in Spain and in Catalonia (AIMC 2013a).[2] Similarly, the choice of the social networks was based on their having the largest number of users in Spain and Catalonia (AIMC 2013b).

Table 4.1 Content variables for audience analysis

Variables	Definition
Platform	This variable categorised publications (posts or tweets) according to whether they were made on Facebook or on Twitter.
Authorship of the publication	First, the author of the first-generation publication was specified, whether this was made by the radio broadcaster or by the audience.Second, the types of replies to the first-generation publication were categorised: broadcaster replies to an initial publication by the audience, audience replies to an initial publication by the broadcaster, or audience replies to a publication by another listener.
Definition of the author	This variable sought to identify the author of the publication.
Synergy with on-air broadcasting	The synergy with conventional broadcasting (on air) was determined by the relationship that publications in social networks had with the content that was broadcast on air.
Typology of content generated	The classification of this variable was based on research by Wardle and Williams (2010), who proposed a category called "Audience Content"—instead of the term 'UGC'—to categorise content generated by the audience, which is divided into four subcategories that have been adapted for this study:

- "Audience Footage" refers to new information on a current news story, breaking news, unknown data, photographs, videos, audios, etc.
- "Audience Experiences" refers to the content derived from personal experiences of the audience that served to respond to news or information submitted by the broadcaster, thus providing additional information to the radio discourse.
- "Audience Stories" refers to stories from the audience that were not part of the thematic and news agenda of the broadcaster, i.e., topics from the audience unrelated to the media agenda.
- "Audience Comments" refers to contributions made by the audience for or against the proposed topic, interpreting facts and/or expressing ideas. In our study, this subcategory is called "Opinion/Comment" as it identifies content of an opinion-giving or judgmental nature, while the previous three categories highlight the informative nature of the content provided by the audience.

  After the pretest, it was decided to add a new subcategory called "Comment out of context," covering all frivolous or trivial publications, insults or onomatopoeias, among others, which had no connection with the radio discourse.

Source: Authors.

The inclusion of the geographic factor in the sample selection from the Catalan radio ecosystem allows the study of elements that may result from the fact that both broadcaster and audience share experiences and other ties, the result of both geographical and emotional proximity, which could determine listeners' behaviour (Bonet 2000).

The research technique used to carry out this study was that of quantitative and qualitative content analysis, for which an ad hoc methodological tool was designed. In this regard, it should be emphasised that the data presented in this paper refer only to the activity of the audience in the Facebook and Twitter profiles of the four programmes analysed, although the full study also addresses the behaviour of the broadcaster. The set of variables designed to study the contribution of the audience focuses primarily on determining the use of one network or another, defining its users, knowing the content that is generated and establishing the level of audience participation in the construction of the radio discourse. Table 4.1 summarises the main variables considered.

Any post or tweet generated by the audience was considered a unit of analysis, be it spontaneous or in response to a post or tweet by the broadcaster or another listener. The study protocol was applied to a total of 5,745 units of analysis, of which 4,872 (84.8%) belonged exclusively to the activity of listeners taking place in the profiles of the selected programmes. Specifically, 2,175 units on Facebook and 2,697 units on Twitter were analysed. The 873 (15.2%) remaining units were publications by the broadcaster.

To validate the results, reliability was calculated with Holsti's intercoder coefficient, which measures the degree of agreement between two or more coders (Wimmer and Dominick 1996). The completed reliability tests yielded a Holsti coefficient of 88.8 on the 17 variables that make up the record of analysis of social networks, far exceeding the minimum level of agreement in this test, based on 80% (Igartua 2006). The next section presents the main trends identified regarding the contribution of the Spanish and Catalan audience, through social media, to the construction of the main radio magazine programmes' information discourse.

RESULTS

Volume of Interaction

Ordering the magazine programmes by the number of users that they had in March 2012 on both Facebook and Twitter shows that those produced by commercial broadcasters had the highest numbers of followers (*El món a RAC1*, 40,252 on Facebook and 35,020 on Twitter; *Hoy por hoy*–Cadena SER, 19,084 on Facebook and 14,606 on Twitter), as opposed to the public broadcasters (*El matí de Catalunya Ràdio*, 13,450 on Facebook and 9,027 on Twitter; *En días como hoy*–RNE1, 13,900 on Facebook, and there is no Twitter profile available at the time of the study). However, the analysis reveals the general lack of a direct relation among the number of followers in the profiles, the volume of publications produced and the on-air audience of magazine programmes. Moreover, the data for the latter underline the local perspective as a determining factor in the activity that listeners carry out in the SNS studied, since the online communities of regional programmes appear to be more participative (with an on-air audience rate of activity in social networks of 0.00194 for *El matí de Catalunya Ràdio* and 0.00227 for *El món a RAC1*)[3] compared with those of programmes with national coverage (with levels of activity of the on-air audience in social networks of 0.00031 for *En días como hoy* and 0.00039 for *Hoy por hoy*), which logically have a higher number of listeners.

Given this situation, there is a need to determine whether the number of posts and tweets from the audience is a consequence of the number of publications by the broadcaster (see Table 4.2). In other words, whether the audience is more likely to interact in those social networks where the broadcaster regularly intervenes and where more calls for dialogue are made or listener-programme conversations take place. The data obtained do not support this cause-effect relationship.

Exploration of the universe of each social network introduces some nuances in relation to the link between the number of followers of the profiles and the number of publications. In the Facebook pages analysed, the volume of activity varies from 1 post per 12 'friends' (*Hoy por hoy* and *El*

Table 4.2　Activity of the broadcaster and of the audience by programme

		Facebook	Twitter	Total publications
En días como hoy (RNE1)	Broadcaster	16	2	18
	Audience	510	34	544
Hoy por hoy (Cadena SER)	Broadcaster	35	175	210
	Audience	821	830	1651
El matí de Catalunya Ràdio (Catalunya Ràdio)	Broadcaster	172	292	464
	Audience	496	649	1145
El món a RAC1 (RAC1)	Broadcaster	30	151	181
	Audience	348	1184	1532
Total SNS	Broadcaster	253	620	873
	Audience	2175	2697	4872

Data: Number of posts and tweets published by the radio programmes and their listeners during the composite week analysed.

NB: The data on Twitter on *En días como hoy* correspond to the corporate profile of RNE, in the absence of a specific profile.

Source: Authors.

matí de Catalunya Ràdio) to 1 post per 26 'friends' (*En días como hoy* and *El món a RAC1*). Consequently, in this social network a correlation is not observed between the profiles of the magazine programmes with the largest number of users and the volume of activity, which might suggest that each audience displays different behaviours depending on the programme.

By contrast, on Twitter, there is some correlation between the number of followers and the number of tweets. Interestingly, the level of user activity is inverse to the number of followers. Thus, in the profile of *El matí de Catalunya Ràdio*, 1 post is published for every 14 followers; in *Hoy por hoy*, 1 post is written for every 18 followers; and in *El món a RAC1*, only 1 message appears per 30 followers. It therefore seems that the more followers on Twitter, the more messages are generated, but the number of followers who do not join in the conversation is also greater.

Dialogue: Participating in the Conversation

One Subject, Two Conversations

By observing how different interactors behave in public communication spaces that radio programmes build in social networks, it has been detected that, in one way or another, most participants follow the discourse of the station and use walls and timelines to construct a conversation. That many-sided conversation takes place in parallel with the radio broadcast and to some extent keeps pace with what is happening on air. Of the messages published in the networks by those responsible for the programmes analysed, 97.1% are neither integrated into any conversation nor respond to enquiries from the audience. By contrast, the publications generated by the audience on its own initiative, without following a previous thread, accounts for 47.8% of its messages. The remaining messages (52.2%) are part of a conversation initiated by the broadcaster or by another user.

Although it has been said that both discourses, on air and online, share a thematic link, there may be some spread in the contributions made by the audience. This spread is accentuated when the station does not take charge of the conversation on the network, when it is not able to guide the comments and does not lead the dialogue. On those occasions, the audience stops acting as a group and individual criteria take centre stage. When this happens, there is an accumulation of disjointed, inconsistent messages, with little connection between them.

In those Facebook spaces where broadcasters pose questions to the audience, ask for their opinion, advertise their content and so on, channelled, ordered, easy-to-follow conversations are established. The common trend is for interactors to use the station's messages as a hook on which to post their comments, as a basis on which to build the dialogue. Audience publications, therefore, appear as responses to the proposal made by the programme. However, when Internet-using listeners do not know where to put their messages on Facebook, they place them in the main timeline, which makes them difficult to respond to and thus limits any potential conversation. Such disordered dialogues also encourage participants to take the initiative and propose other topics. This could be something positive, but it has two major drawbacks. The first and most common of these is that the questions raised at the initiative of the audience may be completely unrelated to the radio discourse and are probably of no interest to other participants, who, in principle, join the social network of the magazine programme precisely because they are also interested in its content and what happens in it. The second drawback is that even assuming that the subject may arouse some interest, the message is quickly lost in all the other wall postings, decreasing the chances of obtaining new answers that would keep the conversation going.[4]

According to the data obtained, listeners' publications on Facebook can be mostly understood as responses to messages generated by the programme (59.3%). The radio programme—the broadcaster—however, places its posts without taking any account of the users' conversation: only 3.9% of its messages can be considered as a response to some intervention from the audience. In fact, for the broadcaster, the wall is basically a showcase that advertises and highlights its own content, showing very little interest in exploiting the possibilities that Web 2.0 offers for interacting with listeners in a more active and collaborative way.

On the other hand, the general trend common to all the analysed spaces is to use Twitter as a communication tool in which the initiative is in the hands of the audience. The timeline of Twitter is a continuous flow in which one message is followed by another and which shows the adaptability of online discourse with respect to on-air discourse. Some of the interventions from the audience respond to calls for involvement from the programme, usually posted on Twitter and also announced on air (24% of total tweets). But most of the tweets posted by the audience (76%) arise spontaneously as a reaction to what they hear on air or after reading other tweets. The accumulation of messages, which happens haphazardly, promotes free interaction. In addition, the conversation mostly takes place between the interactors themselves.

Posting Opinions and Comments: The Main Motivation for the Radio Audience to Interact in Social Networks

The interactions that occur on the Net follow their own dynamics, sometimes unrelated to the evolution of the programme: while messages published by operators, the profile owners, tend to restrict themselves to the programme content (or promote their space or other programmes on the station), the audience's messages do not always form a coherent dialogue with the broadcasts, or even with previous publications.

In the set of morning magazine programmes analysed, most of the audience publications fall into the category "Opinion/Comment" (40.3% of total publications in both networks by all the magazine programmes) and follow a previous publication by the broadcaster, even if this was no more than an announcement of content with no explicit request for any replies. This behaviour is identified in both social networks and each of the profiles of the analysed programmes. There is therefore evidence of a desire on the part of the audience to express their point of view, whether favourable or critical, usually giving reasons of some sort. In this type of intervention, of course, the connection to what happens on air is unquestionable. For example, *HpH*-SER[5] tweets the day's main story along with a link to it: "March: the first big test for Rajoy. The first analysis by Carles Francino http://t.co/FD4xQS0q."[6] Later, the audience reacts by publishing their opinions or comments unsolicited by the radio station, such as "It can't be that hard to criticise labour reform but none of the pundits speak out clearly what country they living in"[7] or "Why don't you do real journalism and investigate what's happening in small firms where the workers are terrified."[8]

The data show a significant volume of opinions and comments from the audience in parallel with 'hard'programme sections, those that delve more deeply into the political and economic news, and in which the broadcaster does not call for any type of intervention from the audience.[9] Nevertheless, the audience do express their views and opinions about the issues addressed on air, despite knowing that their voice will only be heard (read) by the network users. Actually, the opportunities provided by the broadcaster for certain levels of interaction with Internet-using listeners present in the SNS appear in the framework of the 'soft' sections, which are closer to infotainment.

It should not be forgotten that the audience, as a group, is composed of numerous individuals whose personal motives for publishing in an online space, such as social networks, are very diverse. One reason could be precisely to go against the mainstream in order to stand out from the crowd. The Internet community applies the term 'troll'[10] to such individuals, who publish provocative, irrelevant or out of context posts in communication environments like forums, chats, blogs or social networks, with the sole purpose of causing annoyance and diverting the conversation away from the main issue that the community is dealing with. Perhaps, in this study, using the term 'troll' to refer to those who sign "Comment out of context" posts and tweets would be an overstatement, since, largely, such comments merely reflect the audience's discontentment with what is happening on air, criticising pejoratively the programme's production team, collaborators or even guest commentators.

A situation of this kind was detected in the profile of *EMCR*-CR, making the category "Comment out of context" the primary activity (62%) of its audience during the reporting period. Although this result deviates from the values obtained for that category in the profiles of the other magazine programmes (ranging between 22% and 28%), it must be taken into consideration for what it represents in itself. First, the audience has felt provoked by the presence of a public figure on air, which it considers contrary to the ideology of the radio station, and reacts by disqualifying the presenter and the interviewee in question.[11] An example of this type of publication would be the following tweet: "Would someone like to slap the bastard that is speaking."[12] Obviously such comments would never have been recognised so directly and immediately by the broadcaster, or shared with other members of the audience, were it not for social media. Second, the audience's ownership of the spaces generated in social networks makes it easier and simpler to express disagreement, even if it is not done in a very correct way, as illustrated by the following tweet: "But who is this bloke!!"[13] And third, far from what one might think *a priori*, "Comments out of context" are not always anonymous, an aspect that will be addressed later.

However, pointless, trivial publications such as "see you later, I have to go to the vet's, but I'm listening, have good day"[14] or "good morning and welcome springtime"[15] also embody the category "Comment out of context." Due to its characteristics, this kind of writing neither contributes to nor complements on-air discourse, or even the profile itself, but can be seen as indicative of the creation of social communities among different listeners, a circumstance that is especially apparent among the audience of *HpH*-SER.

In relation to the other variables that describe the activities of Internet-using listeners to the morning magazine programmes in the SNS, the percentages reveal various actions that confirm the power of on-air over online in all the cases studied.

Audience interaction is encouraged by the presence of sections that invite the audience to share personal experiences that complement the discourse proposed by the broadcaster ("Audience Experiences") on issues as diverse as "We're again asking you for your wedding stories and anecdotes,"[16] or "What happened to you that night you went to pick up the kid from a party? Did you forget your trousers? Did you end up partying with the kids?"[17] Listeners seem to enjoy recounting their personal life situations, and these may even be taken up on air over the course of the broadcast. This aspect is especially fostered by *EDCH*-RNE1, where the contributions of its audience, categorised as "Audience Experiences" (21.7%), are far greater than those of the other programmes in the sample. Although some of the other magazines also have similar sections, the volume of such publications is significantly lower.

This shows that the opening of on-air sections to respond to what is happening on the SNS is not in itself a factor in determining either the volume or the nature of audience publications. Thus, 18.5% of the publications in the profiles of *EMRAC1* and 15.4% in the *HpH*-SER are seen to correspond to "Audience Footage," indicating that their audiences are usually more active in sharing breaking news, pictures, links, etc. than telling stories of a personal nature that are certainly more susceptible to become on-air content. Perhaps the explanation for this behaviour is related to the experience in the online environment and the level of digital culture of the audience.

Regarding "Audience Stories" content, the rate shown by this category is surprisingly low in all the SNS profiles of the programmes analysed, whose average percentage of posts and tweets is around 0.5%, with the audience publications of the Cadena SER magazine programme showing the highest presence (1.2% of the total) and RNE's magazine programme showing none at all. This variable refers to contributions outside the programme's agenda and presented as a proposal capable of being integrated into its content. In a sense, along with the category "Audience Footage," it is one of those that best define the role of the audience as prosumers, that is, individuals who take the initiative in proposing topics and producing content—outside the radio broadcaster's news agenda—mainly to be broadcast on air. However, the low incidence of this activity is a sign of a lack of interest currently shown by users in initiating topics that the broadcaster could incorporate into its narrative discourse.

Facebook or Twitter? A Dilemma for the Audience

The type of communication seems to determine the selection of one or another social network. The study shows the general preference for using Twitter on the part of listeners (19.7% of total publications of the network) over Facebook (5.1% of total publications of the network) when it comes to sharing new information or other materials ("Audience Footage"). Possibly, the immediacy of the former is the factor that encourages its use for this activity.

On the other hand, the situation is reversed in the case of recounting experiences ("Audience Experiences"), in which Facebook (12.6%) significantly outperforms Twitter (5.5%). The exception is in *EMRAC1*, whose users continue to opt for Twitter even to make direct observations, demonstrating their ability to narrate personal experiences in under 140 characters. It appears, however, that for the audiences of other magazine programmes this is a difficult requirement.

Less significant differences have been detected in the two activities that the majority of morning magazine programme audiences carry out in social networks: "Opinion/Comment" and "Comment out of context." For the first type of publication, Facebook (46.1%) significantly outperforms Twitter (35.6%), which to some extent makes sense, since for the development of a constructive discourse that requires arguments, reflection is a necessary condition, and possibly its publication requires a greater space than that available on Twitter. With respect to the type "Comment out of context," it was seen that Twitter (38.6%) surpasses Facebook (35.7%). Although the difference between both networks regarding this content is relatively small, it should be stressed that such publications reflect an immediate audience reaction to what they are hearing on air and can be expressed concisely—some of these comments on Facebook take up only one or two short sentences.

It is evident that the characteristics of the communication platform tend to favour certain types of publications. Thus, spontaneous, short, reactive messages are found mostly on Twitter; while reflective, well-argued, or expository publications are mainly posted on Facebook. Therefore, the maxim coined by McLuhan (1964) is also true for communication in social networks: "The medium is the message."

To probe this type of singularity further, Figure 4.1 shows the analysis of audience activities for each magazine programme.

According to the data in Figure 4.1, the first finding is that the audiences of each magazine programme act differently in the SNS. Thus, the most active on Twitter belongs to *EMRAC1*, an audience that in all types of activities prefers the microblogging network to Facebook. In fact, more of its audience's publications are made as tweets (77.2%) than posts (22.8%; see Table 4.2). On Twitter, "Comments out of context" proliferate (40.5%) as well as "Audience Footage" (23.1%). In contrast, 85.1% of the publications in the Facebook profile are in the "Opinion/Comment" category, a percentage that places this activity as the favourite in this social network.

Also listeners to *EMCR-CR* interact more on Twitter (56.6%) than Facebook (43.4%), but in a different way. This audience tends to tweet "Comments out of context" (66.9%) and, to a lesser extent, to provide new content

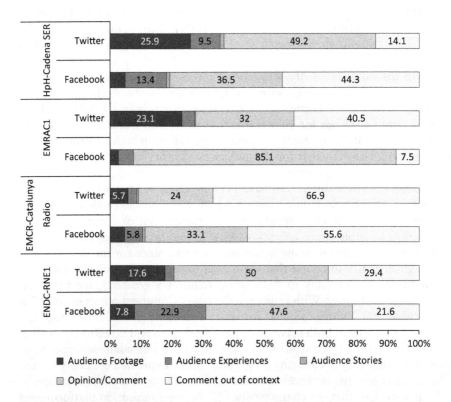

Figure 4.1   Type of audience-generated content in each social network

Source: Authors.

related to the broadcaster's proposed discourse, "Audience Footage" (5.7%), while Facebook is used more to express "Opinions/Comments" (33.1%) on what is happening in the programme on air. Nevertheless, it should be noted that this network also shows a large number of "Comments out of context" (55.6%). In fact, as in the case of Twitter, these are the highest percentages in the sample. As indicated above, this is a result of the audience reacting against the content of the analogue broadcast.

Overall, the audience of *HpH*-SER does not share the habits of the audience observed in the two previous magazine programmes. First, its audience is likely to use both networks equally (Twitter, 50.2%; Facebook, 49.8%; see Table 4.2) to interact with the programme (although it will later be explained that they use them differently depending on their gender, a situation that can be extrapolated to other programmes analysed). However, this relative harmony disappears when the observation is made from the perspective of publication content. A clear preference is observed for using tweets to express mainly "Opinions/Comments" (49.2%) and to provide new information ("Audience Footage," 25.9%). This is also the audience that publishes the fewest "Comments out of context" (14.1%) on Twitter, while most of the contributions in the form of Facebook posts are "Comments out of context" (44.3%) and "Comments/Opinions" (36.5%). However, its audience also selects Facebook to recount its own experiences related to the established news agenda ("Audience Experiences," 13.4%), although number of these publications is relatively small.

Regarding the national public magazine programme *EDCH*-RNE1, it appears that its audience mainly uses Facebook to express "Comments/Opinions" (47.6%). What really sets it apart from the rest, however, is its higher contribution of unpublished content that complements the news discourse proposed by the broadcaster, either in the form of "Audience Experiences" (22.9%) or "Audience Footage" (7.8%). Given that its Twitter profile is the corporate one, users interact primarily by providing "Comments/Opinions" (50%) and offering new data towards the broadcaster's narrative ("Audience Footage," 17.6%), although "Comments out of context" (29.4%) also form part of this social space.

In light of the data, two distinct types of conduct are observed in relation to audience-programme proximity and the sociodemographic characteristics of the two radio ecosystems included in the sample. Regardless of the nuances brought by percentage levels, a greater tendency can be detected towards using Twitter for "Comments out of context" and "Audience Footage" in the audiences of Catalan magazine programmes, while Facebook appears to be reserved for publication of opinions and comments. By contrast, the audiences of the Spanish programmes are inclined to use both networks to make their "Comments/Opinions." However, the behaviour of both audiences differs when posting "Comments out of context" depending on ownership of the radio station. While in both networks this activity is not very high for interactors of the publicly owned magazine programme

(*EDCH*-RNE1), the audience of the commercial magazine programme (*HpH*-SER) is clearly committed to the Facebook wall for this purpose. This peculiarity is not seen in the case of the audiences of the Catalan magazine programmes.

In the context of this study, both sharing the same geographic space and sharing emotional ties are understood as proximity. Therefore, it can be interpreted that proximity to the themes and issues raised on air causes reactions that are perhaps more visceral, justifying the appearance on Twitter of more "Comments out of context." But competency in using the networks also favours the selection of one or the other depending on the activity, reinforcing the idea of a greater digital culture among the Catalan population and, perhaps, a younger user profile: characteristics that have been identified in earlier studies (AIMC 2013c; GESOP 2013).

Another phenomenon to be considered regarding the activity of the audience in SNS is the retweet, when a user publishes a message tweeted by another user, who in this case could be the broadcaster/programme or another listener. Of the total tweets of the morning magazine programmes analysed, 28% were retweets. Regarding the type of retweeted publication, "Audience Footage" leads the ranking (36.5% of the total retweets in the set of all Twitter profiles analysed), followed by "Comments out of context" (33.4%) and "Opinions/Comments" (27.3%). The presence of other variables based on the content generated is almost token. Regarding individual behaviour, it is noticeable that while the audience of *EMRAC1* appears as the most active in this social network, the *HpH*-SER is the one that produces the most retweets. Users of this magazine programme basically replicate in this way new data on the news topic discussed ("Audience Footage") and redistribute reviews or user comments. In *EMRAC1* a trend towards "Audience Footage" is also shown, although "Opinions/Comments" and "Comments out of context" are also retweeted. The "Comments out of context" are the only reason that drives users of *EMCR*-CR to replicate comments on Twitter. In the case of *EDCH*-RNE1, the fact that the programme does not have its own profile is probably the cause of the low activity detected in relation to retweeting, showing a preference for sharing views and opinions.

Again, the analysis shows divergent behaviour among the morning magazine programmes, with a Twitter profile in relation to the type of publication that is retweeted.

Who Publishes? Defining the Audience

On-air interaction involves dialogue with the programme presenter, who usually asks the listener for personal data, such as name and place of residence. This is a minimal amount of information, which can be falsified, but the voice of the listeners on air might be recognised by other listeners who know them. On the Internet, however, there is a perception of acting with greater anonymity (though this is not always the case). True, to create a profile in social networks, users must provide certain personal information. But as there are no checks made on the accuracy of this, they can create a profile with false details and interact in social networks, hiding their true identity.

On this basis, acknowledging the risk involved in equating the gender of authors with the gender of their usernames, the analysis addresses the authorship of publications from the gender perspective, from the name that users adopt in their interaction with the broadcaster. Thus, publications are defined in terms of whether they come with male ("Man"), female ("Woman") or unidentified ("Indeterminate") signatures, the latter referring to authors with 'neutral' profile names (aliases of indeterminate gender, institutions, companies, associations, etc.).

When establishing the authorship of publications on SNS profiles of morning magazine programmes, in general masculine signatures predominate (39.8%), followed by unidentified signatures (33.5%, "Indeterminate") and finally feminine signatures (26.7%), but if the type of social network is taken into account, notable differences become apparent. Thus, unidentified authorship predominates on Twitter (55.8%), which shows a tendency to rely on anonymity in this social network. By contrast, on Facebook there is a greater willingness to identify gender (49.5% masculine, 44.8% feminine).

Once more it seems that "the medium is the message," that the tool exerts an influence and it not only affects what is said or how it is said, but who says it. Or to be more precise, it appears that using one network or another influences how the authors of a publication identify themselves to the rest of the community.

On Facebook, new relationships start out from a person-node that joins one network user to another. To meet someone and be recognised, it is essential to present oneself to the community under one's real identity. On Twitter, however, building relationships does not depend on identity: nicknames, pseudonyms and fictitious names proliferate, and communication does not suffer at all as a result of replacing a real name with a nickname.

Gender, a Key Factor

Analysis of the type of authorship in the profiles of the various magazine programmes and in every social network confirms that in the case of Twitter, the general trend is maintained: unidentified signatures ("Indeterminate") make up the majority in the profiles of all programmes, regardless of their coverage area. Similarly, it can be seen that the Facebook-using audiences of the four programmes clearly reveal their gender identity. As discussed above, the nature of each of these networks affects the way users identify themselves. Thus, Facebook becomes an environment for the 'identified' and Twitter for the 'unidentified.'

When the authorship of listeners in the SNS can be identified, the most active interactors in the Catalan magazine programmes are men in both social networks, while in the case of the Spanish magazine programmes, women are more active on Facebook and men on Twitter. Likewise, the

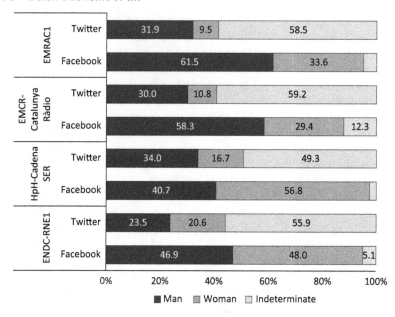

Figure 4.2   Type of authorship by social network and programme
Source: Authors.

female audience of the Catalan magazine programmes is lower than that detected for Spanish magazine programmes, as shown in Figure 4.2.

Just as different preferences can be observed in the magazine programmes analysed for the use of one social network over another, depending on users' gender, the latter's activities—the content generated—are also seen to differ, as summarised in Figure 4.3.

The analysis of activities on the profiles of the magazine programmes according to authorship in both networks highlights the difficulty of establishing common patterns of behaviour. Thus, not on all programmes are most "Comments out of context" anonymous, nor are these exclusive to Twitter. In fact, their conduct is different in each case. On *HpH*-SER, the members of the audience who hide behind pseudonyms when posting on frivolous or delicate matters opt for Facebook, while on *EMRAC1* they prefer Twitter. However, the authors of such anonymous postings on *EMCR-CR* use both platforms with similar frequency. Taking into account that *EDCH*-RNE1 does not have a profile on Twitter, its anonymous Facebook users are seen to prioritise opinions over "Comments out of context."

Male authors display different behaviours depending on the programme. Thus, the most active male Facebook users are on *EMRAC1* (85.5%), opting mostly for publishing their opinions—whether or not solicited by the broadcaster—and they seem to forgo using the wall for trivial comments.

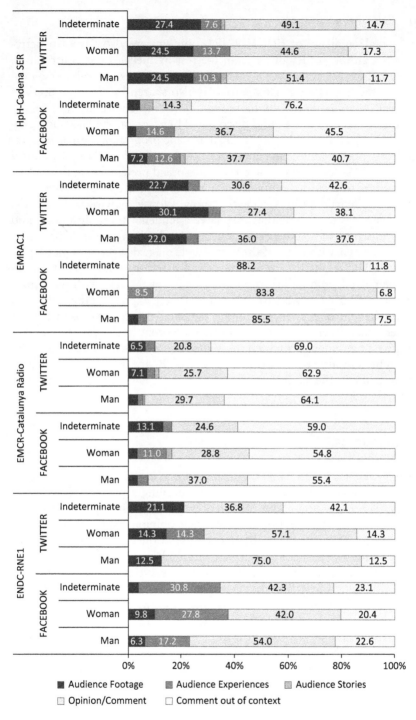

Figure 4.3 Authorship of publications from the audience by type of content, social network and programme

Source: Authors.

For the male audience of *EDCH*-RNE1, opinions are also a priority activity (54%), although they differ from the rest by their greater contribution of personal experiences (17.2%) that complement the news discourse proposed by the broadcaster. This pattern is also shared by the male users of *HpH*-SER, who use Facebook more than Twitter to contribute these direct observations to the online radio discourse. However, on the Facebook profiles of the *HpH*-SER and *EMCR*-CR magazine programmes, male interactors clearly post more "Comments out of context," followed by "Opinions/ Comments." As for Twitter, there is a widespread preference on the part of male authors to provide unpublished news content ("Audience Footage").

Although female authors generally show a lower activity rate than the other users, it is noticeable that they have a tendency to publish posts and tweets consisting of "Audience Experience" on both networks. This is particularly the case with users of the nationwide magazine programmes *HpH*-SER and *EDCH*-RNE1, in which the broadcaster proposes topics that can easily be moved from online to on air. This is not the case with the female audience of *EMRAC1,* who are more interested in expressing their opinions and comments rather than recounting personal experiences. With respect to other content generated, it should be noted that in the case of Catalan magazine programmes, interactions signed by women differ not only by programme but also by network. In *EMCR*-CR, the dominant content in both networks is the "Comment out of context," while users of *EMRAC1* opt for Twitter for such publications.

CONCLUSIONS

The audience has found a communication space in the social network profiles of the radio programmes that, while fulfilling a publicity role for its owners, serves as a megaphone for listeners. These profiles are tools that the audience uses to share and disseminate their opinions and where they feel free to do so. Through them, listeners can send their comments to a large number of followers of the programme and exchange views.

The programme content broadcast on air is subject to the strict supervision of what might be called 'the on-air team' (scriptwriters, producers, presenters and collaborators). This means that the participation of the audience on air is always regulated by the broadcaster, who will decide who intervenes, at what point, how long the intervention lasts and at what moment to interrupt it. By contrast, the messages published on the radio stations' Facebook and Twitter profiles (either in response to the publications of the 'on-air team' or on the author's own initiative) are beyond such control. In other words, Internet-using listeners can express themselves freely in social networks, without restrictions imposed by the broadcaster, which is either less strict in this environment than on air, is unable to apply any censorship for technical reasons or applies *a posteriori* censorship, by eliminating unwanted content that has already been available to other users for some time. No wonder that "Opinion/Comment" and "Comment out of context," whether called for by the broadcaster or not, have become the most common type of publications in all the magazine programmes analysed.

A direct relationship among the ratings, the volume of messages from the radio station and the number of publications in social networks could not be detected. However, the proximity of listeners to the broadcaster has appeared as a factor that encourages them to interact in social networks, as seen in the case of the Catalan magazine programmes. And proximity should be understood as both geographical and emotional closeness. It seems clear that the fact that broadcaster and listeners share a physical, territorial, geographic, linguistic and cultural context leads to topics that are more local and familiar being dealt with. But emotional proximity can also mean greater involvement from the listeners, a greater empathy, and thus, a greater desire to intervene, to become an active part of 'their' community, 'their' programme and 'their' radio station.

The characteristics of Twitter and Facebook make the audience use each platform differently. These features have generally favoured posting comments and opinions on the Facebook wall, while out-of-context comments have gained space on Twitter. Maybe when assessing the pairing of publication type with the chosen social network, attention should be paid to differences in ubiquity of access, ease of publication, ergonomics of mobile devices for short texts or impulsiveness when writing a message. However, another factor that has not yet been addressed could be psychological in nature. Twitter is a social network in which everyone writes in her or his timeline, and it is perceived therefore as a private, personal space, where users can act with relative comfort and feel free to write whatever they like; by contrast, the Facebook wall, despite being public and open to participation, is still an environment created by someone else and which belongs to someone else, and therefore participation could be affected by a feeling of communicatively trespassing or at least occupying a space where some caution should be exercised.

Regarding the authorship of publications, what perhaps stands out the most is the relationship of anonymity with the out-of-context comment formulated as a tweet. This general trend in the Catalan regional magazine programmes is certainly indicative of the degree of digital culture of their younger audience. Indeed, the greater penetration of information technology in this region[18] explains the greater use of social networks, especially Twitter (GESOP 2013), among the Catalan audience.

The gender of the audience becomes a key element in understanding the behaviour of users. Thus, male listeners are generally more participative, prefer Twitter and prioritise making evaluative comments and adding new items of information to the broadcaster's narrative. On the other hand, women are less participative listeners, prefer Facebook and are more willing to tell their life experiences as a complement to the radio discourse.

Regarding the conversations that are built up in social networks, there are two features which stand out. First, the interventions made online, although they keep pace with what is happening in the live broadcast and adapt to on-air content, rarely have an impact on the analogue broadcast. Two discourses are established, on-air and online, which both address the same issues at the same time, but in parallel to each other. The on-air discourse influences the online one, but the online discourse does not influence the on-air one. Facebook and Twitter interventions, when broadcast on air, usually appear in special sections for comments from the network. Outside these sections, reading out listeners' messages on air is a rarity.

The second noteworthy feature of the conversations that are built up on the network is that despite being generated simultaneously with the programme and adapting to it, they do not end when the programme does. These conversations evolve beyond the programme, echoing what has happened during the day and fading as time passes. It could be said that the screen and what happens on it function as a sort of 'augmented radio,' an environment influenced by what is transmitted on air but at the same time independent of it.

This study shows that the level of participation of the Spanish and Catalan audience in the construction of talk radio information's discourse in morning magazine programmes is limited to the interaction mode defined in Carpentier's AIP model (2011b), as it has no power in decision-making processes that could be considered comparable to that of the radio stations. Also, the content generated by the audience that the programme incorporates on air is mainly related to infotainment. Listeners are outside the process of construction of news discourse, which is entirely in the hands of the programme, thus making more participatory journalism a utopia in these radio programmes, in both their on-air and their online dimensions. In this sense, the role played by prime-time magazine programmes in defining the editorial line of the radio stations, and consequently their brand image and credibility, could explain the reluctance to open up these spaces to real participation by the audience. Another aspect that stands out is that the audience usually acts in response to a call from the broadcaster, and the volume of its input in co-creating content is limited. Perhaps, as Carpentier (2011a) points out, the expectations of a hyperactive and hyperproductive audience are overly optimistic in light of the latter's current practices.

NOTES

1. The Catalonia Radio Observatory (OBS) forms part of the Image, Sound and Synthesis Research Group (GRISS) of the Universitat Autònoma de Barcelona (UAB, Autonomous University of Barcelona), recognised by the Government of Catalonia (Grup 2014SGR1674) and attached to the Department of Audiovisual Communication and Advertising at the UAB.
2. According to the *Estudio General de Medios* (AIMC, 2013a), the on-air audience for the national programmes for the period studied (first third of 2012)

comprised 4,285,000 listeners for *Hoy por hoy* (Cadena SER) and 1,742,000 listeners for *En días como hoy* (RNE). The regional programmes had audiences of 675,000 listeners in the case of *El món a RAC1* (RAC1) and 589,000 for *El matí de Catalunya Ràdio* (Catalunya Ràdio).

3. The activity rate for the on-air audience in social networks is obtained by dividing the number of interventions by the audience on the Facebook and Twitter profiles by the number of on-air listeners of the radio programme.
4. During the sample period, Facebook was modifying its graphic appearance. In principle these changes will help page owners to present their contributions in an ordered way that could provide a better structure for the replies generated. These changes may also mean that in future analyses, audience contributions to some programmes on Facebook are presented in a more orderly, i.e., less dispersed, way.
5. Henceforth the following abbreviations are used to identify the different magazines in the study: *EDCH*-RNE1; *EMCR*-CR; *HpH*-SER; *EMRAC1*. The letters represent the names of the programmes and the stations to which they belong.
6. *HpH*-SER, 9 March 2012 at 08.24h.
7. *HpH*-SER, 9 March 2012 at 09.38h.
8. *HpH*-SER, 9 March 2012 at 09.41h.
9. Both in the Spanish and the Catalan morning magazine programmes, between 08.00 and 10.00 a.m., political and economic content predominates. Thus, as well as news, there are interviews with institutional figures appearing in the day's news, and a roundtable with journalists, politicians and other prominent members of society. From 10.00 a.m. onwards the 'soft' sections take over, hinged on infotainment.
10. This definition of 'Troll' is found in the *Cambridge Dictionary Online* among others (http://dictionary.cambridge.org/dictionary/british/troll_2).
11. For the following day a general strike had been called in Spain and during the broadcast of the morning magazine programme this topic was treated superficially.
12. *EMCR*-CR, 28 March 2012 at 10.05h.
13. *EMCR*-CR, 28 March 2012 at 10.08h.
14. *HpH*-Cadena SER, 1 March 2012 at 09.02h.
15. *EMRAC1*, 20 March 2012 at 10.04h.
16. *EMRAC1*, 28 March 2012 (time not indicated).
17. *EDCH*- RNE1, 20 March 2012 at 10.45h.
18. According to the survey on *Equipment and Use of Information and Communication Technologies in Households 2012*, by the National Institute of Statistics (INE), the percentage of Catalans who had ever used the Internet was 78.7%, 5.4 points above the figure for the Spanish territory as a whole, which was 73.3% (from www.ine.es and accessed April 8, 2014).

REFERENCES

AIMC [Asociación para la Investigación de Medios de Comunicación]. (2013a). *Estudio General de Medios*. Madrid: AIMC.

———. (2013b). *Navegantes en la Red 2012*. Accessed March 20, 2014. http:www.aimc.es/-Navegantes-en-la-Red-.html.

———. (2013c). *Marco General de los Medios en España*. Accessed March 20, 2014. http://www.aimc.es/-Descarga-Marco-General-Asociados-.html.

Banks, J. and Deuze, M. (2009). "Co-creative Labour." *International Journal of Cultural Studies*, 12(5), 419–431.

Beer, D. and R. Burrows (2007). "Sociology and, of and in Web 2.0: Some Initial Considerations." *Sociology Research Online*, 12(5). Accessed December 10, 2013. http://www.socresonline.org.uk/12/5/17.html.

Bonet, M. (2000). *La transformació de la ràdio local a Catalunya. Perspectives de futur.* Barcelona: Collegi de Periodistes, Diputació de Barcelona.

Boyd, D. and Ellison, N. (2008). "Social Network Sites: Definition, History and Scholarship." *Journal of Computer-Mediated Communication*, 13, 210–230.

Bruns, A. (2005). *Gatewatching: Collaborative Online News Production.* New York: Peter Lang.

Carpentier, N. (2011a). *Media and Participation. A Site of Ideological-Democratic Struggle.* Bristol, Chicago: Intellect.

———. (2011b). "The Concept of Participation. If They Have Access and Interact, Do They Really Participate?" *CM: Communication Management Quarterly/ Casopis za upravljanje komuniciranjem*, 21, 13–36.

Castells, M. (2001). *The Internet Galaxy: Reflections on the Internet, Business and Society.* Oxford, New York: Oxford University Press.

Cohen, N. S. (2008). "The Valorization of Surveillance: Towards a Political Economy of Facebook." *Democratic Communiqué*, 22(1), 5–22.

Deuze, M., Bruns, A. and Neuberger, C. (2007). "Preparing for an Age of Participatory News." *Journalism Practice*, 1(3), 322–338.

GESOP [Gabinet d'Estudis Socials i Opinió Pública]. (2013). *L'Omnibus: ús de les xarxes socials entre els catalans 2013.* Accessed November 20, 2014. www.gesop. net/images/pdf/ca/Informes/IG37_GESOP_XarxesSocials_Estiu2013.pdf.

Gherhards, J. and Schäfer, M. S. (2010). "Is the Internet a Better Public Sphere? Comparing Old and New Media in the USA and Germany." *New Media & Society*, 12(1), 143–160.

Gutiérrez, M., Ribes, X. and Monclús, B. (2011). "La audiencia juvenil y el acceso a la radio musical de antena convencional a través de Internet." *Comunicación y Sociedad*, XXIV(2), 305–331.

Habermas, J. (1974). "The Public Sphere: An Encyclopedia Article (1964)." *New German Critique*, 3, 49–55.

———. (1996). *Between Facts and Norms. Contributions to a Discourse Theory of Law and Democracy.* Cambridge, MA: MIT Press.

Igartua, J. J. (2006). *Métodos cuantitativos de investigación en comunicación.* Barcelona: Bosch.

Jenkins, H. (2006). *Convergence Culture: Where Old and New Media Collide.* Cambridge, MA: MIT Press.

Livingstone, S. (2003). "The Changing Nature of Audiences: From the Mass Audience to the Interactive Media User." In Valdivia, A. (ed.), *A Companion to Media Studies.* Malden, Oxford, Carlton: Blackwell Publishing, 337–359.

Martí, J. M., Monclús, B., Ferrer, I., Gutiérrez, M. and Ribes, X. (2013). "How Broadcasters Face the Digital Challenge in the Current Context of Economic Crisis? An Approach to the Spanish and Catalan Cases." Paper presented at ECREA Radio Research Conference, London, September 11–13.

McLuhan, M. (1964). *Understanding Media: The Extensions of Man.* New York: McGraw-Hill.

Moyo, L. (2012). "The Digital Turn in Radio: A Critique of Institutional and Organizational Modeling of New Radio Practices and Cultures." *Telematics and Informatics*, 30, 214–222.

Napoli, P. M. (2010). "Revisiting 'Mass Communication' and the 'Work' of the Audience in the New Media Environment." *Media, Culture & Society*, 32(3), 505–516.

Nightingale, V. (2007). "New Media Worlds? Challenges for Convergence." In Nightingale, V. and Dwyer, T. (eds.), *New Media Worlds. Challenges for Convergence.* South Melbourne, Oxford: Oxford University Press, 19–36.

Papacharissi, Z. (2010). *A Private Sphere. Democracy in Digital Age.* Cambridge: Polity Press.

Riffe, D., Aust, Ch. and Lacy, S. (1993). "The Effectiveness of Random Consecutive Day and Constructed Week Sampling. Newspaper Content Analysis." *Journalism Quarterly,* 70, 133–139.

Toffler, A. (1980). *The Third Wave.* New York: Bantam Books.

Wardle, C. and Williams, A. (2010). "Beyond User-Generated Content: A Production Study Examining the Ways in Which UGC Is Used at the BBC." *Media, Culture & Society,* 32(5), 781–799.

Willens, W. (2013). "Participation—in What? Radio, Convergence and the Corporate Logic of Audience Input through New Media in Zambia." *Telematics and Informatics,* 30, 223–231.

Wimmer, R. D. and Dominick, J. R. (1996). *La investigación científica de los medios de comunicación. Una introducción a sus métodos.* Barcelona: Bosch.

5 Sports Broadcasting in the Age of Network Society
Engagement with Listeners and Interaction throughout a Collective Experience

Toni Sellas

INTRODUCTION

Sports have been ever-present throughout the history of radio in Spain, and today sports broadcasting is one of the main products on Spanish talk radio stations. This is even more notable in the case of Catalonia, due to the Barcelona Football Club (BFC, also known as Barça) being one of the region's most important institutions and sports broadcasts having played a key role in normalisation of the Catalan language. Both public and commercial broadcasters spend time and resources on sports news and programming, especially the sports midnight magazine and the live broadcast of BFC matches. These programmes are some of the most popular on the airwaves and the Internet, and they also achieve some success in quantitative terms on social network sites (SNSs).

This study analyses the use of Twitter by the two main sports broadcasting programmes in Catalonia and their followers. Analysis focuses on the broadcasters' interaction with listeners through this social medium and aims to highlight those relationship dynamics which turn a single moment into a collective experience.

SPORTS, MEDIA AND IDENTITY: A CATALAN FRAMEWORK

Catalonia is an autonomous region of Spain, with a population of over 7.5 million inhabitants (16% of the Spanish total).[1] The Autonomous Government of Catalonia—or *Generalitat*—is the institutional system by means of which it has governed itself since 1359 (apart from the period of the Franco dictatorship, which suppressed Catalan institutions). Comprising the parliament, presidency and government, the *Generalitat* has powers in areas such as health, education and public security, among others. It is for this reason that Guibernau (2007, 74) argues: "In many respects, the *Generalitat* acts as a quasi-state, since its devolved powers include the right to introduce socio-cultural policies aimed at regenerating the Catalan nation."

Catalonia is not acknowledged as a nation in international forums either politically or culturally (Guibernau 2007). However, Catalan public para-diplomacy has found in sports a suitable field for building an international reputation and for the symbolic articulation of national identity (Xifra and McKie 2012). One of the organisations with the greatest symbolic significance for Catalonia is indeed the BFC, which throughout its history has often been a vehicle for expressing Catalan identity (Xifra 2008).

Academic research has examined how sport and its media coverage contribute to the construction of personal and collective identities, including national identity (Bernstein and Blain 2003). Sporting events are an opportunity to express this identity, and identification with a particular team or national team brings with it a personal sense of belonging to a community. The media condition this community experience and contribute to the development of a common national memory (Boyle 1992). The symbolism of sport also favours the identification of an 'us versus them' opposition in terms of nationality (Hargreaves 1986). This symbolic dimension is summarised by Hobsbawm (1990, 143), who states: "The imagined community of millions seems more real as a team of eleven named people. The individual, even the one who only cheers, becomes a symbol of his nation himself."

In the case of Catalonia, to the relationship between sport and identity we must add the language factor. It is worth noting that the Catalan language was banned and persecuted during the Franco dictatorship (1939–1975). Therefore, once its democratic institutions were restored, the parliament of Catalonia in 1983 approved the Linguistic Normalisation Act, which was crucial to the recovery of Catalan in official use, education and the media, following the negative effects of the Franco regime. The Linguistic Policy Act of 1998 (replacing the previous one) and the Statute of Autonomy of 2006 reinforced Catalan as Catalonia's own language (having co-official status with Castilian Spanish, the official language of Spain).

Catalonia is one of the stateless nations which have their own media system different from that of the state of which they form part. The Spanish radio market today reflects the political-administrative structure established with the arrival of democracy and is a result of 1980s deregulation (Bonet 2012). It is an industry with statewide, regional, local, public and private radio. Within this context, Catalonia has a specific radio broadcasting model, due, as already mentioned, to the added factor of the region's language (Catalan). Audience leadership for broadcasting stations at both the regional and local levels is very much related to the strength of the language in the region. Catalan is a key element of uniqueness and differentiation. The Catalan radio system has been a factor in the social normalisation of the language and a gradual normalisation of business, having made Catalan a commercial element which acts as an attraction for the audience (Fernández-Quijada, Sellas and Bonet 2013). Regulation has been a key factor in shaping this reality.

In Catalonia, the two most listened to talk stations are regional and in Catalan: the public Catalunya Ràdio and the private RAC1, totalling 1,270,000 listeners (AIMC 2013). As for sports radio, programmes in Catalan are leaders in terms of audience, ahead of state radio programmes, which, as already mentioned, lead the rankings for Spain as a whole.

Sports radio broadcasting has a long tradition in Spain and Catalonia and comprises some of the content to have formed part of the history of the medium since its origins. Sports take on a particularly prominent role on weekend radio, when programming includes the programmes known as *carrusels*, based on the events of the Spanish Football League (Liga BBVA). *Carrusel Deportivo*, broadcast by Cadena SER, was the pioneer of such programmes, beginning back in 1954, and is currently the audience leader on a statewide level. The structure of these programmes includes broadcasting live football matches while keeping an eye on the other results of the day. They are characterised by a dynamic and informal style, the personalities of the match commentators and the participation of a wide range of collaborators, often including former professional players and coaches.

In Catalonia, the broadcasting of BFC matches is one of the radio products in Catalan that has played an important role in normalisation of the language. In this regard, it is worth noting the pioneering role of sports broadcaster Joaquim M. Puyal, who made the first broadcast in Catalan on September 5, 1976, via EAJ-1 Radio Barcelona. From the outset, Puyal was aware that incorporating Catalan into the production of messages for the masses was a way of contributing to the social and cultural recovery of Catalonia (Puyal 2007). His programme has contributed to normalisation of the Catalan language over decades, expanding the language with new words, some of them from traditional Anglicisms, by means of which fans learned football terminology, and using a familiar but correct linguistic register with the audience. This is the model followed by other stations that have increased the supply of football broadcasting over the last 30 years.

RADIO AND SOCIAL MEDIA: TALKING
TO THE NETWORKED LISTENERS

In recent years, social media have been incorporated into the daily lives of many people. Broadly defined as "a group of Internet-based applications that build on the ideological and technological foundations of Web 2.0, and that allow the creation and exchange of user-generated content" (Kaplan and Haenlein 2010, 60), social media have become a space where many of our personal and professional activities take place, to the extent that they "have unquestionably altered the nature of private and public communication" (van Dijck 2013, 7).

In the middle of the first decade of this century, the so-called Web 2.0 and social media grew as technologies within a new participatory culture that allowed mass collaboration among users, thanks to which citizens recovered their central role in the public domain. Half a decade later, however, a critical look at its evolution leads us to add some nuances. Certainly, social media foster the active role of users in the process of circulating content, but their potential for participation depends on social context and the structural factors in which they are developed (Carpentier 2011a). It should also be borne in mind that many projects conceived as community platforms for connection and the exchange of user-generated content have become global corporations that do business primarily via information and user data (van Dijck 2013).

It has now become necessary to evaluate how the media have integrated into the social media ecosystem. The growth of these platforms has led to organisations trying to develop strategies for interacting on them with their audiences. This is particularly true of SNSs, which Boyd and Ellison (2008, 210–230) define as "web-based services that allow users to (1) construct a public or a semi-public profile within a bounded system, (2) articulate a list of other users with whom they share a connection, and (3) view and traverse their list of connections and those made by others within the system." SNSs generate connected audiences, which are defined by the way the network architecture shapes the flow of information and interaction among users (Boyd 2011).

Social networks are a dynamic and hybrid environment in which the mass media, communications professionals and networked individuals share time, space and content. In these structures, the acquisition and consolidation of trust is a key element (Rainie and Wellman 2012), and the media face the challenge of becoming part of the trust network of their audiences. This forces them to focus on relational dynamics, in a context marked by the shift from an appointment-based model of media-based consumption towards an engagement-based paradigm where the boundaries between the culture industries and user production is both porous and filled with tension (Jenkins, Ford and Green 2013).

What kind of relationship are we talking about? Research has shown that media organisations use social networks primarily for promotional purposes (Armstrong and Gao 2010; Ferguson and Greer 2011; Messner, Linke and Eford 2011). The aim is to make content available to audiences wherever they are and bring users to the corporate website, a strategy that reduces the potential of social networking to a minimum. We can take as a framework for analysing these relationships Carpentier's (2011b, 24) AIP model, which distinguishes among access, interaction and participation, based on the consideration of power as a defining element: "The balance between people's inclusion in the implicit and explicit decision-making processes within these fields, and their exclusion through the delegation of power (again, implicit or explicit), is central to discussions on participation in all fields."

To Carpentier, access and interaction are necessary factors for participatory processes in the media but should not be confused with participation, which is linked to power dynamics and decision making. Access is a first stage, based on presence and related in different ways to technology, content, people and organisations. Interaction emphasises the social communicative relationship with other humans or objects within the media sphere. But participation goes still further: "Through this juxtaposition to access and interaction, participation becomes defined as a political—in the broad meaning of the concept of political—process where the actors involved in decision-making processes are positioned towards each other through power relationships that are (to an extent) egalitarian" (Carpentier 2011b, 31). Social networks offer a new means of relationship between the media and their audiences, but beyond technology, the question is, which mindset do they want to relate to them with?

RESEARCH DESIGN AND METHOD

This chapter examines the relationship established via Twitter between the two main Catalan radio stations and their audiences based on live broadcasts of Barcelona Football Club matches. Twitter is a micro-blogging service that allows users to publish short messages (maximum 140 characters) on a network comprising other users. It combines the potential to publish blogs, the immediacy of instant messaging and the connectivity of social networks. The programmes studied are *La transmissió d'en Puyal—LaTdP* (on the public broadcaster Catalunya Ràdio) and *El Barça juga a RAC1* (on the private broadcaster RAC1). We aim to determine the type of engagement these programmes have with their listeners through Twitter and uncover the relational dynamics they have with their followers. To do so, we start from the following research questions:

RQ1: How do they use Twitter? What strategy do they adopt?

RQ2: What kind of relationship is established between broadcasters and listeners?

RQ3: What is the role played by listeners on this social medium?

The fieldwork combined different data collection techniques in different phases. The first step was to conduct a content analysis of tweets published by the broadcasters, focusing on the principal objective of the messages. Following a research model developed in previous studies (Bonini and Sellas 2014; Sellas 2013) and taking into account the characteristics of a sports broadcast programme, we understand that these can be encoded in accordance with the following main purposes: (a) broadcasting the match; (b) broadcasting a press conference or statements by the main participants; (c) broadcasting news and information; (d) broadcasting opinion/analysis; (e) promoting and/or distributing content; (f) inviting users to participate and/or informing them about their participation; (g) responding to questions or comments from users; (h) disseminating content to users. Beyond the purpose of the messages, however, we aimed to observe the relationship between broadcasters and receivers. We therefore also encoded those elements characteristic of Twitter that we considered to be significant: retweets (publishing a message tweeted by another user), replies (replies to messages from other users) and links (which may be to content linked to the programme or externally).

Our analysis of Twitter profiles covered two weeks from November 25 to December 8, 2013. We selected this period because we consider it to be standard for a regular BFC season: it includes three matches corresponding to the three main competitions in which the club competes (Liga BBVA, Copa del Rey and Champions League), as well as training days and days prior to and after a match; at the same time, we avoided exceptional events that might condition the results. The analysis was done by encoding the total number of tweets published ($n = 927$) by the two profiles studied—@LaTdP and @ FCBRAC1—using the aforementioned categories. An initial analysis was first conducted of a sample of 120 tweets by two PhD students, with the aim of evaluating the data-gathering tools. Reliability was calculated manually according to the percentage of agreement index (Neuendorf 2013), which was 92%.

The second step was to study those tweets that mention the users @LaTdP and @FCBRAC1. To this end, we collected messages posted on this channel by users of Twitter—whether followers of these two profiles or not—that included explicit references to the accounts of one or both radio programmes (that is, the message included the username: @LaTdP, @FCBRAC1). In this case, the instrument used for data collection was Topsy, a social media search tool focused primarily on Twitter and Google+ which allows the customisation of search parameters (keywords, domains, sentences, Web address) and results to be filtered by date, relevance or language. In our case, we monitored tweets that referred to @LaTdP and @FCBRAC1 on the dates included in the previous phase. All messages ($n = 1,129$) were encoded into three categories: (a) automatic retweets (the user replicates the original tweet by @LaTdP or @FCBRAC1); (b) modified tweets (the user replicates the original message but adds content); (c) mentions/replies (original user tweets addressed to @LaTdP or @FCBRAC1 that do not replicate content from these two profiles).

The third step consisted of an analysis of tweets published around a particular topic, in this case, the broadcasting of BFC matches, with the aim of mapping the activity generated. One Twitter convention is the use of hashtags—a short keyword preceded by the hash symbol #—to label messages and organise content. In this case, we analysed the hashtags used by the two programmes under study: #latdp (*La transmissió d'en Puyal*) and #frac1 (used by @FCBRAC1 to refer to *futbol a RAC1*). For this analysis, we monitored tweets by means of Tweetbinder, a Web-based application for sorting and measuring Twitter information. This tool allows users to search for and categorise tweets on particular subjects, using key terms or hashtags, and store them in 'binders.' The resulting tweets are automatically sorted by replies, retweets and images as well as any custom binders defined by the user. This platform allows users to collect data pertaining to the activity of a given week, or a maximum of 3,000 tweets. In this study, we monitored the two hashtags from November 25 to December 2, 2013 (number of tweets: 2,927).

Finally, in order to contextualise the data obtained, we complemented the fieldwork with a fourth phase, consisting of two in-depth interviews: one with Raül Llimós, head of RAC1 sports; the other with Marcos Garcia, coordinator of *La transmissió d'en Puyal—LaTdP*. The interviews took place in Barcelona on January 14 and 21, 2014 and took about an hour on average. They were semi-structured interviews, based on three foundations: corporate criteria for the use of Twitter, relationship with users and account management.

The aim of the research conducted in these four phases was to obtain a comprehensive and complete overview of the activity of broadcasters and listeners on Twitter based around BFC match broadcasts. For this reason, we considered it appropriate to combine different complementary techniques. The analysis of tweets made by the programmes was necessary in understanding the normal dynamic between broadcasters and their audience. But we also wished to focus our attention on the possibilities available to listeners, to determine whether Twitter is merely a channel that facilitates access to technology and messages or, contrarily, is a truly social environment in which the relationships among the different actors is situated in the field of interactivity or even participation (Carpentier 2011a). This approach led us to study tweets posted by the audience in response to or mentioning the programmes and those messages which used key hashtags. Finally, the in-depth interviews aimed to provide a better contextualisation and interpretation of the trends revealed in the previous phases. The combination of these four stages was also aimed at drawing some conclusions regarding the correlations among the various results.

FINDINGS

Number and Main Goals of the Tweets

Upon conclusion of this research, @LaTdP had 52,629 followers and followed 375 users itself, giving a ratio of 84.14. This proportion is slightly lower in the case of @FCBRAC1 (72.81), which had 39,872 followers and followed 214 users. Although it is true that Twitter does not require reciprocity and nothing requires users to follow those who follow them, the data show a significant imbalance and lack of interest in other users.

With regard to the activity of the two accounts in the period analysed, @LaTdP published 728 posts, while @FCBRAC1 published 199. The profile of RAC1 broadcasts restricts the programme to posting on match days, as the rest of the week it disappears from the Net. In contrast, @LaTdP shows greater regularity on Twitter, with a daily presence and an average of 52 tweets per day, which doubles on match days and falls the rest of the week, although not excessively. If we take a more detailed look at the content published (see Figure 5.1), almost 50% of the tweets by @LaTdP were for information purposes. These were messages with general breaking sports news or news specific to BFC, news summaries, press reviews and reports of the team's activities. This focus on disseminating information is what allows the programme to maintain communication with the audience throughout the week, whether there is a Barça match or not.

Match days bring other important purposes for @LaTdP, such as broadcasting the game itself (89 tweets). The average is almost 30 tweets per broadcast. These are simple messages, citing the minute of play and the incident, and incorporating the characteristic tag #latdp. A significant number of tweets (172) also correspond to the broadcasting of press conferences or statements, relayed in real time via Twitter. Similarly, the post-match statements of leading protagonists are also broadcast using this channel. However, the number of tweets that seek some audience response or interaction is lower. Over the same period, @LaTdP published only 29 messages encouraging participation. Of other content, there is the "Fotojoc" competition—in which followers have to guess the person or the historical moment from an image—calls for followers to give their line-up of the Barça team, questions

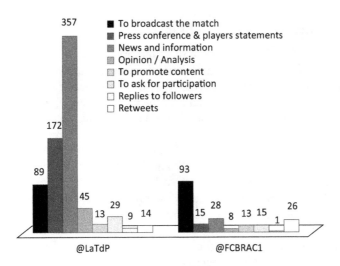

Figure 5.1 Aim of the tweets

Source: Own data.

regarding how the team has played or and questions regarding opinions of some of the players' performances. Beyond that, we find 9 tweets which are direct replies to followers and 14 retweets (mostly of tweets by players in the hours prior to or after the match).

As for @FCBRAC1, the profile of *Barça de RAC1* broadcasts does not extend beyond match days and its main purpose is the broadcasting of the match (93 tweets, almost half of the total) or related aspects, such as statements by the protagonists or the dissemination of opinion and/or analysis. Of the data collected, we also note that those messages asking questions of other users (46 tweets) represent 21% of the total. This is due to a number of practices routinely followed by @FCBRAC1. Firstly, it is a profile that retweets many tweets published by BFC players on the same social network, and even some tweets by club executives, messages which often include images taken by players on their mobile phones. Additionally, the programme invites fans via Twitter to discuss or give their opinion on some tactical aspects, or on certain players, and to participate in different types of competitions and draws, some linked to the programme sponsors. However, we found only one single direct response to another user.

The two programmes therefore display different dynamics in terms of frequency of publication and the main purpose of their messages. They do, however, basically coincide in having a one-way constant, with few mentions of users (beyond BFC players or journalists linked to the programme) and scant response to their followers' questions on Twitter. Tweets addressed at the audience to encourage participation have little continuity then, beyond simply resolving who has won the competitions they organise.

Using Mentions, Retweets and Links

Another way of analysing programmes' activity on Twitter is to observe their use of some conventions characteristic of this social network, such as mentions (of other users) and retweets (reposting a tweet originally published by another user). We collected data on the number and types of mentions— according to whether the mentioned user has some links to the programme or is an external user, or whether the message included both types of mention— and retweets (to users with links to the programme or external users). Of the 927 messages published by @ LaTdP and @FCBRAC1, 887 were original in terms of content. As for references to other users, we find only 68 mentions, half of which are of users related to the programme. Mentions or retweets to other types of user are only occasional.

It is also interesting to observe whether the two profiles analysed enrich their messages with additional content. @LaTdP included links in most of the messages it posted (418 tweets, 58% of the total), almost all to other areas of the programme: the latdp.cat website, its YouTube channel, its Instagram or Twitpic photos, its audio content on uWhisp, or the Catalunya

Ràdio live website. In contrast, only 17% of @FCBRAC1's tweets incorporated links. These were basically audio content uploaded to its Soundcloud profile or photographs published by the Barcelona players on their social network profiles. Again, we see how the two profiles fail to take advantage of the platform's features to generate more interactivity with users. Hypertext and hypermedia extend beyond the limits of the message and allow content to be linked from outside one's own profile. But the links used by the two programmes are self-referential: a demonstration of a more promotional purpose than one aimed at dialogue with the audience.

The Role of the Networked Audiences in Twitter

Let us now take a look at the activities of Twitter users in relation to the two programmes. We analysed 1,129 tweets posted by users in the period of study that mentioned the two radio programmes' profiles. For @LaTdP there were 749 tweets, 427 (57% of the total) of which were retweets, whereby the user merely reproduced the original message posted by the programme. This is an action that can be done with a simple right click or manually. By doing so, users show interest in the original message, as they decide to reproduce it, while not adding any content of their own, acting as a kind of speaker or repeater for the programme. Some common retweets are team line-ups, commentary for a goal, Web content of the programme or competition questions.

A further 82 tweets (11% of the total) were modified retweets. These are messages in which users replicate the original tweet but modify it by adding their own content, basically text. This type of action represents a greater involvement of users, who do not limit themselves to reproducing a message by the broadcaster but also incorporate their own nuances, which may be of various different kinds, such as approval, congratulations, disagreement, clarification or enrichment of the original content. That said, this action is in the minority. By contrast, 240 user tweets (32% of the total) are users' own posts. In this case, the user mentions or replies to the programme. This is the action that involves the greatest commitment and a proactive attitude by the user.

With regard to @FCBRAC1, we collected 280 tweets that mention the BFC broadcast on RAC1. Of these, most are users' own posts. This is, therefore, the third type of action we have established. There were 171 tweets, or 61% of the total. As for other types of action, we find 96 retweets (34% of the total) and only 13 modified retweets (5%). The @FCBRAC1 audience is therefore quantitatively less active but more involved when providing own content, with such messages a majority.

Given the above results, let us now pay some attention to analysing the tweets we have categorised as genuine messages and users' own messages, grouped under the name mentions/replies: 240 for @LaTdP and 171 for @FCBRAC1. Analysis of these tweets leads us to extract three types of post:

1. Posts responding to a call for participation. This may be to participate in some of the programme's competitions, to comment on the BFC line-up, to predict a score, to assess the performance of the players or the coach, or to give an opinion on the match, among others.
2. Posts providing opinion and/or criticism, on the user's own initiative. Basically, there are two types: tweets assessing sporting elements and tweets assessing, either positively or negatively, the professional work of the journalists on the programme, the match broadcast and technical details (for example, synchronisation with the HDTV signal). In these messages, the user takes the initiative in communication, usually to express criticism or an opinion, but also for spontaneous displays of emotion, such as messages of support, 'shouting' the name of a player or celebrating a goal.
3. Posts that provide content and bring added value to the broadcast and timeline: documentation, archived information, audiovisual material, historical or present data and even user-generated content (see Images 5.1 and 5.2). In this regard, in some cases users become an information source for the programme. This is qualitatively the most important contribution of those observed.

Image 5.1   Examples of tweets that mention @LaTdP

Source: Own, using Topsy.com data.

Image 5.2 Examples of tweets that mention @FCBRAC1

Source: Own, using Topsy.com data.

Tweeters and Tweets around the Key Hashtags

To complement the above information, we shall now observe activity around the key tags associated with the two programmes: #latdp and #frac1. We begin from the general consideration that the hashtag is a means of coordinating a distributed discussion between more or less large groups of users, who do not need to be connected through existing '"follower" networks' (Bruns and Burgess 2011, 1). By monitoring the two hashtags, we show the fragmentation of the conversations around them. During the period for collecting data on this element, 388 users generated 927 tweets with #latdp, averaging 2.38 tweets per contributor, with 288 users posting just 1 tweet. As for the hashtag #frac1, we find that 939 users generated 2,000 tweets, averaging 2.12 tweets per contributor, with 608 users posting a single tweet. In both cases few users posted 6 tweets or more: 14 in the case of #latdp and 46 in that of #frac1 (Image 5.3). In both cases, most users limit themselves to posting a single tweet, and the user that posts most is specifically the programme itself. The use of hashtags is therefore sporadic. It allows us to follow what many people say about a common element, but we are not able to deduce any conversations constructed around this content.

Data on contributors also reveal the type of activity these users are involved in. Tweets that involve some interaction with others are in the minority. In the case of #latdp, we find 29% retweets and 2% replies; for #frac1 these figures are 20% and 3%, respectively. These percentages show

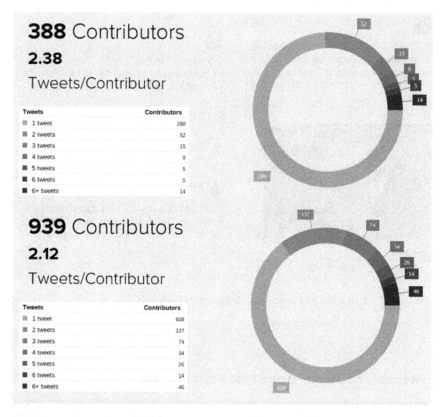

388 Contributors

2.38

Tweets/Contributor

Tweets	Contributors
1 tweet	288
2 tweets	52
3 tweets	15
4 tweets	9
5 tweets	5
6 tweets	5
6+ tweets	14

939 Contributors

2.12

Tweets/Contributor

Tweets	Contributors
1 tweet	608
2 tweets	137
3 tweets	74
4 tweets	34
5 tweets	26
6 tweets	14
6+ tweets	46

Image 5.3   Contributors to #latdp vs. contributors to #frac1

Source: Tweetbinder.

that the activity around the analysed tags is not only highly fragmented, with many tweeters posting just a few messages each, but is also focused on the diffusion of many tweets, posted by many different users and collected under one umbrella theme but which do not generate communication flows between different tweeters.

Broadcasters' Strategies to Engage with Followers on Twitter

On the preceding pages we have discussed the results of our observation of both the analysed programmes and users that interact with them via Twitter. The dynamic of the relationship between these two actors responds in part to the approach broadcasters take to social networks. In the interviews conducted with programme managers, we find that both @LaTdP and @FCBRAC1 consider Twitter a channel for the dissemination of content and interaction with the audience. However, our exploratory study reveals the difficulties radio companies and their professionals have in implementing what they aim to do in theory.

According to the discourse of their managers, the programmes see social networks as an opportunity to spread content, advertise the station, foster the relationship with users and encourage participation. But in the everyday reality of the profession, their postings on Twitter still respond more to a broadcasting than a relational model.

In the case of @LaTdP, the programme's team is well aware of the station's public service vocation. This is why they try to keep the profile active all week, with quality content and information that go beyond mere audio content. As for interaction, @LaTdP looks for responses from its followers and tries to encourage debate through surveys, requests for opinions, a weekly discussion question and a competition during the match. The goal is to keep the audience informed and active. In this respect, Twitter is another channel for making all the information and breaking news about BFC available to the audience. The aim is for the LaTdP brand to be an unofficial, but professional, reference point for the *Culer* (a nickname for Barça fans) universe.

As we have seen, however, the LaTdP audience's response on Twitter is more that of a faithful follower than an interlocutor. Most of the tweets posted by users are repostings of tweets by @LaTdP. This can certainly be considered a sign of approval of the programme content, a relevant factor given that it is a public broadcaster and that its managers highlight the goal of informing its audience. Furthermore, it is a constant and quantitatively important audience. These are users who post often and do so throughout the week, in line with the constant presence of the profile, not only when there is a match. Yet it is also a user profile that chooses to use the simplest of actions, the retweet. That said, we do sometimes find users providing valuable own content to the programme and the timeline, and sometimes with messages that indicate what we might consider some 'joint responsibility' with the public service (concern for the quality of language and vocabulary, demanding accurate data, interest in historical references).

As for @FCBRAC1, the managers are very aware that Twitter is a channel that allows them to extend the reach of content, as well as a means of interaction with the audience. However, it is still a profile very much linked to match days and therefore reproduces conventional programme dynamics. Regarding the relationship with followers, initiatives of the programme on this social network include the use of specific hashtags for draws, competitions, trivia and other mini-sections, along with experiments like *#relatbarça* (listeners complete a story via Twitter).

As we have seen, users are more interactive in broadcasts by the commercial radio station RAC1. In quantitative terms, it is an audience that posts less (we collected 280 tweets that mention @FCBRAC1, and 749 mentioning @LaTdP) and whose activities are limited to match days (in correlation with the dynamics of @FCBRAC1). Qualitatively, however, it is an audience that takes more initiative (and does not limit itself to reacting to the programme's numerous calls for participation) but does so largely via tweets containing its own original messages.

DISCUSSION AND CONCLUSION

Our study reveals Twitter as a channel that provides access to content and allows for user presence. Users are both present on the network (@LaTdP and @FCBRAC1 total 92,500 followers on Twitter) and active; in the period of analysis, we collected more activity by users than by the two radio programmes: 1,129 user tweets mention the programmes, and 1,137 users posted 2,927 tweets with the hashtags #latdp or #frac1, with only 927 posts by the programmes. Numbers aside, however, our research shows notable trends that go beyond a quantitative assessment.

If we analyse it in terms of Carpentier's AIP model (2011b), access is required as a first necessary step prior to interaction, in its various different forms: audience-to-media technology interaction, audience-to-content interaction, audience-to-audience interaction or interactions from audience to media organisations and communities. As we have commented throughout these pages, Twitter is a new space for the relationship between broadcasters and listeners. For now this relationship is more a sum of dispersed messages than a dialogue via tweets, and the role of listeners remains limited. Among the audience, an attitude of what we might call a 'retweet culture' still prevails. This is especially true of users interacting with @LaTdP, consistent with the dynamic of the programme's profile, given its dedication to public service and commitment to providing relevant information and content. In the case of @FCBRAC1, there are also many retweets, but its audience is more dynamic and involved, with more original messages from listeners. Here the style and the structural characteristics of radio stations are relevant factors. RAC1 is a station with less human and material infrastructure than one the size of the public station Catalunya Ràdio. RAC1 came into being in 2000 and its staff comprises young professionals who have evolved in consonance with the birth and growth of social networks. In many cases, and especially in sports writing, they have been pioneers in a commitment (often personal) to integrating the Internet and social media into their daily routines. The casual style of the presenters also helps to build relationships with an audience profile that uses social networks naturally. The approach adopted by @FCBRAC1 to Twitter contributes more to this interaction with users. In this regard, we note a clear correlation between the character of the station, its relational dynamic with its followers and the response of users on the social network, who through their posts often show a certain sense of a joint participation in a common project and a certain way of being a Barça fan.

However, in both cases we have observed very few mentions and replies by the programmes to their followers. They are invited to participate, and listeners are present, say things and contribute their opinions and content. But they then receive little response from the programmes themselves. Moreover, the problem is that the potential for conversation on Twitter is very fragmented. Results on the use of hashtags confirm this: we found many users posting messages, but most of them with a maximum of two tweets. Furthermore, mentions or replies among users are also scarce.

The relational dynamic between programmes and users on Twitter therefore makes it difficult to allow relevant and valuable content to stand out from the crowd of different kinds of messages. Interviewees representing the programmes expressed their willingness to bring interesting contributions from listeners to the airwaves, to take advantage of the dynamics generated on the Net. But they acknowledge that for now they are following a constant process of trial and error, often conditioned by structural factors that hamper efforts to achieve a more profound engagement with listeners on these new channels.

On social media it is always easier and takes less commitment to simply click than to contribute content (the retweet on Twitter, the like on Facebook, the +1 on Google+). Social networks are now a reality via which the opinions of thousands of listeners/users are channelled. In this respect, there is a greater presence of the audience, which is visible and can express itself easily. But this sum of posts still bears the impression of the coffee shop or pub debate. Indeed, throughout this study we tested the potential and possibilities for the audience to have an important role in its relationship with broadcasters. For this to happen, however, stations and programmes will have to promote a culture of change, both internally and among their audience. This change will allow for the transition of social media, still marked by quantitative considerations, towards an environment where more qualitative considerations predominate. And this requires time, resources and dedication, as well as a commitment to training and integration of new professional roles, which might be content curators, digital anthropologists and/or data mining specialists. Connected publics require a new media culture on social networks.

NOTE

1. IDESCAT (Catalan Institute of Statistics). Data from January 2013. Accessed January 30, 2014. http://www.idescat.cat/pub/?id=aec&n=245.

REFERENCES

AIMC [Asociación para la Investigación de Medios de Comunicación]. (2013). *Resumen general de resultados EGM. Febrero a Noviembre de 2013*. Accessed April 11, 2014. http://www.aimc.es/-Datos-EGM-Resumen-General-.html.

Armstrong, C. L. and Gao, F. (2010). "Now Tweet This: How News Organizations Use Twitter." *Electronic News*, 4(4), 218–235.

Bernstein, A. and Blain, N. (eds.) (2003). *Sport, Media, Culture: Global and Local Dimensions*. London: Frank Cass.

Bonet, M. (2012). "Spanish Radio: When Digitalization Meets an Analog Business." In Hendricks, J. A. (ed.), *The Palgrave Handbook of Global Radio*. New York: Palgrave Macmillan, 176–192.

Bonini, T. and Sellas, T. (2014). "Twitter as a Public Service Medium? A Content Analysis of the Twitter Use Made by Radio RAI And RNE." *Communication & Society/Comunicación y Sociedad*, 27(2), 125–146.

Boyd, D. (2011). "Social Network Sites as Networked Publics: Affordances, Dynamics, and Implications." In Papacharissi, Z. (ed.), *A Networked Self. Identity, Community, and Culture on Social Network Sites*. London: Routledge, 39–58.

Boyd, D. and Ellison, N. (2008). "Social Network Sites: Definition, History, and Scholarship." *Journal of Computer-Mediated Communication*, 13(11), 210–230.

Boyle, R. (1992). "From Our Gaelic Fields: Radio, Sport and Nation in Post-Partition Ireland." *Media, Culture & Society*, 14(4), 623–636.

Bruns, A. and Burgess, J. E. (2011). "The Use Of Twitter Hashtags in the Formation of Ad Hoc Publics." Paper presented at 6th European Consortium for Political Research General Conference, University of Iceland, Reykjavik, Iceland, August 25–27.

Carpentier, N. (2011a). "New Configurations of the Audience? The Challenges of User-Generated Content for Audience Theory and Media Participation." In Nightingale, V. (ed.), *The Handbook of Media Audiences*. Malden, MA: Wiley-Blackwell, 190–212.

———. (2011b). "The Concept of Participation. If They Have Access and Interact, Do They Really Participate?" *CM: Communication Management Quarterly/Casopis za upravljanje komuniciranjem*, 21,13–36.

Ferguson, D. and Greer, C. F. (2011). "Local Radio and Microblogging: How Radio Stations in the U.S. Are Using Twitter." *Journal of Radio & Audio Media*, 18(1), 33–46.

Fernández-Quijada, D., Sellas, T. and Bonet, M. (2013). "Media Systems and Stateless Nations: Catalan and Welsh Radio in Comparative Perspective." *Trípodos*, 33, 13–32.

Guibernau, M. (2007). *Catalan Nationalism: Francoism, Transition and Democracy*. London: Routledge.

Hargreaves, J. (1986). *Sport, Power and Society*. Oxford: Polity Press.

Hobsbawm, E. (1990). *Nations and Nationalism since 1780: Programme, Myth, Reality*. Cambridge: Cambridge University Press.

Jenkins, H., Ford, S. and Green, J. (2013). *Spreadable Media. Creating Value and Meaning in a Networked Culture*. New York: New York University Press.

Kaplan, A. M. and Haenlein, M. (2010). "Users of the World, Unite! The Challenges and Opportunities of Social Media." *Business Horizons*, 53(1), 59–68.

Messner, M., Linke, M. and Eford, A. (2011). "Shoveling Tweets: An Analysis of the Microblogging Engagement of Traditional News Organizations." Paper presented at *International Symposium on Online Journalism*, Austin, Texas, April 1–2.

Neuendorf, K. A. (2013). *The Content Analysis Guidebook*. Thousand Oaks: Sage.

Puyal, J. M. (2007). "Del carrer a les ones. De com el futbol català va conquerir la ràdio." *Quaderns del CAC*, 28, 53–61.

Rainie, L. and Wellman, B. (2012). *Networked. The New Social Operating System*. Cambridge, MA: MIT Press.

Sellas, T. (2013). "La ràdio a les xarxes socials: els magazins matinals a Twitter." *Quaderns del CAC*, 29, 23–33.

van Dijck, J. (2013). *Platformed Sociality. The Culture of Connectivity. A Critical History of Social Media.* Oxford: Oxford University Press.

Xifra, J. (2008). "Soccer, Civil Religion, and Public Relations: Devotional-Promotional Communication and Barcelona Football Club." *Public Relations Review: A Journal of Research and Comment,* 34(2), 192–198.

Xifra, J. and McKie, D. (2012). "From Realpolitik to Noopolitik: The Public Relations of (Stateless) Nations in an Information Age." *Public Relations Review: A Journal of Research and Comment,* 38(5), 819–824.

Part II
Productive Publics

6   The Automatic DJ?
Control, Automation and Creativity in Commercial Music Radio

Fredrik Stiernstedt

INTRODUCTION

The first decade of this century saw a lot of changes in the production of commercial music radio. These changes were to a large degree spurred by technological developments such as digitisation, the rise of social media and 'the culture of connectivity' (van Dijck 2013). Established radio companies struggled to adjust to the 'shock of the new.' New strategies for increased interactivity and communication with listeners—for example, through social networking sites—were developed and new forms of radio distribution, such as the Internet and mobile phone applications, were developed. There has been discussion about how these changes affect listeners, the economics of radio commercials and both text and radio aesthetics (cf. Berry 2006; Bonini 2012; Freeman, Klapczynski and Wood 2012; Freire 2007; Menduni 2007; Moreno, Costa and Amoedo 2010; Murray 2009; Wall 2004). However, there has not been sufficient work on how these technological changes affect the organisation of work and labour conditions within the radio industry. We know from studies of other sectors of the media industry that similar processes of media change (digitisation, platform expansion, etc.) have had implications for workers in the industry (Nygren and Zuiderveld 2011). For example, it has been reported that tension is created among employees, that conflicts in relations between media company management and staff can arise (Erdal 2007; Westlund 2012) and that the experiences of work and of power relations within the workplace have been transformed (Mayer 2009).

In this chapter I will analyse transformations in the organisation of work and labour in music radio production that have come about due to technological change; the implementation of social network media in production and the push towards more interactivity and user-generated content. What effects do these phenomena have on the organisation of work and for labour relations? What new roles are assigned to producers and audiences? What does this mean for the creative potentials of music radio work?

To explore these questions I have studied Sweden's largest commercial radio company, MTG-Radio. I have conducted ethnographic field work (interviews and observations) in the editorial department and amongst the DJs and producers during the period of 2006 to 2010. I have combined this approach with analysis of internal production documents, external texts about the company (e.g., newspaper articles, government investigations, official reports) and of the media texts produced at MTG-Radio. Through these various materials I have assembled an account of how new media technologies, both as a material and a discursive reality, have affected work and production in the company.

The study of technological change, new competition and organisational changes from an ethnographic perspective makes it possible to discuss, examine and deepen previous theories of media work. Theoretically the chapter takes as its starting point the issue of the up-skilling and de-skilling of media work (Barrett 2005; Braverman 1999; Knights and Willmott 1990; McKinlay and Smith 2009; Örnebring 2010; Roberts 2007). Sociological research of media work has shown how new production technologies have been used to push for increased automation of work in the media industries. This risks reducing employees' craft knowledge, bureaucratisation of creative processes and increasing management's power and control over production.

The concept of de-skilling is controversial, however, and a range of other studies have indicated how work in general has become more knowledge intensive, how employees have been given more control over work processes and have become more independent in relation to management and bureaucratic systems of control with the help of new (digital) technologies, a process which is usually labelled up-skilling (Edgell 2012). Studies of de-skilling and up-skilling are usually carried out on a macro level by using survey methods and statistical data (Fraser 2010). Such methods, however, give limited information of how workers actually use technologies and say little about how they experience technological restructuring of work. Through observations and interviews it will be possible to expand our understanding of how new technologies and new organisational principles create opportunities for more or less qualified work, creativity and control and how technologies shape power relations in the everyday life of media production.

MEDIA WORK, SKILLS AND CREATIVITY

What has happened in the commercial music radio and in the media industries in general during the last decade can be described as a technological restructuring of work. Production practices and work organisation have been transformed, both directly by the implementation of new technical production tools and indirectly as a response to new media technologies and platforms and the competition they create (Cottle 2003; Marjoribanks 2000; Ursell 2000). This restructuring must, however, be understood in relation to the specific nature of media work and media production.

Work and production within the media industries share many traits with other forms of white-collar labour. However, as noted by many scholars, media work is also different from many other forms of production. Theodor

W. Adorno (1976, 39), perhaps most famous for his relentless critique of commodification and standardisation of cultural products in the industrial capitalist era, wrote in his *Sociology of Music*: "[Media production] is not industrial mass production in a strict literal sense . . . even though it in part is shaped by industrial production logics, the process is still more artisan." The specific form of media production has to do with what usually is called the art/commerce relation, and the ground for the art/commerce relation is the particular commodity form of media content. Successful media commodities, which can attract large audiences, have to be—in some way—unpredictable, innovative and creative: the (pseudo)individuality (to use yet another reference from Adorno) of media commodities is hence a precondition for their attractiveness on the market. In order to create such (pseudo)individuality of media commodities, producers within the industries have to have some form of creative autonomy and manoeuvring space within production arrangements that also have to be relatively predictable. It is hence irrational for media companies to rationalise production too much (Banks 2007; Deuze 2007; Hesmondhalgh 2007; Huws 2010; Miège 1989). This fact has led media industries to develop their own models for management, organisation and production that try to produce and enhance creativity, unpredictability and standardisation at the same time. To manage this balance is, according to Mark Banks (2007, 30), the "essence of the labour process in the cultural industries."

In this chapter I analyse the technological restructuring of media work through the concepts of up-skilling and de-skilling. The debate around these concepts has been ongoing since the publication of Harry Braverman's (1999) book *Labor and Monopoly Capital*. The argument put forward by Braverman was essentially that in more advanced and bureaucratic capitalism, companies increasingly invest surplus in machinery that automates labour and design labour processes which standardise work and make it into more of a machine-based and powerless activity (cf. Brynjolfsson and McAfee 2014). Workers are increasingly deprived of skill, autonomy, self-determination and professional judgement. There are hence essentially three steps in the process of de-skilling as outlined by Braverman: firstly, machines and production protocols usurp knowledge previously harbored in humans; secondly, production is increasingly automated; and thirdly, management control and centralised decision making is installed within the labour process. There has been some empirical support for the thesis on de-skilling (cf. Boddy and Gunson 1996), and in relation to work in the media industries, empirical studies have shown how new technologies have been implemented to automate a range of production practices (Greenbaum 2004; Marjoribanks 2000; Morris-Suzuki 1997). Studies in relation to digital technologies have also shown that the degree of autonomy in media work has become lower (Tyrkkö and Karlqvist 2005) and that the labour process as well as the content itself have become more standardised (Kidd-Damarin 2010; Nygren 2008).

De-skilling is, however, a contested notion. Several studies have found no evidence for the process of de-skilling and in other studies authors have pointed to the very opposite tendency: that technological restructuring of work can lead to up-skilling. Up-skilling means that more skills, and importantly, more sophisticated skills are needed in a more technologically advanced workplace (Edgell 2012). Studies have shown how routine tasks are increasingly handed over to machines but that this, in contrast to Braverman's argument, gives employees more space to initiate, plan and organise their own work (Allvin 2006). More advanced technology also calls for a better educated workforce, which creates better skilled personnel and, in turn, improves the bargaining position of employees in relation to management and owners (Gallie et al. 1998). A more general argument concerns the nature of the economy and society in general. The fact that the economy in general is more knowledge intensive and that a larger portion of societal production is focused on producing 'intellectual,' 'mental' or 'immaterial' commodities (such as information, symbols, knowledge, etc.) will, according to some commentators, naturally lead to a more autonomous, self-fulfilling and creative working life for many and raise the skill level in the labour force in general (cf. Florida 2002).

The question of de-skilling and up-skilling is intertwined with the notion of creativity and the art/commerce relation in media work. Arguably de-skilling ought to hamper creativity, as work processes are more standardised, automated and controlled. In contrast it would be reasonable to believe that up-skilling could expand and enhance the creativity of media producers, since they gain skills, and that professionalism and autonomy hence might be strengthened. In previous studies, however, de-skilling and up-skilling have been investigated mainly with statistical methods (Gade 2008; O'Doherty and Wilmott 2000). The implementation of new and advanced technologies in production has often been used as an indicator of up-skilling per se. In what remains of this chapter, I will tackle the question of what happens with work and labour relations in commercial music radio from an ethnographic viewpoint, which also includes the employees' actual experiences, uses and negotiations of the ways in which new technologies and new media platforms are introduced in media work. I will aim to demonstrate that there are certainly tendencies of up-skilling among the producers I have interviewed and in the production I observed. At the same time, there is an ongoing redefinition and renegotiation of the very notion of creativity as such, which in many ways seems to undermine traditional understandings of professionalism, creativity and autonomy and fundamentally transforms the very nature of the balance between art and commerce in media production.

NEW FORMS OF AUDIENCE ENGAGEMENT IN MUSIC RADIO

For a long time, radio has been a medium characterised by a rather high degree of audience interaction and interactivity, especially when compared with television. Since the 1960s, telephone technology has been frequently used—internationally—to allow for members of the radio audience to participate and 'talk back.' In the 1970s, when programming philosophies and broadcasting ideals (as well as institutions) changed in many countries, to more localism and increased closeness to the audience, interactivity, audience participation and experiments with 'citizen journalism' became commonplace (Forsman 2014).

Another form of audience participation, often not recognised as such, comprises the various forms of audience research undertaken by broadcasting institutions. Audience research has been commonplace in both public service and commercial radio since the inception of the medium in the 1920s. Since the 1980s, however, new market ideologies and increasing commercialisation have gradually increased the importance and impact of audience research (Bjur 2010).

The last decade has seen rapid developments of social network media as well as a more general digitisation of production and reception of radio. This has further increased the development of audience participation and interactivity in radio and has created new frameworks and patterns for audience engagement with radio content. Podcasting has allowed for time shifting and made it increasingly simple for listeners to become producers of their own content (Berry 2006). Social media has lowered the threshold for participation, and in many radio shows, the DJ and presenter is increasingly a form of moderator, choosing and assembling content produced by members of the audience (opinions on different matters, song requests, etc.) (Bonini 2012).

Social media facilitates communication among members of the audience, thus contributing to a group understanding of themselves as part of an audience community (Stiernstedt 2010). New media technologies have changed how audiences can participate as members in research and surveys. Listening in itself creates a lot of data which is possible for the broadcaster to process if done digitally, and social media can be used to let the audience 'vote' and tell their opinions in different matters (Stiernstedt 2008).

Naturally there are still a minority of the radio listeners that partake in these new forms of engagement with radio stations, but it is a group that it is growing. At MTG-Radio, all of the changes outlined above took place during the period in which I did my fieldwork: to create new forms of audience engagement was seen as a key strategy for survival, as explained by one of the producers in the study:

> [We have to do this] since right now we are losing listeners. The two latest ratings reports have confirmed it very clearly. Normally we can see movements of listeners between different radio stations. If we lose some listeners, they turn up somewhere else. But now . . . they have just disappeared. And then our strategy is to find new arenas to meet the audience. More digital media platforms, more Web-based services.
>
> (Informant F)

The producers at MTG had, however, no clear idea about what new forms of audience engagement they had to offer. They just had the feeling that they had to do something. Early on, two main interpretations of the situation took hold in the organisation, which represent two different roles assigned to the listener: the role of 'informant' and the role of 'socialiser.'

The first role assigned to listeners is tied to the usage of new media technologies to refine and simplify methods of audience research. New digital platforms were interpreted mainly, at least by management, as new tools to survey and better understand audience taste patterns. As explained by one of the top managers at MTG-Radio:

> We can know a lot of people listening and participating online. If they for example register to get access to bonus or extra materials, then we could use it as audience research. . . . And through social media, and in discussion forums, etc., we basically get focus groups. For free!
>
> (Informant L)

Members of the audience participating or engaging in communication with the radio station on digital platforms were seen mainly as informants. Much of the information gathering was done without the knowledge of the informants, but social media and digital platforms were also used for more traditional forms of audience research, such as questionnaires. This type of more traditional research was, however, increasingly rebranded as contests to take part in for fun, as a form of playful extra material possible to access through the radio stations' websites and other digital arenas (Stiernstedt 2008).

The second role assigned to listeners was that of 'socialiser,' meaning that they were understood as resources for increasing the sociability of radio output. This understanding of the possibilities of new media was strongest among the DJs and other staff directly involved in broadcasting and does not correspond to a new role assigned to radio audiences. On the contrary, it has for long been one of radio's main purposes with 'call-ins' and other forms of participation from the audience taking place in music radio. In fact, the argument at MTG-Radio, among the producers, was precisely that social media and new platforms for interaction and participation would help return format radio to its 'roots,' allowing it to regain a 'soul.' In the general confusion and institutional processes of sense-making that took place as new digital media and social media were implemented in the production process at MTG-Radio, a turn to the medium's history and a revived understanding of radio as the 'original social media' became widespread among my informants:

> Lot of stations are on Facebook, Twitter and social media. But they don't know what they are doing there. . . . It should not be one-way communication. It should be conversation and you should listen to what the listeners are saying. Facebook is like broadcasting!
>
> (Informant M)

I have always said that a TV personality or a movie star stands on a stage above the audience and the audience looks up to them. A radio presenter, on the other hand, stands with his or her audience, they are in the audience, so to say. That's why social media and radio works naturally together.

(Informant K)

The idea of radio as a 'direct' and 'social' medium was widespread and often discussed among my informants, and for them, new media platforms were understood as a way of connecting radio to its roots and to use audience engagement and participation to strengthen the sociability of radio, enhancing its closeness to listeners by letting members of the audience participate in broadcasts and talk-back to the radio station.

In the following, I will look closer into how these technological changes, the implementation of digital platforms and social media, as well as the general digitisation of production affected the organisation of work and the power relations within production.

NEW MEDIA PLATFORMS AND TENDENCIES OF DE-SKILLING

This chapter is about commercial music radio, which is often called 'format radio' due to the fact that the majority of commercial music stations produce 'programmes' according to a format. A format is a pre-defined set of rules and models for choice of music and DJs, covering what the latter are supposed to say and do between songs. The format is meant to create the station's identity (Barnard 1989; Hendy 2000; McCourt and Rothenbuhler 2004). Formats are defined and chosen in relation to the preferred target group and are often understood as a 'machine' for delivering the right audiences to advertisers. In many ways format radio, which began in the 1950s, is in itself a tool for de-skilling. It creates automation, standardisation and central control over output, hence limiting the space for individuality and creativity whilst increasing the replaceability of employees in the music radio industry.

However, it was not until the development of digital systems for broadcasting and music scheduling that the tendencies of de-skilling became more fully developed in commercial music radio. The digitisation of production tools gained speed in the 1980s and 1990s. The reasons for this were both technological (i.e., increasing processing speed and falling prices of computer technology) and political (deregulation which led to increased syndication and hence an increasing demand for automation). In this period it was mainly the music scheduling that was being automated, with the help of digital technologies such as the market leading software RCS Selector®. Music scheduling software promises stricter control over both format and staff, greater predictability, fewer errors and lower costs. The software manual, in a passage clearly intended to be read by managers, states the following: "Humans are human. Selector works without human problems or limitations. Selector will never schedule a song that breaks any of your unbreakable rules and will always work according to your instructions" (Lee n.d., 32).

One of my informants further underlines that de-skilling is a direct consequence of music scheduling software:

> When it is installed and running, all that has to be done is basically to record some new songs in the system once in a while. The rest is all done by the software. This makes it much easier to get a good output even from a non-skilled music director.
>
> (Informant A)

In the early 2000s, the possibilities for control and automation were further advanced through the implementation of digital studio technologies and on-air systems for broadcasting. Among these is the well-known voice track practice which makes it easier to pre-record large amounts of output. One DJ can therefore do much more work and the staff can be downsized (Ala-Fossi 2005). Digital broadcasting systems, such as RCS MasterControl, further automate the actual broadcasting of content and increase the possibility for managers to visually monitor and control what goes on in the studio. The automation has gone so far that, as one informant states: "I do not see myself as a DJ anymore. I'm just someone who gets a packet of songs, a playlist and instructions for when and how to play them" (Informant B).

The connection between these technologies and the push for de-skilling and staff redundancies are by no means a secret among the employees I interviewed in this study:

> For example, the voice track application came towards the end of the 1990s. On-air staff did not like it at all. (. . .) But those higher in the hierarchy with responsibilities for budgets think it's perfect. And it has been used to cut costs. And to increase centralisation of control and foster so-called rationalisations. These software are used to save money.
>
> (Informant A)

In the middle of the 2000s the media landscape in general changed substantially due to new digital and connective media. New competition—for example, Internet-radio, P2P sharing of music, and social media in general—challenged traditional commercial music radio. New media platforms also increasingly became tools used for communication with audiences and to increase 'interactivity' and foster relationships with listeners. This also had consequences for the organisation of work within commercial music radio. In many ways, as I will discuss in the next section of this chapter, the implementation of new digital technologies and the expansion to new media platforms (i.e., social media and new distribution technologies) counteracted tendencies of de-skilling. If de-skilling ultimately is a technique for increasing the intensity of work (getting the staff to produce more with less resources), the introduction of new media platforms increases the general labour time.

> Previously, like in the 1980s, working in a studio, doing live radio was intensive. You had to have 100% focus. Everything was done manually, it was stressful and intense. But nowadays . . . it's all automatic. On the other hand, it is intensive in another way now. Nowadays you have to work all the time. You're supposed to handle Twitter, Facebook, you're supposed to record, edit and publish bonus materials for the Internet platforms. It goes on and on. You're basically on air 24/7.
>
> (Informant C)

This was also a reason for the initial hesitation, or even resistance, of many of the informants to start working with new media platforms. The arguments they presented in the interviews for not using new media platforms and not implementing them in production were that it took "too much time" (Informant D), that it was a "constant pressure to produce content" (Informant E) and that they were "supposed to do it in our free time" (Informant F).

The push for increased control and automation with the help of digital technologies had quite obviously economic motives within the organisation I studied. In the early 2000s, after the implementation of new digital production technologies, there were several rounds of staff cuts, and profit margins slowly grew. These changes were, however, not uncontested among the staff. Many complaints were put forward that this development led to less creativity, less personal input and less interesting output. In the middle of the 2000s ratings started to drop and the criticism of de-skilling became louder and was heard more within the organisation. Change was on the way.

NEW MEDIA PLATFORMS AND TENDENCIES OF UP-SKILLING

The changes that took place in production, which I in the previous section described as instances of de-skilling of media work, could, at least by some researchers, also be interpreted as examples of up-skilling. For some, the introduction of computer technologies in production in itself represents up-skilling. This is due to the fact that it is hypothesised that more skills are needed to operate more advanced computers and software. I have, however, shown how increased control, increased automation and reduced need for a skilled and professional creative workforce were the actual end results of the digitisation of radio production. Nonetheless, around the year 2010 there was an actual renaissance of the idea of a skilled and professional workforce, with a larger degree of professional and creative autonomy at

MTG-Radio. This was also a general tendency in the industry around this time. And this change was most certainly connected to new media technologies and processes of digitisation.

The rapid transformations of the media landscape, with the rise of digital social media and new platforms for distributing media content created new competition. Audience figures, especially among younger audiences, started to drop. Several 'crisis meetings' were held in the production at MTG-Radio. Not only did commercial music radio experience new competition from other media that distributed music, but the notion was that the mentality and demands of "a new media generation" (Informant G) had to be met with changes in content. This had some general consequences. Management slowly moved away from centralised control and automation, the DJs and the audience got more direct influence over content and playlists, DJs were given expanded manoeuvring space for producing and distributing content and control through so-called 'temporal cueing' (i.e., tight time frames) was loosened. One quote from a station manager I interviewed illustrates this development:

> We have been investing more and more in content and characters. We have DJs who can say what they want, talk about what they want, and even pick their own songs. Nowadays it has to be authentic, honest, forreal. That's the only way to reach the younger audiences. (. . .) Already some years ago it was obvious that competition in commercial music radio is no longer about the music. It's about what you do between the songs. And it's becoming clear that the tone and mentality is changing, even among the most conservative within this company and within the industry.
>
> (Informant H)

In FM broadcasts, it became more important to create content that could 'go viral,' which often meant that DJs got more space for developing their ideas for gags, stunts and talk. At the same time other media forms, such as written blogs, online video and photography, became more important and integrated into production at MTG-Radio: "It was some sort of . . . it wasn't really an order, but it was much encouraged from the management. That we [DJs] should do blogs. Management thought that it was important that we were visible in social media in general" (Informant I).

The strict control over the form and content of the material produced at MTG-Radio (the idea behind format radio) became gradually looser. The general focus on music as such was also increasingly questioned—for example, at staff meetings. One of my informants remembers how: "I remember very well all these times I had a meeting with my boss and we decided to take away one more song per hour. So that the percentage of talk gradually increased. Slowly but steadily it became more content, so to say" (Informant J).

One of the strategic consultants working with the company in question to improve its programming and develop new ideas wrote on his company blog:

> I have for some time noted that radio's future comes from three and only three areas:
>
> 1. Between the songs
> 2. Instead of the songs
> 3. In addition to the songs
>
> (. . .) Invariably this 'call for content' will push radio in spoken word directions, on air or off. And every spoken word direction has natural tentacles across platforms.
>
> (Ramsey 2012)

The new technologies integrated into radio production led to a general re-skilling of the workforce: editing, moving images or writing blog entries required new skills. In effect this was also an up-skilling, since the skills required were more advanced than before. Also, the general tendency in production was to enhance self-determination among staff (decrease control) and to allow more autonomy in the production practices (decrease automation). In order to meet the increased competition and to attract new listeners (as well as ones lost to other media), creativity became a new buzz-word at MTG-Radio. To facilitate and enhance creativity among the workers, especially in their handling of new media platforms, became, at least for a short period of time, almost the overarching goal of management.

THE CONTESTED NOTION OF CREATIVITY

Creativity and innovation became, as I demonstrated above, more embraced values at MTG-Radio around 2010. This had strategic and commercial reasons, as it was an attempt to handle new competition, to develop new content and production practices in relation to interactive and social media technologies and to form a new 'multiplatform organisation' at the company. Management tried in various ways to foster creative approaches to work and to foster new 'creative subjects' among the producers, DJs and content managers at the company. It did so through courses and workshops, inviting management consultants to give talks and prescribing reading of various books on how to foster a creative personality (including books authored by senior management at MTG-Radio). Furthermore, management did so by reorganising the production facilities, distributing weekly newsletters on the theme of 'how to be creative,' setting up 'innovation contests,' etc.

In this process, as I will discuss, the very concept of creativity and the practices connected to the notion of 'being creative' gradually changed.

Creativity has for a long time been a celebrated value among media workers throughout the media and cultural industries. The so-called creatives (i.e., staff producing content) have also, as analysed by Keith Negus (1999), defined themselves in relation and opposition to the 'suits' of the media industry (management, marketing, sales, etc.). At MTG-Radio, the suits were now paradoxically pushing for more creativity among the creatives.

Creativity became a buzz-word and an object of discourse within the media organisation in which the creative subject or personality—the creative performance and how to be (and who is) creative—was elaborated on. Interestingly, the people who were singled out as creative in the organisation very seldom belonged to the 'creative' parts of the company in the traditional sense. It was not the content producers who were said to be creative but rather the management, marketing and sales departments. They were—for example, in the weekly newsletter distributed to all employees—repeatedly described as "creative gods" who "delivered creative solutions" and "come up with creative ideas" (Informant F). During the period of my fieldwork, one of the top managers of the company wrote a book with the title *Two magic years of thoughts* (*Två magiska år av tankar*) that he distributed to all employees at the company (as well as to clients and customers outside of it). The book can be described as a mix of pop philosophy, management ideology and communication theory. One of his general ideas with the book is that: "Just a few years ago commercials and commercialism was seen to be something very different from culture and aesthetics. Just some years ago it was unthinkable for most artists and creatives to do commercials or work with PR. It was looked down on. That's not the case anymore" (Bacoccoli 2011, 36).

Throughout the book the author elaborates on the consequences of this alleged shift. Administrative and economic processes in cultural and media production, he argues, are the truly creative elements of this work and are described in terms of 'sharing' and 'collective meaning making'—or in other words as cultural processes. Marketers, salespeople, etc. are compared to 'poets,' 'artists' and 'oracles,' their job is to create the 'new and unexpected' that is more interesting than the 'so-called editorial content' and that 'opens doors to new worlds of experience.' This view of media production and this self-understanding by management were heavily propagated within the company. This was the type of creativity that was enhanced and embraced within production, and it was arguably an ideological move to co-opt the positive and celebrated values of creativity in order to be able to use it as a tool for increased dominance of the commercial parts of the media company.

At the same time there was another and parallel idea of creativity fostered and propagated within production, the idea of creativity as collaboration. In the history of the idea of creativity, the creative subject has often been interpreted (and branded) as the 'lonely genius,' and in economic terms this notion, originally stemming from Romanticist thought, has been inscribed in copyright law as the individual rights holder (Woodmansee 1994). To make visible and emphasise the collaborative and ordinary aspects of creative cooperation is, in such a context, often a sobering or even radical exercise. In the context of media production at MTG-Radio, collaborations and acts of 'sharing' are seen as the essence of creative behaviour.

One of the management texts used in production states: "We have to build a culture that encourages and finally demands from the employees that they engage in the practice of giving, to share everything, with everyone, all the time" (Farber 2009, 126).

Those who do not "connect and share with everyone else" are in the same text labelled as "empty", "dead" and "selfish" (Farber 2009, 126). In theory, to emphasise the collective efforts of creative work can be a good thing, and to enhance and stimulate sharing of ideas and knowledge is important and valuable in organisations of all kinds. In practice, however, these mantras had mainly two implications for the employees. The first was that they were increasingly pushed to give away their 'creative capital' (their ideas) for free. Ideas and knowledge are the most important skills in media production. The push for 'sharing your ideas' could hence be understood as a technique for de-skilling in itself. Secondly, and more importantly, the idea of collaboration turned out to be rather one-sided. In practice, to "collaborate and create new connections and networks" (Bacoccoli 2011, 53) meant that the creative parts of the company (content production) should be increasingly open to include the administrative parts (sales and marketing) in developing new ideas for content and in planning broadcasts based on 'advertiser funded content.' A whole new division was set up within the company with this sole purpose (to better integrate creative and sales) and was given the telling name 'Creative Sales'. This new strategy was something that became a constant source of agony among the staff producing content at MTG-Radio:

> Our goals and purpose are naturally divergent. My primary task is to create as entertaining radio as possible. Their primary task is to sell air time and make money. This leads to collisions and conflicts. They think that we have to collaborate on this. I think we have two different missions. What we mean by the concept 'good radio' is essentially two totally different things.
>
> (Informant K)

As I have aimed to show in this part of the chapter, the very notion of creativity became a buzz-word in production at the beginning of the 2010s. Creativity and autonomy are often understood as antithetical to de-skilling and to automation and control. The way that this concept was discussed and introduced in the production at MTG-Radio can rather be understood as an attempt from management to 'co-opt' a celebrated value from cultural production and media work and to use it as a tool for de-skilling and for increased commercial control over media content and media work.

CONCLUSION

During the last decade, music radio has seen rapid changes. New technologies have facilitated new forms of production, new media platforms have fostered new modes of audience engagement and new organisational forms—as well as business models—have been developed in the industry. Against this background, the structure of media work within commercial music radio has been evolving.

This case study, in line with previous works (Örnebring 2010), finds evidence for simultaneous de-skilling and up-skilling in media production due to the implementation of digital technologies. Digital tools for production generated more automation and control, while the rise of interactive, social media and its implementation within commercial music radio production, on the contrary, increased the staff's access to more advanced skills, developed multi-skilling and, in general, raised the levels of autonomy and self-determination in production. Creativity, to 'be creative,' increasingly became a celebrated value, or even a buzz-word, within production.

Quite paradoxically however, the general up-skilling runs in parallel with a deepened commodification of labour and more ideological forms of control over media workers through to co-optation of the very concept of creativity. Creativity and innovation strangely end up meaning to "follow the management's directions," to "simplify the capitalisation of media products," to "connect sales, marketing and 'creative' parts of the company and integrate them more deeply" (Informant H). The radio worker in this study is hence paradoxically both up-skilled and 'creative' and at the same time strictly subsumed under management control in the media factory of the social media age.

REFERENCES

Adorno, T. W. (1976). *Inledning till Musiksociologin. Tolv teoretiska föreläsningar* [Introduction to the Sociology of Music. Twelve Theoretical Lectures]. Kristianstad: Bo Cavefors Bokförlag.
Ala-Fossi, M. (2005). *Saleable Compromises. Quality Cultures in Finnish and US Commercial Radio*. Tampere: Tampere University Press.
Allvin, M. (ed.). (2006). *Gränslöst arbete: socialpsykologiska perspektiv på det nya Arbetslivet* [Limitless Labour: Socialpsycological Perspectives on New Forms of Work]. Malmö: Liber.
Bacoccoli, T. (2011). *Två år av magiska tankar.* [Two Years of Magical Thinking]. Stockholm: MTG-Radio.
Banks, M. (2007). *The Politics of Cultural Work*. Hampshire, New York: Palgrave Macmillan.
Barnard, S. (1989). *On the Radio: Music Radio in Britain*. Milton Keynes: Open University Press.
Barrett, R. (2005). *Management, Labour Process and Software Development. Reality Bites*. London, New York: Routledge.
Berry, R. (2006). "Will the iPod Kill the Radio Star? Profiling Podcasting as Radio." *Convergence: The International Journal of Research into New Media Technologies*, 12(2), 143–162.

Bjur, J. (2010). *Transforming Audiences. Patterns of Individualization in Television Viewing.* Gothenburg: Department of Journalism, Media and Communication University of Gothenburg.

Boddy, D. and Gunson, N. (1996). *Organisations in the Network Age.* London, New York: Routledge.

Bonini, T. (2012). "Doing Radio in the Age of Facebook." In Oliveira, M., Portela, P. and Santos, L. A. (eds.), *Radio Evolution. Conference Proceedings.* Minho: CECS University of Minho, 17–26.

Braverman, H. (1999). *Labor and Monopoly Capital: The Degradation of Work in the Twentieth Century.* New York: Monthly Review Press.

Brynjolfsson, E. and McAfee, A. (2014). *The Second Machine Age: Work, Progress, and Prosperity in a Time of Brilliant Technologies.* New York: W.W. Norton & Company.

Cottle, S. (ed.). (2003). *Media Organization and Production.* Los Angeles, London: Sage.

Deuze, M. (2007). *Media Work.* Cambridge: Polity Press.

Edgell, S. (2012). *The Sociology of Work. Continuity and Change in Paid and Un-Paid Work.* Thousand Oaks, London: Sage.

Erdal, J. I. (2007). "Negotiating Convergence in News Production." In Storsul, T. and Stuedahl, D. (eds.), *Ambivalence Towards Convergence. Digitalization and Media Change.* Gothenburg: Nordicom, 73–85.

Farber, S. (2009). *Greater than Yourself. The Ultimate Rule of Extreme Leadership.* New York: Random House International.

Florida, R. (2002). *The Rise of the Creative Class: And How It's Transforming Work, Leisure, Community and Everyday Life.* New York: Basic Books.

Forsman, M. (2014). "Talk Back and Participate: The Making of the Active Audience Within Swedish Local Radio 1977–2000." In Djerf-Pierre, M. and Ekström, M. (eds.), *A History of Swedish Broadcasting. Communicative Ethos, Genres and Institutional Change.* Gothenburg: Nordicom, 127–153.

Fraser, D. (2010). "De-skilling Revisited: New Experience on the Skill Trajectory of the Australian Economy 2001–2007." *SSRN Electronic Journal*, 1–17. Accessed November 26, 2012. http://ssrn.com/abstract=1804618.

Freeman, B., Klapczynski, J. and Wood, E. (2012). "Radio and Facebook: The Relationship between Radio and Social Media Software in the U.S., Germany & Singapore." *First Monday*, 17(4). Accessed May 17, 2014. http://firstmonday.org/ojs/index.php/fm/article/viewArticle/3768.

Freire, A. M. (2007). "Remediating Radio: Audio Streaming, Music Recommendation and the Discourse of Radioness." *The Radio Journal: International Studies in Broadcast and Audio Media*, 5(2–3), 97–112.

Gade, P. J. (2008). "Journalism Guardians in a Time of Great Change: Newspaper Editor's Perceived Influence in Integrated News Organisations." *Journalism & Mass Communication Quarterly*, 85(2), 371–392.

Gallie, D., White, M., Cheng, Y. and Tomlinson, M. (1998). *Restructuring the Employment Relationship.* Oxford: Clarendon House.

Greenbaum, J. (2004). *Windows of the Workplace: Technology, Jobs, and the Organization of Office Work.* New York: Monthly Review Press.

Hendy, D. (2000). *Radio in the Global Age.* Cambridge: Polity Press.

Hesmondhalgh, D. (2007). *The Cultural Industries*, 2nd edn. London: Sage.

Huws, U. (2010). "Expression and Expropriation: The Dialectics of Autonomy and Control in Creative Labour." *Ephemera: Theory & Politics in Organization*, 10(3/4), 504–522.

Kidd-Damarin, A. (2010). *The Network-Organized Labour Process: Control and Autonomy in Web Production Work.* Paper presented at 28th Annual International Labour Process Conference, Rutgers University, New Brunswick, NJ, March 15–17.

Knights, D. and Willmott, H. (1990). *Labour Process Theory*. London: Macmillan.

Lee, K. (n.d.). *Selector Manual*. New York: Radio Computing Services Inc.

Marjoribanks, T. (2000). *News Corporation, Technology and the Workplace: Global Strategies, Local Change*. Cambridge: Cambridge University Press.

Mayer, V. (2009). "Bringing the Social Back in Studies of Production Cultures and Social Theory." In Mayer, V., Banks, M. and Caldwell, J. T. (eds.), *Production Studies. Cultural Studies of Media Industries*. London, New York: Routledge, 1–13.

McCourt, T. and Rothenbuhler, E. W. (2004). "Burnishing the Brand. Todd Storz and the Total Station Sound." *The Radio Journal. International Studies in Broadcast & Audio Media*, 2(1), 3–14.

McKinlay, A. and Smith, C. (ed.). (2009). *Creative Labour. Working in the Creative Industries*. Basingstoke, New York: Palgrave Macmillan.

Menduni, E. (2007). "Four Steps in Innovative Radio Broadcasting: From Quicktime to Podcasting." *The Radio Journal: International Studies in Broadcast & Audio Media*, 5(1), 9–18.

Miège, B. (1989). *The Capitalization of Cultural Production*. New York: International General.

Moreno, E., Costa, M. P. and Amoedo, A. (2010). "Radio and the Web: Communication Strategies of Spanish Radio Networks on the Web (2006–2008)." *Observatorio (OBS*) Journal*, 10, 121–137.

Morris-Suzuki, T. (1997). "Capitalism in the Computer Age and Afterword." In Davies, J., Hirschl, T. and Stack, M. (eds.), *Cutting Edge: Technology, Information, Capitalism and Social Revolution*. London, New York: Verso, 57–71.

Murray, S. (2009). "Servicing 'Self-Scheduling Consumers': Public Broadcasters and Audio Podcasting." *Global Media and Communication*, 5(2), 197–219.

Negus, K. (1999). *Music Genres and Corporate Cultures*. London: Routledge.

Nygren, G. (ed.). (2008). *Nyhetsfabriken: journalistiska yrkesroller i en förändrad medievärld* [The News Factory: Journalistic Working Roles in a Changing Media World]. Lund: Studentlitteratur.

Nygren, G. and Zuiderveld, M. (2011). *En himmla många kanaler: flerkanalpublicering i svenska mediehus* [A Lot of Channels: Multiplatform Publishing in Swedish Media Houses]. Gothenburg: Nordicom.

O'Doherty, D. and Willmott, H. (2000). "Debating Labour Process Theory: The Issue of Subjectivity and the Relevance of Poststructuralism." *Sociology*, 35(2), 457–476.

Örnebring, H. (2010). "Technology and Journalism-as-Labour: Historical Perspectives." *Journalism*, 11(1), 57–74.

Ramsey, M. (2012). *TV's Digital Lesson for Radio*. Accessed September 27, 2012. http://radiointelligence.com/?s=push+to+content.

Roberts, J. (2007). *The Intangibilities of Form. Skill and Deskilling in Art after the Readymade*. London: Verso.

Stiernstedt, F. (2008). "Maximising the Power of Entertainment. The Audience Commodity in Contemporary Music Radio." *The Radio Journal: International Studies in Broadcast and Audio Media*, 6(2/3), 113–127.

———. (2010). "Announcing in Multiplatform Broadcasting: Self-Referentiality, Buzz and Eventfulness in a Commercial Music Format." *Radio-Leituras*, 1(1), 131–153.

Tyrkkö, A. and Karlqvist, L. (2005). *Arbetsvillkor och arbetsbelasting i journalistiskt arbete: en studie av tidningsredaktioner* [Working Conditions and Work Effort in Journalistic Labour: A Study of Newspapers]. Stockholm: Arbetslivsinstitutet.

Ursell, G. (2000). "Television Production: Issues of Exploitation, Commodification and Subjectivity in UK Television Labour Markets." *Media, Culture & Society*, 22(6), 805–825.

van Dijck, J. (2013). *The Culture of Connectivity: A Critical History of Social Media.* New York: Oxford University Press.

Wall, T. (2004). "The Political Economy of Internet Music Radio." *The Radio Journal: International Studies in Broadcast and Audio Media,* 2(1), 27–44.

Westlund, O. (2012). *Cross-media News Work: Sensemaking of the Mobile Media (R)evolution.* Gothenburg: Gothenburg University Press.

Woodmansee, M. (1994). *The Author, Art, and the Market: Rereading the History of Aesthetics.* New York: Columbia University Press.

7 Redefining Co-production in German Radio

Incorporating the Listener in German Radio Plays

Golo Föllmer

INTRODUCTION

Besides a vast amount of 'common,' mostly literary, productions, the German radio play[1] has a long history of drawing ideas, activities and voices from the audience, involving the public in productive and communicative processes, altering the outcome from a product into a communicative setting that offers multiple entries. Bertolt Brecht's *Lindberghflug* (1929) is a prominent landmark in this approach, and it may be assumed to have inspired many later examples with its spirit of radically questioning radio's distributional character by developing communicative on-air processes. But, as I would like to show, this is only one approach in a long row of varied concepts, each operating different processes and each aiming for different results.

In order to grasp the variety of 'incorporative' practices in the radio play, I begin in Part A by giving an overview of the medium's conditions and implications for such uses. In Part B, I deduct different factors and dimensions of co-production between professional producers and listeners, of the inclusion of verbal activity or corporeal presence of listeners, and of listeners' participation in a radio play. As these descriptions suggest, a precise use of terminology and modelling of the findings is central to my discussion and will be investigated in depth, resulting in a general model of listener incorporation in radio play.

To avoid terminological problems, I will employ the less used and therefore the more open term 'incorporation' in this essay as a neutral description of the range of possible forms of activity, interaction, participation, etc. As the term is linked semantically to processes of social inclusion, mental involvement and physical integration, it appears to be most appropriate.

In Part C a number of examples will be assessed in order to test the capacity of the proposed model to explain the processes involved.

TECHNOLOGICAL, INFRASTRUCTURAL AND CULTURAL CONDITIONS OF RADIO

For the purpose of this discussion, the conditions of radio can be divided into technological, infrastructural and cultural. This assumption follows Shawn Gary VanCour (2008), who differentiates among technology, economy, regulation and culture. Aiming to keep the categories simple and appropriate to the topic, I contend that for Germany, at least until the mid-1980s, when private radio was allowed, the categories of economy and regulation can be grouped together, as there have been few essentially economic influences in German radio history. Even today, Public Service Radio, especially in areas such as the radio play, still has a strong position that makes it somewhat independent of market considerations.

Technology

Since radio's inception as a mass medium in the early 1920s, there have been numerous discussions about the technological characteristics that lend radio its own communicative structure and aesthetics—what is today termed "radiogenic" (Chignell 2009, 93–94). In Germany, discussions about 'arteigene Rundfunkmusik' (a radio music 'native' or 'characteristic to the [media] species') (Scherchen 1991), 'radiophone Kunst' ('radiophonic art') or 'funkische Musik' (translating into something like 'radiotic music') (Amzoll 1994, 27) focused mainly on the aesthetic qualities emerging from transmission. Examples of these include the eerie presence of static noise as an almost physically felt sensual experience (Chlebnikov 1993) and the vicinity of international programmes on the frequency dial, either in cross-talk or in simply switching from a programme in one language to another language, as stated by Rudolf Arnheim (1936, 14): "This is the great miracle of wireless. The omnipresence of what people are singing or saying anywhere, the overlapping of frontiers, the conquest of spatial isolation, the importation of culture on the waves of the ether (. . .)."

Besides phenomena of technological and transnational encounters, attention was also given to the effect of 'switching' between successive broadcast elements in the programme flow of single radio stations and, in some cases, the possibilities presented by filmic montage. Friedrich Walter Bischoff focused on these effects when he produced the much discussed radio montage experiment *Hallo! Hier Welle Erdaball!* at Schlesische Funkstunde in 1928 (Döhl 1981), and Alfred Braun (1930, 54) from Berliner Funkstunde correspondigly described the genre as a

> (. . .) broadcast play [*Funkspiel*] which consciously transfers cinematic technology to radio in a rapid sequence by way of fantastically colourful, rapidly floating and bouncy images, foreshortening and overlapping (in the pace), switching from close up to long shot with fade-ins, fade-outs and cross-fades.[2]

As far as the radio play was concerned, the constraints to sound transmission and auditive perception were discussed at great length. In fact, these discussions were focused not so much on the auditive sense itself—rather, what dominated these discussions were the immensely irritating exclusion of visual clues and the cognitive processes of replacing them with content from the listener's own visual memory. Ernst Hardt (1930, 69–70), director of the Westdeutsche Rundfunk AG, stated in 1929:

> Do we miss the scenic image? Do we miss trees, the sea, castle halls, the factory floor? Not at all! The eternally alert potency of the human brain gives us, including the simplest among us, a treasury of living, constantly changing imagery against which the static, unfamiliar construction of a cardboard and wooden stage pales into insignificance. . . . I can never get rid of this image of Ophelia whom I never saw, . . . whose sweet image arose within me, yet the image of an unearthly being.[3]

Furthermore, it was repeatedly claimed that the auditive sense had to be understood as the more archaic one, giving access to the more intuitive imagination, as stated by Hans Roeseler (1930, 24): "I believe that sound is the primary sense, that it alone gives us the possibility to create certain irrational experiences by activating our fantasy in order to lead us into the fourth dimension."[4]

The consequences Richard Kolb drew from these findings became most influential for the development of the German radio play. Excluding radiophonic realities, such as the closeness to filmic montage and collage, Kolb interpreted the radio play purely as a continuation of the stage drama—however, with the important difference that it was the only dramatic form capable of staging the metaphysical, timeless human questions:

> As a consequence of being independent of space and material [the bodiless nature of the voice] is projected through the willingness of the listener out into infinity and the universal which it reflects.
>
> (Kolb 1933, 240)

> The word of the radio play author is no longer tied to a material image. It is unfettered and free of subject matter. It leads us out into the absolute through the abstract.
>
> (Kolb 1933, 243)[5]

One explanation as to why Kolb's ideas were so convincing can be found in recording and transmission technologies of the time. The whole signal chain offered low quality, especially for fragile sounds, and the monophonic signal lacked spatial transparency necessary to identify individual sound sources in complex and noisy atmospheres. Assembling and mixing sounds in the studio was possible in only extremely simple ways, since everything had to happen live, either from live sources or from the hard-to-handle gramophone.

Even though technology had evolved after WWII, Heinz Schwitzke, an influential managing editor and theoretician of radio play in Germany, continued to insist on basing the radio drama of the 1940s and 50s on the acoustically easy to handle metaphysicality of the spoken word, marginalising sounds and music, and even more so any concepts of using radio in communicational settings, other than the mass media paradigm (Schwitzke 1963).

Infrastructure

By definition, interaction between producers and users in mass media is eliminated by technical means (Luhmann 2000). Any resistance to this is rejected by controlling technical channels through economic owners or public representatives in power. In some cases, such as pirate radio activities, even executive force of law is used.

The United States of the 1910s and early 1920s had seen an immense growth of radio amateurs receiving and casting freely on the ether, based on the 1912 Radio Act. Then, interaction between producers and users was eliminated, and the actual division into these roles was done in 1921/22 by a re-regulation of the broadcasting frequencies and stricter rules on the use of technology on the different frequency bands (VanCour 2008). In 1927, new FCC regulations weakened the non-commercial sector of broadcasting to the effect that ". . . the commercial monopoly of the airwaves was legislatively assured" (Lacey 2002, 26). However, whoever was financially potent was able to run a radio station and express his or her opinion.

In Germany, by contrast, a very different system, based on strong political restrictions, was established according to the definition of radio as a state-controlled institution from the ground up. This was partly due to the political crises in 1918, when revolutionary soldiers who had gathered in the Zentralfunkleitung (Central Radio Administration), occupied the state-run news agency, Wolff'sches Telegraphen Bureau in Berlin (an event remembered as the *Funkerspuk*, the 'radio operators spook'), and used the agency's technical infrastructure to distribute political demands and orders (Hagen 2005; Koch and Glaser 2005). Fearing similar usage of the established and well-working radio infrastructure in 1923, the government ruled out any private broadcasting activity. In 1925 it set up a system of regional broadcasting institutions under state control, concerning both technical operations and contents. That became even more entrenched in 1926 when all stations were obliged to broadcast only those political news items produced by the state-owned news agency, Drahtloser Dienst AG (Koch and Glaser 2005), thereby avoiding political debate and increasingly conceptualising radio as a neutral "cultural instrument" (Hagen 2005, 80). In July 1932, still half a year before the NSDAP came to power and took control of all media in Germany, centralised state control was again greatly strengthened by applying new guidelines to programming under the direct supervision of state officials (Koch and Glaser 2005).

Bertolt Brecht's *Radiotheorie (1927–1932)* (Brecht 1967) emerged from the context of this heavily restricted radio infrastructure and the corresponding limited courage of the responsible editors and broadcasting commissions (Amzoll 1994). Our modern public service–broadcasting ethos of a balance among fact-based information, cultural advancement, education and entertainment was still far away, even though it was clearly in discussion. Cultural and political pioneer Bertolt Brecht was one of those who fought for this idea in theory and in practice.

In his essay *Radio—eine vorsintflutliche Erfindung?* from 1927, Brecht (1967, 121–124) criticised the quality of the existing programmes as being truly embarrassing[6] and coined the humorous phrase that radio was the first medium ever which, precisely because it was restricted to giving a voice to only those in power (the 'bourgeoisie,' as he put it), was clearly enabling a global audience to realise that this "caste had nothing to say" (123). In 1930[7] he emphasised this point again by insisting that the public hadn't been waiting for radio, but radio was still waiting for the public, and radio was therefore still disoriented as to material appropriate to its concept of culture and communication (Brecht 1967).

Brecht (1967, 136) opposed the therein implied concept of culture: "All our ideology-producing institutions [represent a] concept of culture in which the creation of culture is already completed and culture does not require continuous efforts."[8] Contrary to this concept of culture, Brecht requested opportunities to conduct experiments in aesthetic as well as instructive programming, instead of simply repeating what had already been created. Bearing in mind that radio had shown how it could be used for political participation during the revolts in 1918 throughout Germany and elsewhere, Brecht (1993, 15) now made his famous demand: "Change this apparatus from distribution to communication."

In 1931 Walter Benjamin (2005, 543) strengthened Brecht's critical perspective on the quality and communicational misconception of German radio programmes:

> The crucial failing of this institution has been to perpetuate the fundamental separation between practitioners and the public, a separation that is at odds with its technological basis. A child can see that it is in the spirit of radio to pull as many people as possible in front of a microphone on *every* possible occasion; the public has to be turned into the witnesses of interviews and conversations in which now this person and now that one has the opportunity to make himself heard.

Benjamin, just like Brecht, does not have in mind to let each and every man and woman from the street do a broadcast or state his/her opinion, but—contrary to the non-political attitude of radio at that time—to mirror public discussions on political and cultural affairs more closely and to allow the original words and actualities of the multitude of public figures to come through more.

Exceptions to the rigorous restrictions did exist. In 1928 the Rund-funkversuchsstelle was founded at the Berlin Music Academy (Hochschule für Musik zu Berlin), which combined an experimental studio and basic practical radio courses, fulfilling to some degree what Brecht and others had demanded.[9] As the Rundfunkversuchsstelle was situated at a music academy, its most influential outcome turned out to be the development of a musical instrument, Friedrich Trautwein's Trautonium (Hagen 2005). However, the largest amount of classes dealt with pragmatic skills and technically based aspects of speech and music production in radio, with foundation courses on *funkisches Sprechen* ('radiophonic speech') for different kinds of radio-journalistic genres. Experiments also played a crucial role, as demonstrated by courses on remote orchestra directing, test broadcasts over a shortwave frequency and an attempt by Paul Hindemith to creatively use the gramo-phone as a musical instrument (Schenk 2004).

Other important exceptions include a number of literary, audio poetical and musical experiments on radiophonic forms of reporting and narration by Fritz Walter Bischoff, Alfred Braun and others. Bischoff's radio montage *Hallo! Hier Welle Erdball!* [Hello! Here Frequency Earth!] from 1928 used four gramophones to mix music and probably also location recordings from different geographical origins over an assemblage of 'found' literary texts, dramatic scenes, poetry, nursery rhymes, news catchlines and original pas-sages by Bischoff and his co-author Werner Milch. As an allegory to radio's outstanding capacity to instantly combine auditive elements from hetero-geneous origins, the 'aural symphony' (as it is named in the subheading) repeatedly states: "Just an excerpt, a snapshot. But life is like that, dear lady. There is no logic to it, it does with us what it will . . ." (Döhl 1981, 136).[10] According to Daniel Gilfillan (2009), Bischoff ". . . captures the modernist mood of fragmentation and incompletion that both accompanied and was itself produced and reproduced by new technologies like the radio." Rein-hard Döhl (1981, n.p.) construes it as a playful representation of radio in its entirety, portraying the semantic constructiveness of its mix of entertain-ment, news and cultural elements.

Culture

While in the USA the pre-history of radio listening was shaped by an active culture of ham radio amateurs, Germany experienced the regulative closure of communicative freedom soon after WWI. Even social movements, such as the Arbeiter-Radio-Bund (Workers Radio Association), gradually turned away from its previous central demand for freedom of radio broadcasting in 1928 and voted primarily for freedom of radio reception, i.e., mainly lower fees for radio reception (Koch and Glaser 2005). Radio got dragged into the nationalist ideology, forbidding any forms of equal participation or political representation. This, in effect, was contrary to what was regarded by some as a particularly important role of radio: "One of radio's most admirable functions is its ability to bring the different classes together. The nation [*Volk*]is torn apart by ideology and party politics. . . . In this situation only radio can help. Radio alone is nonpartisan" (Gosler, cited in Lacey 2002, 30).

Contemporary art music of the 1920s and 1930s by contrast developed a strong interest in open social encounters, which also promoted the role of radio. In 1929 a special issue of the musicologist journal *Die Musik* focused on 'Gebrauchsmusik' ('utility music'), taking over the label given to a fashionable movement that had thrived since the early 1920s. This was an attempt to end the perceived isolation of and lack of response to contemporary art music (Krabiel 1993). The term 'utility music' denotes a music that is incorporated into ordinary, everyday life on a functional basis. Eberhard Preussner defined it in opposition to opera and concert music from the nineteenth century, which, more in its forms of presentation and reception than in the music itself, appeared to be reduced to a refinement of life but is completely detached from it and results in an ". . . art form that runs parallel to life . . ." (Preussner 1929, 416).[11] The 'Gebrauchsmusik' of that time, on the other side, was meant to be a necessity of life, incorporating and incorporated into work, political activity, religious worship, education and into the internal logic of media, such as film, radio and gramophone (Danuser 1984). According to Curt Sachs, it was meant to be akin to cult music from the cradle of humanity, when music arose from communal activity, giving form, order and tangibility to activities such as hunting, healing and all sorts of social interaction (Sachs 1929).

Heinrich Besseler (1925) proposed the phenomenologically inspired term 'Umgangsmusik' for this paradigm in order to highlight a line between what he considered an often submissive use of commercially produced music by its listeners and the more cognitively active and responsible involvement with music of artistic rank. Similar to Preussner, Besseler compared both types of 'functional music' to autonomous 'Darbietungsmusik' ('presentational music'), which he characterised as being established on a strict distinction of roles between (active) musicians and (passive) listeners (Besseler 1925).

Germany's most influential forum for contemporary music, then and today, the *Musikfest* in Donaueschingen (intermittently named *Kammermusikfest* and held in Baden-Baden and Berlin and later renamed *Donaueschinger Musiktage*), chose 'Gebrauchsmusik unterhaltenden Charakters' ('utility music of entertaining character') in 1926 as one of two special topics and continued this focus in different forms over several years. It included commissioned works by Ernst Krenek, Paul Hindemith (who worked at the previously mentioned Rundfunkversuchsstelle from 1927 onwards), Kurt Weill and others. Also included were 'concerts' that integrated the audience into choirs organised in Fritz Jöde's 'Musikantengilden' ('musicians guilds'), part of a lay musician's movement that advocated the concept of a

'Gemeinschaftsmusik' ('communal music'): "Music that was not meant for the concert recital, but for use by singing and instrumental groups—for the purpose of getting involved in music" (Krabiel 1993, 14).[12]

Similar attention was given to the media of the time, focusing on mechanical musical instruments, film and—with the Reichsrundfunkgesellschaft in 1929 for the first time as the festival's co-producer—'Originalkompositionen für den Rundfunk' ('original compositions for radio'), which aimed at the previously mentioned idea of a 'funkspezifische Musik,' which takes technical as well as social and communicational elements into account (Krabiel 1993). As discussed further below, Brecht's *Lindberghflug* seized upon and influenced these ideas decisively.

MODELLING RADIOPHONIC INCORPORATION

In the following analyses, I will take up Nico Carpentier's concept of 'participation,' which he defines as effectively occurring only in cases when the invited listener is equal to the producer in his power of decision making (Carpentier 2011). Following Carpentier, a weaker form of 'listener incorporation' is described by the concept 'interaction,' a relationship established by a mutual exchange of opinions or material between listener and producer, with the producer having sovereignty over the majority of formal and aesthetic characteristics. Carpentier sees the weakest form of incorporation described by the concept of 'access,' which is put into effect as soon as a listener is able to contribute singular pieces of material or action, thereby achieving perceivable presence in the resulting work, but without the option of directly influencing the producer's decisions, let alone having equal power in decisionmaking (Carpentier 2011).

Carpentier derives his precisely refined definition of 'participation' from political and social theory, basing his convincing argument on the notion that all spheres of human life are potentially political. However, applying his three-step model to media examples quickly reveals its limitations. For instance, the model does not differentiate among different modes of 'access' occurring when listeners achieve presence in different spheres of the reality built by an incorporative radio play, in one case making listeners heard on air, in the other case only amongst listeners in a local setting.

Obviously, there can be categorically different modes of listener activity leading to 'access,' 'interaction' and 'participation,' depending on the technical channels used; on whether material, action or communication of the listener is incorporated; on the general nature of the entities exchanging information, etc. Carpentier's model does not offer concepts that represent these types of different modes. I therefore propose to complement the model with further characteristics relevant to our subject matter. Since we are discussing media used by individuals and groups, I will focus on concepts from the fields of media studies, psychology and game studies.

Modes of Activity and Contemplation

First, it should be stated that active and passive roles are found on both sides of every medium, i.e., on the side of the media producers and on the side of the recipients. While producers are understood as being 'the active ones,' they are in fact in a passive role as far as framing infrastructure (business model, practical standards) and expectations of the recipients are concerned. Recipients by contrast have an active role (as the findings of cultural studies have shown extensively) when they select and elaborate media content in the sense of assembling different elements into something individually meaningful (Rusch 2002). That leads to the assumption that—as Besseler (1925) also implied—media products allow different degrees of freedom for cognitive activity.

When talking about interaction, we have to take into account that acting entities can follow categorically different types of internal plans. Heinz von Foerster (1993) draws the dividing line between models of trivial and non-trivial machines. The first one behaves always identical to the same input, which means that it can neither purposefully nor arbitrarily alter or adapt its rules of behaviour. This trivial machine follows transformational rules that cannot be changed, unless the machine breaks down. A vivid example of the trivial machine is a light switch. The non-trivial machine, on the other side, has an additional set of transformational rules that describe how the system can modify its 'regular' set of transformational rules, those which handle the input values and determine its reaction to them. This machine can react differently to the same input value, depending on interactions that occurred in the past. Von Foerster names nature, the psyche and any kind of living being as examples of this type of machine (von Foerster 1993).

As far as media concepts like those of early German radio are concerned, a central statement of von Foerster can be critically applied here. He points to the fact that much too often the world is classified as a trivial machine because this model promises comprehensibility and predictability: "It is therefore not unexpected that we want all observations, every behaviour, our environment, even the whole universe to be seen represented through a trivial machine" (von Foerster 1993, 24).[13]

But even if we can assume to have non-trivial machines at work in an interaction, this interaction can still be far from an open, equal exchange, represented by 'mutual contingency' in which the partners of a dyadic (two-sided) interaction are open to change their individual rules of behaviour in reaction to the actions or communications of the other *and* their own convictions. If only one participant is open to change his rules, an 'asymmetrical contingency' is at work. 'Reactive contingency,' on the other hand, describes situations where partners are guided in their behaviour only by assumptions drawn from the communications of the other and not by their own rules. 'Internal contingency' refers to when both partners are guided in their behaviour only by their internal rules and not by those of the other (Piontkowski 1976).

Independent from the type (or depth) of dyadic interaction, instances of incorporation also differ according to the kind of sensual and diegetic experience offered by the system in use. Game theory has described such sensual opportunities in detail, and I will try to apply some of its concepts to our topic. Alison McMahan (2003) chooses the term 'engagement' to describe non-diegetic incorporation of the game user, whereas 'involvement' stands for diegetic incorporation (McMahan speaks of inclusion). 'Presence' and 'immersion' form another interlinked pair of terms, the first one (a term also used by Carpentier) refers to the outer world, meaning the perception of physically 'being there' in a virtual world. The latter term,'immersion,' refers to self-perception, describing the impression of being "(. . .) caught in the game's story . . ." (McMahan 2003, 68), or the joy of contemplating the game's realm, or motoric activity therein.

Furthermore, I would argue that aesthetic qualities of incorporative structures should be acknowledged as much as social or political ones. This could be described as a difference in the 'type of contemplation' at stake. According to Rudolf Brandl (2006), one type of contemplation is a mental awareness awakened by a media product, pointing to a concept 'behind' the concrete content of this product and therefore focusing on an independent idea (*theoría*). The other type of contemplation is a physical awareness, i.e., an actual perception (*aísthêsis*) (Brandl 2006). It is assumed here that both types occur, each following different rules, building different structures and leading to different experiences on both sides, the side of the author and the side of the listener.

A Comprehensive Model of Listener Incorporation

It appears that a complex mix of factors is at work in different forms of incorporative structures used in radio play—in fact too many to grasp easily. Table 7.1 shows the questions on which the characteristics focus, the respective choices they provide and how they could be grouped into three categories, namely Productivity, Interactivity and Sociability.

Based on this grouping, I propose a comprehensive model of audience incorporation into media production that builds from Carpentier's three-step model but includes it in only one of the three resulting dimensions and uses the term 'interaction' differently. Figure 7.1 shows how the characteristics refer to the higher-level categories, 'productivity,''interactivity'and 'sociability', which are assumed to represent independent dimensions.

Table 7.1 Grouping of characteristics

Type	Questions	Choices
Productivity	Do listeners produce sound or material that is turned into sound?	No: receptive activity Yes: productive activity
	Does the incorporation influence the outcome?	No: engagement Yes: involvement
	Is the focus on the inner world or the outer world?	Inner world: immersion— Outer world: presence
Interactivity	Which depth of incorporation takes place?	Access—interaction—participation
	Is the incorporation trivial (reactive) or complex (interactive)?	Trivial machine—non-trivial machine
	Do the systems incorporate aspects of each other?	Mutual contingency—asymmetrical contingency
Sociability	What is the primary value for listeners/users?	Aesthetic value—functional value
	Is the audible result produced by one or by several persons?	Individual activity—collective activity

Source: Author's own elaboration.

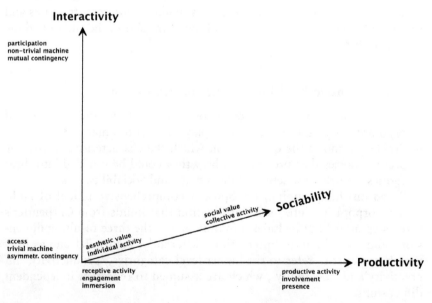

Figure 7.1 Three-dimensional model of listener incorporation

Source: Author's own elaboration.

I will apply this three-dimensional model to a choice of German examples discussed as follows.

EXAMPLES

Der Lindberghflug

The *Lindberghflug* was developed as a commission for the *Kammermusikfest* Baden-Baden in 1929 by Kurt Weill for the Berliner Funkstunde under Hans Flesch. This was the first time the Reichsrundfunkgesellschaft was the joint organiser of the festival. Bertolt Brecht became involved in the project via a subcommission for the libretto and Paul Hindemith was included as co-composer. Flesch was convinced that radio had no alternative to developing its own aesthetics on the basis of its genuine, technically based principles, and he insisted that experimentation was the only way to get there (Hagen 2005).

The libretto gave an account of Charles Lindbergh's sensational Atlantic crossing in 1927, which Brecht saw as a symbol for the power of the individual—a power the individual could develop only as a part of society. The piece was commissioned specifically for one of that year's festival topics, 'Original compositions for radio.' The premiere on July 27, 1929 was staged in a room prepared as a broadcast studio with the audience seated in surrounding rooms to which the music was transmitted. The now famous second performance was set up spontaneously because an originally planned public final rehearsal in a concertante version (with the audience in the same room) had been dropped. Brecht insisted on a chance to compensate for the cancellation with a performance on the following day, July 28, which would be capable of demonstrating the communicational setting he envisioned. The stage was divided into two parts. 'The radio' with ensemble, choir and narrator were positioned on the left. A singer, representing 'the listener,' was positioned on the right, exemplifying the listener's part in the piece in actual broadcasts, which declaims the vocal part of the hero, Charles Lindbergh (Krabiel 1993).

Bertolt Brecht clearly thought along the lines of the 'Gebrauchsmusik' concept, which was strongly advocated by Kurt Weill, but gave it his own imprint. He defined the music's 'utilitarian value' as 'didactic value' (Krabiel 1993, 20), for which the *Dreigroschenoper* [Threepenny Opera], premiered the year before to tremendous success, had proved the template for his Epic Theatre:

> Free-roaming feelings aroused by music . . . are all distractions from music. To avoid these distractions the individual shares in the music, by following the music with his eyes as printed, and contributing the parts and places reserved for him by singing them for himself or in conjunction with others (school class).
>
> (Brecht 1993, 16)

The first broadcast was done the next day, July 29, but the earliest version is a transmission from the Berliner Funkstunde on March 18, 1930, again in the concertante version, including all vocal parts. In fact, in the long and winding history of the *Lindberghflug* (Brecht renamed it twice and Weill composed a version that replaced Hindemith's parts), its incorporative concept hardly played a role. The idea of leaving the airman's vocal part out of the transmission so that school classes could fill it on the basis of the libretto printed in the programme guide was realised far less often than concertante broadcasts or local recitals.

The idea did, however, receive attention. Klaus-Dieter Krabiel (1993) suggests that broadcasts of chamber music omitting one (usually the lead) instrument ('Musizieren mit unsichtbaren Partnern'—'Making music with invisible partners'), starting in 1931 at Deutsche Welle, were inspired by the *Lindberghflug*, and the same could apply for 'Music minus one' broadcasts popular later in the USA.

The *Lindberghflug* is mainly characterised by its functional, more precisely didactic value of listener incorporation, even though the piece's history of concertante recitals suggests it was mostly misunderstood as an aesthetic experience. When addressing individual radio listeners, it does not allow interaction or participation, but only access and diegetically (and compositionally) irrelevant, immersive engagement and asymmetrical contingency with an obviously trivial machine (the radio can only be switched on or off or turned louder or softer). This is true as long as the productive activity is done individually. If, on the contrary, the user does not think of the radio as being his or her counterpart but shifts focus to a local group of people, this paints a different picture. We then witness mutual contingency in an interaction with a complex non-trivial machine that allows presence in a collectively produced result. Here, the functional value clearly lies in strengthening social bonds and—as Brecht pointed out—no longer in an aesthetic experience.

Nachkriegswinter. Der 29. Januar 1947
[Postwar Winter: January 29 1947]

Ernst Schnabel's dramatic feature *Der 29. Januar 1947* documents an insignificant Wednesday in postwar Germany. The Nordwestdeutsche Rundfunk had invited listeners, advertising prize money and publication of the best submission, to cooperate in the production of a programme by portraying an arbitrarily chosen date from their individual perspective: "The Nordwestdeutsche Rundfunk challenges all its listeners to participate in a programme. . . . Everyone should provide a realistic depiction of his or her daily routine" (cited in Gerlinger 2012, 71).[14]

The response was tremendous. Approximately 35,000 entries reached Ernst Schnabel, who requested help from the University of Hamburg. Supposedly 70 students aided him in viewing, choosing and arranging letters, of which only between 40 and 100 letters (0.1% to 0.3%) were used in the end. According to Christian Gerlinger, depending on the texts' focus and characters, Schnabel used some of them mostly unaltered, having them read in the style of an interior monologue. Others were employed to build dramatic scenes, including acted dialogues and background sounds (Gerlinger 2012). Others were collaged into more general reflections on the tragic postwar situation, often commented on by passages from an observer that took on the role of a reporter, teacher or critic, addressing the listener and not the characters in the piece (Wagner 1990).

Wolfram Wessels classifies the piece as a literary work that attempts to approach reality with the letters remaining as only a tool, even if an essential one (Gerlinger 2012). Schnabel applied strict criteria during the selection process, one being the mention of a love relationship, the other consisting in a hint at democratic commitment (Gerlinger 2012). The actual authorship was also of great importance. Schnabel later commented with irritation on the fact that amongst the 35,000 entries, there was not a single one from a wealthy businessman, a politician, a lawyer, judge, doctor or theologist. "No one wrote to us saying, we are doing well. Instead numerous domestic employees wrote and said that their employers were doing well" (Gerlinger 2012, 89).[15]

Schnabel repeated his experiment in 1950, this time receiving 80,000 entries for his similarly built *Ein Tag wie morgen. Der 1. Februar 1950.* Later remakes did not nearly reach this interest level. The 1997 production for the 50th anniversary of this groundbreaking piece drew only 1,200 entries.

As a piece with literary quality, *Der 29. Januar 1947* offers strong aesthetic value. The included texts received access to and presence among the public, merging a diegetic involvement of their authors into a product that represents a collective mind, though filtered through the lens of Schnabel. The machine 'radio' appears non-trivial to the chosen authors, as they probably wondered about the hidden 'rules' that transformed their individual texts into a complex, composite result. Contingency, however, is asymmetrical, as Ernst Schnabel could not interact with individual authors but certainly perceived their texts as closed and to a degree hermetic.

However, we can discover yet another layer of incorporative activity, this time internally, i.e., inside the individual listener. Hans-Ulrich Wagner insists that Schnabel's montage technique avoids numbing, identificatory empathy and, on the contrary, aims to evoke critical thinking in the listeners. "Because the play is not based on character development or a discernible plot, the author allows individual relationships to be traced, so that a critically conscious examination of one's own world can emerge" (Wagner 1990, 177).[16]

Klaus Schöning would later, using the same argumentation, criticise the 'deficit of communication' in the German 'literary radio play' of the 1950s and request a distanced listening attitude in order to avoid any touch of commodity aesthetics: "The consumer is potentially a creator by listening to a production made identifiable as a construction which does not reproduce, but changes, designs and creates; which is not unique, but can be reproduced and is available 'to everyone' " (Schöning 1974, 21).[17]

With reference to Helmut Heißenbüttel, he insists that standards in the radio apparatus must be avoided: "It is necessary to oppose it with disruptive elements, to irritate rather than to endorse" (Schöning 1974, 22).[18] From the perspective of the 1960s 'Neues Hörspiel,' 'O-Ton' (actualities) is understood as revealing the fact that each and every journalistic activity is inevitably manipulative, and thereby emancipating the listener.

Rosie. Ein Radio-Spektakel zum Mitmachen für Stimmen, Musik und Telefonierende Hörer [Rosie: A Radio Spectacle in which Voice, Music and Telephoning Listeners Can Join In]

Rosie, when first broadcast in 1969 by Radio Bremen und Südwestfunk, was clearly a product of the '68 generation. In its introduction, the notorious band Insterburg & Co. humorously introduced the programme as a sophisticated high-brow product, while at the same time hinting at discussions about the balance between entertaining versus critical content: "Nobility instead of rawness exists once again today through radio. . . . You won't get revolt, rebellion, or no sex, who wants that? . . . Radio listeners, ladies, gentlemen, today we do not want to bawl about what is so awful in our times. Today we bring you something really sweet."[19]

When Richard Hey comes live on the microphone, he first repeats the invitation for the listeners to join in. He then very casually and contrary to custom introduces the studio team, including the audio technicians as well as the lady on the telephone, clearly signalling the anti-hierarchical conduct of the time. This attitude is later confirmed in a performative way, when the studio crew publicly discusses how to deal with incoming callers.

> Hey: Perhaps, I don't know Helmig, maybe one minute per caller . . .
> Helmig: Yes.
> Hey: . . . say, or should we say two minutes?
> Helmig: One minute is enough.
> von Einem [over a studio microphone from the technical room]: I
>   think we shouldn't limit it.
> Hey: We shouldn't limit it?
> von Einem: No-no, as it happens.
> Hey: As it happens?
> von Einem: Yes-yes.
> Hey: [telephone rings] Good. Meanwhile, then, broadcast the interlude.
> [To the first caller:] Hello.[20]

Here, the listener's position intermittently changes from being addressed to eavesdropping on a conversation normally not meant to be overheard by the audience. Andrew Tolson (2006, 120) terms this kind of practice "zoo aesthetic" because it makes "backstage matters" public. Exposing normally firmly hidden studio processes and consequently offering insider knowledge, the listener is privileged over 'regular' listeners. This can be interpreted as enhancing the listener's status in order to lower the barrier between producers and audience, and thereby increasing the likelihood of call-ins. The opportunity to join in is explained to the listener earlier in the programme with reference to Bertolt Brecht's *Radiotheorie* (1967), admitting that incorporation is limited and thus, once more, lowering the barrier by acknowledging the limitations of professional possibilities:

> You, the listener, will have three opportunities during the broadcast to influence the continuation of the programme. . . . Unfortunately, we have not yet reached the point where every transmitter is a receiver and every receiver a transmitter. Therefore, we have to use the telephone as an aid.[21]

The team prepared two alternative versions for each of the three decision points in the story line. When the first of the three decisions is later due, Hey points out that callers are asked not only to vote for an option and justify their opinion, but also to freely state their opinion of the programme's concept as a whole.

> We now have the situation in which the kitchen boy has been slapped across the face. The question now is, should he now conform, accept the slap and see whether he will somehow get along in the business, even make a career there, or should he defend himself, hit back? We are directing these questions at you. Give us a call. . . . A simple majority decides how it will continue. . . . Of course we are delighted when you don't just help decide the question about how it continues, but also tell us what you find noteworthy in relation to the programme.[22]

The radio play *Rosie* does not offer the listener a large degree of productivity or interactivity. The few who get through on the phone achieve presence on air to give their opinion, but since all choices have been pre-produced, they interact with a trivial machine that offers only two choices and cannot change its *modus operandi* in reaction to the callers' arguments. However, if we understand the story only as the inducement for call-ins, then sociability, interactivity and even productivity can be seen to take place on a higher level. Callers get deeply involved for the short moment they are on the air; they decide collectively on the continuation of the story line; and the discussions accentuate values (like the non-hierarchical attitude emphasised by the makers and taken up by several callers) and individual perspectives (personal experience brought in as evidence for a decision), as well as humour and rhetorical wit, as elements making the communication witnessed by all listeners worthy in itself.

Der Ohrenzeuge [The Earwitness]

In the course of 12 years, from 1993 to 2005, Radio Fritz and the media production company Raumstation broadcast 623 two-hour episodes of the live role-playing game *Der Ohrenzeuge*.[23] Based on whodunit plots around the detectives Paule, Oscar Schombrutzki and Cleo Fischer, callers had to cooperate by interrogating characters, distributing tasks and solving the crime of the day. Some episodes were staged in real places, such as *Etikettenschwindel* from 2002, which incorporated, apart from regular callers, participants visiting the annual Berlin gardening and food exhibition, *Grüne Woche*. The largest part of the episodes, however, was confined to the radio studio and phone lines.

   Der Ohrenzeuge combined pre-produced storytelling snippets with live interactions between callers talking to the presenter (acting as their friendly host and advisor), the characters (asking them questions on certain facts) and each other (in order to team up in search of evidence and when having to make decisions). Thanks to the advance in digital technology, as opposed to the technical situation in 1969 when *Rosie* was produced, live improvisations of the actors speaking to callers could now be turned into lively dramatic situations with the ad hoc use of archived Foley and atmospheric sounds.

> Cleo: Moritz?
> Moritz: Yes.
> Cleo: Hi Moritz, Cleo here. . . . Gee, Moritz, listen, you are at Green
>   Week, aren't you?
> Moritz: Yes.
> Cleo: Listen, I've just taken a bite of a strange organic apple. . . . You
>   really are at Green Week. It must be possible to find out if
>   it's really organic when it's labelled organic . . . Should we
>   maybe take another look at the crates of apples?
> Moritz: Yes, maybe there is something in there.
>   [Swooshing sound signalling change of scenery]
>
>
> Cleo: Danilo! Hi Danilo! . . .
> Danilo: Will you maybe take a look at the crate and see if perhaps the
>   place or origin is on it?
> Cleo: That's a good idea. Let's have a . . . Wait a second, maybe take
>   the apples out first, then we can take a look as to whether
>   there is something in there we can . . . What, man, take a
>   look at this, if the whole time the apples here . . . I just can't
>   believe this, clear out everything and the apples!

Danilo: Yes.
Cleo: Man, take a look at this . . . It's really burning!
Danilo: Yes, totally![24]

Obviously, several physical and virtual realities overlap here. Moritz is actually, 'physically' visiting the *Grüne Woche*, calling from a phone set up by the radio crew there, while Danilo is probably calling from home. There are certainly high levels of involvement, presence, collective activity and social value at stake, but productive activity is restricted to communicating one's ideas, not producing any original storytelling elements. Interactivity, by contrast, is confined to access and asymmetrical contingency, since the callers cannot change the overall run of events but have to stick to the producers' plot. While the interaction between the actual participants is lively and the radiogenic effect of listener 'co-presence' (Chignell 2009) is reinforced by emphasising the real-time character of the events, interaction between listener and the medium remains hierarchical in principle. However, in the given framework this appears necessary in order to establish a working game structure. With reference to game theory (Perron 2003), a rule-based 'game' activity that serves the given narrative to make the system work is necessary here, rather than a freely creative activity of 'play.'

Radioortung [Locating Radio]

Radioortung[25] was a production of Deutschlandradio Kultur using the infrastructure of Udo Noll's audio geolocation system *radio aporee*.[26] In 2010 and 2011 the two art groups, Ligna and Rimini Protokoll, produced individual pieces for the system set in and around Berlin's Alexanderplatz.[27] *Radioortung*'s interaction scheme seems to be strictly of a receptive nature. Listeners carry Global Positioning System–equipped Android smartphones that play sounds 'located' at the place they are actually at, sometimes also mixing in adjacent sounds and consequently creating collages of spatially arranged sound objects.

Referring back to Klaus Schöning's perspective mentioned above on the use of actualities and building radio plays in an open manner, the effect of cognitive activity in the setting of a public city center is complemented by epistemic and communicative effects of watching others using the same system, expressing what they hear in their facial expressions, in their movements and possibly even in verbal communication. These effects once again reinforce the above mentioned effect of 'co-presence' by limiting 'radio' (which in effect it ceases to be in the technical *and* communicative sense) to one single physical location. Again, we encounter a dual system. On the one hand (the individual listener using the smartphone), it offers a trivial machine with asymmetrical contingency, engagement and immersion, but also a high degree of receptive activity when using the very openly arranged audio snippets. On the other hand (users watching each other), there is a complementary layer of collective, performative activity of visually exchanging ideas on how to play with the technical system and of possibly communicating directly with each other.

OUTLOOK

The above analyses have shown that multiple elements are present when we examine incorporative radio plays. A narrative structure is meant to be experienced in a specific interplay of (1) certain modes of interaction, (2) enjoyment in creative and sometimes performative productivity and (3) the experience of social encounter. As the examples above have shown, the three-dimensional model with its subcategories can help us grasp the workings of such systems more precisely. To test and develop it further, it might be interesting to compare it to models developed for other modes of incorporative nature, for example in music, film, stage drama, etc.

Within the context of radio it would be particularly worthwhile to examine music and sound art–based examples, such as Hartmut Geerken's *hexenring* from 1994 (Vowinckel 1998). In this piece, incoming calls, bearing whatever sound the callers wished to produce, were recorded onto tape loops that were broadcast continually, a principle akin to Max Neuhaus' radio works, *Public Supply* and *Radio Net*, from 1966 to1977 (Föllmer 2005a, 117f.). Geerken here referred to theoretical groundings for an "interactive radio play as non-narrative radio art" (1992, 1) he drafted in the early 1990s.

Another influential example that applies a similar approach is *Horizontal Radio* from 1995. This is a large-scale cooperative performance which includes many European artists casting sound elements from public service radio stations that are interconnected via the networks of the European Broadcasting Union and using websites and phone lines to incorporate listeners. Similar to *hexenring*, it can be understood as applying musical instead of narrative principles, and as such it has had many successors.[28] As Antje Vowinckel (1998) for the radio play and I for music (Föllmer 2005b) have pointed out, approaches such as these expose general communicational and social aspects of listener incorporation into the medium they use but tend to lack transparency with regard to interaction, which might discourage listeners' inclination to interact.

Another interesting non-narrative field of analysis are journalistic forms of listener incorporation. The German Web radio, channel detektor.fm, uses the *CrowdRadio* smartphone app[29] to seamlessly incorporate listeners' opinions into programmes on controversial topics.[30] While users record and upload their voices at length without a journalist's intervention, in the end, of course, a journalist chooses which files and which passages to play on air, thereby diminishing the degree of participation of those contributions which prove insufficiently professionally structured and spoken and do not fit the rhetoric of the programme flow.

Fully participative in Carpentier's sense is the documentary website *Dokublog*, initiated by and regularly integrated into the on-air programme *Mehrspur* at Südwestrundfunk's SWR2.[31] Users are asked to upload actualities (interviews, atmospheres, observations) and are allowed to use all files they find in the database to produce short features of up to 10 minutes. Around 1,500 snippets so far have been accumulated on mostly biographical, oral history and everyday life topics and were turned into approximately 500 short features, which can all be listened to online *and* turned into new content without restrictions.

Even though it proves difficult to continually motivate listeners to contribute high-quality elements, the high level of individual productivity found here makes these concepts a promising object of research in the future.

NOTES

* A re-edition of the documentation of the workshop 'Dichtung und Rundfunk' held at Kassel-Wilhelmshöhe on November 30–October 1, 1929 can be found under mediaculture-online.de.
1. I prefer the term 'radio play' before the more common term 'radio drama' because it is closer to the German 'Hörspiel' (lit. 'hear play') and omits the almost compulsory implication of an Aristotelian 'dramatic' form.
2. Translation by the author.
3. Translation by the author.
4. Translation by the author.
5. Translation by the author.
6. This essay is the first in a series of five essays together forming what was post-humously named Brecht's 'Radio theory' (Brecht 1967, 119–140).
7. The first publication of the speech *Der Rundfunk als Kommunikationsapparat* dates it to 1932. However, Klaus-Dieter Krabiel (1993) corrects the date of origin to November 1, 1930.
8. Translation by the author.
9. In his 1927 essay *Vorschläge an den Intendanten des Rundfunks*, Brecht (1967, 125–126) had demanded: "You have to equip a studio. It is completely impossible to fully assess your technical devices without experiments." Translation by the author.
10. Translation by the author.
11. Translation by the author.
12. Translation by the author.
13. Translation by the author.
14. Translation by the author.
15. Translation by the author.
16. Translation by the author.
17. Translation by the author.
18. Translation by the author.
19. Transcript and translation by the author.
20. Transcript and translation by the author.
21. Transcript and translation by the author.
22. Transcript and translation by the author.
23. www.raumstation.de/?p=303.

24. Transcript and translation by the author.
25. www.dradio-ortung.de.
26. www.aporee.org.
27. Ligna: *Verwisch die Spuren!* (2010), presenting future archaeological perspectives on the history-charged location; Rimini Protokoll: *50 Aktenkilometer* (2011) playing interviews with witnesses of and original reports from observations the GDR intelligence and oppression service 'Stasi' made on the respective locations.
28. The most important one today is 'Art's Birthday,' which is celebrated yearly on January 17 as a networked radio art event; however, listener incorporation does not play a central role in it.
29. www.crowdradio.de/en.
30. www.detektor.fm.
31. www.dokublog.de.

REFERENCES

Amzoll, S. (1994). "Die Republik lauscht. Faszination früher künstlerischer Radiophonie." *Neue Zeitschrift für Musik*, 155(1), 26–33.

Arnheim, R. (1936). *Radio*. London: Faber & Faber.

Benjamin, W. (2005). "Reflections on Radio." In Jennings, M. W. (ed.), *Walter Benjamin: Selected Writings, Volume 2 Part 2, 1932–1934*. Cambridge: Belknap, 543–544.

Besseler, H. (1925). "Grundfragen des musikalischen Hörens." In Schwartz, R. (ed.), *Jahrbuch der Musikbibliothek Peters für 1925*, 32, 35–52.

Brandl, R. (2006). *Musik als kommunikative Handlung*. Göttingen: Cuvillier.

Braun, A. (1930). "Hörspiel." In Sektion für Dichtkunst der Preußischen Akademie der Künste (ed.), *Dichtung und Rundfunk. Reden und Gegenreden*. Kassel: v. Holten, 53–57.*

Brecht, B. (1967). "Radiotheorie (1927–1932)." In *Schriften zur Literatur und Kunst I*. Frankfurt/M.: Suhrkamp, 121–140.

———. (1993). "The Radio as an Apparatus of Communication." In N. Strauss (ed.), *Radiotext(e)*. = Semiotexte 16, 6(1), New York, 15–17.

Carpentier, N. (2011). "The Concept of Participation. If They Have Access and Interact, Do They Really Participate?" *CM: Communication Management Quarterly/Casopis za upravljanje komuniciranjem*, 21, 13–36.

Chignell, H. (2009). *Key Concepts in Radio Studies*. Los Angeles: Sage.

Chlebnikov, V. (1993). "The Radio of the Future." In N. Strauss (ed.), *Radiotext(e)*. = Semiotexte 16, 6(1), New York, 32–35.

Danuser, H. (1984). *Die Musik des 20. Jahrhunderts*. Laaber: Laaber.

Döhl, R. (1981). "Versuch einer Geschichte und Typologie des Hörspiels in Lektionen." *Rundfunk und Fernsehen. Wissenschaftliche Vierteljahreszeitschrift*, 29(1), 127–141.

Föllmer, G. (2005a). *Netzmusik. Elektronische, ästhetische und soziale Strukturen einer partizipativen Musik*. Hofheim: Wolke Verlag.

———. (2005b). "Electronic, Aesthetic and Social Factors in Net Music." *Organized Sound*, 10(3), 185–192.

Geerken, H. (1992). *Das interaktive Hörspiel als nicht-erzählende Radiokunst*. Folkwang-Texte 2 = Beiträge zu Musik, Theater, Tanz, 6.

Gerlinger, C. (2012). *Die Zeithörspiele von Ernst Schnabel und Alfred Andersch (1947–1952). Von der Aufhellung der Aktualität zu ihrer dichterischen Durchdringung*. Münster: LIT.

Gilfillan, D. (2009). *Pieces of Sound*. Minneapolis: University of Minnesota Press. Kindle File.

Hagen, W. (2005). *Das Radio. Zur Geschichte und Theorie des Hörfunks-Deutschland/ USA*. München: Fink.

Hardt, E. (1930). "Drama." In Sektion für Dichtkunst der Preußischen Akademie der Künste (ed.), *Dichtung und Rundfunk. Reden und Gegenreden*. Kassel: v. Holten, 43–48.*

Koch, H. J. and Glaser, H. (2005). *Ganz Ohr. Eine Kulturgeschichte des Radios in Deutschland*. Koln: Bohlau.

Kolb, R. (1933). "Die neue Funkkunst des Hörspiels." In Kolb, R. and Giesmeier, H. (eds.), *Rundfunk und Film im Dienste nationaler Kultur*. Düsseldorf: Friedrich Floeder, 228–246.

Krabiel, K-D. (1993). *Brechts Lehrstücke. Entstehung und Entwicklung eines Spieltyps*. Stuttgart: Metzler.

Lacey, K. (2002). "Radio in the Great Depression. Promotional Culture, Public Service, and Propaganda." In Hilmes, M. and Loviglio, J. (eds.), *Radio Reader. Essays in the Cultural History of Radio*. New York: Routledge, 21–40.

Luhmann, N. (2000). *The Reality of Mass Media*. Stanford: Stanford University Press.

McMahan, A. (2003). "Immersion, Engagement, and Presence." In Wolf, M. and Perron, B. (eds.), *The Video Game Theory Reader*. New York: Routledge, 67–86.

Perron, B. (2003). "From Gamers to Players and Gameplayers. The Example of Interactive Movies." In Wolf, M. and Perron, B. (eds.), *The Video Game Theory Reader*. New York: Routledge, 237–258.

Piontkowski, U. (1976). *Psychologie der Interaktion*. München: Juventa.

Preussner, E. (1929). "Der Wendepunkt in der modernen Musik." *Die Musik*, 21(6), 415–418.

Roeseler, H. (1930). "Epik." In Sektion für Dichtkunst der Preußischen Akademie der Künste (ed.), *Dichtung und Rundfunk. Reden und Gegenreden*. Kassel: v. Holten, 16–19.*

Rusch, G. (2002). "Kommunikation." In Rusch, G. (ed.), *Einführung in die Medienwissenschaft. Konzeptionen, Theorien, Methoden, Anwendungen*. Wiesbaden: Westdeutscher Verlag, 102–117.

Sachs, C. (1929). "Alte und ältere Zweckmusik." *Die Musik*, 21(6), 429–430.

Schenk, D. (2004). *Die Hochschule für Musik zu Berlin. Preußens Konservatorium zwischen romantischem Klassizismus und Neuer Musik, 1869–1932/33*. Stuttgart: Steiner.

Scherchen, H. (1991). "Arteigene Rundfunkmusik." In Lucchesi, J. (ed.), *Hermann Scherchen. Werke und Briefe*. 1. Bern a.o.: Lang, 67–73.

Schöning, K. (ed.). (1974). *Neues Hörspiel O-Ton. Der Konsument als Produzent. Versuche. Arbeitsberichte*. Frankfurt/M.: Suhrkamp.

Schwitzke, H. (1963). *Das Hörspiel. Geschichte und Dramaturgie*. Köln: Kiepenheuer & Witsch.

Tolson, A. (2006). *Media Talk. Spoken Discourse on TV and Radio*. Edinburgh: Edinburgh University Press.

VanCour, S. G. (2008). *The Sounds of 'Radio'. Aesthetic Formations of 1920s American Broadcasting*. Madison: University of Wisconsin Press.

von Foerster, H. (1993). "Das Gleichnis vom Blinden Fleck. Über das Sehen im allgemeinen." In Lischka, G. J. (ed.), *Der entfesselte Blick*. Bern: Benteli, 14–47.

Vowinckel, A. (1998). "Online—Offline. Ansätze eines interaktiven Hörspiels." In Helbig, J. (ed.), *Intermedialität. Theorie und Praxis eines interdisziplinären Forschungsgebiets*. Berlin: E. Schmidt, 93–107.

Wagner, H-U. (1990). "Die künstlerischen Ausdrucksmöglichkeiten des Features— NWDR-Beispiele aus den ersten Nachkriegsjahren." *Studienkreis Rundfunk und Geschichte. Mitteilungen*, 16(2/3), 174–183.

8 Radio Ambulante

Narrative Radio Journalism in the Age of Crowdfunding

Manuel Fernández-Sande

CROWDFUNDING: AN ALTERNATIVE VEHICLE FOR FINANCING NEW RADIO ENTERPRISES?

Crowdfunding has grown significantly over the past few years, especially since the 2009 debut of digital platforms designed to facilitate direct interaction between promoters of new media projects and prospective donors (Lambert and Schwienbacher 2010).

As this novel form of financing has gradually gained traction, it has provided a major impulse for projects in almost every sector imaginable. Strictly speaking, crowdfunding is not a new concept. The practice of raising funds for a specific project or goal through some form of popular subscription is almost as old as humanity itself. Perhaps the earliest example of crowdfunding in the modern sense of the term was a campaign mounted by *New York World* publisher Joseph Pulitzer in 1884 to raise money for the construction of a pedestal for the Statue of Liberty. In slightly more than five months, the newspaper raised close to $100,000 for this cause. The massive response of New York's working-class citizens to Pulitzer's call to action is clear by the monetary value of individual donations to the campaign, 160,000 of which were less than a dollar (Pitts 2010).

Crowdfunding can be defined as a means of financing projects through many small individual donations. In practice, it generally involves selling a concept to a large number of donors, each of whom contributes a small percentage of the total capital needed to finance a proposed venture (Belleflamme, Lambert and Schwienbacher 2013).

Crowdfunding has been a perennial means of financing communications enterprises and has been a fixture of radio broadcasting from its very emergence as a mass medium. Early radio programmes in many countries were underwritten by listener contributions until the fledgling market for broadcast advertising became firmly established. In some cases, fundraising took the form of subscription campaigns organised at the grassroots level by radio clubs and groups of listeners themselves in support of local radio programming. In other instances, the impetus for public financing came from broadcasting companies seeking to bridge the gap between the flow of advertising revenue and their actual operating costs. However, once advertising revenues reached a level that not only covered overhead costs but also guaranteed steady profit margins, radio broadcasting companies gradually ceased to regard their listeners as direct financial stakeholders.

The popular subscription financing models for radio broadcasting prevalent in most countries during the 1920s fit the three main criteria for what is known today as crowdfunding in that they (1) involved a critical mass of stakeholders eager to financially support a project they regarded as mutually beneficial, (2) the greater part of the funding that enterprises received was provided by individual listeners rather than other organisations and (3) fundraising campaigns employed various communications channels to reach out to potential donors. There were several examples of popular subscriptions in Spain and Brazil during this period that are particularly worth noting.

Radio Ibérica, which was one of the first broadcasting ventures in Spain to offer regular programming, sought financial support from the Federación Nacional de Aficionados. Later, its parent company, the Sociedad Nacional de Radiodifusión Española, made direct appeals to audiences for financial support. Early on, Radio Barcelona also relied on listener support via contributions from the Asociación Nacional de Radiodifusión. In 1925, the Unión de Radioyentes Españoles devoted a percentage of the membership dues it received to underwriting the operating costs of Unión Radio, a network that played a dominant role in the early history of Spanish broadcasting (Fernández-Sande 2006).

As the concept of radio advertising was slower to catch on in Brazil, early broadcasting ventures in that country were financed through dues paid by members of legally registered societies and clubs. Radio Sociedade, launched in Rio de Janeiro in 1923, and Radio Educadora Paulista, launched a year later in Sao Paulo, were both financed by means of membership support (Tota 1990).

It is therefore possible that radio was the first mass medium to use crowdfunding as a major means of financing its initial phase of development. In addition to the criteria noted above, there are other aspects of early radio fundraising campaigns that clearly put them into the category of what we now refer to as crowdfunding activities. The promoters of early radio stations were pioneers in the development of incentive marketing. In addition to offering the possibility of enjoying a higher quality of programming than that provided by amateur radio clubs, radio stations lured potential subscribers and donors with insider incentives available exclusively to contributors, which ranged from subscriptions to in-house magazines to complementary theatre tickets, opportunities to attend live studio broadcast sessions and promotional items that bore the emblem and call letters of the broadcaster. Offering incentives and promotional items was a powerful way of creating a strong feeling of complicity between radio stations and their listeners. According to Eric Rivera (2012), there are a number of different models of crowdfunding, the most popular of which are:

- The equity investment model, through which individuals contribute to the financing of a project with the expectation of receiving a part of the financial profits it may eventually generate.
- The donor model, through which people support a cause (usually of a social or cultural nature) without any expectation of seeing a material or financial return in exchange for their contribution.
- The loan model, by which promoters receive financial support from community investors with the understanding that once their projects are up and running, the lenders will receive not only the original sums they committed, but also a modest return on their investment, which is usually based on a lower the rate of interest than that charged by commercial banks.
- The subscription or 'pre-pay' model, which is contingent upon the commitment of a critical mass of interested individuals willing to pay in advance for a product still in the financing stage.
- The final 'incentive/reward' model, which involves financing a project by means of the pooled contributions of many individuals who expect to benefit in some way from the end result. This is the method most commonly used to finance cultural and communications activities and projects. As previously mentioned, it has become the most viable means of financing radio start-ups and other audio projects through crowdfunding channels.

Historically, private radio stations abandoned listenership fundraising efforts once they consolidated their sources of advertising revenue. However, public radio stations and networks have continued to rely on the contributions of individual listeners, either as their sole means of support or as a complement to the government funding that makes up a large part of their operating budgets. Public radio and television networks in European countries such as Great Britain, Italy and France receive government financing through two different mechanisms: either directly through the mandatory licensing of home receivers or by means of taxes on the advertising revenues of commercial networks, or indirectly as a percentage of tax revenue. In any event, all of these methods suppose the mandatory use of taxpayer money. The third method of financing radio broadcasting, which in the majority of cases is employed by stations and networks that offer predominantly culturally, socially or community oriented programming, involves direct appeals to listeners. This system of listener-based funding has become popular in many countries, the most outstanding example being the United States, where listeners support a nationwide network of local stations affiliated with National Public Radio (NPR) (Gallego 2012).

The first attempt to provide an independent, non-commercial radio broadcasting service funded by listeners in the United States was the brainchild of Lewis Hill. His Pacifica Foundation, created at the close of the Second World War, was specifically conceived to promote the launch of independent, alternative media outlets that were politically unaligned and provided culturally diverse programming. His first venture, Radio KPFA in Berkeley, California, began broadcasting in April 1946. Hill's intention was to launch a radio network that did not rely on advertising to cover its operating costs or seek to appeal to a mass audience. He was more interested in using radio broadcasting to create a community of radio listeners interested in the type of socially and culturally oriented programming he sought to provide. KPFA relied entirely on listener donations. As such, it is considered to have been the first example of listener-supported radio in the United States and an important precedent for the crowdfunding carried out today.

Lewis Hill invented a new model for financing independent, alternative radio broadcasting in the United States that was to have a major impact on the quality and content of radio. Contributors were offered a monthly magazine he christened *The Folio*, which kept them informed about upcoming programmes (Lasar 2000; Walker 2001; Whiting 1992). With an enviable track record of seventy consecutive years of listener-supported broadcasting, the Pacifica Radio Network now comprises a total of six stations: in addition to founder station KPFA, it includes KPFK in Los Angeles, KPFW in Washington, DC, WBAI in New York and KPFT in Houston.

Radio Pacifica's financing model has been successfully adopted by other public radio ventures such as NPR, which supplements listener contributions with public and private grants and sponsorship agreements (Gallego 2012; Mitchell 2005).

THE DEVELOPMENT OF CROWDFUNDING AS IT IS KNOWN TODAY

Crowdfunding has been gaining traction as an alternative financing vehicle for a wide range of cultural, social and business enterprises. A number of different factors have led to the renaissance and exponential growth of this time-honoured method of fundraising. There is no doubt that the current international financial crisis and the consequent tightening of credit conditions in many countries have both contributed to the search for alternative funding mechanisms. The technological revolution and globalisation have also made crowdfunding much more viable and attractive. Both the interactivity of communications in the digital era and their global reach have vastly enhanced entrepreneurs' possibilities of forging direct connections with potential donors and funders. Lastly, the crowdfunding model fits perfectly in a new global culture driven by social entrepreneurship, exchange networks and a greater interest in personal participation (Bannerman 2013).

The emergence of online platforms devoted exclusively to crowdfunding campaigns has fuelled the growth of this type of microfinancing. The first online platform specifically designed to promote crowdfunding activities was probably Kiva (Flannery 2006). The concept really began to take off in 2008 with the appearance of Indiegogo, which was quickly followed by scores of other platforms designed to facilitate project promotion and fundraising management. A few, such as Kickstarter, now provide a truly international meeting point for entrepreneurs and potential funders scattered across the globe, while others serve smaller, national markets. There are many generalist crowdfunding sites such as Gofundme that provide an umbrella for almost any type of project or cause and others that concentrate on specific areas of interest. The majority of these operate on an 'all or nothing' principle, meaning that contributions are only processed and ceded to the poster if his or her campaign has succeeded in generating pledges sufficient to meet a pre-determined funding target within a designated period of time (Ramos 2013). Others, adhering to the 'everything counts' principle, allow project promoters to collect funds committed even if the total amount pledged falls short of their original goal. A few, such as Indiegogo and Projeggt, offer both promoters a choice between these options when they post their proposals, although this greater level of flexibility usually supposes the imposition of higher commissions.

In 2012 there were approximately 170 online crowdfunding platforms vying for potential funders' attention (Valiati and Tietzmann 2012) and they continue to proliferate, driven by a strong demand for this type of service. Lawton and Marom (2012) assert that these websites function as agents of democratisation by eliminating intermediaries and allowing anyone in the world with Internet access to participate in the world of online investment.

There are crowdfunding models for every type of promoter, investor and contributor. Wefunder is a platform that lists projects in search of funding whose promoters are willing to offer people a return on their investment. Prosper and Zopa are two others that facilitate peer-to-peer loans. Youcaring and Justgiving, which concentrate on charitable giving, channel funds pledged by altruistic donors interested in new, non-commercial ideas and social causes. Kickstarter and Indiegogo stand out among the various websites that focus on fundraising for creative projects. Promoters who use this type of platform generally offer some kind of non-monetary incentive or compensation to donors.

Some of the platforms that provide forums for funding creative, educational and cultural initiatives are highly specialised. For example, Spot.us, Indie Voice and Mediafinders match promoters and funders of independent journalism projects, Emphasis.is focuses on photojournalism and audiovisual projects, Sellaband concentrates on music and both Cinemashares and Kifund are centred on filmmaking and other audiovisual initiatives.

Since its launch in 2009, Kickstarter has become the world's most successful fundraising platform for projects in a wide variety of creative fields. The categories it covers include art, comics, dance, design, fashion, film and video, gastronomy, games, music photography, publications, technology and theatre. Promoters pay the platform a 5% commission on the total raised for their projects. Over $1 billion was raised through this website between 2009 and 2014, and the website is enjoying steady year-over-year revenue growth.[1] Kuppuswamy and Bayus (2013), who have analysed patterns of contributor behaviour during fundraising campaigns carried out via this platform, have noted that donor response lulls and peaks at different points of a campaign. They have observed that campaigns with modest targets are the most successful and that donors tend to jump on the bandwagon during the final week of a promotion. The quality of the project proposed, the viability of stated time frames and economic goals, a promoter's ability to roll out an effective communications strategy during the fundraising period and geographic considerations are also strong factors in whether or not a given proposal receives crowdfunding (Mollick 2013). To date, the projects that have attracted the highest amounts of funding via Kickstarter have been the Pebble smartwatch, which received more than $10.2 million in pledges, and the Ouya Android-powered game console, which ranks a close second with a take of over $8.5 million.

Given that it allows promoters to develop an active, interested community of followers, crowdfunding has become much more than a low-cost means of financing projects. The intensive communications campaigns required to make crowdfunding activities successful also create a high level of visibility for projects well before they get under way. Mounting a crowdfunding campaign is also a way of testing a target market's real level of interest in a given product or service (Schwienbacher and Larralde 2012). It must also be pointed out that the very nature of this alternative fundraising process tends to generate collateral feedback that can potentially boost the innovative aspects of the product originally proposed. Collective financing also enhances the viability of 'out of the box' projects that may not fit into traditional sector frameworks. Sørensen (2012) has pointed out the impulse this new means of fundraising has given to the production of documentary films. Other scholars have analysed the impact that this type of financing has had on a wide range of projects related to journalism (Aitamurto 2011; Cabrera 2014; Carvajal, García-Avilés and González 2012). Some have even coined the term 'journalistic crowdfunding' to describe the fundraising efforts of journalists seeking to make direct funding a part of their formulas for making online journalism financially viable (Cea-Esteruelas 2013).

The ramifications of this fundraising alternative in terms of both the innovation it can add to a project and the new category of consumer-investor it has generated have had great implications for this study on the use of crowdfunding to finance radio ventures.

As previously mentioned, although crowdfunding has been used to finance projects in a vast range of business sectors, it has proved to be an especially useful vehicle for raising money for culturally oriented initiatives, a large number of which have been related to journalism and communications (Burtch, Ghose and Watkal 2013). A closer look at the contenders for funding in this category reveals a dramatic upward trend in funder support for radio and audio projects that are not conceived to be merely showcases for musical entertainment.

Audio-related crowdfunding proposals tend to be posted on platforms that specialise in promoting cultural initiatives. So far, large radio broadcasting companies have not used these platforms for fundraising purposes. The majority of proposals one sees in these environments are for financing community or alternative radio stations, online broadcast operations, podcasts, improvements to stations' existing facilities, applications for frequency permits, books on the history of radio or music festivals linked to specific radio stations. The projects proposed are usually modest in scope and promote alternatives to standard mainstream radio (Gallego and Fernández-Sande 2013). The crowdfunding campaign launched in 2012 by San Francisco–based Roman Mars to finance *99% Invisible*, an ongoing series of podcasts devoted to design and architecture, is an especially relevant example of how audio start-ups can be financed through Kickstarter, as his success directly inspired the founders of Radio Ambulante to run a campaign on the same platform when it was time to finance their project.[2] The proposal Mars posted on Kickstarter in 2012 attracted 5,661 donors who contributed a total of $170,477. A second Kickstarter campaign launched in November 2013 to finance a second season of *99% Invisible* was even more successful than the first: 11,693 listeners[3] donated more than $375,000—an international landmark in podcast fundraising via this method.

On the whole, commercial radio offers little in the way of innovation and tends to cling to the formulas that have traditionally delivered the profit margins and audience quotas station owners have come to expect. However, crowdfunding has opened up new fundraising and financing channels for people interested in offering innovative types of radio programming. That said, proposals for radio projects still make up only a small percentage of the total proposals posted on crowdfunding platforms for communications initiatives. Nevertheless, the modest but steady growth in the number of proposals being floated by radio entrepreneurs in search of funding on these websites could be a signal of a nascent trend. As of April 2014, 355 fundraising campaigns for radio or podcast proposals had been posted on Kickstarter.[4]

Collective financing is a good alternative for radio professionals with local experience under their belts looking for more creative freedom. These new radio entrepreneurs are making their mark in a number of countries. Some examples of interested projects in Europe include Alessio Bertallot's online *Casa Bertallot* project in Italy and DJ Tango's *IslaFM* in Spain, both of whom have managed to make the shift from commercial radio to personal online broadcasting thanks to crowdfunding campaigns.

DJTango made his move after working for fourteen years as a disc jockey and radio presenter for dance music stations in Spain. In September 2012, when his show *La Isla* was dropped by Loca FM after a 6-year run, he decided to launch his own online programme under the same title.

Early in 2013 he mounted a crowdfunding campaign on a platform backed by the media conglomerate Prisa called Mymajorcompany that brought in almost €15,000 donated by 324 music fans—an amount well above his original €12,000 target and enough to support his operating costs for a year.[5] A second campaign, run a year later on the crowdfunding platform Mola.FM,[6] confirmed the loyalty of the programme's followers: 315 donors contributed €13,000 to keep the project on the air.

Alessio Bertallot divides his time between his career as a musician and his work as a radio presenter and DJ. From 1996 to 2010 he was presenter for *B Side*, a programme broadcast by the Milan-based national private station Radio Deejay. In 2010 he moved on to Rai Radio 2's *Raitunes* programme, for which he was awarded a Premio Flaiano.[7] When *Raitunes* was pulled by the public radio station in June 2013, Bertallot made the decision to launch *Casa Bertallot*, an online radio programme that would allow him a greater margin of creative freedom. To finance the new project, he mounted a fundraising campaign on Musicraiser that convinced 521 fans to donate a total of €20,500.[8] Bertallot's programme is available on the Internet via Spreaker and Soundcloud and is also distributed by a number of Italian private local radio stations.

These are two cases of individuals with solid industry experience who took advantage of loyal audiences to create their own projects when commercial stations dropped their shows. Crowdfunding allowed them to connect with their listeners and transform them into communities that have provided ongoing support for their new endeavours.

These examples are proof that financial implication on the part of listeners is paving the way for alternative radio projects that don't fit into mainstream sector moulds. Alternative radio projects have two major characteristics that make them good candidates for crowdfunding (Giudici, Guerini and Lamastra 2013): the first is their ability to attract target audiences of established and potential listeners and the second is the much lower start-up and maintenance costs they suppose compared with other types of audiovisual projects such as films, which require far higher levels of investment.

In this sense, crowdfunding not only constitutes a new channel for financing projects that are of no interest to mainstream commercial radio broadcast organisations but also serves as a driver of sector innovation. The combination of a greater margin of creative freedom and financial independence and an active implication on the part of listeners changes the very processes of production and fosters experimentation with the narrative elements of programming, both of which broaden the scope of radio broadcasting.

It is clear that the number of radio initiatives financed through crowdfunding is still too low to provide leverage for major changes in the sector. However, there are a few groundbreaking projects worth analysing in depth for their future import. One of them is Radio Ambulante.

RADIO AMBULANTE'S FINANCING AND PRODUCTION MODEL

This chapter focuses on a case study of Radio Ambulante, which serves as one of the best recent examples of how crowdfunding can be used to launch a new radio broadcasting venture. It is partially based on a series of in-depth interviews conducted with Carolina Guerrera, executive director and co-founder of Radio Ambulante.[9]

The inspiration for Radio Ambulante dates back to when *Lost City Radio*, a novel written by one of the venture's founders, Daniel Alarcón (2007), hit the bookstands. Alarcón, who was born in Lima, Peru in 1977 but has lived in the United States from early childhood, began forging a distinguished career as a fiction writer and journalist soon after earning a degree in anthropology at Columbia University. He is associate editor of the Peruvian magazine *Etiqueta Negra* and has written work published by periodicals such as *The New Yorker*, *Harper's* and *The Virginia Quarterly Review*.[10] Up until 2007, he worked primarily in the field of print journalism and had no experience in radio.

However, shortly after the release of his novel *Lost City Radio*, the BBC asked him to direct a radio programme about Andean migration to Lima. While working on location, he had the opportunity to experiment with the possibilities that radio offered. Delighted by the experience but frustrated that many of the interviews he had conducted in Spanish never made it into the finished English-language documentary, Alarcón began to play with the idea of putting together a narrative radio journalism project that would specifically showcase the accents and voices of Latin America (Red Cultural FNPI 2012).

A few years later, in January 2011, Daniel Alarcón and Carolina Guerrero revisited the idea and made the decision to create a narrative radio project that would provide a showcase for Latin American stories. Their objective was to produce a diverse series of radio podcasts that reflected the Latin American experience and captured the linguistic richness of Latin American culture.

Radio Ambulante is a good example of how the new possibilities for financing and distributing quality audio content can be creatively and successfully exploited. It offers an emerging business model that not only takes full advantage of digital convergence and the multiple platforms now available for the dissemination of journalism but is also geared towards making the production of digital content financially viable (Fernández-Sande and Peinado 2012).

As we shall see, Radio Ambulante goes well beyond being a mere crowd-funding success story. It also represents a new paradigm for radio journalism and production that is well aligned with the characteristics of today's digital economy.

Alarcón invested $25,000 of his own money in the launch of the project and the creation of two pilot programmes. However, when Radio Ambulante failed to win any foundation grants in 2011, he decided that crowdfunding was the logical next step. According to executive director Carolina Guerrero, a full year's work went into the planning of the crowdfunding campaign, during which she and Alarcón were also busy lining up the production staff and journalists who would bring Radio Ambulante to life.

Their decision to run their crowdfunding campaign through Kickstarter turned out to be a propitious move: during the January through March 2012 fundraising period, 600 donors pledged a total $46,032. As the original target had been $40,000, the campaign was considered a great success. After commissions to Kickstarter and Amazon were deducted from the total sum pledged, they had $41,000 in seed money—enough to see the project through its first few months.[11]

The first content to be published on the website included two pilot podcasts produced by Gabriela Wiener and Cristian Alarcón that gave listeners a taste of programming to come. As incentives had been pitched to prospective donors during the campaign, the promised CDs, T-shirts and books were distributed to their respective new owners once the fundraising period had concluded.

The founders of Radio Ambulante started out on the premise that the contents they wanted to offer and the creative path they planned to take would not be feasible within the framework of commercial radio, and it would therefore be necessary to explore alternative methods of financing the project as conceived.

Although Radio Ambulante was registered as a non-profit organisation, it still needed to develop a business model that would ensure its viability. Its immediate expenses included the salaries of core staff members and a few permanent external collaborators, commissions paid to contributing journalists, costs related to the design and maintenance of the Radio Ambulante website and the purchase of technical equipment.

In addition to the $41,000 in seed money obtained through its debut campaign on Kickstarter, Radio Ambulante received between $5,000 and $6,000 in additional direct listener contributions during its first year on the air. There are plans to mount another Kickstarter campaign, with a higher target of $60,000, in late 2014.

However, Radio Ambulante's business model anticipates balancing listener donations and crowdfunding with revenue from other sources. The venture actively seeks grants available to non-profit organisations. To date it has received funding from the Ford Foundation, the Panta Rhea Foundation and Culture Strike. Radio Ambulante also has a contract to supply contents for Public Radio International's programme *The World*.

Alarcón and Guerrero are also developing other sources of revenue, which may include advertising (Rodríguez 2013), subscriptions that offer premium content and sessions with live audiences. It has already organised audience programmes in Los Angeles, San Francisco and New York.[12]

Making Radio Ambulante a reality required innovation and creativity every step of the way, from the planning of the venture's organisational structure and financing model to decisions regarding production processes, its approach to narrative journalism and multichannel distribution.

As Radio Ambulante's executive producer, Daniel Alarcón is responsible for content. Executive director Carolina Guerrera handles the financial and administrative aspects of the venture. Radio Ambulante also has an advisory board.

Another aspect of Radio Ambulante's management model is a strategy of establishing alliances that open new doors and put the enterprise on a more solid footing. The most important of these is a close affiliation with Radio Ambulante's hometown public radio station KALW 91.7 FM in San Francisco, where its podcasts are produced.

Radio Ambulante is gaining visibility and having an impact worldwide through the inclusion of its podcasts in BBC World's regular programming. Daniel Alarcón and his staff have also forged collaboration and distribution agreements with an ever-growing list of partner broadcast organisations and publications. Radio Ambulante podcasts are broadcast by Radio Bilingüe (a national public radio network that serves listeners in the United States and Mexico), UABC Radio (a three-station, campus-based network run by the Universidad Autónoma de Baja California), RMX in Mexico, Radio Sur FM 88.3 in Buenos Aires and Radio Universidad de Rosario (also in Argentina). Radio Ambulante has also established cooperation agreements with magazines in Peru (*Etiqueta Negra* and *Cometa*) and Argentina (*Anfibia*).

The same corporate strategy of creating networks and alliances that broaden the scope of Radio Ambulante's listenership and strengthen its impact is applied to its internal organisation and operations, which rely heavily on crowdsourcing. This term was coined by Jeff Howe (2006) to describe how today's businesses are taking advantage of digital connectivity to engage a dynamic pool of independent external talent through collaboration agreements, exchanges and alliances rather than relying on traditional outsourcing contracts. Radio Ambulante has successfully implemented the crowdsourcing model to broaden its content, which is produced in the field by an external pool of forty collaborating journalists and radio producers located throughout the United States and Latin America. This loosely woven team of collaborators and contributors works hand in hand with a core staff of twelve producers and editors, the latter of whom coordinate the final production aspects of the podcasts.

Radio Ambulante is a product and reflection of digital culture. Daniel Alarcón openly asserts, "without the Internet and all the digital tools available, Radio Ambulante wouldn't exist" (Red Cultural FNPI 2012). It was assumed from the venture's very conception that radio programmes would be produced as podcasts that could be enjoyed on demand by a geographically dispersed listenership. Up-to-date technological equipment and collaborative software facilitate file transfer and the joint preparation of audio scripts.

The venture's successful strategy for digital audio content distribution could be a paradigm for other organisations seeking a model to emulate.

Although it is a relatively new project whose full development and maturity have yet to be seen, at present it stands out as a prime example of a radio start-up that has managed to integrate innovative ideas and techniques into every aspect of its operations and functions in synergy with the dynamics and inner logic of the Internet and the market for digital content.

Its methods and strategies for distribution have been very successful. In addition to forging collaboration agreements with radio stations that feature the podcasts it produces, Radio Ambulante has taken full advantage of the possibilities offered by digital multiplatform distribution to broaden its audience base. In addition to its own website, it currently offers content through Itunes, Soundcloud, Ivoox and Stitcher. It currently attracts a monthly audience of between 50,000 and 70,000 listeners by means of these platforms, approximately 20,000 of whom listen to podcasts via the Radio Ambulante website.[13]

Facebook, and to an even greater degree Twitter, are being used to spread the news about the launch of new programmes and generate interaction among listeners. However, according to Carolina Guerrero, direct communication with listeners is an area that requires further development.

NARRATIVE JOURNALISM AND CREATIVE NONFICTION

When Daniel Alarcón first conceived of the idea of creating radio podcasts that would 'narrate real stories (about Latin Americans) in a literary way,' *This American Life* was one of his main references.

This American Life is a weekly public radio programme hosted and produced by Ira Glass. After a highly successful launch in Chicago in 1995, the show was nationally syndicated in 1996. Produced by Chicago Public Media and distributed by Public Radio International, *This American Life* is broadcast by more than 500 public radio stations throughout the United States and attracts an average weekly audience of more than 2 million radio listeners. The show is a classic example of narrative radio journalism, a genre that applies the techniques of fiction to news production to give the settings, human subjects and topics addressed in a news story a heightened sense of drama, emotion or entertainment value that makes it more compelling to listeners.

Daniel Alarcón was looking to produce something with a similar aesthetic and began to explore the possibilities of narrative radio journalism. He saw Radio Ambulante as an extension of his own experience as a writer—another vehicle for telling stories (Carelli 2012). He was also attracted by the greater creative freedom projects financed through crowdfunding and foundation grants enjoyed, compared with that allowed in commercial radio. Alarcón and his team were interested in producing podcasts that would narrate the everyday life of Latin American people using their own words and voices—programmes that would be global in scope in that they spoke of the transnational Latin American experience, yet intimate and local in terms of topics and content.

The result of their efforts is a top-notch programme completely unlike anything offered by large commercial radio networks. Radio Ambulante produces creative radio podcasts that fully exploit the potential of the medium and the power of radio to engage listeners' emotions.

Although Radio Ambulante has a well-defined format and aesthetic, it gives the members of its network of collaborating independent producers—most of whom are professional journalists based in Latin America—a lot of leeway in how they individually approach their stories. The organisation's interest on working on projects in close collaboration with contributing freelance journalists is another facet of Radio Ambulante that sets it apart from its commercial competitors.

Collaborating producers are invited to submit ideas to Radio Ambulante's editorial team. Once an idea has been given the green light, story development gets under way. Every podcast produced grows out of an initial pitch or summary that covers the main points of a programme a producer has in mind. Once these presentations have been made, the editorial team vets the various proposals submitted and makes a selection. Each producer is assigned an editor who coordinates and supervises that particular project from start to finish.

This editorial oversight ensures that all of the stories broadcast by Radio Ambulante have an identifiable style. Every podcast conforms to the canons of narrative journalism: each is structured with an introduction, climax and denouement, has its clearly defined main characters, establishes the setting for the story to be related, and provides enough context to enable listeners to grasp the full gist of the overall narrative. Almost all of the podcasts produced by Radio Ambulante are built around interviews conducted by journalists that provide the guiding thread and bulk of the information conveyed. Journalists are expected to build on the feelings and emotions expressed by the subjects interviewed in the form of the anecdotes, descriptions of places or incidents and testimonies.

Radio Ambulante's production manual (Radio Ambulante 2013) sets out a series of specific guidelines for the production of every programme. High standards of sound quality and the inclusion of ambient sound recordings that give listeners a feeling for the environment in which the story is taking place are two important production requisites.

As Radio Ambulante has now completed its third season of programming, enough recorded material is available to trace the evolution of the narrative structure and the length of its productions. The initial plan was to release a new, hour-long programme every other month, but editors quickly realised that programmes needed to be spaced more closely together to ensure listener loyalty. The solution was to produce shorter programmes that varied between eight and ten minutes in length but nonetheless featured fairly complex narratives and contained a wealth of information. Although all of the podcasts produced during Radio Ambulante's second season were shorts, this policy was loosened the following year in order to experiment with longer programmes, a few of which were over thirty minutes in length and allowed producers to explore certain stories in greater depth.

In line with Alarcón's initial vision for Radio Ambulante, the producers of every programme are asked to reduce their use of voice-overs to a minimum so as to highlight the voices and accents of the people being interviewed. Interviewers are also requested to employ a direct and clear style of delivery that brings them and their stories closer to their audiences.

As Daniel Alarcón puts it:

> There is no set format. We offer simple, short chronicles with very few trappings that are sustained by a single narrative voice as well as occasional longer chronicles that are more complex, contain multiple interviews and are richer in terms of sound and production values. We look for good stories.
>
> (Carelli 2012)

Scripts for all podcasts tend to follow the same structure: the voices of the central figures of the story lead into an introduction by Daniel Alarcón, which is followed by a narrative provided by the lead presenter/interviewer assigned to a specific programme. The voices of its main subjects, punctuated by ambient sounds and silences, rise to the fore as the story unfolds. Music is used to ease transitions between scenes or reinforce given messages. Each podcast ends with a concluding statement and a short wrap-up delivered by its producer.

The goal for the next few seasons is to produce enough podcasts to maintain a weekly release schedule. At present, new podcasts are released on a monthly basis. Alarcón would also like to broaden his network of collaborators in Latin American countries. Brazil is one of his top targets in terms of recruiting new talent. Radio Ambulante has also branched out into other kind of activities, which include workshops on narrative radio journalism for media professionals offered through organisations such as the Fundación Nuevo Periodismo de Cartagena de Indias.

Radio Ambulante is, in effect, an ambitious laboratory of ideas, whose format has evolved from what was initially a straightforward narrative radio programme to a more flexible vehicle that incorporates a variety of different genres. Among other recent additions to its line-up, it now features pieces of fiction such as Mexican writer Guadalupe's story *La Comuna* and interviews conducted by Daniel Alarcón.

CONCLUSIONS: CAN RADIO AMBULANTE SERVE AS A MODEL FOR OTHERS INTERESTED IN PRODUCING AUDIO CONTENT?

The story of Radio Ambulante provides a case study in how today's alternative channels of audio content distribution can be successfully exploited to build financially viable organisational structures through which creative audio content can be produced and delivered to the public. Perhaps the most interesting aspect of the model this enterprise has pursued is how it has been structured to take advantage of many of the opportunities that have emerged with digital convergence and the new role that audiences can play in the launch and development of new audio initiatives. Its strategic competitiveness lies mainly in the high quality of its programming, which is a result of its implementation of innovation at every stage of production.

By crowdsourcing its external collaborators and crowdfunding a large part of its financing, Radio Ambulante has developed a novel model of management and production that has little in common with those employed in commercial radio.

Radio Ambulante is global, digital and Web based: the three main characteristics that companies need to prosper in the new economy. Production costs are low, in part, because its small core team of in-house professionals collaborate with a wide network of geographically dispersed collaborators by means of all the digital tools available to them.

Another essential element of its business strategy is its emphasis on developing mutually beneficial collaborations, content sharing alliances and agreements with other companies and organisations that compensate for its limitations as a new enterprise still working towards consolidation. Although new to the radio scene, Radio Ambulante has demonstrated a prodigious talent for detecting and developing synergies with other organisations that fulfil its own financing, production and distribution needs.

Radio Ambulante is a product of the shifts in listener behaviour and consumption patterns brought on by the emergence and development of the Internet. Its choice of podcasting as a principal presentation format (although its programmes are also available via more traditional distribution channels) is fully aligned with consumer demand for more profound audio experiences in this format. As José Ángel Esteban has aptly observed, "Podcasts are naturally linked to the use of earphones, an individual and attentive way of listening and a full enjoyment of all the nuances and richness of the sound being reproduced" (Romero 2012).

Another interesting angle is Radio Ambulante's ability to reconcile the local focus of its programming (stories about people in specific places and situations) with its overall transnational approach. Its editors have deftly achieved a balance between the local and the global, a communications imperative in a digitised world.

The cultural richness of the project stems from its emphasis on diversity as a differentiating element. The founders' own personal histories as cosmopolitan Latinos who have put down roots in San Francisco have been factors in their determination to break down stereotypes of what Latina Americans are all about.

The independence from the pressures of commercial radio that Radio Ambulante's financing model affords is obvious in the product it produces and its commitment to narrative journalism. Its producers have been free to mix elements of journalism and Latin American chronicle writing with other literary conventions.

One is impressed by the novel narrative structures and high sound quality of the podcasts this team produces, which are drawn from a variety of sources to create engaging stories that have a deep emotional appeal to listeners.

Another striking qualitative aspect of Radio Ambulante's podcasts is the manner in which they exploit all the expressive possibilities of radio to vividly evoke the atmosphere of different settings and situations and bring listeners closer to the story being told.

Among the few valid criticisms of this project that one could offer is that its minimal success in generating user interactivity stands out. While it is true that 600 fans and listeners played an active role and even provided financial support for its launch, one does not get the impression that the staff of Radio Ambulante has pursued all the possibilities offered by available communications platforms to boost the level of its interaction with users and foster listener participation in the generation of new audio content. In line with the theories of Carpentier on this subject, we consider the level of Radio Ambulante's interaction with its audience to be minimal. It still has not managed to strike a balance required between the control its producers have over the content it features and the possibilities for active listener input to give it credit for fully exploiting the medium's potential for interactivity (Carpentier 2011). Although listeners do have the opportunity to interact, suggest topics for new stories and post comments about recent podcasts through Radio Ambulante's social network profiles and its website, the production processes themselves are completely controlled by the journalists who produce the programmes. Experimenting with user interactivity and working out ways to boost audience participation will be one of the venture's most important challenges going forward.

Radio Ambulante's capacity for further growth remains unknown. For the moment, it has achieved financial stability and its directors are contemplating the possibility of initiating another crowdfunding campaign at the end of 2014 to raise the money needed to consolidate the enterprise. The quality of its podcasts is attracting a growing flow of traffic to its website and the other platforms where its programmes are featured. Its importance and prestige are also on an upward trend.

It is still too early to judge whether the model employed by Radio Ambulante qualifies as a case study of how audio content in today's changing market can be successfully distributed. To reach any definitive conclusions, it will be necessary to track its evolution over the next few years. However, there is no doubt that some of the principles on which it has based its financing, organisation, system of production and its novel narrative approach to radio programming could be applicable to other new initiatives involving audio content in search of alternatives to the traditional formulas of commercial radio.

NOTES

1. Figures based on data published on https://www.kickstarter.com/. Accessed February 23, 2014.
2. Guerrero, Carolina. Interviews by author conducted on February 18 and April 21, 2014.
3. Data obtained from https://www.kickstarter.com/projects/1748303376/99-invisible-season-3. Accessed April 25, 2014.
4. Data obtained from https://www.kickstarter.com/projects/1748303376/99-invisible-season-3. Accessed April 25, 2014.
5. Data obtained from http://mymajorcompany.es/laisla-fm. Accessed February 12, 2014.
6. Data obtained from http://www.mola.fm/project/laisla. Accessed February 15, 2014.
7. Information contained on Alessio Bertallot's website http://www.bertallot.com/. Accessed March 4, 2014.
8. Data obtained from https://www.musicraiser.com/it/projects/1685-casa-bertallot. Accessed March 4, 2014.
9. Guerrero, Carolina. Interviews by author conducted on February 18 and April 21, 2014.
10. Daniel Alarcón is the author of *War by Candlelight: Stories* (2005), *Lost City Radio* (2007), *The King Is Always Above the People* (2009), *The Secret Miracle: The Novelist's Handbook* (2010) and *At Night We Walk in Circles: a Novel* (2013).
11. Guerrero, Carolina. Interviews by author conducted on February 18 and April 21, 2014.
12. Guerrero, Carolina. Interviews by author conducted on February 18 and April 21, 2014.
13. Guerrero, Carolina. Interviews by author conducted on February 18 and April 21, 2014.

REFERENCES

Aitamurto, T. (2011). "The Impact of Crowdfunding on Journalism." *Journalism Practice*, 5(4), 429–445.
Alarcón, D. (2007). *Lost City Radio*. New York: Harper Collins.
Bannerman, S. (2013). "Crowdfunding Culture." *Wi: Journal of Mobile Culture*, 7(March), 1–30. Accessed November 29, 2013. http://wi.mobilities.ca/crowdfunding-culture/.
Belleflamme, P., Lambert, T. and Schwienbacher, A. (2013). "Crowdfunding: Tapping the Right Crowd." *Journal of Business Venturing, Forthcoming*. CORE Discussion Paper No. 2011/32. Accessed March 10, 2014. http://ssrn.com/abstract=1578175 or http://dx.doi.org/10.2139/ssrn.1578175.
Burtch, G., Ghose, A. and Watkal, S. (2013). "An Empirical Examination of the Antecedents and Consequences of Contribution Patterns in Crowd-Funded Markets." *Information Systems Research, Forthcoming*. Accessed February 12, 2014. http://ssrn.com/abstract=1928168.
Cabrera, M. A. (2014). "Crowdfunding y nuevos proyectos periodísticos en España. Análisis de la innovación y el éxito de casos." Paper presented at the XV Foro Universitario de Investigación en Comunicación, Universidad de Vigo, Vigo, España. Accessed April 12, 2014. http://www.foro2014.com/wp-content/uploads/2014/02/49.-Cabrera.pdf.

Carelli, G. (2012). "Del libro a la radio, los cronistas que quieren registrar la voz de América." *Clarín*, February 20, 2012. Accessed January 8, 2014. http://www.clarin. com/sociedad/libro-cronistas-quieren-registrar-America_0_649735084.html.

Carpentier, N. (2011). "The Concept of Participation. If They Have Access and Interact, Do They Really Participate?" *CM: Communication Management Quarterly/ Casopis za upravljanje komuniciranjem*, 21, 13–36.

Carvajal, M., García-Avilés, J. A. and González, J. L. (2012). "Crowdfunding and Non-Profit Media. The Emergence of New Models for Public Interest Journalism." *Journalism Practice*, 6(5–6), 638–647.

Cea-Esteruelas, M. N. (2013). "Economía de los cibermedios: modelo de ingresos y fuente de financiación." *El Profesional de la Información*, 22(4), 353–361.

Fernández-Sande, M. (2006). *Los orígenes de la Radio en España. Vol. II*. Madrid: Fragua.

Fernández-Sande, M. and Peinado, F. (2012). "La empresa radiofónica actual." In Gallego, J. I. and García-Leiva, M. T. (eds.), *Sintonizando el futuro: Radio y producción sonora para el siglo XXI*. Madrid: Instituto RTVE, 29–58.

Flannery, M. (2006). "Kiva and the Birth of Person-to-Person Microfinance." *Innovations*, 2(1–2), 31–56.

Gallego, J. I. (2012). "La audiencia en la radio: viejos roles, nuevas funciones." In Gallego, J. I. and García-Leiva, M. T. (eds.), *Sintonizando el futuro: Radio y producción sonora para el siglo XXI*. Madrid: Instituto RTVE, 209–227.

Gallego, J. I. and Fernández-Sande, M. (2013). "Crowdfunding of Audio and Radio Contents: Sustainability and Viability of this Finance Concept." Paper presented at ECREA Radio Research Conference, London, September 11–13.

Giudici, G., Guerini, M. and Lamastra, C. R. (2013). "Why Crowdfunding Projects Can Succeed: The Role of Proponents' Individual and Territorial Social Capital." *SSRN Electronic Journal*, 1–20. Accessed February 2, 2014 http://ssrn.com/ abstract=2255944 or http://dx.doi.org/10.2139/ssrn.2255944.

Howe, J. (2006). "The Rise of Crowdsourcing." *Wired*, 14(6), 1–4. Accessed December 12, 2013. http://archive.wired.com/wired/archive/14.06/crowds.html.

Mollick, E. (2013). "The Dynamics of Crowdfunding: An Exploratory Study." *Journal of Business Venturing*, 9–14. Accessed April 10, 2014. http://dx.doi. org/10.1016/j.jbusvent.2013.06.005.

Kuppuswamy, V. and Bayus, B. (2013). "Crowdfunding Creative Ideas: The Dynamics of Project Backers in Kickstarter." *SSRN Electronic Journal*, 1–37. Accessed April 14, 2014. http://funginstitute.berkeley.edu/sites/default/files/V.Kuppuswamy_ Crowdfunding%20-%20UCBerkeley.pdf.

Lambert, T. and Schwienbacher, A. (2010). "An Empirical Analysis of Crowdfunding." *SSRN Working Paper*, 1–23. Accessed October 15, 2013. http://www. crowdsourcing.org/document/an-empirical-analysis-of-crowdfunding-/2458.

Lasar, M. (2000). *Pacífica Radio: The Rise of an Alternative Network*. Philadelphia: Temple University Press.

Lawton, K. and Marom, D. (2012). *The Crowdfunding Revolution: How to Raise Venture Capital Using Social Media*. New York: McGraw Hill.

Mitchell, J. W. (2005). *Listener Supported: The Culture and History of Public Radio*. Westport: Praeger Publishers.

Pitts, J. B. (2010). "Pulitzer Crowdfunded the Statue of Liberty?" *The Daily Crowdsource*, October 20, 2010. Accessed January 2, 2014. http://dailycrowdsource. com/2010/10/20/earth/geography/pulitzer-crowdfunded-the-statue-of-liberty/.

Radio Ambulante. (2013). *Manual de productores de Radio Ambulante*. Accessed January 9, 2014. http://radioambulante.org/wp-content/uploads/2013/09/Manual_ Productores-RA.pdf.

Ramos, J. (2013). *Crowdfunding. Cómo conseguir financiación en Internet*. Los Gatos: Smashwords. Epub.

Red Cultural FNPI (Colombia). (2012). *Cómo funciona Radio Ambulante: crónicas radiales latinoamericanas.* May 5, 2012. Accessed March 23, 2014. http://reddeperiodismocultural.fnpi.org/2012/05/08/como-funciona-radioambulante-cronicas-radiales-latinoamericanas-entrevista-con-daniel-alarcon-su-fundador/.

Rivera, E. (2012). *Crowdfunding: La eclosión de la financiación colectiva, un cambio tecnológico, social y económico.* Sant Pol de Mar (Barcelona): Microtemas.

Rodríguez, V. (2013). "El desafío de mantener una empresa financiada por crowdfunding." *Metro*, October 10, 2013, Puerto Rican edition. Accessed November 15, 2013. http://www.metro.pr/economia/radio-ambulante-el-desafio-de-mantener-una-empresa-financiada-por-el-crowdfunding/pGXmji!dbM8zl16bjJQU/.

Romero, L. (2012). "Radio y arte sonoro: ¿Es posible la integración?" In Gallego, J. I. and García-Leiva, M. T. (eds.), *Sintonizando el futuro: Radio y producción sonora para el siglo XXI.* Madrid: Instituto RTVE, 239–257.

Schwienbacher, A. and Larralde, B. (2012). "Crowdfunding of Small Entrepreneurial Ventures." In Cumming, D. (ed.), *Handbook of Entrepreneurial Finance.* New York: Oxford University Press, 369–392.

Sørensen, I. E. (2012). "Crowdsourcing and Outsourcing: The Impact of Online Funding and Distribution on the Documentary Film Industry in the UK." *Media, Culture & Society*, 34(6), 726–743.

Tota, A. P. (1990). *A locomotora no ar. Rádio e Modernidade em Sao Paulo 1924–1934.* Sao Paulo: Secretaria de Estado da Cultura do Estado de Sao Paulo.

Valiati, V. and Tietzmann, R. (2012). "Crowdfunding: O Financiamento Coletivo como Mecanismo de Fomento à Produção Audiovisual." Paper presented at XIII Congresso de Ciências da Comunicação na Região Sul. Chapecó, Santa Catarina, Brasil, May 31–June 2. Accessed December 10, 2013. http://www.intercom.org.br/papers/regionais/sul2012/ resumos/R30–1090–1.pdf.

Walker, J. (2001). *Rebels on the Air. An Alternative History of Radio in America.* New York: New York University Press.

Whiting, J. (1992). "The Lengthening Shadow: Lewis Hill and the Origins of Listener-sponsored Broadcasting in America." *The Dolphin*, 23(Autumn), 183. Accessed January 9, 2014. http://www.kpfahistory.info/hist/lengthening_shadow.htm.

9 User-Generated Playlists
Radio Music Programming in the Age of Peer-to-Peer Production, Distribution and Consumption

J. Ignacio Gallego

INTRODUCTION

In 1955 Todd Storz and Bill Stewart started the first Top 40 selection KOWH-AM in Omaha, Nebraska (Keith 1987). This was the beginning of a format that would systematise the capacity of music radio stations to become the main gatekeepers for phonographic products, Contemporary Hit Radio.

Radio stations that follow this format construct their playlists through several inputs that have evolved over 60 years. They have a fundamental goal: to gather the greatest amount of listeners for the most popular songs in each moment.

These programming formulas constantly changed, displaying an interactive dynamic with the emergent phonographic industry. They became a key element in constructing and defining the taste of audiences and legitimating the work of disc jockeys in music radio in a systematic fashion. For example, in the beginning of the 1940s, Duncan MacDougald (1941) highlighted how the radio and the music industry had a decisive influence in the success of songs produced by Tin Pan Alley.

Within both the commercial and public realms—the former exemplified by the US radio stations or the first charts in Spain and the latter inspired by the ultimate representative of the European model, the BBC—radio turned into the most important music adviser (Gallego 2011).

At the end of the 1990s, the music industry was strong and well established, reaching its greatest success in terms of sales (Wikström 2009). Within this scenario, each medium knew the role it played in the value chain that established music hits. This status quo broke down with the popularisation of the Internet and the emergence of services that radically transformed music broadcasting and distribution.

Consequently, one of the goals of this chapter is to analyse the influence of audiences in the programming strategies of music radio stations, contributing to the evaluation and questioning of the deterministic and cyberfetishist discourse that endows digital social networks and the consumers with key power as music advisers and playlist co-creators.

PROGRAMMING MUSIC RADIO

Selecting, organising and creating the right tone in each moment, everyday: those are the main functions of a music programmer. Storz and Stewart built up the first Top 40 model, taking as a point of departure the observation of the reproduction routines in a jukebox at their favourite bar (Keith 1987).

These first programming formulae placed the listener at the centre of the selection process within a logic that is still at work in commercial music radio and which Rothenbuler (1987, 78) describes as follows: "The music that is played on commercial radio stations to attract audiences that contribute to ratings that are attractive to advertisers that are in turn attractive to radio station management." Therefore, the logic of commercial music radio had as its main selling product not the playlists that shaped programming but rather the audiences themselves.

This music—through its capacity to build identities and links to juvenile culture—turned into the ideal cultural product to define an audience type, namely the objective audience that believed it was creating trends through its listening practices, despite the fact that, in reality, there was a well-oiled machinery in charge of music programming.

Aside from the first purely music radio format, linked to the emergent rock and roll, other formats related to other genres developed by big labels started appearing: soul and urban, country, dance, oldies—each type of music had a radio format, each format catering to a specific audience.

As Ien Ang (1991) points out in *Desperately Seeking the Audience* when referring to the internationalisation of TV audiences, commercial music radio managed to develop research strategies that facilitated the configuration of a specific idea about radio audiences. Consequently, consumers became objects of study, scrutiny and control.

Hence, music radio programming practices have been diametrically different depending on the country, the station's ownership and the programming format. Keith Negus (1993, 66) singled out the differences between US commercial music stations and BBC Radio 1 in terms of the selection of music:

> In Britain records are prioritised according to the musical tastes, public personas and specific requirements of disc jockeys and their producers. (. . .) In the United States the priorities have more to do with the format categories; tracks that do not fit—'where nobody knows what to do with it'— and recordings that are not receiving wider commercial support (albums, tours and widespread advertising) are de-prioritised or simply ignored.

Aside from these two approaches to programming, it is important to highlight the development of research on music radio audiences. Historically, this has been a widespread practice in the United States. In Spain, this type of study has become popular amongst radio owners only since the first decade of 2000. Focus groups, call-outs or telephone research and music testing are practices that, one way or another, evaluate the taste of audiences and search for the most adequate playlist depending on the programming format (Keith 1987). In addition, in the last decade, online feedback studies have exponentially grown (Schramm and Knoll 2012). The predominance of audience studies to programme music directly intervenes in the creativity of lists and the appearance of new artists, standardising the scheduling of commercial music radio. Programmers take fewer risks due to the increasing importance of research and the consideration that listeners look for known songs that have been previously tested. This has been brought to the extreme in some US markets where the introduction of the PPM—Portable People Meter—six years ago allows for knowledge on the number of connections to and disconnections from a station depending on the song playing (Karp 2014).

The progressive concentration of the radio market (Lee 2004) and the music industry, along with the practices of programming and researching audiences mentioned previously, has caused a significant reduction of diversity in radio schedules. Apart from the historical influence of commercial music radio over the big labels' repertoires (Negus 1993), it is necessary to add the reformulation of radio when confronting new ways of discovering music online. Radio owners have chosen to reduce risks, concentrating artists on a rotation. For example, in the last decade, the most played songs on US radio have doubled their exposure. In 2003, the song most played reached the play frequency of 442,160 in comparison to the 749,633 play frequency for 2013 (Karp 2014). In Spain, the level of rotation in "Los 40 Principales"—the most important music radio station with over 3.4 million listeners (AIMC 2014)—has also followed this trend: in 1992, a song would on average last 4 weeks in the radio chart; in 2012 it reached an average of 13.5 weeks.

Moreover, in the private sector, which depends on advertising for funding, we should mention the importance of paid services since they have understood audiences as customers, developing other programming formats that have been perfected within the currently existing online paid services. In this context, it is essential to mention the "Hilo Musical" (tubed music service), which was fundamentally used by business companies as background music in office spaces. It offered a selection of thematic channels and a remarkable diversity of music. Satellite radio platforms such as Sirius XM also utilise different radio formats and channels where the programmer/trademark is a pop-rock star (E Street Radio, Pearl Jam Radio or Grateful Dead Channel).

As opposed to this mainstream radio/music, in which audiences are limited to the role of institutionalisation and sale—both in terms of the commercialisation of advertising spaces and the promotion of phonograms—there are modes of resistance that have historically attempted to promote music diversity and fight against standardisation. It is thus necessary to, on the one hand, analyse the role of public radio, and, on the other hand, highlight community and free radios as key players in the development of different music subcultures.

Public radio has historically treated popular music as a public good, justifying its existence and important role in the dissemination of music (Wall

2012). In a 2004 document, the regulating institution of British media, Ofcom, defended the role of the radio in promoting the diversity of specialised music: "The nature of radio arguably makes it better at providing all sorts of music, from classical to folk, from jazz to rock, and at providing opportunities for new talent and for live performances" (Ofcom 2004, 49). In Spain, the 2006 law (Law 17/2006, June 5), which regulates national media, highlights that public service should promote a type of programming that satisfies the cultural needs of citizenship, disseminating Spanish identity and cultural diversity (BOE 2006). Given all this, traditional public radio stations (BBC, Rai, CBC, RNE, RF, NPR) have favoured a form of programming based on the work of their specialists. Even if, on occasion, this way of programming and understanding audiences has been labelled elitist or paternalist (Jacka 2003; Williams 1976), the truth is that in the countries where public media play a decisive role, their stations have been fundamental in the consolidation of a local industry and the promotion of music genres and artists that have no space within the context of commercial music radio. In this context, it is worth noting those public policies that have established broadcasting quotas in private radio to favour local artists and labels. In an attempt to guarantee music diversity in their stations and protect the local industries, countries such as France, Canada, Nigeria and Australia have established these policies (Stein-Sacks 2012).

Finally, it is worth noting the role of audiences in third sector stations, since they are essential in developing specific types of music. These are community, free and university radio stations where listeners are in charge and use the air waves to disseminate their favourite music. This type of station is where, in reality, audiences have a direct participation in the programming of songs outside the limits established within private and state media.

Therefore, we can categorise music programming taking as a point of departure the manner in which we understand audiences from a political economy point of view. Table 9.1 summarises this approach.

Table 9.1   Audience typology

Type of audience	Consumer audience	Customer audience	Citizen audience	Community audience
Type of station	Commercial music radio	Paid radio	Public radio	Community/ university radio
Programming style	Programming songs that attract the maximum audience	Programming songs that attract audiences willing to pay for content	Programming songs depending on the work of specialists and the promotion of diversity	Programming songs following the taste of a community that has real access to the air waves

Source: Prepared by the author.

PARADIGM SHIFT: THE TRANSFORMATION
OF SOUND CONSUMPTION

From the beginnings of radio broadcasting and the subsequent consolidation of the music industry, the role each link played in the value chain was perfectly defined. The relationship between both industries was clearly established so that the prescriptive function of the radio was the perfect showcase for the novelties stemming from the phonographic industry. Whereas commercial and public radio gave access to music, different distributors and sales venues controlled the purchase of sound equipment. Following this logic, a single with a continuous rotation made the listener go to the store and buy a whole record.

In 1945, Adorno approached the relationship between both industries in *A Social Critique of Radio Music* (Adorno 1996), criticising the standardisation of music radio programmes and their remarkable effect on consumption, given the commercial character that music had acquired.[1] In *Noise*, Jacques Attali (1977), on his part, defined the importance of the *hit parade* and the radio in the concentration of sales within a limited roster of greatest hits and how specific works only acquired value due to their overexposure in the air waves.

This status quo started to break down upon the digitisation of sound contents and the consolidation, during the 1990s, of the Internet as a content distribution network. If in the 1980s audiences received the recording master in 1's and 0's through the compact disc, in the 1990s the developments in the sound codification of audio files (mp3, ogg, wav, aiff) were key to the dematerialisation of sound artefacts, facilitating the distribution of these files. From the emergence of streaming in the mid-1990s (McCauley 2002) to the appearance of Napster in 1999—the first remarkable platform for P2P files—these new forms of distribution radically changed not only the way we understand the circulation of sound but also the access and exchange of all types of content (Gallego 2013). Therefore, it was not only phonography that changed but also the different gatekeepers and forms of consumption, radically affecting how we understand the working mechanisms of the different cultural industries and their interrelations.

Thus, the circulation of cultural products drastically changed. In Flichy's (1980) paradigm, the phonographic industry could be considered as an editorial industry and the radio industry was mostly devoted to the programming of content flows. With the arrival of digital, the difference between these two models becomes increasingly blurry. Their complementarity turned into competition. On the one hand, the reproduction of music through a physical support mutated towards an access model. On the other hand, radio products began to complement conventional programming with the reproduction of contents through services such as the podcast and pay-per-view, hence acquiring an editorial character.

This shift in the circulation of products entailed the consolidation of a new way of accessing content for audiences, with new practices rapidly identified by the different gatekeepers that have attempted to extract a surplus from new forms of creation and distribution of sound content. In the beginning of radio broadcasting, the transmission of music through Hertzian stations was seen as a potential competitor for phonographic reproduction and live music. This threat has also appeared with the rise of P2P networks and the exchange of files between peers. Those initial fears turned into almost perfect complementarity for the different cultural industries. Today, we are still analysing how the process of digitisation affects the different segments of the conventional value chain of the music industry.

This analysis takes as a point of departure two fundamental viewpoints, apocalyptic and digitally integrated; what Robert McChesney (2013, 7) defines as "celebrants and sceptics." There are those authors who, in a tremendously deterministic and utopian perspective, defend that free access to the diverse forms of cultural creation places the latter in a unique position that would ultimately make them profitable (Benkler 2006; Shirky 2008; Anderson 2009). On the other side of the spectrum, there are those who question the goodness of the Internet and speak of how certain opportunists of the digital world destroyed the music business and, above all, put an end to a just form of paying authors and music performers; Levine (2011) or Lanier (2010) would be paradigmatic examples of this viewpoint.

In addition to these discourses, framed within a purely capitalist analysis in which everything is measured against the economic value of these transformations, we find other, intermediate approaches that evaluate the possibilities of new forms of production and distribution within informal structures, what Hermano Vianna (2003) labelled "Música Paralela/Parallel Music." These structures have fostered the development and commercialisation of genres such as dancehall, rio funk, tecnobrega, huayno pop, cumbia villera or champeta (Yúdice 2012).

With these three approaches in mind, this chapter analyses the influence of radio audiences in the creation of music playlists, evaluating whether we are really facing important changes in music programming or simply facing a cyber-utopian mirage in which the conventional power structures do not allow for a real transformation of the relationship between broadcasters and listeners.

AUDIENCES AND MUSIC PROGRAMMING WITHIN THE NEW PARADIGM

Scholarship and the industry have widely studied the evolution of audiences' behaviour within the media in the last 20 years. It seems clear that a great part of the citizenry has changed the ways it relates with the media. Nonetheless, after a decade and a half of digital utopia, there are more and more discourses that cast doubt over the alleged benefits that these changes have brought to citizens.

Focusing on the field of analysis of this article, it is obvious that listeners search for and find music in different ways, when we compare the present situation with previous eras. If the specialised media previously played the role of fundamental advisers, the de-centralisation and the ability to access a great amount of sound content nowadays has transformed the ways in which music is circulated. In the US, the studies developed by Edison Research observe an annual growth in the listening of online radio and podcasting. In addition, even if AM/FM continues leading the way in which music is discovered by 75%, different services such as YouTube (59%), Pandora (48%) and Facebook (39%) grow steadily. Amongst young people between 12 and 24 years of age, data show how these social networks have grown in relation to conventional radio (65%), YouTube (83%) and Pandora (71%) (Edison Research 2014). In both cases, the non-digital networks—family and friends—occupy the second position amongst advisers. This number has grown within youth cohorts, a fact that may be related to this sector's constant interaction through social networks (Figures 9.1 and 9.2).

The fall in the impact of conventional radio in music prescription is evident. In this respect, several commentators have pointed out the decline of young audiences who listen to the radio (Franquet 2008; Gallego 2010), as well as their emotional distantiation and the reduction of listening time (Martí et al. 2010). Different studies of institutions, such as the European Broadcasting Union (EBU), have also highlighted this decline. In a study on public service and social networks, the EBU pointed to a fall of 27% in youth consumption between 2006 and 2010, which was reflected in the spectacular growth

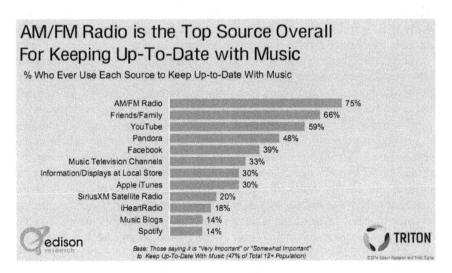

Figure 9.1 Percents who ever used each source to keep up-to-date with music

Source: Edison Research (2014).

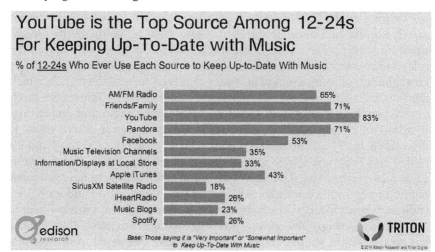

Figure 9.2 Percents of people age 12–24 who ever used each source to keep up-to-date with music

Source: Edison Research (2014).

of Spotify (EBU 2011). In Spain, the group PRISA confirms the remarkable rise of the average age of music radio listeners, linking these data to the lack of migration to conventional radio and the absence of new young listeners within some brands traditionally geared towards adolescents.[2] Finally, the BBC also confirms that their most juvenile-friendly station, BBC Radio 1, has an audience whose average age is 32, and remarks that there has been a drop of 50% in listening time in a decade, more precisely from 10 hours 30 minutes to 6 hours 20 minutes per week (Burrell 2014).

Aside from these new tendencies in music listening, we need to focus on how audiences have changed their behaviour vis-à-vis radio itself. Contemporary audiences create, remix and finance content in different ways, using the radio for social activism and, on some occasions, for intervention in the programming of content (Gallego 2012). The traditional form of intervening in sound consumption implied changing stations, turning off the radio (Macfarland 1997) or choosing to listen to other types of sound vibrations that came from other devices or audiovisual media. Today, listeners combine in their own playlist radio contents originating in different devices. And this is perhaps the most radical way in which they intervene in the programming of consumption. The editorialising of radio shows allows for customised consumption, anywhere and at any time, altering the conventional listening practice that stems from the programming flow. Services and applications such as Spanish Ivoox, German Soundcloud, British Mixcloud and Audioboo and US Stitcher, Swell and Slacker allow for both access to a great amount of content and the creation of an ad hoc playlist for each listener. In some of these services, the configuration of streaming that stems from different podcasts is achieved automatically through the consumption patterns of users or their pre-defined preferences; others, in turn, support a fully customised playlist.

The concept of playlist is increasingly present thanks to services such as Spotify and Deezer. Large online phonoteques allow for accessing a great variety of music content. In this long queue, users define lists with their favourite songs in different contexts. In this way, users become the programmers of the sound flow, with significant impact amongst their peers thanks to the socialisation of content in the digital social networks. Redefining the use of music to build one's identity, the playlists turn into the album cover for users, who, in addition, prefer this type of fragmented consumption of songs rather than long records. As Rossana Reguillo (2012, 139) argues:

> (. . .) today, the documentable consumption of *singles* is giving way to the so-called *playlist*, which, in the Ipod, computer or other means of reproduction, constitute repertoires configured by the subjectivity of the young person, each in whom taste is less related to the idea of a specific (music) identity and much more to taste or mood.

This way of presenting taste and mood has been especially developed through YouTube and its interaction with other networks. Clips are embedded, emerging within the flow of contents of the Facebook wall or timeline. In this way, YouTube is becoming a key element in music training and information, exceeding the limits determined by the mainstream (Reguillo 2012).

If, in the analogue era, the compilation of songs on cassettes was the way to share taste and introduce your favourite bands to friends and family members, digital playlists are linked to the streaming services that facilitate this work. This form of programming, related to the user effort to choose a variety of songs, allows individuals to follow in real time the play queue of friends when it is streaming. Other platforms, such as Last.fm, automatically generate recommendations through a series of connections with other users. In this type of network, the official labelling or *folksonomy* is essential, creating an informative database that breaks apart traditional forms of music prescription (Amaral and Aquino 2009).

And given this dynamic, what kind of decisions are Hertzian stations taking? Aside from the previously discussed concentration of songs, there are very few novelties in terms of their programming. On some of the main Spanish music radio stations, there is an important growth in the programming of non-music content. In fact, most media attempt to preserve young audiences but mostly through non-music content. Moreover, they are also expanding into the audiovisual field. BBC Radio 1 launched an audiovisual channel in the iPlayer (Burrell 2014). In Spain, the most remarkable shows launched last year by two of the most important stations—Los 40 Principales and Europa FM—have started developing cross-media artefacts.[3]

A study written more than five years ago highlighted the lack of innovation within Spanish commercial music radio in its use of the Internet (Amoedo, Martínez-Costa and Moreno 2008). Indeed, if we focus on the issue of audience participation in the design of charts, there are no special novelties. Looking at the UK, it is worth noting the strategy of Absolute Radio on three fronts:

1. Playlist meetings where some audience members are invited to participate in the weekly selection of songs.
2. The section "Influence Our Music" connects listeners with the platform Song People,[4] an online consumers' panel that, according to the station's website, has influence on music programming: "Songpeople is Absolute Radio's panel of listeners that have the power to change what is played. Using Songpeople, we make sure that we play what YOU want" (Absolute Radio 2014).
3. "I Haven't Heard It for Ages"[5] offers listeners a questionnaire to request a song. In this case, each listener is interpellated in the following fashion: "But rather than playing the songs we like (which sounds like a great idea!), we'd like to know which songs YOU want to hear" (Absolute Radio 2014).

In the last two Absolute Radio actions we can see how "YOU" is in uppercase. In reality, if one observes the Absolute Radio playlist (for the week of November 7, 2013), it coincides with 84% of the songs played by its most important private competitor, XFM, even though there are certain variations in the rotation. Besides, 68% of the songs in the playlist belong to three great multinationals (Warner, Sony and Universal) or their subsidiaries. If we add the songs released by Domino Recordings (a transnational independent company), songs belonging to the four of them compose 92% of the list. This reveals how standardisation in private stations is increasing. Beneath the 'participation' discourse, the 'most prominent' are increasing their programming control.

Within the processes of adaptation of Spanish commercial stations, it is worth noting the PRISA purchasing and relaunching of Yes.fm.[6] This service allows different types of customised radio or playlists for free and via subscription. It offers songs from previous playlists and thematic radios, on demand music or non-musical contents (sports, weather and news) created by PRISA's conventional station, Cadena SER.

One of the last private projects is *Jelli Radio*,[7] a service that gathers (since April 2014) twelve US stations under the slogan "100% User Controlled Radio." It allows listeners to intervene in the FM broadcast playlist in real time. Michael Dougherty, the company's CEO, defines the service as follows: "We wanted to make radio more social and more fun. (. . .) We're trying to make something new, a new experience that really shows the audience they're in control" (Gross 2011). In actuality, audience control of Jelli is limited because the company exercises its editorial right over the artists that

Figure 9.3   Jelli 101 FM (Oregon)

Source: Taken on April 16, 2014.

can be voted in and the songs that can be included on a playlist. Listeners, apart from offering both qualitative and quantitative data in real time, can only alter the order of the playlist and automatically get the tune's name on the air waves when they click on a specific song (Figure 9.3).

In terms of public radio, several stations have tried to involve listeners in the creation of playlists. The study *Public Media and New Media Platforms* (EBU 2011) presents diverse case studies of the participation and good use of social networks by several European public radio stations. Among them, it is worth noting *Raitunes* on Italian RAI and *La Tweet-Liste* in the Le Mouv' channel of Radio France. *Raitunes* offers listeners the chance to continuously interact with its Facebook wall, which has a remarkable activity of YouTube videos insertion—between 60 and 100 videos per day on average. These videos allow the station to track down audiences'taste in order to design the playlist. The weekly show *La Tweet-Liste* builds playlists on the basis of listeners' suggestions, and the interactions between the host and the audience in a reformulation of the classic 'listener's request' system.

More recently, in this respect, the launching of the BBC Playlister service[8] in the summer of 2014 is notable. It establishes a new relationship with some of the most important music services—Spotify, Deezer and YouTube. Playlister offers users the possibility of labelling content and creating their own playlists following the DJs' advice and the songs that play in the station. Once the playlist is created, you can choose to listen to it on any of the services mentioned previously, outside the BBC site. In this case, there is no direct participation of the listeners in the programming of public radio. Once again listeners offer quantitative and qualitative data on the broadcast and selected content. In this way, the BBC attempts to benefit from its historical capacity as adviser (Sweney 2013), establishing links to other digital services that are becoming increasingly relevant.

In terms of community media, the development of groups of users within social networks and peer-to-peer services is transforming the ways in which citizens relate to music. Focusing on users' intervention in content that has been historically developed on free and community radio stations, new forms of production and distribution such as podcasting and streaming allow citizens today to programme and distribute music content worldwide. In this way, Net-only radio is the refuge for specific subcultures that question the system with a discourse similar to punk (Baker 2012). The great problem this type of content faces is the capacity to gain visibility in the long queue of sound content given that big media exercise unavoidable control due to their capacity to invest large amounts of money and develop cross-media strategies.

USER-GENERATED PLAYLIST: REALITY OR FICTION?

After the 2000s, a decade of digital effervescence and utopian discourses on the possibilities of technological development, the great world crisis and disaffection with the Internet have brought to the fore critical discourses in relation to the goodness of the digital.

Authors such as David Harvey (2010) have pointed out that instead of free culture, we are increasingly confronted with the mercantilisation of culture and the expansion of copyright laws. In this context, pop music "is notorious for the appropriation and exploitation of grassroots culture and creativity" (Harvey 2010, 245). Online audiovisual consumption and the capacity to select content have also been questioned. Rendueles (2013, 177) remarks: "The capacity to choose has not allowed us to develop and appreciate new aesthetic forms; instead we massively consume what the market offers, identifying this as our own project." For example, quickly browsing the Top 100 streaming services offered by Promusicae in Spain reveals how 90% of the songs played on Spotify, Deezer and XboxMusic are by artists who belong to the three great transnational companies (June 2013 data). Online audiences are tracked down and commercialised thanks to the activities of Internet consumers (Albornoz 2011). In terms of streaming services, this is exemplified by news on how Pandora is attempting to get revenue by selling user profile information on voting intentions, resulting from the crossing of data on user zip codes and preferred musical tastes, to political parties (Dwoskin 2014).

Lastly, Tim Wall (2012, 345) questions the idea that Internet music services "make it easier to control access and to make some or all of the services subject to subscription models" on the grounds that such services "are taking the radio-like experience away from the public status of over-the-air radio."

Taking into consideration these critiques, the reality is that the technological possibilities for audience participation in music programming have not triggered key changes in the way radio broadcasters and music distributors operate. On the basis of the previously mentioned framework to categorise audiences, I draw a series of conclusions on the real transformations that have impacted music programming and services:

1. The *consumer audience* continues to be one of the main sales assets of advertising companies. However, there is increasing sophistication in tracing profiles. In the era of big data, free services capture the audiences' attention. Free labour—from user-generated content to user free work—and audiences' data, which are in turn commercialised, have become increasingly important. 'Likes,' songs added to a 'playlist' or content added to social networks are actions that benefit companies. Consequently, today the key is to create and programme content that allows for both information flows stemming from the audience, as well as data on traditional exposure, search navigation and user response and participation (Napoli 2011).

2. The *customer audience* has turned into an object of desire for paid online music services in which there is access to large music collections. These services have taken a great amount of the money audiences previously invested in phonograms. And, in this case, we can really appreciate a transformation in participation in terms of creating a playlist. This possibility, in some platforms, such as Yes.fm, is available only to customers who pay for these services and can hence share content in different networks or, internally, within specific services.

3. The *citizen audience* has not substantially changed, because public radio services have not significantly modified the forms of participation in the music services they offer. In addition to the asynchronous access to podcast services and content exclusively created for the European public radio networks, the European Union should contribute to boosting this kind of service. The question, then, becomes whether or not it is possible to develop the concept of public service in the music sector with important citizen participation? In actuality, the lack of sustainability of many music projects could trigger this type of state intervention.

4. The *community audience* has undergone a far greater transformation than other kinds of audience, having transferred its participatory logic to the Internet, which has in turn led it to globalise much of its content that previously could only be broadcast using the Hertzian network. Therefore, it now operates through wider circulation networks.

Taking this approach as a point of departure to different audience typologies, the attempt to forecast the development of music radio programming becomes tremendously complex. The feeling that music format radio is about to disappear is given additional weight due to the decline registered both in young audiences as well as in radio's hitherto pivotal role as adviser. The different digital networks and services have come to occupy this position. A fundamentally music medium such as radio needs to re-evaluate its place. From a public perspective, it is imperative to develop policies that strengthen the exposure of new artists and the development of local industry, reflecting new production practices based on do-it-yourself (DIY) practices. In the case of privately owned radio, it seems obvious that the two emergent tendencies are the rise of talk shows and a decrease in the lists' diversity. In both the public and private cases, the absence of strategies to involve audiences seems outstandingly clear. In addition, there is a lack of innovation in a media sector that develops programming strategies following a top-to-bottom logic. This may trigger an upsurge of community media that strengthen the real participation of citizens in defining the music offer. Within the music industry, we have already witnessed projects developed horizontally as well as the appearance of parallel markets that take advantage of different technological possibilities. The radio (on air and online) and music distribution networks (webcasting or access to music collections) may follow this path, reflecting the real diversity of music creation.

NOTES

1. "Our second axiom—increasing standardisation—is bound up with the commodity character of music. There is, first of all, the haunting similarity between most musical programmes, except for the few non-conformist stations which use recorded material of serious music; and also the standardisation of orchestral performance, despite the musical trademark of an individual orchestra. And there is, above all, that whole sphere of music whose life-blood is standardisation: popular music, jazz, be it hot, sweet or hybrid" (Adorno 1996, 232).
2. Fernando Fernández Pablo, head of research at Cadena Ser. Interviews by author, conducted October 1, 2013.
3. The projects *Yu* (Los 40 Principales) and *Un lugar llamado mundo* (Europa FM), broadcast live audiovisual version through different platforms—online and TV.
4. http://www.songpeople.com/absolute-radio-signup.

5. http://www.absoluteradio.co.uk/djs_shows/i_havent_heard_it_for_ages/index.html.
6. http://www.yes.fm.
7. http://radio.jelli.com/.
8. http://www.bbc.co.uk/music/playlister.

REFERENCES

Absolute Radio. (2014). *The No Repeat Guarantee*. Accessed March 25, 2014 http://www.absoluteradio.co.uk/onair/no-repeat-guarantee/.

Adorno, T. W. (1996). "A Social Critique of Radio Music. From The Kenyon Review, spring 1945." *The Kenyon Review*, 18(3–4), 229–235.

AIMC [Asociación para la Investigación de Medios de Comunicación]. (2014). *Estudio general de medios*. Madrid: AIMC.

Albornoz, L. A. (2011). "Redes y servicios digitales. Una nueva agenda político-tecnológica." In Albornoz, L. A. (ed.), *Poder, medios, cultura*. Buenos Aires: Paidos, 221–246.

Anderson, C. (2009). *Free: The Future of a Radical Price*. New York: Harper Collins.

Amaral, A. and Aquino, M. C. (2009). "'Eu recomendo . . . e etiqueto': práticas de folksonomia dos usuarios no Last.fm." *Líbero*, 12(24), 117–130.

Amoedo, A., Martínez-Costa, M. P. and Moreno, E. (2008). "An Analysis of the Communication Strategies of Spanish Commercial Music Networks on the Web: los40.com, los40principales.com, cadena100.es, europafm.es and kissfm.es." *The Radio Journal— International Studies in Broadcast and Audio Media*, 6(1), 5–20.

Ang, I. (1991). *Desperately Seeking Audiences*. London: Routledge.

Attali, J. (1977). *Noise. The Political Economy of Music*. Minneapolis: University of Minnesota Press.

Baker, A. (2012). "Exploring Subcultural Models of a Discursive Youth Net-Radio Hierarchy." *Continuum: Journal of Media & Cultural Studies*, 26(3), 409–421.

Benkler, Y. (2006). *The Wealth of Networks: How Social Production Transforms Markets and Freedom*. New Haven: Yale University Press.

BOE. (2006). *Ley 17/2006, de 5 de junio, de la radio y la televisión de titularidad estatal*. España: Boletín Oficial del Estado. Accessed March 25, 2014. http://www.boe.es/boe/dias/2006/06/06/pdfs/A21207–21218.pdf.

Burrell, I. (2014). "Radio on the TV: Radio 1 Comes to Iplayer for the First Time in 47 Years of Being Audio-Only." *The Independent*, February 21, 2014. Accessed February 21, 2014. http://www.independent.co.uk/news/media/tv-radio/radio-on-the-tv-radio-1-comes-to-iplayer-for-the-first-time-in-47-years-of-being-audioonly-9142251.html.

Dwoskin, E. (2014). "Pandora Thinks It Knows if You Are a Republican." *Wall Street Journal*, February 13, 2014. Accessed April 5, 2014. http://online.wsj.com/news/articles/SB10001424052702304315004579381393567130078.

EBU. (2011). *Public Media and New Media Platforms*. Geneva: European Broadcasting Union.

Edison Research. (2014). *Infinite Dial 2014*. Arbitron & Edison Research. Accessed March 26, 2014. http://www.nzonair.govt.nz/document-library/the-infinite-dial-2014-edison-research/.

Flichy, P. (1980). *Les Industries de l'imaginaire. Pour une analyse économique des média*. Grenoble: PUG.

Franquet, R. (2008). *Radio digital en España: incertidumbres tecnológicas y amenazas al pluralismo*. Madrid: Fundación Alternativas.

Gallego, J. I. (2010). *Podcasting. Nuevos modelos de distribución para los conteni-dos sonoros.* Barcelona: UOC Press.

———. (2011). "Novas formas de prescrição musical." In Herschmann, M. (ed.), *Nas bordas e fora do mainstream musical. Novas tendências da música indepen-dente no início do século XXI.* San Pablo: Estação das Letras e Cores Editora/ FAPERJ, 47–59.

———. (2012). "La audiencia en la radio: viejos roles, nuevas funciones." In Gal-lego, J. I. and García-Leiva, M. T. (eds.), *Sintonizando el futuro: Radio y produc-ción sonora para el siglo XXI.* Madrid: IRTVE, 209–227.

———. (2013). "Radio e musica popolare in rete: distruzioni, trasformazioni e ri-mediazioni." In Bonini, T. (ed.), *La Radio in Italia.* Roma: Carocci, 303–318.

Gross, D. (2011). " 'Rocks' or 'Sucks'? Radio Lets Radio Listeners Play DJ." *CNN. com,* March 1, 2011. Accessed April 15, 2014. www.cnn.com/2011/TECH/web/03/01/jelli.radio/index.html.

Harvey, D. (2010). *The Enigma of Capital and the Crises of Capitalism.* New York: Oxford University Press.

Jacka, E. (2003). "Democracy as Defeat: The Impotence of Arguments for Public Service Broadcasting." *Television & New Media,* 4(2), 177–191.

Karp, H. (2014). "Radio's Answer to Spotify? Less Variety." *Wall Street Journal,* January 16, 2014. Accessed April 4, 2014. http://online.wsj.com/news/articles/SB10001424052702303754404579313150485141672.

Keith, M. C. (1987). *Radio Programming. Consultancy and Formatics.* Boston: Focal Press.

Lanier, J. (2010). *You Are Not a Gadget.* New York: Vintage.

Lee, S. S. (2004). "Predicting Cultural Output Diversity in the Radio Industry, 1989–2002." *Poetics,* 32(3), 325–342.

Levine, R. (2011). *Free Ride: How Digital Parasites Are Destroying the Culture Business, and How the Culture Business Can Fight Back.* New York: Random House.

Martí, J. M., Gutiérrez, M., Ribes, X., Monclús, B. and Martínez, L. (2010). "La cri-sis del consumo radiofónico juvenil en Cataluña." *Quaderns del CAC,* 34, 67–77.

McCauley, M. (2002). "Radio's Digital Future." In Hilmes, M. and Loviglio, J. (eds), *Radio Reader: Essays in the Cultural History of Radio.* New York: Routledge, 505–530.

McChesney, R. W. (2013). *Digital Disconnect: How Capitalism Is Turning the Inter-net Against Democracy.* New York: The New Press.

MacDougald, D. Jr. (1941). "The Popular Music Industry." In Lazarsfeld, P. F. and Stanton, F. N. (eds.), *Radio Research.* New York: Duell, Sloan and Pearce, 65–109.

Macfarland, D. T. (1997). *Future Radio Programming Strategies.* Mahwah: Law-rence Erlbaum Associates.

Napoli, P. M. (2011). *Audience Evolution. New Technologies and the Transforma-tion of Media Audiences.* New York: Columbia University Press.

Negus, K. (1993). "Plugging and Programming: Pop Radio and Record Promotion in Britain and the United States." *Popular Music,* 12(1), 57–68.

Ofcom. (2004). *Radio—Preparing for the Future. Phase 1 Developing a New Frame-work.* London: Ofcom.

Reguillo, R. (2012). "Navegaciones errantes. De músicas, jóvenes y redes: de Face-book a YouTube y viceversa." *Comunicación y Sociedad,* 18, 135–171.

Rendueles, C. (2013). *Sociofobia. El cambio político en la era de la utopía digital.* Madrid: Capitan Swing.

Rothenbuler, E. W. (1987). "Commercial Radio and Popular Music. Processes of Selection and Factors of Influence." In Lull, J. (ed.), *Popular Music and Com-munication.* Newbury Park: Sage, 78–84.

Schramm, H. and Knoll, J. (2012). "Contemporary Music Programming of German Radio Stations. The Impact of Traditional and Interactive Market Research." Paper presented at ECREA International Conference, Istanbul, Turkey, October 24–27.

Shirky, C. (2008). *Here Comes Everybody: The Power of Organizing without Organizations*. New York: Penguin.

Stein-Sacks, S. (2012). "On Quotas as They Are Found in Broadcasting Music." Canadian Radio-Television and Telecommunications Commission, February 9, 2012. Accessed April 16, 2014. http://www.crtc.gc.ca/eng/publications/reports/rp120309c.htm#s5.

Sweney, M. (2013). "Will Playlister Be Enough to Keep Young Music Fans Tuned to BBC?" *The Guardian*, October 10, 2013. Accessed March 20, 2014. http://www.theguardian.com/media/media-blog/2013/oct/10/bbc-playlister-music-service-radio-1.

Vianna, H. (2003). "A música paralela: Tecnobrega consolida uma nova cadeia produtiva, amparada em bailes de periferia, produção de CDs piratas e divulgacáo feita por camelos." *Folha de São Paulo,* October 13, 2003. Accessed April 13, 2014. http://www1.folha.uol.com.br/fsp/mais/fs1210200306.htm.

Wall, T. (2012). "Música popular y radio en el siglo XXI." In Gallego, J. I. and García-Leiva, M. T. (eds.), *Sintonizando el futuro: Radio y producción sonora para el siglo XXI.* Madrid: IRTVE, 329–350.

Wikström, P. (2009). *The Music Industry.* Cambridge: Polity Press.

Williams, R. (1976). *Communications.* London: Penguin Books.

Yúdice, G. (2012). "New Social and Business Models in Latin American Musics." In Sinclair, J. and Pertierra, A. C. (eds.), *Consumer Culture in Latin America.* New York: Palgrave Macmillan, 17–33.

10 Community Radio and Participation
Listeners as Productive Publics

Salvatore Scifo

INTRODUCTION

Active participation by audiences in production processes constitutes one of the distinctive features of community radio practices worldwide, marking its distinction when compared with the majority of practices in place in mainstream public and commercial radio stations. This has also been reflected in academic debates that have remarked on the value of participatory media production processes in the context of the discussion on democratic media systems, and, more generally, in the campaigns that support the concept of communication as human right.

Bruce Girard, a community media scholar and an important contributor in the campaigns that have promoted the idea of communication as a fundamental human right, compiled the anthology of community radio initiatives, *A Passion for Radio*. He argues that community radio is

> A type of radio made to serve people; radio that encourages expression and participation and that values local culture. Its purpose is to give a voice to those without voices, the marginalized groups and to communities far from large urban centres, where the population is too small to attract commercial or large-scale state radio.
>
> (Girard 1992, ix)

The dual role of the community as listener/producer is also emphasised by Frances Berrigan, a community media consultant for the United Nations Educational, Scientific and Cultural Organization (UNESCO) who had edited several reports by the end of the 1970s, including one of the first comparative research studies in the field (Berrigan 1977). In researching the use of community media for development, *Community Communications*, Berrigan describes this sector as:

> (...) intended to be based on more than assumed audience needs and interests. Community media are adaptations of media for use by the community, for whatever the community decides. (. . .) They are media in which

the community participates, as planners, producers, performers. They are the means of expression *of* the community, rather than *for* the community.

(1979, 8, emphasis added)

Berrigan's report can be seen in the wider context of the 1970s, a decade when the gaps and fallacies of mainstream media were widely discussed in UNESCO's forums. During these discussions, representatives of developing countries were critical of the fact that a few global conglomerates located in the West controlled most of the media traffic around the world. Those were discussed in detail in the *MacBride Report* (UNESCO 1980), which, among other things, stressed the importance of participatory and locally originated content in the developmental process as a tool for activating participation in democratic processes and fostering cultural identity.

In the following decade, media activists campaigned for more open, accessible and wide-ranging public service, as well as claiming the right to open their own radio outlets. Legally or illegally, there is no doubt that the total number of radio stations grew exponentially both in the US and in Europe, where, in countries like Italy and France, their number went well over the thousands (see, for example, Dark 2009; Downing et al. 2001; Lefebvre 2008; Lewis 2006; Lewis and Booth 1989; Opel 2004). Downing and colleagues (2001, 188) have remarked that despite the commercialisation of the radio sector that has followed the rise of 'free radio' in Italy and France, the participation of listeners in production processes at least led to the coverage of topics outside the limits of dominant discourses, demonstrating that many citizens wanted access to the media directly or through the activists involved in them, so that they could be "tuned to the public's wavelengths rather than the parties' or the state's or the churches'."

The importance of participation in the media production process, as well as in wider political processes, has been also discussed by the scholar Clemencia Rodriguez (2001, 19) in her conceptualisation of 'citizen media.' Following an exploration of theoretical definitions of the concept of citizenship, which, she suggests, "is not a status granted on the basis of some *essential* characteristic" and has to be enacted "on a day-to-day basis" through participation in everyday political practices, Rodriguez maintains that 'citizen media' implies that a "collectivity is *enacting* its citizenship by actively intervening and transforming the established mediascape" (2001, 20). Two other implications in this model are, first, that "these media are contesting social codes, legitimized identities, and institutionalised social relations" and, second, that "these communication practices are empowering the community involved, to the point where these transformations and changes are possible" (2001, 33–34). Moreover, Rodriguez (2001, 3) reconceptualises how these media can impact on the participants' sense of themselves:

It implies having the opportunity to create one's own images of self and environment; it implies being able to re-codify one's identity with the signs and codes that one chooses, thereby disrupting the traditional acceptance of those imposed by outside sources; it implies becoming one's own storyteller (. . .); it implies reconstructing the self-portrait of one's own community and one's own culture (. . .); it implies taking one's own languages out of their usual hiding place and throwing them out there, into the public sphere and seeing how they do, how they defeat other languages, or how they are defeated by other languages.

In other words, the homogenisation of culture on a global scale, as a result of the action of the private global media corporations, can be balanced by community media that support local cultural production and local heritage and improve social and political participation in those communities, in their own language and on their own terms.

Although this could be realised with any kind of media, community radio has some comparative advantages among other solutions: it is cheap, it is pertinent in terms of language and content, and it reaches those who are illiterate. It is also relevant to local practices, traditions and culture and has a better outreach in terms of geographic coverage in a local area (Gumucio Dagron 2001). But despite all the virtues described by its advocates, academics have drawn attention to the ways that community media in general have to continuously challenge the views of mainstream broadcasters and policymakers who see community radio as parish pumpery, and believe that media production should be limited to professionals in order to achieve the highest quality. This, they argue, has resulted in non-dominant groups being prevented from participating in the process and from circulating their views through the airwaves for a long time.

An early example of this critique comes from Raymond Williams (1980), who describes the structural characteristics of mass media institutions acting as barriers to wider social participation in media practices. These structural characteristics were defined as professionalisation, capitalisation and institutionalisation (Williams 1980). More recently, echoing Williams, James Hamilton in 2001 argued that media should also be "available to ordinary people without the necessity of professional training, without excessive capital outlay and they must take place in settings other than media institutions or similar systems" (quoted in Atton 2002, 25). These issues have been further conceptualised by McQuail (1987, 121) in his *democratic participant media theory,* where he argues that "communication is too important to be left to professionals." He goes on to argue that groups, organisations and local communities should all have their own media (1987, 121–123).

In this view, small-scale, interactive and participative media should exist primarily for their audiences, who would in this way exercise their rights of access to media in order to communicate, and their content should not be subject to centralised political or state bureaucratic control. McQuail envisages the democratic participant as someone who searches for his or her way of social and political action outside of the traditional channels of participation, such as a political party, and he points out the failures of the mass media system in engaging with the communicative needs of citizens, especially in minority groups. He thus suggests locally originated media that use horizontal structures of production: communication should not be left only in the hands of professionals.

So far, then, we can say that conceptualising community radio does not merely involve a consideration of the process of allowing audiences to participate in the production for access, as described by Williams, for their own sake. The access of community groups to the media is seen as important because these small-scale stations, with their local outreach, can be tools that allow these communities to speak for themselves and shape their own identities and discuss issues relevant to them through their own channel of communication.

In the next section, the community radio's constitutive concepts of access and participation will be analysed further to unravel the meaning behind these concepts and its application in the context of community media. This involves moving on from the description of the broad arguments in favour of community radio to an evaluation of the critiques that have been applied to them.

ACCESS AND PARTICIPATION

Even if community stations highlight their democratic characteristics, they then need a kind of structure on which their participants can agree and in which they can believe, for such 'democracy' to work. Fairchild (2001, 93) argues that "democracy in communication is the most amorphous yet omnipresent ideal that defines community radio" and that a radio station can be considered more or less democratic only if it facilitates participation and is reasonably accessible to the local population. Moreover,

> The politics of specifying practical working definitions of these concepts depend entirely upon achieving some measure of equity in the distribution of power between numerous entities including the state, broadcast regulators, dominant media institutions, community media organizations themselves, and various community groups competing for representation and some measure of control.
>
> (Fairchild 2001, 93)

The kind of model envisaged here can be seen, for example, in the stated policy of the British community broadcaster ALL FM in Manchester, a station that was set up to contribute to the social regeneration of south-eastern Manchester's neighbourhoods:

All of the programme ideas at ALL FM are generated by the local residents and groups within the community who make up our volunteer base. The staff supports the volunteers to generate and produce their ideas. We engage in outreach work with various community organisations and networks and offer the opportunity through this for individuals or groups to get involved and make programmes for their community. We train groups to produce their own radio programmes and generate their own content. (. . .)

(ALL FM 2004, 25)

As can be seen, this definition does stress the element of *process*, as opposed to *product*, the output of a community radio station itself. On this matter, Duncombe, for example, in 1997 argued that it is the "position of the work with respect to the relations of production that gives it its power" (cited in Atton 2002, 18) and it is this that might enable social change at a local level. It is also important to remember that radio production is less technically complex than other media, and that creates the possibility of relatively 'inexperienced' individuals producing whole programmes by themselves.

The key internal characteristic of community radio, then, is assumed to be some form of an equitable distribution of power, and beyond that, an equitable distribution of activity, in which it becomes possible for anyone to engage with any level of production or management. However, again, as with broader issues of creating a more democratic public sphere *outside* the station, the creation of a democratic culture *within* the station has been seen as fraught with conceptual, as well as practical, difficulties. Fundamentally, the degree of participation can vary from total ownership to a merely marginal engagement in programming. As Gumucio Dagron (2001, 16) reports, there are in fact very few examples of radio stations that have "been conceived, set up, managed, technically run, financed and maintained by the community." One relatively isolated example cited is a miners' station in Bolivia in the late 1940s (analysed in detail in O'Connor 2004). Furthermore, even if a community radio station has the most inclusive policy on access and participation, there are several concerns that arise in the everyday management of its operations. Hochheimer (1993), for instance, identifies some central concerns on the organisation of the democratic structures of community media management. In practice, where some of them are (or can be) more active, others remain marginalised, and at times there can be emotional, economic and cultural issues that affect collective action. These are time-consuming and can potentially create conflicts inside the station. Moreover,

Community radio stations differ from traditional, mainstream stations not only in their world-view, broadcast policies and content. They also differ in their structure. (. . .) Alternative media which fashion themselves as 'democratic media organizations' bear little resemblance to their more formally structured siblings. Yet they need some structure to maintain themselves.

(Hochheimer 1993, 478–479)

Who gets to speak, hear and mediate are very important issues to be dealt with, or as Fairchild (2001, 98) puts it, what is meant by community radio in a particular community is "the result of the arduous task of political organisation and the endless task of forging alliances within a particular set of social circumstances." Nevertheless, Lewis (1984, 141) argues, the effort is worth it: "Though the workings of such stations are never easy, the structure does offer the possibility of accountability to the audience/user in a way state and commercial stations do not."

In his study, Hochheimer (1993) also refers to stations in very mixed areas. Again, ALL FM offers a good example of this, as it broadcasts to an ethnically mixed area in the south-eastern Manchester boroughs of Ardwick, Longsight and Levenshulme—hence 'ALL.' This is what the station stated in its application for a full-time licence with regard to its accountability towards the served community:

> Any member of the local community can apply to become a volunteer at ALL FM and can choose what roles they wish to undertake. We publicize this regularly on air using a recruitment trailer. Some volunteers choose to work as production staff and some as broadcasting staff. We also have volunteers who help with the general running of the station, such as administration. (. . .) The Steering Group has been constituted to be representative of the local community by following the demographic (Census Information) of the local community in its recruitment policy. (. . .) The main way ALL FM intends to make its service accountable to the community is through the work of the Steering Group which will recruit and maintain a representative body of people to discuss and guide programming policy. (. . .) We hold regular Open Days where the Public can come into the station, meet the presenters and staff and let us know what they think of the service we provide.
>
> (ALL FM 2004, 36–37)

At least in its intention, ALL FM claims to put in place a structure that can potentially accommodate the communicative needs of a (possibly changing) community, where different actors could ask for access. As van Vuuren (2006, 383) points out, "In this scenario, the primary function of a community radio management might be an equitable allocation of airtime, subject to the particular needs and extent of support for the groups in question, as well as some basic principles to which the groups are required to adhere."

Indeed, as Carpentier (2011, 131) has stated in the discussion of his access, interaction and participation (AIP) model, participation is also about "equal(ized) power relations in decision-making processes," including the participation in the content of media production itself, the participation in management and policies of a media organisation and the fact that an organisation that claims to be participative, as ALL FM, does allow the people, here in their role as both listeners and producers, to have a say in the decisions of the station.

As a community radio station should be accountable much more to the community it serves than mainstream broadcasters, careful consideration of its access and participation policies must be made. Due to social and cultural differences, some groups may have problems in coming forward and asking for a slot in the schedule. In this sense, a thorough knowledge of the demographics and social dynamics of the community, eventually supported by a full-time community outreach developer, would be likely to help in involving the more marginalised groups. The schedule should try to reflect the composition of the targeted community, balancing the voices and allocation and, as van Vuuren suggests, an equitable allocation of airtime.

There remains, however, tension between Hochheimer's concerns, Carpentier's AIP model and van Vuuren's findings in the application of the ideals of democracy in a community radio station's everyday practice. In other words, while in principle a station might have the mission to be inclusive, participatory and outreaching, putting these concepts into practice might be difficult and work intensive and require robust governance structures. For a radio station, a claim to speak for any particular community of place, of interest or ethnic group is a strong assertion, and accountability here is key for both the targeted community and relations with media regulators.

ALL FM, MANCHESTER

To discuss the practical implications of the implementation of access and participation policies in a radio station, here the focus will be on the case of the British community radio station ALL FM, based in the south-east Manchester neighbourhood of Levenshulme.

The station was chosen as part of a doctoral research project of the author of this chapter that aimed to research the development of community radio stations in Britain under New Labour between 1997 and 2007. The objective was to provide a case of an urban, multicultural broadcaster that relied extensively on public funding mainly oriented towards social policy objectives as inner-city regeneration, to show the opportunities and challenges of such a model of community radio (see Scifo 2011). The source material for that research included grey literature reviews, observation in the field research and oral history methods in the form of semi-structured in-depth interviews.

ALL FM was originally part of a wider group, Radio Regen, a charity based in Manchester that encouraged the use of radio as a tool for the cultural and social regeneration of the city's most deprived neighbourhoods.

The station began originally with a three-day broadcast as Radio Longsight in May 2000, with subsequent limited broadcasts, through the Restricted Services Licences (RSL) scheme (see Ofcom 2014), that expanded to the neighbouring areas of Ardwick and Levenshulme.

In 2001 the then regulating body for radio broadcasting in Britain, the Radio Authority, released a call for an Access Radio pilot project that would precede the introduction of full-time community radio, and ALL FM applied successfully for such a licence, starting broadcasting on June 5, 2002 (Everitt 2003) and becoming in fact part of the 15 pioneering stations of the forthcoming third sector.

In the evaluation of the pilot project, published in March 2003, Anthony Everitt (2003) cited ALL FM's volunteer Nadia Ali as an example of how community radio could boost self-confidence and personal development. A British Asian woman, her experience as a single parent had been particularly tough as she was then living on benefits, after her separation from her husband. After a radio production training course with Radio Regen, she had become a Project Officer for ALL FM and, with her programme *The Independent Woman*, "instigated strong debates on issues such as forced marriages, which led to the setting up of a community group to address the issue" (Everitt 2003, 109).

During the Access Radio pilot project phase, Ofcom (2004a) also commissioned research to get further information on what listeners were making of the sector, which included stations Forest of Dean Radio, Awaz FM, Angel Radio and ALL FM. Among other findings, listeners of ALL FM seemed to appreciate the diverse music mix offered by the station, and its music programming proposal above all, followed by its usefulness of having a station broadcasting in their language, *from, about, and by* members of the local communities living in the area.

Ofcom's research findings highlighted some of the challenges of a multi-cultural station that tried to reflect the diversity present in its catchment area through a diverse music schedule. With the sense of communities of interest (e.g., based on ethnic groups, age groups or music genre) arguably stronger than the sense of community of place, listeners often tuned in for specialist programmes, but very few of them continuously listened to the station throughout the whole day.

While this meant that a lot of work had to be done to get the message across to large parts of the local community, it was also true that the possibilities of access and the degree of localism and of content diversity that were starting to emerge were surely stronger than in any other local broadcaster, with the *process* of broadcasting assuming increasingly more importance than the *content*.

Following the successful evaluation of the pilot project, the British Parliament introduced Community Radio as the third sector of radio broadcasting through the Community Radio Order 2004 (United Kingdom Parliament 2004), approved on July 19 (later amended in 2010, see United Kingdom

Parliament 2010) and with full-time application forms that were made available by the new media regulator, the Office of Communication (Ofcom) on September 1, 2004 (Ofcom 2004b).

In its application for a full-time licence, ALL FM (2004, 43) described how it aimed to provide more local speech programmes focusing on the "ultra-local content on what is happening in Ardwick, Longsight and Levenshulme," also because "There is very little non-BBC speech content on radio in Manchester" (27), and to do so in both English and foreign languages. However, the station recognised that "While it is not possible to reflect the exact demographic [based on the 2001 census data] of the area in the schedule, this is what we aim for in the makeup of our volunteer body and the programmes we air" (ALL FM 2004, 30). This is also shown by targeting subgroups in the ethnic communities, like Asian women, given that among other radio shows in the area "there are very few programmes which feature women as the main presenter, and which focus on the issues faced by Asian women in the community" (ALL FM 2004, 30). Programmes done *by and for* ethnic minorities with refugee status, especially the increasing number of Somalis, had the aim "to integrate with the community and feel that there is a place for them in the City" (ALL FM 2004, 34). Furthermore, ALL FM remarked that it would also be the only station "where school children are given the opportunity to make radio" (2004, 43).

To comply with statutory requirements of community radio regulation in terms of participatory structures of management, ALL FM planned to establish a steering group to enhance the possibility of the local community to also have a say in programming policies. This was going to be formed by local residents, who would liaise with the station's board of directors and would base its recruitment policy on the demographic representation given by the 2001 census data. Its overall aim would be to

> (. . .) ensure that the representative body for ALL FM has influence over the executive group regarding editorial matters. The Steering group will be comprised of members of ALL FM. As such, these members will have voting rights at the Annual General Meeting for ALL FM and will have a say over the appointment of Directors and other constitutional matters. This group will also be responsible for devising a programme of community consultation events.
>
> (ALL FM 2004, 37)

This body would then help to ensure that, as stated in the intentions of ALL FM in the application, the "service is different from other local radio services in the area as it recruits local people and trains them to make radio. As such, the content of ALL FM's schedule is a true reflection of the community, *made by the community for the community*" (ALL FM 2004, 43, emphasis added).

ALL FM was eventually granted its full-time community radio licence by Ofcom on September 5, 2005, and the regulator's Radio Licensing Committee (RLC) motivated the award by stating:

> This is an experienced group with a proven track record of securing funding. It provides extensive evidence of local support. Its social gain objectives are well thought-through, and its experience in the provision of training is a particular strength of this group. It has sensible plans to develop a steering group as a mechanism for ensuring greater community involvement in the management and operation of the station.
>
> (Ofcom 2005)

The station continued to broadcast with the Access Radio licence until the end of 2005 and started under the new regime on January 1, 2006, further extended after its first five-year term for another five years and until December 31, 2015.

In terms of integration of social media tools into the station's outreach, ALL FM uses its Twitter profile (https://twitter.com/allfm) to provide further information about its upcoming programming, the possibility to listen again to broadcasted shows on MixCloud, as well as lending support to local community and grassroots initiatives. Indie bands and local artists, as well as local community groups, that are given broadcasting space in the station do also often use it for thanking the station for allowing them on air space often unavailable elsewhere and provide Web links for further information to the public. The Facebook page (https://www.facebook.com/ALLFM) is used for similar purposes, as well as for promoting donations and the possibility to advertise to support the station. Some individual shows also use their own Facebook page to communicate more specifically with their base of listeners and give space to new and independent musicians, as *The Unsigned Show* (https://www.facebook.com/allfmunsigned) and *Radio Daisie* (https://www.facebook.com/radiodaisie).

Multiculturalism: Challenges and Opportunities

The UK experience has shown how multicultural radio stations do encounter more difficulties in getting funding, especially from advertising sources, as opposed to stations oriented to a particular ethnic community, as the Everitt report had already demonstrated in the early days of the pilot project. ALL FM's station manager claims that even though 'inclusive' stations like ALL FM aim to facilitate social cohesion and bring different communities together, they are in a very difficult position, which threatens their financial survival and even the prospect of a radio landscape where

> You will end up in a situation where 'ghetto-radio' will work, with single radio for single community and where multicultural ones won't

work on a sustainability issue and I think that's a tragedy, actually, it's a shame. In ALL FM, you can see the benefits in cultural mixing, also simply on an internal basis where volunteers come in from different backgrounds, meet and talk with each other. There is a reason to interact.
(Interview, Alex Green, station manager, September 29, 2006)

Indeed, bringing different cultures together had a beneficial effect on the volunteers presenting at the station: "I have learned so much about many cultures in doing this job. . . . We live in a multicultural society and these are the issues we need to deal with" (interview, Gavin White, administrator, September 29, 2006). "ALL FM brings us together and helps to embrace other cultures, that's how we develop an understanding about each other and become more tolerant" (interview, Stevie Fly, presenter, *Caribbean Connections*, September 30, 2006).

It could be argued that these members of ALL FM might have had a positive attitude towards multiculturalism *prior* to the participation at the stations, given that they did not say that they had been *changed* by their participation. However, they underlined the process of *learning* about other cultures and being part of a platform that facilitated such processes. Green likewise reported changes of attitude that had taken place because of the involvement in the station: "I have seen people with racist views changing their opinion while getting involved with the station. You put them with the people to whom they object and then you can put them in a room and get them to talk to each other. You can have transformations" (interview, Green 2006).

Earlier in this chapter, issues around democratic management processes (Hochheimer 1993) and risk of enclosure of the local public sphere (van Vuuren 2006) were discussed, highlighting how uphill is the task of making abstract concepts work in practice. While these issues are continuously negotiated by more homogeneous community broadcasters, with stations like ALL FM, these tensions may tend to go even higher.

While Green recalls that "it is great to facilitate a sense of community ownership that people feel is accessible, is responsible and responsive to them, so if they want to get involved they can" (interview, Green 2006), in some cases the main drive was the editorial control. Among the shows, ALL FM broadcast one produced by members of a Muslim literary association, which had as its main objective the promotion of Muslim literature and greater education in the Muslim community. No problems occurred until they reached the point where they wanted to exercise more control over other shows, until a meeting where they demanded full control of all the Asian content in the station. This was demanded on the grounds that the management of the station allegedly did not understand the languages and their culture well enough. The group claimed that since they understood these languages far better, they should be in charge of the Hindu and Sikh programmes (the Indians' broadcast output), even though they were a

Pakistani group of Muslims. At that meeting, the management made it clear that it was not its job, nor that of the group, to dictate what could or could not be broadcast. Green maintains, "I don't have editorial control over the station. If something is wrong on air I will stop it, I will do it in those terms, but I don't drive content and this is the whole point. This is a platform, it is not anyone's editorial path" (interview, 2006).

ALL FM activities happened to receive media attention for its positive contribution to the dialogue between the Muslim community and the larger community in the area, with the programme *Knowledge Is Power: The Islamic Hour,* reviewed three times in 2005, in *The Guardian's Society* supplement (Benjamin 2005a, 2005b) and *The Independent's Media Weekly* (Byrne 2005).

National Health Service women's health development worker and radio presenter Faiza Chaudri explained that the programme had been created because of her personal interest as a young British Muslim woman: "There were a lot of things I didn't know about being Muslim and I had no one to ask. My parents are [from] a different generation and from Pakistan, whereas I was born here. The imams often don't speak English, and anyway I don't go to the mosque—it's for men" (in Benjamin 2005a). She also stated how listeners who contacted her were not only Muslims, as "lots live in Muslim areas and want to know more about their neighbours" (in Benjamin 2005a), receiving "positive responses because we've made it so straightforward that people can understand what our religion is all about" (in Byrne 2005).

Chaudri believes that the programme can also help, on the one hand, to stimulate discussions and get answers to topics that are not discussed openly in her religious group, such as marriage and domestic violence, as well as, on the other hand, to combat a negative depiction of Islam in the media: "The media has got a big role to play in the perceptions people have about Muslims. It's really easy to give a negative image of the Muslims, which sells papers. They need to combat that by giving positive responses. The Muslim community do feel let down by the media" (in Byrne 2005).

ALL FM also had the merit of demystifying access to broadcasting: "It's not something I would have gone into, but ALL FM has equipped me with the skills to open my wings. I just thought the media was really negative," said Chaudri (in Byrne 2005). Moreover, the aural nature of radio makes the conditions of such dialogue easier, as "I can go on air and talk about anything and people don't know whether I'm wearing a headscarf or what colour I am" (in Byrne 2005). What emerges here is the fact that the aural nature of radio helped some of the presenters to go on air with a greater confidence because it allowed them to be judged for what they *said*, rather than for how they *looked*. This would have helped to bring forward perspective, to counterbalance negative depictions in the media and to provide new angles from which to tackle current issues in their community.

Alternative Journalism

> Whereas the mainstream has a tendency to privilege the powerful, alternative media set out to privilege the powerless and the marginal: to offer a perspective "from below" and to say the "unspoken". Alternative and mainstream media not only use different casts of sources, they tend to have a different relationship *between* producers and sources, with alternative media sometimes blurring the lines between the two.
>
> (Harcup 2003, 371)

ALL FM's schedule included what its presenters described as 'Manchester's alternative/radical show,' *Under the Pavement: Anarchy on the Airwaves*. Presented by two 'vegan anarchists,' known to the public by the names David and Spike, the shows included 'alternative/leftfield eclectic playlist covering indie, punk, folk, experimental, hip hop, electronic and pop,' news from the Indymedia Network and 'reports on direct action and grass roots resistance in the Manchester area' (Under the Pavement 2014). The show was originally broadcast on Monday evenings and, echoing similar critiques that have circulated in scholarly circles, the station's manager Alex Green commented that at that hour, the programme was basically "preaching to the converted", those "who listened to it were activists, there was no one who wasn't" (interview, 2006).

Indeed, looking at the programme's website, enthusiastic feedback from the audience included a radical media blog, a punk performance poet and hosts of vegan radio shows from the USA. Arguably, to a critical eye, it would have been more interesting to know *who else* had been listening to the show apart from people who would be expected to listen. In other words, "One would imagine that they [alternative media producers] above all would be passionately concerned with how their own media products were being received and used" (Downing 2003, 625–626).

The station management felt that the timeslot did not involve a larger listening group, and as Green said:

> Because we felt that if it's going to be an activists' show, they have to talk with people who are not engaged in their issues, who don't understand those issues. In [the] daytime, they wouldn't broadcast only to their own community, but to everybody else, being provocative, and we thought 'Let's give it a go.'
>
> (Interview, 2006)

With the BBC's standards of 'impartial' journalistic values also permeating ALL FM, Green saw "balanced reporting" as one of the challenges of *Under the Pavement*:

> The most difficult thing with that show is that, if you take a group of activists and you get them to do a radio show about issues that are

highly political, or they feel really passionate about, then it is very hard to be balanced. They are struggling really hard to be journalists, they think that if they try to be balanced or question the activists, they are endorsing the point of view of the government, the opposing viewpoint.

(Interview, 2006)

Green recalled one episode of the programme covering a campaign against a company based near Brighton that allegedly was an arms manufacturer. Locally, activist groups had organised a campaign aiming to close the factory down, using tools like roadblocks and switchboard campaigns. The arguments against this company were highly emotive and the allegation was that the company was producing bombs, and that these bombs were dropped in Lebanon in strikes conducted by Israel earlier that year (2006), resulting in the killing of innocent people. The presenters interviewed the leader of this campaign, asking him about it, and he went on talking almost uninterrupted for half an hour, without the presenters challenging his views once, or asking for factual details: "They just gave him a half-hour platform to put [across] that viewpoint and then,'Nice one mate! That is fantastic, smash those bastards,' whatever . . ." (interview, Green 2006). At the time, a producer in the BBC's Religion and Ethics Department, Manchester-based Vanessa Baldwin, had been seconded for a few hours a week to ALL FM, where she was listening to programmes and providing informal feedback.

She happened to listen to the show and spoke to the management of the risks of being sued for libel if the claims were not substantiated by evidence. Indeed, Green did some background research on the company and found out that it did not make bombs but rather that it made the equipment used in planes to hold bombs. Even though the difference might seem subtle to an activist eye, there was a factual distinction, and as Green commented, "the whole emotive charge of their campaign was wrong" (interview, 2006). At a subsequent meeting with the station management, the presenters did not immediately understand what was wrong with the show, even though they admitted they had not done much background research about the company. In fact, they had been given a platform to campaign, on the basis of incorrect information.

While on participation, ALL FM has proven to be very inclusive and proactive in trying to achieve this objective, its degree of *radicalness* has a certain number of limitations that are embedded in a station with a broadcast licence, when compared with an Internet-only station. As Green underlines: "I think this is one of the difficulties of doing radical radio. You know, we could lose our licence or get a fine that will close the station down. Probably one Ofcom fine will sink us and that is why we have to be very careful" (inerview, 2006). Such concerns were also echoed in the area of participatory journalism research applied to online media:

. . . A conversation is not 1,000 people shouting at once. Good conversation is two-way, among a few people. If viewers are allowed to post anything they want on the message board I host, it invites all sorts of dangers, not the least of which is a defamation lawsuit.

(Lasica, quoted from 2003 by Lievrouw 2011, 110)

On the presenters' journalism practices, Green added: "We want them to be journalists, but they find it very hard to challenge the McDonalds campaigners, they find it hard [to find] flaws in their argument . . . but an activist Internet radio station is going to be listened [to] only by activists!" (interview, 2006). A similar example was discussed by Atton and Hamilton (2008), referring to the case of a video report by arms control activists for the Web-based alternative media outlet Undercurrents. They questioned whether such examples threatened standards of journalism and argued that perhaps this was "the wrong question to ask" (2008, 88). They stated that the primary aim of such a report was to mobilise public opinion and that "the presence of explicit mobilizing information is an enduring characteristic of alternative media, the aim of which is to suggest possibilities for social action to audiences" (2008, 88). In other words, "the primary audience for such work, it was assumed [by the presenters], would be the activist community itself" (Atton and Hamilton 2008, 89). The way *Under the Pavement* reported itself seems to indeed suggest that the primary public was to report "direct action and grass roots resistance" to like-minded activists, rather than trying to extend the awareness of counter-hegemonic practices to a larger number of people in the area. As Downing (2003, 633) has noted:

We need to admit in all frankness that there have been only too many examples of people . . . who started alternative media ostensibly to allow 'other voices' but actually only to express their own, and where the term 'dialogic' has definitely been honoured far more in the breach than in its observance.

In fact, when interviewing one of the presenters of the programme, David, 'dialogue' did not seem to be at the top of their priorities, where the aim of the programme was talking to "people taking action on issues," trying to "get things across that you would usually not hear on mainstream radio that are relevant to our communities" (interview, David, presenter, *Under the Pavement,* September 27, 2006) and linking global with local issues. The week before my visit, there had been the annual UK-wide Labour Party conference in Manchester, and the programme had reported on the initiatives of the *Stop the War* coalition and the Campaign for Nuclear Disarmament. The emphasis was again to "cover things not covered by mainstream radio and give space to people more involved in direct action" (interview, David 2006). The approach that privileges covering, in principle, *only* what is not covered by mainstream radio makes one think that this corresponds to what Downing (2003, 627) described: "Just because people think their voice is not represented does not mean they are interested in other voices than their own."

It is useful, in this context, to point again to van Vuuren's discussion of the struggle inherent in the production of knowledge and the representation of the community. The example discussed in this section illustrates that "far from being an open-access sphere . . ., a community public sphere is a more or less bounded domain," where the access is in fact determined by "cultural orientations, norms and values" (van Vuuren 2006, 389).

> We don't see ourselves as a radical station. We don't see ourselves as how Indymedia views a radical station. We think we are radical in the way we do our work. If you have that diversity of voices, then you should achieve some degree of democracy, representation and integration.
>
> (Interview, Green 2006)

What I have tried to reveal here is how ALL FM takes the issue of representation and participation very seriously, by giving space to 'alternative' and 'radical' voices within the community and actually making a further effort to make such voices reach a larger public, among its listeners. It also reveals the challenges of doing 'partisan' broadcasting when reporting about events, and the importance of accuracy in the world of licensed broadcasting, when compared with the alternative media content available via the Internet. The station actually needs to be accurate because false allegations could risk putting it in danger, where it could receive an irreparable blow to its finance or lose its licence altogether. It is also interesting to see how it challenges notions of 'radical' and 'alternative' by highlighting the limits of such approaches to the use of radio, by local activists. ALL FM is sincerely committed to including a plurality of voices and viewpoints, by providing a platform where the local community has the 'radical' option (possibly unlike other broadcasters in the area) to get their voices heard in programmes done *by* them and *for* them.

CONCLUSIONS

In this chapter, we have seen how a variety of different approaches, both at the theoretical and at the empirical level, have contributed to different articulations of community radio, including the importance of a high degree of participation of the targeted community in its management, programming and ownership.

Besides democracy, access and participation, the 'need' for a distinct third sector has been claimed, in order to ensure a media outlet for a local community, to create a tool that puts at the centre of its mission the aim of promoting and preserving local identity and local cultures and to act as a forum to discuss local issues in a two-way mode of communication.

As argued throughout this chapter, the concept of access and participation, when applied to community radio, brings with it a number of problems and tensions. Organising democratic models of community media, as Hochheimer (1993) and van Vuuren (2006) demonstrate, can be problematic when dealing with claims of being representative and speaking on behalf of a whole community of place or of interest.

Overall, despite all the structural challenges, ALL FM is still broadcasting after more than ten years. The station has proven to be resilient and adaptive in challenging funding circumstances, giving voice to hundreds of listeners based in their transmission area. Across the country, New Labour governments that ruled Britain between 1997 and 2010 failed to provide solid financial foundations for the sector, but it could be said that a 'quiet revolution' has been taking place in local broadcasting across the UK.

British media scholar Nick Couldry (2010, vi) has argued that "voice as process—giving an account of oneself and what affects one's life—is an irreducible part of what it means to be human." In this chapter, I hope to have demonstrated how community radio, despite its limitations, and far from being a perfect model, has begun to offer a tool for self-expression, for making the use of one's voice meaningful and for encouraging local communities to take the important step in transgressing the barrier that separates listening from producing.

REFERENCES

ALL FM. (2004). *Community Radio License Application Form*. Accessed January 24, 2005. http://www.ofcom.org.uk/radio/ifi/rbl/commun_radio/tlproc/archives/applications/England/NorthWest/allfm.pdf.
Atton, C. (2002). *Alternative Media*. London: Sage.
Atton, C. and Hamilton, J. (2008). *Alternative Journalism*. London: Sage
Benjamin, A. (2005a). "Faiza Chaudri." *The Guardian*, October 5, 2005. Accessed February 24, 2014. http://www.theguardian.com/society/2005/oct/05/guardian societysupplement3.
———. (2005b). "Hour of Need." *The Guardian*, December 7, 2005. Accessed February 24, 2014. http://www.theguardian.com/society/2005/dec/07/guardians ocietysupplement.
Berrigan, F. (1977). *Access: Some Western Models of Community Media*. Paris: UNESCO.
———. (1979). *Community Communications: The Role of Community in Media Development*. Paris: UNESCO.
Byrne, C. (2005). "Heard the One about the Mickey Mouse Hijab?" *Media Weekly— The Independent*, October17, 2005. http://www.independent.co.uk/news/media/heard-the-one-about-the-mickey-mouse-hijab-320202.html.
Carpentier, N. (2011). *Media and Participation. A Site of Ideological-Democratic Struggle*. Bristol: Intellect.
Couldry, N. (2010). *Why Voice Matters. Culture and Politics after Neoliberalism*. London: Sage.
Dark, S. (2009). *Libere! L'epopea delle radio italiane degli anni '70*. Viterbo: Stampa Alternativa.

Downing, J.D.H. (2003). "Audience and Readers of Alternative Media: The Absent Lure of the Virtually Unknown." *Media, Culture & Society*, 25, 625–645.

Downing, J.D.H., Villarreal, T., Gil, G. and Stein, L. (2001). *Radical Media: Rebellious Communication and Social Movements*. London: Sage.

Everitt, A. (2003). *New Voices. An Evaluation of 15 Access Radio Projects*. London: Radio Authority.

Fairchild, C. (2001). *Community Radio and Public Culture: Being an Examination of Media Access and Equity in the Nations of North America*. Cresskill: Hampton Press.

Girard, B. (1992). *A Passion for Radio. Radio, Waves and Community*. Montreal: Black Rose Books.

Gumucio Dagron, A. (2001). *Making Waves: Stories of Participatory Communication for Social Change*. New York: Rockefeller Foundation.

Harcup, T. (2003). " 'The Unspoken—Said': The Journalism of Alternative Media." *Journalism*, 4(3), 356–376.

Hochheimer, J. L. (1993). "Organizing Democratic Radio: Issues in Praxis." *Media, Culture & Society*, 15, 473–486.

Lefebvre, T. (2008). *La bataille des Radios Libres.1977–1981*. Paris: Nouveau Monde.

Lewis, P. M. (1984). "Community Radio: The Montreal Conference and After." *Media, Culture, & Society*, 6, 137–150.

———. (2006). "Community Media: Giving a 'Voice to the Voiceless.' " In Lewis, P. M. and Jones, S. (eds.), *From the Margins to the Cutting Edge. Community Media and Empowerment*. Cresskill: Hampton Press, 13–39.

Lewis, P. M. and Booth, J. (1989). *The Invisible Medium: Public, Commercial and Community Radio*. Basingstoke: Macmillan Education.

Lievrouw, L. A. (2011). *Alternative and Activist New Media*. Cambridge: Polity Press.

McQuail, D. (1987). *Mass Communication Theory: An Introduction*, 2nd edn. London: Sage.

O'Connor, A. (ed.). (2004). *Community Radio in Bolivia: The Miners' Radio Stations*. Lewiston, New York, Lampeter: Edwin Mellen Press.

Ofcom. (2004a). *Ofcom. Community Radio Final Report*. London: Ofcom/Research Works Limited.

———. (2004b). *Community Radio Licence Application Form*. London: Ofcom.

———. (2005). *Ten Community Radio Licence Awards: September 2005*. Accessed January 10, 2014. http://licensing.ofcom.org.uk/radio-broadcast-licensing/community-radio/current-licensees/awards-05–06/communr210905/.

———. (2014). *Radio Restricted Service Licences*. Accessed January 10, 2014. http://licensing.ofcom.org.uk/radio-broadcast-licensing/restricted-service-licences/.

Opel, A. (2004). *Micro Radio and the FCC: Media Activism and the Struggle over Broadcast Policy*. Westport, London: Praeger.

Rodriguez, C. (2001). *Fissures in the Mediascape: An International Study of Citizens' Media*. Cresskill: Hampton Press.

Scifo, S. (2011). *The Origins and Development of Community Radio in Britain under New Labour (1997–2007)*. Ph.D. thesis. London: University of Westminster.

Under the Pavement. (2014). *Under the Pavement, Anarchy on the Airwaves*. Accessed January 12, 2014. http://www.underthepavement.org/ Accessed January 12, 2014.

UNESCO. (1980). *Many Voices, One World. Towards a New, More Just and More Efficient World Information and Communication Order*. Paris: UNESCO.

United Kingdom Parliament. (2004). *The Community Radio Order 2004* (Statutory Instrument Number 1944, 19 July 2004). London: HMSO.

———. (2010). *The Community Radio (Amendment) Order 2010* (Statutory Instrument Number 118, 21 January 2010). London: HMSO.

van Vuuren, K. (2006). "The Enclosure of the Community Public Sphere." *Media, Culture & Society*, 28(3), 379–392.

Williams, R. (1980). *Problems in Materialism and Culture: Selected Essays*. London: Verso.

Interviews

David, presenter, *Under the Pavement,* September 27, 2006.

Stevie Fly, presenter, *Carribean Connections*, September 30, 2006.

Alex Green, Station Manager, September 29, 2006.

Gavin White, Administrator, September 29, 2006.

11 Radio Wnet

From Mainstream to Grassroots: A Case Study of Productive Listeners

Grażyna Stachyra

INTRODUCTION

This article is a case study of Radio Wnet, a radio station turned social network and citizen consortium as well as a site of diverse social and media-related initiatives. A case study of Radio Wnet, which is a combination of broadcast radio and an Internet portal, would be incomplete without an outline of the specific factors influencing or enabling its creation. These include technological factors (such as the availability of broadcasting via the Internet) as well as the economic and political ones resulting from the transformation of the media market in Poland over the last two decades.

The first part of this text outlines the media landscape in Poland and introduces research showing a fall in the level of public trust the Polish media enjoy. The second part discusses the origin of Radio Wnet, along with its legal and organisational structure and its ideological profile. This is followed by an analysis of the functioning and contents of the radio's channels. The theoretical framework for the analysis utilises the notions of access–interaction–participation (Carpentier, 2011), 'produser' (Bruns, 2008), 'prosumer' and 'conducer' (Ritzer and Jurgenson, 2010), all of which are applied here in the context of the production and consumption of media. The chapter then discusses the notion of community in the context of the social group revolving around Radio Wnet and the social actions this group undertakes, to conclude with a summary of the challenges faced by the station in the near future.

THE CONTEMPORARY MEDIA MARKET IN POLAND

The media market in Poland is relatively young, having emerged in the early 1990s, when political and economic transformations led to the end of state monopoly on media ownership, the abolition of censorship and the introduction of the freedom of economic activity. These factors were decisive in the shaping of the media landscape in post-Communist Poland, which is typified by a shift from centralised towards decentralised communications. The watershed moment was the passing of the Broadcasting Act by the Polish parliament and the subsequent establishment of the National Broadcasting Council (KRRiTV—Krajowa Rada Radiofonii i Telewizji) as the regulator of broadcast media tasked with allocating broadcasting frequencies and granting radio and television broadcasting licences (Jędrzejewski 2003). No such regulator was established for the press market; this resulted in the privatisation of newly created titles, while regional ones were almost entirely taken over by multinational media corporations.

The daily newspaper market is dominated by the 'big four': Axel Springer Poland (with a 20.4% market share), Agora SA (18.3%), Polskapresse Publishing Group (18.05%, corresponding to the largest publisher of local press) and Orkla/Media Regionalne (13.6%). The combined sales of daily titles published by these four corporations are estimated at 75% of the total daily circulation. The magazine market is an oligopoly, with Bauer Publishing Poland taking up about 50% of market share, while the combined market share of the next three largest publishing houses, Axel Springer, Gruner & Jahr and Edipresse, is about 5–8%. Notably, most of these media conglomerates are multinational media corporations, with significant German ownership (Godzic 2010).

The radio and television markets have undergone a slightly different process. In the nationwide free to air (FTA) market, the two public (state-owned) television channels, TVP1 and TVP2, were joined by two other Polish broadcasters, Polsat and TVN, both of which obtained nationwide broadcast licences. As these two grew, numerous local TV stations ceased broadcasting and closed down. Twenty years since the first commercial TV stations started operations, the television market is dominated by the four largest broadcasters: TVP1, TVP2, Polsat and TVN; their joint market share in the first quarter of 2013 was over 51.3%, having dropped by 7.2 percentage points since 2012. The market share held by thematic TV channels belonging to these four broadcasters is about 20%; other, smaller broadcasters have a combined market share of 30%, although their individual share is estimated at less than 1% each (KRRiTV 2013a).

Similarly, in the radio market, four public stations were joined by two commercial ones, RMF FM and Radio Zet. These two radio stations are now the two most popular in Poland, with an audience share of 22.12% and 16.08%, respectively, according to quarterly reports of a Radio Track survey for the period between December 2013 and February 2014 (Millward Brown SMG/KRC 2014). They quickly became part of larger media groups, as RMF FM was taken over by Bauer Media, and Radio Zet (along with several other station networks) became the property of Eurozet. Local radio stations, initially numerous (there were around 160 in 1993), have been absorbed by larger networks (Agora, which took over 13 stations in 2013; Time Radio Group, and others). As a result, their programming has largely been made uniform and stripped of local flavour (with the exception of local or traffic news and weather). Thus, among licensed local broadcasters with a combined audience share of over 28%, truly local broadcasters constitute as little as 10% (KRRiTV 2013b), and their combined audience share across the country is lower than 3%.

Neither Polish legislation nor European Union regulations offer specific solutions to counteract the concentration of media ownership. Article 11 of the Charter of Fundamental Rights states that "the freedom and pluralism of the media shall be respected" (Charter of Fundamental Rights 2000, 11), but this proclaimed 'respect' is not tantamount to a guarantee or an assurance. Attempts to adopt an EU directive aiming to prevent the concentration of media ownership have not been successful yet. While this chapter was being written, the European Initiative for Media Pluralism found itself still gathering signatures to call for such an EU directive.[1] After over twenty years, the Polish TV and radio markets have arguably been recentralised, with respect to both capital and content, as local (in terms of capital) media have been replaced by multinational media corporations. Formally, the plurality of opinion and freedom of expression are not threatened; however, many viewers or listeners feel deprived of their voice in the media. Social media have, thus far, not stepped in to fill this vacuum; paradoxically, religious broadcasters—Radio Maryja and TV Trwam—are attempting to fulfil such a role to some degree, often being criticised for their one-sided view.

As a result, research shows that Poland has some of the lowest levels of trust in the media in Europe, with Poles also being the most distrustful of political parties, newspapers, both houses of parliament, the government, television, courts of law and civil servants. According to the report titled *Zaufanie społeczne* [Public Trust] by the Public Opinion Research Centre, a major Polish opinion polling body, trust in the media has been falling over the last few years; this concerns both television and the press (CBOS 2012). Although trust in radio was not surveyed, it seems unlikely that it would be exempt from this trend. A similar survey in 15 European countries showed that Poles display significantly less trust in the traditional media than the respondents from other countries (European Trusted Brands 2012). As few as 37% of Poles trust radio and television, compared with every second respondent on average in the other countries. The level of trust in these media is particularly high in Sweden (82%) and Finland (70%). Poles also exhibit low levels of trust in the press (38%), although this does not significantly diverge from the European average of 40%. The Internet enjoys exceptionally high levels of trust in Poland, with 56% of Poles trusting information from online sources, against the European average of 45%. It thus seems justified to state that the way to (re)gain public trust in the media is through the Internet, the strategy adopted by the journalists who founded Radio Wnet. It is in fact a social network built around and functioning through radio and a Web platform.

RADIO WNET—A RESPONSE TO PUBLIC MEDIA: FOUNDATION

"Who was dissatisfied with old media?" ask Lister and colleagues (2009, 66); they follow this question with:"what were the problems to which new communications media are the solutions?" Their explanation is twofold: "First, the socio-psychological workings of the *technological imaginary*; second, earlier 20th century traditions of media critique aimed at the *mass* broadcast media and their perceived social effects" (2009, 66). It is difficult to establish whether the origin of Radio Wnet lay in a sense of disappointment with the traditional media or resulted from the specific political and economic conditions of the time. Both of these factors appear to have been relevant, although the political context of the Polish media directly affected the course of events.

In early 2009 Krzysztof Skowroński was dismissed as director of Polish Radio's Program, a position he had held since 2006; the reason cited was financial irregularities.[2] An early contributor to Radio Zet, the first nationwide commercial radio station in Poland, Skowroński went on to work with the state-owned television broadcaster TVP1 and with Polsat, the largest commercial television broadcaster in the country. Over some twenty years of his career, he had built up a reputation as an independent journalist, and in 2011 was elected head of the Polish Journalists Association. Some journalists believed his dismissal was politically motivated (he was appointed director of Program III before a government change, although he never publicly stated his political preferences), all the more so because the radio station increased its audience share during his time as director, and most of its employees expressed their support for Skowroński.[3] A letter protesting his dismissal was signed by almost one hundred opinion journalists representing various political views; artists, scientists and—online—thousands of listeners; this, however, had no impact on management's decision. Several other journalists quit Program III as a gesture of solidarity. Several months later Skowroński announced the establishment of a new entity, Radio Wnet. He was joined by several well-known journalists, among them longtime contributors to Program III, such as Grzegorz Wasowski and Jerzy Kordowicz, as well as Jerzy Jachowicz, a pioneer of investigative press journalism in Poland.

This was the first spectacular case in Poland of mainstream journalists transferring to what was in fact a social medium. The founders of Radio Wnet intended it to be an attempt to build "a truly public & truly social medium," free from political interference but deeply interested in public matters. The mission of the radio was to "increase the level of freedom in the Polish media" (Stachyra 2012, 407).

The democratic deficit in the media and the credibility and responsibility of the media have been much debated, both by journalists and media and communication scholars (Dróżdż 2012; Groenhart 2012; Hamerlink and Nordenstreng 2007; McQuail 2003; Rossi and Meier 2012, to name but a few). The issue of "who has, and should have, access to and control over mediated public debate" (Livingstone and Lund 1994, 4), posed as early as twenty years ago, still remains topical.

Critics of postmodern societies point out that as large holdings or corporate groups, often active in the media market, grow in importance, and as their connections with the political system become stronger, public life is dominated by the rules of the market; at the same time, however, the market is becoming politicised through its strong connections with the political establishment. Therefore, on the one hand, this mass quality of the media has led to a widening of the public sphere; on the other, however, this public sphere has evolved by becoming more commercialised and by excluding from the mainstream those views which are inconvenient to the leading political and economic powers. Arguably, although the public sphere has become a sort of "a platform for advertising" (Habermas 1991, 181), where products and ideas are being marketed, not everyone can afford to advertise. Civic activity in the media appears an attempt to regain some of that sphere, and an opportunity to do so is afforded by the new technologies, in particular the growth of the Internet as a broadcasting platform, exempt from the legal regulations binding other media.

Although the plurality of opinions and freedom of speech have been protected by legal regulations in Poland since 1989, many citizens, including journalists, believe the media system not to be fully free and democratic. The clinical example is article 212 of the Polish Penalty Code, about defamation. According to the Helsinki Foundation for Human Rights, which appealed unsuccessfully to the Ministry of Justice and the president of Poland to remove the article from the legal system in 2012, this regulation is more often being used against both journalists and ordinary citizens who comment on current affairs, write blogs or even call petitions to administrative or judiciary authorities.[4] In response to the previously described crisis of trust in the mainstream media, a number of grassroots initiatives have developed, creating an 'alternative circulation' of ideas, beliefs and opinions underrepresented in the traditional media.

Radio Wnet is an important exponent of this phenomenon, informing the debate on how the media can help citizens learn about the world and participate in debate and how to make decisions based on various sources of information (Dahlgren 1997). The radio station's founders intended it to be a truly public and social medium, free from political interference but strongly interested in issues important to the wider community. Commercial stations, some of which expressed at their inceptions a wish to shape public debate (an example being Radio Zet, co-created by Skowroński), in time abandoned this intention and, with the exception of very few individual programmes, almost entirely focused on entertainment. Public radio (as well as television), on the other hand, has often been denounced as heavily politicised (Godzic 2010), and as such unwilling to bring into the debate contents inconvenient to those in power. Therefore, Radio Wnet defined its mission as "acting to extend freedom in the Polish media" (Radio Wnet website n.d.).

It is important to note that while Wnet is a radio station in both spirit and name, it functions mainly online; thus, the technological aspect was crucial for its broadcasting structure. What is exceptional, at least in the Polish context, is that the construction of a social medium and a social network began with the idea of radio. Kate Lacey comments on the crucial role of the practice of listening as an element constituting the public sphere, expressing the view that "the auditorium is offered as a convenient metaphor for the public sphere, the space in which the political is literally sounded out" (Lacey 2013, 159). Radio Wnet explicitly refers to the public sphere in calling itself on its website "a truly public medium" (Radio Wnet website n.d.); at the same time, it stresses its distance from the public—in name—media or the state-owned broadcasters, which, in the opinion of the station's founders, have failed to fulfil their statutory role. Thus, Radio Wnet positions itself as the on-air voice of "the forgotten man in the street" (Loviglio 2002, 94), thereby, in a peculiar way, attempting to fulfil the mission radio used to follow in its heyday.

ACCESS, INTERACTION, PARTICIPATION AND . . . HIERARCHY?

"For the People and by the People"

Since its foundation in the autumn of 2009, Radio Wnet has evolved from a small group of experienced radio, television and press journalists to a more complex, multilevel organisational structure, with important elements of interaction and participation. These two notions are not always strictly demarcated; Nico Carpentier (2011) analyses them with reference to four criteria, 'technology, content, people and organisation,' viewed from the angle of production and reception. Here, participation is always understood as co-deciding at each of the four previously mentioned levels (Carpentier 2011). Radio Wnet can be argued to have evolved from the mainstream towards grassroots journalism, made 'for the people and by the people.' This process, observed in the late twentieth century United States by Gillmor (2004), was somewhat delayed in Poland. Salon24, a blogging platform established by Igor Janke, a former journalist from the broadsheet daily *Rzeczpospolita*, constitutes a similar phenomenon, although the organisational structure of Radio Wnet appears to be more complex and thus provides an interesting object for analysis.

The name of the radio station, Wnet, is based on a wordplay drawing on associations with the term 'net,' short for Internet. In Polish, the preposition 'w' means 'in,' 'into' or 'inside'; thus, 'wnet' can be read as 'something that is in or goes into (the Inter)net'; literally, the word 'wnet' means 'soon.' While Wnet is primarily a radio station, it strongly converges with other media. The portal radiownet.pl contains audio content, fragments of individual programmes and transcripts of some audio material, as well as films, video news reports and other video content. This is accompanied by *Kurier Wnet*, an irregularly published print magazine (issue 3 was published in early 2014). All of these contents are co-created by listeners, although the mode and extent of their involvement and co-deciding have differed depending on the specific medium.

Legal Form and Ideological Profile

Radio Wnet was founded as a limited liability company in the autumn of 2009. Its start-up funds were provided partly by the founders and partly by the European Regional Development Fund as part of the European Union Operational Programme Innovative Economy project. In December 2011 a new entity was created, Wnet Cooperative Media (Spółdzielcze Media Wnet), with the legal status of a cooperative. This was an enterprise initiated by communities functioning around Radio Wnet. The radio station's consumers and supporters thus became its co-owners, in a process which could be described as a shift from the 'conducer' (more of a consumer than a producer) stage to that of 'prosumer,' which denotes the kind of person who is equally a producer and consumer, as *"prosumption* involves *both* production and consumption rather than focusing on either one or the other" (Ritzer and Jurgenson 2010, 14). Importantly, the radio station's listeners—the members of the community—were now able not only to publish their content on air and online, but also to co-decide about the new entity's future.

The manifesto of Wnet Cooperative Media stated:

> We are not interested in playing master and servant, nor in playing the elites who are in the know and the masses who have to foot the bill. We want to ensure that responsibility for words, the truth, and values such as honour, homeland, community, and friendship return to the public debate. We are creating a new form of media, one in which we will have access to the facts. (. . .) We must all act together to show the strength and the joy within us.[5]

The founders of the group made a clear reference to the ideas of Solidarność ("Solidarity"), the trade union cum social movement established in 1980 under the Communist regime, whose key demand (number 3 on a list of 21[6]) was freedom of speech: "Our ideological foundations (. . .) are freedom, responsibility and solidarity, rooted in the republican and Christian traditions of the Republic of Poland and of the social movement around *the first Solidarity*."[7]

The founders of Radio Wnet believed that the legal form of a cooperative, which combines economic activity with fulfilling the deeper needs of its members, would provide the strongest bond between the broadcaster and the listener; at the same time, it would be the best expression of the idea of solidarity. Members of a cooperative have a material influence on the future of the medium they jointly own. This appears to be a robust attempt at implementing the ideal of participation and joint decision making by participants, co-deciding on/with technology, content, people and organisational policy (Carpentier 2011).

The choice of the cooperative seems significant, constituting a reference to the ideas of cooperation and co-decision, transferred from the sphere of technology to that of interpersonal relationships and organisations. Early cooperative societies, such as the nineteenth-century Rochdale Pioneers, were established for the "benefit and the improvement of the social and domestic conditions of its members" (Bailey 1960, 19–20), with each member having only one vote whatever his shareholding, and profits from the enterprise being distributed to members in proportion to the goods they purchased. The cooperative movement which started to develop in Poland in the early nineteenth century was characterised by the presence of an ideological dimension; this was mostly patriotic and in favour of national liberation but also stressed the need for interpersonal cooperation and the protection of tradition and culture as ties holding an unfree nation together. When Poland regained independence in 1918, the development of the cooperative movement continued. After World War II, the Communist People's Republic of Poland incorporated cooperative societies into the planned economy, where they played a major role, employing 11.5% of the workforce (Maliszewski 2009). The fall of Communism in the 1990s marked a decline in the importance of cooperatives. Paradoxically, it was Solidarność which had initiated the process of liquidating cooperatives and allowed the very people they had opposed politically to appropriate them (Maliszewski 2009). In this respect, Radio Wnet draws on economic ideas popular in the interwar period but subsequently abandoned during the rebuilding of the capitalist system, thus positioning itself outside the mainstream in yet another way—by means of its organisational structure.

Model of Broadcasting

As noted previously, Radio Wnet is an instance of converged media. Part of the station's programme is broadcast live from a provisional studio in Warsaw and aired by friendly local radio stations: Radio Warszawa in Warsaw, Radio Nadzieja in Łomża and Art Radio in Bogatynia, as is the case for the daily morning show, *Poranek Radia Wnet* [Radio Wnet's Morning], scheduled between 7 and 10 a.m. The day's programming is streamed live, 24/7, at the Radio Wnet website, with reruns played at night. Although music is an important part of the programming, the radio station proclaims to have no music format, in accordance with its philosophy. In that, it resembles the first non-state-owned radio stations in Poland created in the early 1990s, whose music repertoire depended on the personal taste of programme hosts, radio DJs and presenters.

The structure of the Wnet portal is organised around four functional-ities: listen–watch–read–publish. The first three are categories of journalistic content available on the website. In early January 2014, their count was as follows:

- Audio content: 9,320 items
- Video content: 1,757 items
- Textual content: 25,696 items

It should be noted that some of the textual contents consisted of tran-scripts from programmes broadcast by the radio.

The fourth category, 'publish,' is characterised by interaction and, to a certain degree, participation. This relates to the radio station's categories of content providers. They include:

- 'Republicans' (members of 'Radio Wnet Republic')—2,734 persons (as of January 2, 2014)
- Students at 'Wnet Academy' (*Akademia Wnet*)
- 'Open Air' (*Wolna Antena*) members
- The editorial team, consisting of the employees or contributors to the station

'Republicans' are all registered users of the portal, who can access a chan-nel known as @R (pronounced 'ether,' which in Polish means also 'radio waves'), where they can create their own programmes, be they podcasts, videocasts or blogs. They can contact or work jointly with other users; the number of individual or collective channels is not limited. Thus, the 'Wnet Republic' embodies the idea of a prosumer. The name of the community is not a coincidence; rather, it is informed by the egalitarian ideology of the broadcaster, since the community itself comprises ordinary citizens as well as members of parliament, journalists, scientists, artists and social activists, co-existing on equal terms. It is where "participation becomes defined as a political—in the broad meaning of the concept of the political—process where the actors involved in decision-making processes are positioned towards each other through power relationships that are (to an extent) egali-tarian" (Carpentier 2011, 31).

If the egalitarian structure of the 'Republic' resembles a network, the 'Wnet Academy' is more hierarchical. In accordance with its name, this is a place where trainee journalists are schooled by masters of the trade. Initially, entry to the 'Academy' was based on the recommendation of a professional Radio Wnet journalist or a personal invitation issued to a participant due to the quality and quantity of the contents he or she had published on the @R channel. However, as of 2014, admission became contingent on filling in a form, with a fee charged for participation. At the same time, the model of tuition has changed, with one-on-one tutoring based on a master-apprentice relation supplemented by lectures and seminars conducted by experts; subjects include cultural, political and civilisational issues.

Completing the Academy training is a gateway to 'Open Air,' where graduates (nearly 60 persons so far) are allocated their own airtime on equal terms with professional journalists. 'Open Air' has been functioning since 8 July 2010. It therefore appears that within the loose organisational structure of Radio Wnet, horizontal elements (of participatory and network-like character) co-exist with the vertical model of the Academy, the latter oriented towards the educational component. If the radio station were visualised as a pyramid, the editorial staff of the radio and the permanent contributors (who themselves produce audio content which is then broadcast) would be at the top and the 'Republicans' at the base, while the middle part would consist of the contributors to Open Air, often drawn from the ranks of the Academy. This hierarchy, however, is not fixed, as the same individuals often publish their content at multiple levels at the same time.

The difference in the subject areas explored by the different categories of content producers is shown in the content analysis below.

Content Analysis

To establish the major content of issues represented both on the @R channel and Wnet Academy, the quantitative content analysis methodology was adopted. It included all the materials published online during given periods (two months and one year, respectively). Timespan was different in each case in order to receive comparable numbers of programmes (253 and 284). The whole content was divided into nine main categories, as indicated in Figures 11.1 and 11.2.

Subject area	Item count	Percent
International politics	72	28.46
History	38	15.02
Domestic politics	36	14.23
Economy	33	13.04
Social issues	29	11.46
Media	14	5.53
Arts and culture	14	5.53
Religion	8	3.16
Other	9	3.56

Figure 11.1   Radio Wnet's @R: programme content between November 15, 2013 and January 14, 2014

Source: Personal research. Radio Wnet, free antenna website (n.d.).

Subject matter	Item count	Percent
Arts and culture	97	34.15
History	61	21.48
Domestic politics	36	12.68
Social issues	20	7.04
International politics	16	5.63
Media	14	4.93
Economy	12	4.23
Religion	8	2.82
Other (technologies, leisure, etc.)	20	7.04

Figure 11.2 Radio Wnet's Open Air: programme content between January 1, 2012 and January 15, 2014

Source: Personal research. http://www.radiownet.pl/#/wolna_antena.

The Figures show the breakdown of subject areas in the content published by the radio. For the @R channel, the material analysed spans two months, from November 15, 2013 and January 14, 2014. Two hundred fifty-three podcasts were published during this period.

The main issues within these include:

- The situation in Ukraine and the Euromaidan protests in Kiev against the refusal of the government to sign an EU association agreement (85% of items on international politics).
- The popularisation of recent history; these were mainly items on the history of the People's Republic of Poland and the anti-Communist opposition therein, as well as World War II, the anti-Nazi resistance movement and Stalinism.

The analysis shows that the Republicans are not primarily providers of news; even items related to current political affairs are mostly comment, opinion or analysis pieces and interviews rather than breaking news. An exception was the focus on the events in Ukraine; some Republicans reported from Ukraine, which resulted in a higher frequency of items focusing on that country.

Open Air, where participation is more restricted and programmes are produced at Radio Wnet's studio, has a lower output; therefore, the material analysed spans two years, between January 1, 2012 and January 15, 2014. Over that period of time, 284 items were published; an amount comparable to the two months of output by the Republicans we have analysed.

Compared with @R, the output of Open Air is far more oriented towards arts and culture. This is partly explained by the existing series of programmes on music; nonetheless, it is evident that items on international events are outnumbered by those concerning 'internal affairs.' An important similarity is the strong presence of history, where the thematic profile overlaps. Thus, both of Radio Wnet's channels can be stated to perform an educational role, not only through the audio channel, but also by means of video and text content. The radio website thus resembles an open educational resource which can be utilised not just in learning or teaching history, but also economics, or in social education.

Financing

Originally, Radio Wnet was based on the principles of free participation and free education; however, new sources of financing have become necessary to maintain and develop the enterprise within the Wnet Cooperative Media consortium. Membership fees paid by the members of the cooperative society, who include journalists, contributors, listeners and supporters, help cover the cost of social actions and media events. The amounts depend on the goodwill of the supporters and vary from 100 zł (about €24) upwards. At the beginning of 2014, the total number of cooperative members was nearly 700, having gathered a sum of 267,580 zł (€63,710).[8] Radio Wnet Ltd., in turn, gathered an initial shared capital of 22,000 zł (€5,240).[9] However, both of these funds are insufficient to ensure the long-term functioning of a non-profit medium. Cooperatives "rely on low amounts of upfront member-contributed equity capital and therefore depend on passive or quasi-passive internally generated capital" (Chaddad 2009, 12); thus, Radio Wnet found it necessary to put this capital into circulation and at least partly monetise online contents while preserving free on-air and website access. This was done by introducing a ticketing system, where the cheapest ticket, priced at 7 zł (about €1.5) and bought by text message or bank transfer, pays for 30 days of access to the full online archive. Access can be extended by buying more expensive tickets, the most expensive one priced at 78 zł (around €18).

The use of micro payments has allowed the radio station to continue to function after EU financing ended, despite drawing away from the principle of open access. As such, this marked the end of the free economy at Radio Wnet, which has since become a medium based on a cooperative self-financing system. The ongoing economic crisis makes this difficult, causing the station to try to find sponsors and advertisers. This in turn has exposed it to criticism: becoming financially dependent on the main opposition party (Law and Justice), which has bought advertising worth 150,000 zł (around €35,700) from the Wnet portal, is one charge levelled at the radio station.[10]

SOCIAL ACTIVISM: NETWORK, COMMUNITY AND PARTICIPATION

Social activism is an important dimension of both radio and the portal Wnet. The members of Wnet often undertake social actions apart from journalism. Some of the most important ones include:

- 'Radio Wnet's Farmers Market' ('Jarmark Radia Wnet'), consisting of a regular event promoting organic produce; Radio Wnet is its media partner.
- 'Save the Farmer' (*Uratuj rolnika*), which can be described as a happening built around the direct sales of Polish farm products; it started September 6, 2012, as a raft carrying farmers from the Ponidzie region along with their fruit, vegetables, herbs and preserves entered Warsaw. The farmers had travelled for six days, covering 379 kilometres on the Vistula river, in order to highlight the plight of Polish farmers. The motto of the event was "3,000 per cent disappears between the farmer and the middleman."[11]
- Protests against a proposed act of parliament which would allow genetically modified crops to be grown in Poland. With private and state-owned media devoting little attention to the issue, social media and numerous NGOs, most of which opposed the act, stepped in. Radio Wnet was active in the campaign, and the issue was one of the main subjects debated on air. The act in its proposed form was eventually vetoed by the president of Poland.
- The Online Store of Wnet Cooperative Media, corresponding to a store catalogue that lists a number of goods and services (such as books, printing, car repairs, furniture) offered by entrepreneur-members of the cooperative; these goods and services are available at a discounted rate to other members, with the seller transferring 25% of the discount to Wnet Cooperative Media. Any member of the cooperative can list a (discounted) offer in the catalogue.

An important element of these actions is consumer patriotism, an idea frequently espoused by the cooperative movement, as it boosts demand for goods made in the home country (Gurtowski 2012). Further, the origin of capital is not the only criterion, as the entities supported by the actions are not large corporations but entities whose economic position is often weak. Therefore, the community around the radio is extended beyond the configuration listeners—broadcasters—receivers/consumers (or prosumers) to include groups which are disenfranchised, in this case in the economic sense. The radio station thus extends social inclusion to those 'excluded' from the media mainstream, addressing those who may not be listeners but with whom the listeners have an emotional bond, based on the membership in the same historical, cultural or religious community. Similarly, Radio Wnet broadcasts programmes describing the situation of the Polish diaspora in Lithuania, Ukraine and Belarus. These are expressions of the civic quality of radio, where, in accordance with Benjamin Barber's theory of strong democracy, 'participation' and 'community' are two aspects of one social phenomenon, that of citizenship (Barber 1984). The previously described off-air activity indicates that Wnet is a real rather than a virtual community, a dilemma discussed by Rheingold (2000).

The Wnet cooperative may be analysed as, literally, a community which co-operates, or acts together. The scope of the activities undertaken by the members and supporters of Wnet positions them as a 'distributed community' rather than merely an 'online community,' as described by Gochenour (2006). The former "uses an extended communications infrastructure to allow interaction and coordination of behavior among its members, each of which functions as a node within the overall system" (Gochenour 2006, 46–47). Other notions applicable in this context are *communitas* and *societas* as defined by Turner, Harris and Park (1974); these are distinguished by the role of the principle of reciprocity in social interactions. "This principle obliges an individual to act to the advantage of others because of their earlier actions towards the individual rather than due to their social features or positions" (Bierówka 2009, 18).

The actions of an individual to the advantage of others, undertaken because of their social features and positions, are described as non-reciprocal relations of the *societas* type (Bierówka 2009). The activities undertaken by Wnet show features of both *communitas* (the cooperative, networking within the 'Republic') as well as *societas* (support for farmers or the Polish diaspora). The foundation of cooperative and self-help groups can, however, be clearly classified as a reaction against the institutionalised *societas*, which dominates in postmodern societies. Radio Wnet admits that the ideas of *communitas* are close to its heart:

> Saving freedom of speech requires the cooperation of people of good will. The framework of a cooperative, which combines business activity with the fulfilling of more profound needs of its members, will provide the strongest bond between the broadcaster and the listener; at the same time, it is the best expression of the republican spirit and the idea of solidarity.
> (From the radio station's manifesto at the Radio Wnet website n.d.)

The manifesto highlights the egalitarian and bond-forming quality of the radio station; in contrast, mainstream institutions (which now also include state-owned and commercial radio) show symptoms indicating that the reciprocity principle has lost its bond-making quality. These institutions thus resemble a *societas*, resulting as they do from interactions based on non-reciprocal economic exchange. These interactions are usually motivated by a profit-loss calculation on the part of the participants; one example is on-air game shows, utilised by radio stations to boost their audience figures. Some of the conversations between the presenters and listeners in these shows can be quite intimate, but they do not result in lasting bonds among the participants. This is not the case for Radio Wnet: here, although interlocutors may act on behalf of *societas* external to themselves, they become part of a real community and try to include in it the objects of their actions (farmers, the Polish diaspora, and so on).

The increasing tendency of media companies to merge and form large conglomerates causes the weakening of reciprocal ties also in relations among the employees of these companies. They become alienated from the specific radio or TV station they work for; instead, they dissolve into the so-called media group, where they face division of labour (the production and broadcasting departments are often separate units) on the one hand; on the other, the economy of labour requires that they develop their presenter, reporter or producer skills, which will mean fewer persons involved in the creation and broadcasting of a programme. Radio Wnet seeks to overcome these obstacles chiefly by means of the Academy and Open Air, as well as by hosting numerous open meetings or initiating social actions, with listeners encouraged to participate in all these.

An opportunity to come together may be afforded by other initiatives, such as 'Możemy Więcej!' [We Can Do More], 'the Internet city of Wnet media,' where all registered members who include their email address in the membership form can interact. Whether this would be a virtual community functioning in "cyberspace" (Barbatsis, Fegan and Hansen 1999) or another element of 'network society' is an open question. In their work on qualitative network analysis, Martina Löblich and Senta Pfaff-Rüdiger (2012) outline the different approaches to network in scholarship:

- Network as based on informal relations and a horizontal and decentralised structural pattern (Christopulos 2008)
- Network as a distinct, new governing structure, providing a way to coordinate actions of agents (Adam and Kriesi 2007)
- Network as describing different types of interactions among public and private actors (Kenis and Raab 2008), corresponding to a more general approach

Regardless of the theoretical model of network which is adopted, it is evident that the community of Radio Wnet has qualities of a complex network and, as such, deserves a separate qualitative analysis. It combines horizontal elements with hierarchical ones and online involvement with social activism; moreover, the productivity of audience has a double meaning here, applying both to the production of contents in the journalistic sense and to the literal production of goods and services by members of the Wnet cooperative.

CHALLENGES FOR THE FUTURE

Although Radio Wnet has been broadening its offer since its inauguration at the end of 2009, it remains a niche medium. It is not directly listed in Radio Track surveys, but Radio Warszawa, which facilitates broadcasting of *Radio Wnet's Mornings*, gathers a small audience of 0.7% in the Warsaw region (Millward Brown SMG/KRC 2014). As for website traffic, estimates are that there are about 92,000 unique users every month.[12] No general statistic about the online traffic is published, although individual posts and podcasts have their own counts. The years to come will undoubtedly test the endurance of the cooperative as well as define, to a certain degree, the position of citizen media in public debate in Poland. Key challenges lying ahead for the broadcaster seem to include:

- Financing

As described earlier, Radio Wnet lacks a stable financing source and relies mainly on the micro payments made by the audience and on cooperative members' support. Therefore, there are new initiatives like the online store,[13] which sells books and CDs to make profit. Another source of funds, especially in the beginning, was the European Union programme Innovative Economy, which has supported the creation of Radio Wnet's Internet platform since 2009. Nevertheless, all these sources may not be sufficient for further development.

- Widening the availability of on-air programming

Only three on-air radio stations broadcast Radio Wnet's programmes. All of them are relatively small and offer only a couple of hours of air time. Obtaining a separate licence from the National Broadcast Council (KRRiTV) may be a difficult task due to lack of free frequencies as much as of solid financial background.

- Development of educational offers for up-and-coming journalists

The number of trained scholars at Wnet Academy is still somewhat unimpressive. Although certainly important from the professional point of view, the journalism workshops do not entitle the alumni to a bachelor's or master's degree. Founding a proper school, which issues a respected diploma might be a way to attract more interest from individuals able to finance such studies. But, undoubtedly, it is again a matter of money as well as proper infrastructure (i.e., buildings, studios, equipment and, last but not least, teachers).

- Increasing its opinion formation reach

Despite Radio Wnet programmes being often visited by prominent figures, with some highly professional analyses of political and economic situations, particularly from an international coverage viewpoint (i.e., in Ukraine), the radio station is rarely quoted by mainstream media. Therefore, its opinion formation reach is still very limited.

- Broadening the network of cooperating media and affiliated institutions (at present the network is limited)

What may be said about Radio Wnet is that it is a medium growing from the inside, which generates its own ideas and submedia (i.e., *Kurier Wnet*, @R, etc.); however, it does not sufficiently take recourse to the possibility of network cooperation with other media and other platforms (with the exception of the conservative magazine *Fronda* or the labour union's Radio Solidarność in the programme schedule). It may be worth asking why so many alternative channels of communication and media initiatives still have not acted in synergy, having yet to achieve the required strength so as to reach wider publics. This question is important because the force of Wnet and its growth potential reside in the current dissatisfaction with mainstream media on the part of a considerable section of the public.

As has been observed by Sharon Meraz (2008, 701): "the independent political bloggers' outside status from *beltway* or *mainstream* media has afforded them greater freedom to utilize other citizen media sources when building critiques of traditional media's news reports." Wnet's signature critique of the dominant discourse alongside the opportunities provided by the network-like cooperation of diverse citizen and social media may in the future contribute to increasing its opinion formation reach. However, without stable financing, Wnet will find it hard to successfully compete with public and commercial broadcasters. What appears to be an interesting challenge is the attempt to build a strong foundation for citizen media through the joint effort of educational activity and off-air social initiatives.

CONCLUSIONS

Radio Wnet is a niche, yet inspiring, enterprise on the Polish media market. A combination of broadcast radio and a Web portal, it is a unique instance of the construction of a social medium with recourse to the Internet, but with radio as the main marker of identity for the converged platform. Radio Wnet evinces a combination of left-wing and right-wing characteristics: it uses left-wing strategies (the cooperative) to broadcast a fairly conservative message on politics, society, tradition, national heritage and religion. It is not, however, one-dimensional in political terms, blending a civic activism, reminiscent of socialism and drawing on the pre-war traditions of the Polish Socialist Party, with the classical liberal views voiced by the Adam Smith

Centre or with the libertarian views espoused by the representatives of the Congress of the New Right who occasionally appear on air. All of these remain outside of and in opposition to the main public discourse dominated by Polish and multinational media conglomerates; the exponents of these views also remain critical of the current media landscape. Socialist, ultra-liberal and conservative politicians all appear on air on equal terms; the hosts of Open Air programmes include amateur aficionados of radio as well as artists who identify with the counterculture and are at odds with the Christian values professed by the radio station.

Radio Wnet evinces some elements typical of mainstream media:

- The organisational structure of the radio station based on experienced journalists
- Participation in professional associations representing a segment of professional journalists (Polish Journalists Association, whose current head is Krzysztof Skowroński)
- Some programmes broadcast on air

Grassroots elements include:

- An open, participatory formula of the presence of the audience as content providers within the @R channel and the Wnet Republic
- 'Wolna Antena' as a radio studio open to those with some radio experience
- The networking of the Wnet community
- Non-media initiatives, social activism

Radio Wnet's formula appears to corroborate Denis McQuail's (1997, 2) statement that "audiences are both a product of social context (. . .) and a response to a particular pattern of media provision." The community of receivers/consumers, who are at the same time broadcasters and often co-owners, is largely the by-product of a lack of trust in the official circulation of information and in media discourse. The benefit from the functioning of Radio Wnet can be classified as a 'social gain,' defined by the British Community Radio Order of 2004 as, among additional elements, delivering programmes to individuals who are overlooked by other broadcasters, enabling debate and the expression of opinion and ensuring the availability of education or training to persons not employed by the station (Doliwa 2012).

The radio station's organisational structure has robust elements of participation under the four dimensions of technology, content, people and organisation (Carpentier 2011). Despite this, Radio Wnet does not create a flat network; rather, it is a structural hybrid: on the one hand, the network structure, constantly growing in every dimension, dominates; on the other, the vertical hierarchy of the editorial staff, Academy and "Free Ether" is still relevant. The station and the cooperative will continue to evolve, although time will tell what direction will be taken; what is certain is that the "audiences' constructive and interpretative practices represent a vital link in the societal circulation and reproduction of meanings" (Livingstone 1998, 238) and they will remain an inspiring subject of further analyses.

NOTES

1. http://www.mediainitiative.eu/stop-mediacide/.
2. http://wyborcza.pl/1,76842,6528268,Skowronski_zwolniony_dyscyplinarnie.html.
3. http://jankepost.salon24.pl/269,skowronskiego-bronia-prawie-wszyscy-szefowa-tok-fm-tez-i-na.
4. http://www.hfhr.pl/apel-do-prezydenta-ws-zniesienia-artykulu-212-kk/.
5. The address delivered by Krzysztof Skowroński on October 21, 2011 during a meeting of 'the Radio Wnet Republic,' after: http://www.radiownet.pl.
6. http://www.solidarnosc.org.pl/pl/21-postulatow-1.html.
7. The address delivered by Krzysztof Skowroński, as quoted.
8. http://www.mediawnet.pl/index/form/.
9. http://www.radiownet.pl/strony/regulamin.
10. http://www.rp.pl/artykul/1020592.html?print=tak&p=0.
11. http://rolnikwnet.pl/.
12. http://www.trafficestimate.com/radiownet.pl.
13. http://www.sklep.radiownet.pl/.

REFERENCES

Adam, S. and Kriesi, H. (2007). "The Network Approach." In Sabatier, P. (ed.), *Theories of the Policy Process*. Boulder: Westview Press, 129–154.

Bailey, J. (1960). "The British Co-operative Movement." In Robertson, N. (2010), *The Co-operative Movement and Communities in Britain, 1914–1960*. Burlington: Ashgate Publishing Company.

Barbatsis, G., Fegan, M. and Hansen, K. (1999). "The Performance of Cyberspace: An Exploration into Computer-Mediated Reality." *Journal of Computer-Mediated Communication*, 5(1). Accessed October 6, 2014. http://onlinelibrary.wiley.com/doi/10.1111/j.1083-6101.1999.tb00332.x/full.

Barber, B. (1984). *Strong Democracy*. Berkeley, Los Angeles: University of California Press.

Bierówka, J. (2009). *Zasada wzajemności w społeczeństwie informacyjnym*. Kraków: Oficyna Wydawnicza AFM.

Bruns, A. (2008). *Blogs, Wikipedia, Second Life, and Beyond: From Production to Produsage*. New York: Peter Lang.

Carpentier, N. (2011). "The Concept of Participation. If They Have Access and Interact, Do They Really Participate?" *CM: Communication Management Quarterly/Casopis za upravljanje komuniciranjem*, 21, 13–36.

CBOS [Public Opinion Research Center]. (2012). *Zaufanie społeczne*. Warsaw: Fundacja Centrum Badania Opinii Społecznej.

Chaddad, F. R. (2009). "Both Market and Hierarchy: Understanding the Hybrid Nature of Cooperatives." Paper prepared at the international workshop "Rural Cooperation in the 21st Century: Lessons from the Past, Pathways to the Future." Accessed June 12, 2013. http://departments.agri.huji.ac.il/economics/en/events/p-chaddad.pdf.

Charter of Fundamental Rights. (2000). *Official Journal of the European Communities 2000/C 364/01*. Accessed March 23, 2014. http://www.europarl.europa.eu/charter/pdf/text_en.pdf.

Christopulos, D. C. (2008). "The Governance of Networks: Heuristic or Formal Analysis? A Reply to Rachel Parker." *Political Studies*, 56(2), 475–481.

Dahlgren, P. (1997). "Introduction." In Dahlgren, P. and Sparks, C. (eds.), *Communication and Citizenship: Journalism and the Public Sphere in the New Media Age*. New York: Routledge.

Doliwa, U. (2012). "Od duetu do tercetu. O rozwoju trzeciego sektora radiowego w Europie." In Jaskiernia, A. and Adamowski, J. (eds.), *Systemy medialne w XXI wieku. Wspólne czy różne drogi rozwoju?* Warsaw: Aspra JR, 307–322.

Dróżdż, M. (2012). "The Phenomenon of Catholic Radio Broadcasting—the Public Mission in the Area of Freedom." In Baczyński, A. and Dróżdż, M. (eds.), *Convergence: Media in Future*. Kraków: Institute of Journalism and Social Communication, Pontifical University of John Paul II, 111–129.

European Trusted Brands. (2012). *Reader's Digest*. Accessed 24 March, 2014. www.rdtrustedbrands.com.

Gillmor, D. (2004). *We the Media: Grassroots Journalism by the People, for the People*. Sebastopol: O'Reilly Media.

Gochenour, P. H. (2006). "Distributed Communities and Nodal Subjects." *New Media & Society*, 8(1), 33–51.

Godzic, W. (2010). "Sytuacja polskich mediów audiowizualnych w latach 1989–2008." *Raport o Stanie Kultury*. Warsaw: Ministerstwo Kultury i Dziedzictwa Narodowego.

Groenhart, H. (2012). "Users' Perception of Media Accountability." *Central European Journal of Communication*, 5(2), 190–203.

Gurtowski, M. (2012). "Patriotyzm konsumencki i ekonomiczny a ruch spółdzielczy." *Pieniądze i Więź*. Sopot: Spółdzielczy Instytut Naukowy.

Habermas, J. (1991). *The Structural Transformation of the Public Sphere*. Cambridge, MA: MIT Press.

Hamerlink, C. J. and Nordenstreng, K. (2007). "Towards Democratic Media Governance." In De Bens, E. (ed.), *Media Between Culture and Commerce: An Introduction*. Bristol: Intellect, 225–240.

Jędrzejewski, S. (2003). *Radio w komunikacji społecznej*. Warsaw: Profi-Press.

Kenis, P. and Raab, J. (2008). "Politiknetzwerke als Governanceform: Versuch einer Bestandsaufnahme und Neuausrichtung der Diskussion." In Schuppert, G. F. and Zürn, M. (eds.), *Governance in einer sich wandelnden Welt*. Wiesbaden: VS, 132–148.

KRRiTV (2013a). *Rynek telewizyjny w I kwartale 2013*. Warsaw: Departament monitoringu.

———. (2013b). *Udział w rynku i wielkość audytorium programów radiowych w II kwartale 2013*. Warsaw: Departament monitoringu.

Lacey, K. (2013). *Listening Publics: The Politics and Experience of Listening in the Media Age*. Cambridge: Polity Press.

Lister, M., Dovey, J., Giddings, S., Grant, I. and Kelly, K. (2009). *New Media: A Critical Introduction*, 2nd edn. London, New York: Routledge.

Livingstone, S. (1998). "Relationships between Media and Audiences: Prospects for Audience Reception Studies." In Liebes, T. and Curran, J. (eds.), *Media, Ritual and Identity: Essays in Honor of Elihu Katz*. London: Routledge, 237–255.

Livingstone, S. and Lund P.K. (1994). *Talk on Television: Audience Participation and Public Debate*. London: Routledge.

Loviglio, J. (2002). "Vox Pop. Network Radio and the Voice of the People." In Hilmes, M. and Loviglio, J. (eds.), *Radio Reader*. New York: Routledge, 89–112.

Löblich, M. and Pfaff-Rüdiger, S. (2012). "Qualitative Network Analysis: An Approach to Communication Policy Studies." In Just, N. and Puppis, M. (eds.), *Trends in Communication Policy Research*. Bristol, Chicago: Intellect, 195–215.

Maliszewski, A. (2009). "The Fall of the Co-operative Movement in Poland, International Co-operative Information Centre."*International Co-operative Information Center*, Vol. 88. University of Wisconsin. Accessed December 18, 2013. http://www.uwcc.wisc.edu/icic/orgs/ica/pubs/review/vol-88/poland.html.

McQuail, D. (1997). *Audience Analysis*. London: Sage.

———. (2003). *Media Accountability and Freedom of Publication*. Oxford, New York: Oxford University Press.

Meraz, S. (2008). "Is There an Elite Hold? Traditional Media to Social Media Agenda Setting Influence in Blog Networks." *Journal of Computer-Mediated Communication*, 14, 682–707.

Millward Brown SMG/KRC. (2014). *Radio Track*. Accessed March 27, 2014. http://www.radiotrack.pl/index.php/wyniki.html.

Radio Wnet website. (n.d.). Accessed March 22, 2014.http://www.radiownet.pl

Radio Wnet, free antenna website. (n.d.). Accessed March 22, 2014.http://www.radiownet.pl/#/wolna_antena

Rheingold, H. (2000). *The Virtual Community: Homesteading on the Electronic Frontier*. Cambridge, MA: MIT Press.

Ritzer, G. and Jurgenson, N. (2010). "Production, Consumption, Prosumption. The Nature of Capitalism in the Age of the Digital Prosumer." *Journal of Consumer Culture*, 10(1), 13–36.

Rossi P. and Meier, W. A. (2012). "Civil Society and Media Governance: A Participatory Approach." In Just, N. and Puppis, M. (eds.), *Trends in Communication Policy Research*. Bristol, Chicago: Intellect, 381–400.

Stachyra, G. (2012)."The Radio Afterlife. Three Spheres of Communication and Community." In Oliveira, M., Portela, P. and Santos, L. A. (eds.), *Radio Evolution. Conference Proceedings*. Minho: CECS University of Minho, 401–412.

Turner, V., Harris, J. C. and Park, R. J. (1974). "Liminal to Liminoid in Play, Flow, and Ritual: An Essay in Comparative Symbology." *The Rice University Studies*, 60 (3), 53–92.

Online Sources

http://jankepost.salon24.pl/269,skowronskiego-bronia-prawie-wszyscy-szefowa-tok-fm-tez-i-na (accessed March 22, 2014).

http://rolnikwnet.pl/ (accessed January 12, 2014).

http://www.hfhr.pl/apel-do-prezydenta-ws-zniesienia-artykulu-212-kk/ (accessed March 21, 2014).

http://www.mediainitiative.eu/stop-mediacide/ (accessed March 24, 2014).

http://www.mediawnet.pl/index/form/ (accessed December 14, 2013).

http://www.radiownet.pl (accessed March 22, 2014).

http://www.radiownet.pl/strony/regulamin (accessed March 26, 2014).

http://www.rp.pl/artykul/1020592.html?print=tak&p=0 (accessed January 2, 2014).

http://www.sklep.radiownet.pl/ (accessed January 11, 2014).

http://www.solidarnosc.org.pl/pl/21-postulatow-1.html (accessed November 14, 2013).

http://www.trafficestimate.com/radiownet.pl (accessed March 24, 2014).

http://wyborcza.pl/1,76842,6528268,Skowronski_zwolniony_dyscy plinarnie.html (accessed November 14, 2013).

12 Getting Listeners Involved
Rádio Ás, a Community Web Project

Stanislaw Jedrzejewski and Madalena Oliveira

THE COMMUNITY NATURE OF RADIO

The idea of community is usually associated with radio today in the context of what Bart Cammaerts (2009, 635) classifies as a "third type of broadcast, namely participatory radio, complementary to both commercial and public media." Following Ellie Rennie (2006, 3), community radio corresponds, as all other forms of community media, to non-profit media that provide "community members with an opportunity to participate in the production process." For the International Association for Media and Communication Research, which supports a research group on Community Communication, this area includes media that originate from, circulate and resonate with the sphere of civil society.[1]

Although in formal terms this taxonomy corresponds to how radio stations are seen from a political economic viewpoint, the relationship between radio and community in a wider approach is much more deeply rooted in this medium's 'temperament.' Unlike the press, the focus of radio is not exclusively on the transmission of information. Radio is therefore much more a means of communication than it is a means of information, notwithstanding its favourable position towards the instantaneous dissemination of news. Information is part of the communication process because it is the formal content of a communicative situation. According to Shannon and Weaver's theory (1949), information is what circulates in the flow of communication between the source and the receiver. But radio is no longer only the transmission channel invented by Marconi. Radio is communication in the sense that communication is contact, relationship and interaction, sharing not only ideas and information but also emotion, feelings, and sensations. Comprising all these actions, radio has no other spirit but to build communities, here defined according to Martin-Barbero's (1993, 29) understanding, as close and concrete human ties and by a collective identity.

At the beginning of radio broadcasting, in the 1920s and 1930s, families and neighbours used to get together around a radio set to listen to shows, music and theatre. There was a capacity of radio to aggregate people and give them motives to extend their conversations. In other words, in its golden years, radio favoured the conditions for preliminary forms of current media communities.

With the diversification of commercial radio stations and their technological advancement—which created ever smaller radio sets—listening to radio individually became increasingly frequent. Perhaps some working contexts provide an exception to private listening. But the concept of community was not erased from these changing habits. Though in a different way from the past, when someone tunes in to a radio station, a community of listeners becomes widened. The audience of a radio station can indeed be described in terms of a community, given that it implies sharing the same music preferences, sometimes the same religion and the same humour sensibility. Classical reception and audience studies are usually particularly concerned with the sociodemographic characterisation of the listeners. Indeed, some of these features may constitute a portrait of those groups that to a certain extent create specific communities. The history of radio is full of examples of radio programmes whose listeners are part of fan groups; currently, the latter have blogs or pages on Facebook and interact outside the broadcast, normally in social networks, creating platforms to share additional information on a specific kind of music or sportive group or any other common interest. The natural community profile of all radio stations encourages these forms of community dynamics.

Carpentier, Lie and Servaes (2003, 54) remember that community can "refer predominantly to geography and ethnicity as structuring notions of collective identity or group relations." According to the authors, "a community is actively constructed by its members and those members derive an identity from this construction" (Carpentier et al. 2003, 54). A radio community is nothing different. It usually develops on a geographical and/or ethnic basis. Moreover, its listeners have always contributed to the construction of a shared social identity.

Some local radio station programmes still work today as a kind of café where people meet together to chat.[2] Talking to the host by telephone, listeners actually talk to each other, feeding into a sense of community that exists in the majority of radio projects. Moreover, the intimate relationship that can be built between radio producers and listeners also contributes to the feeling of belonging to a group. Incomparable to any other medium, radio is the space for more than a relationship with a mass of anonymous listeners. It consists indeed in "almost an interpersonal relationship that is established between radio professionals and the listeners" (Oliveira 2013, 186). Aggregation is hence a characteristic that should be added to the depiction of radio as a medium, justifying Ellie Rennie's (2006, 4) position that "radio is the dominant medium for community expression in most parts of the world." Besides being universal, simultaneous and instantaneous (Portela 2011), radio also works as an aggregator.

THE WEB CHALLENGE

The technological transformation of radio broadcasting is a permanent process which, despite occurring from its invention, has nevertheless become accentuated since the 1990s. Digitisation systems were absolutely revolutionary, and sound editing with specific software radically changed the manipulation of sound elements and the possibilities for radio narrative. Improving the quality of the broadcast and of the message at the receiver end, the digitisation process made a particular impact, however, on the production side. It was the production context that was extraordinarily affected by the conversion from an analogue to a digital environment. The new editing paradigm, introduced by the digitisation of sound, represented and facilitated new creative conditions and contributed extensively to the development of the artistic dimension of radio production. Digitisation brought advantages to journalistic audio productions, making it easier to select and edit excerpts of interviews, include them in news features and collect them in easily accessible archives.

The most important change in radio history, however, was introduced by the Internet. In a certain sense, radio was born again after the Internet. The blind medium was given a kind of clean slate due to the extension of the transformations affecting radio as it was known before.

Reconfiguring the notions of time and space, the Internet accelerated the evolution of radio by promoting the integration "in multimedia systems and the interactivity, the hypermediality and the possibility of creating web radios" (Cebrián Herreros 2008, 11). The worldwide Net brought in podcasts and channels for participation, in combination with images, written text and online archives. Over the previous eighty years, radio had not faced such a metamorphosis. Some authors still argue that, though transforming radio, digitisation and the immersion in the Internet will not separate radio from its traditional functions, and it will go on being a predominantly sound vehicle (Almeida and Magnoni 2010). The preliminary results of research carried out within the scope of the NET Station project[3] demonstrate, however, that websites of traditional radio stations are much more similar to other websites (created by other media) than their 'sound' nature would suggest. The research team (Communication and Society Research Centre), to which the authors of this chapter belong, realised that sound is hidden in the websites of mainstream radio stations. It is indeed the last content that users find while surfing on radio websites. The first contact is with images and text. Sound keeps its invisible essence and appears as an additional element, rather than being the predominant component of such websites, as radio's origin would seem to recommend.

The Internet is still a challenge insufficiently explored by radio. If in traditional broadcasts there was a geographic limitation concerning the physical range of Hertzian waves, the Web radio is no longer limited to a local, regional or national spectrum. Without depending on the power of transmission towers, radio broadcasting through the Internet gains a global dimension unparalleled by any of the largest international corporations. Benefiting from the almost costless fluxes of information, radio on the Internet has an unimaginable opportunity for expansion, not only in territorial terms but also as concerns the storage of content that used to be ephemeral. Beyond linear broadcast limitations, radio could also find the Internet to be an opportunity to make available information and other sound formats that would not fit conventional programming (longer programmes or interviews, for example).

Many authors have insisted that the major advantage of the Internet for radio is the emergence of an interactive type of communication. Cebrián Herreros (2008, 207) recognises that "the radio's model of traditional diffusion has been converted into an interactive model," which means that the 'traditional' listener becomes an interactive user with a stronger capacity to participate in the narrative or, at least, of choosing what he/she wants to listen to. In many cases, radio live streaming is available in fragments (podcasts), that is to say, radio programming is now available in audio-on-demand mode. Thus, there is "a combination between the sequence of 24 hours broadcast and the non-sequential or juxtaposed programming" (Cebrián Herreros 2008, 51).

Besides these opportunities offered by the Internet, which are not the focus of this chapter, radio of the Web generation may also be seen as a fresh opportunity in terms of community media. For its technological simplicity, radio is probably the most democratic and generous medium. The Internet and the generalisation of editing software put a special accent on this characteristic. Traditional radio broadcasts were already cheap when compared with other media, and much more accessible than television or even newspapers. Defined by simple language, radio production does not require very complex skills and is therefore particularly well suited to initiatives coming from nonprofessional groups.

Although not well regulated, the Web works currently as a kind of lab where new experiences sprout up like mushrooms. New economic models, new formats and increasingly specialised content for more specialised audiences have been appearing, in part sponsored by individuals having no professional background. Expressions of newly empowered groups' interests, these exploratory projects contain some indications of radio's future or, in Guy Starkey's (2006) terms, suggest a revision of erroneous predictions usually associated with this medium. The Internet provides confirmation of the relevance of radio in the media landscape, stressing the democratic, inventive, ingenious and involving role it can still play.

THE COMMUNITY CHALLENGE AND
THE PORTUGUESE LEGAL VACUUM

Unlike the well-known experiences across many countries (such as Brazil, United Kingdom, France, Spain and Ireland), where community radio is very common, the Portuguese radio landscape almost ignores the existence of this kind of project. There is no tradition of community media in the country, and the format is not legally defined well enough, in regard to either FM broadcasts or the Internet. As stated by Cammaerts (2009, 638),

> an exclusive focus on the political economy and regulation of the media and communication 'industry' and/or on public service broadcasting systems tends to exclude alternative or community media, often very local, embedded in civil society and thus situated in-between or relatively independent from state and market.

According to the Portuguese Law on Radio, which was revised and republished in 2010 (Law no. 54/2010, December 24), "the activity of radio consisting of the organisation of general or informative thematic programming services in the local scope can only be practiced by collective people who have the exercise of social communication activities as the principal object" (§15, 2). The initiative of creating a radio station is, however, also allowed for "associations or foundations with humanitarian, educative, cultural, scientific or academic purposes, if their programming services contribute significantly to value these activities" (§15, 3). In addition to these provisions, §16 states that "the activity of radio cannot be practiced or funded, directly or indirectly, by political parties or political associations, trade unions or public professional associations, unless this activity is exclusively practiced on the Internet, and consists in the organisation of programming services of a doctrinal, institutional or scientific nature" (§16, 1).

Although not absolutely clear, the process of creating a non-commercial or non-public radio station does not seem to be specifically stated in the law. The word 'community' appears in the Portuguese Law on Radio only three times, always concerning the specific obligations of the public service broadcast to immigrant communities in Portugal and Portuguese communities in other countries. Unlike what happens in Brazil, for instance, where community radio is regulated by a specific law that created the Community Radio Broadcast Service (Law no. 9.612/1998),[4] community radio in Portugal does not represent a specific category of radio and is not a principle of the law.

In terms of categorisation, the Portuguese Law on Radio refers to two main typologies. On the one hand, it concerns the coverage area (§7), stipulating that programming services can be (a) international if they cover the territory of other countries, (b) national when they cover the national territory in general, (c) regional if the area concerns a small group of counties or a metropolitan area, and (d) local when the radio station covers only a municipality or a small group of municipalities.[5] On the other hand, two categories define the type of programming service, according to broadcast content and editorial policy. In this context, the law distinguishes between general-interest radio and thematic stations. While the former should present diversified programming and include an informational component that targets the general public, the latter should present programmes focusing on specific matters, such as music or specialised information (§8).[6]

Although community radio is usually local and more or less thematic, given that it is targeted at a more specialised audience, these categories neither properly admit nor adequately define the idea of community media. Community radio is indeed more than local and thematic. The Brazilian law, for example, defines that it is supposed to represent "an opportunity for the diffusion of ideas, cultural elements, traditions and social habits of the community" (§3). There is also an expectation of education promotion, given that community radio in Brazil should "offer mechanisms for the community's training and integration, stimulating leisure, culture and social intercourse" (§3). The Brazilian law also clearly defines that community radio should "allow for the empowerment of citizens in terms of expression rights" (§3). Nothing similar is determined by the Portuguese law, except in relation to the public broadcasting service.

In geographic terms, communities are very often local. Cammaerts (2009) is inspired by the perspective of Howley (2005), who wrote *Community Media: People, Places and Communication Technologies*, to remind us that localism is one of the defining characteristics of community media and radio. However, the Portuguese concept of local radio is not equivalent to what community radio is supposed to be. Deconstructing seven equivocal theses on community communication, Marcos Palácios (1990, 106) suggests that it is inaccurate to consider that "the community is a socially small-sized unit, characterised fundamentally by the physical proximity of its members." According to the author, the concept of community has to be taken outside the ties of local communities, because "community is not only a place on a map" and "people can have diversified experiences of community no matter whether they are living close to each other or not" (Palácios 1990, 107).

Only a small number of community radio projects are well known in Portugal, all of which are on the Internet. Despite the silence of the law on this matter, community radio in Portugal cannot be described as illegal. Perhaps the right term would be *a*legal, considering that it neither exists against the law nor appears within any specific legal framework. Community radio in Portugal today represents more or less what pirate radio did in the 1980s, although such a comparison might be exaggerated due to the former still not having the same impact as the latter. In general, they flourish from private initiative, are very often started by amateurs, are not intended to be profitable and represent a certain emancipation of the audience.

RÁDIO ÁS, LINKING PORTUGUESE-SPEAKING COMMUNITIES

The Rádio Ás project was launched in Portugal, promoted by the local government of Aveiro municipality (located in the centre-north coastside of the country). With a global policy oriented towards investing in the production of content for the Internet, the municipal executive led by the major centre-right Social-Democratic Party (PSD), during the 2009–2012 mandate executed the Aveiro 21 Programme aiming to foster digital citizenship, civic participation and social interaction. A set of sixteen actions, such as the creation of a newsletter, a TV and a community of photographers called *Image 21*, were planned to achieve the objectives of this programme, whose main purpose was to endorse proximity among citizens. Constituting part of this plan, Rádio Ás was hence created in 2011 as a community and inter-municipal Web radio station (http://www.cm-aveiro.pt/radioas).

Although integrated in a strategy of improving the visibility of Aveiro's local culture, this radio station was meant to enlarge the municipality's net of interconnections with other communities. Consistent with this purpose, the project brought together three municipalities of three Portuguese-speaking countries, Aveiro (Portugal), Santa Cruz (Cape Verde) and São Bernardo do Campo (Brazil), with three main goals, according to the mission statement of the station:

> (a) to motivate the civic participation in public space and to open the programming to associative organizations of citizens; (b) to reinforce the communities' cohesion and to sponsor programming related to community life; and (c) to deepen the approach to urban culture and local identity and to promote the diffusion of tradition trends and local modernity through this medium.[7]

This project is exclusively online, as contemplated by §16 of the Law on Radio, according to which radio broadcasts are not allowed for political parties or political associations (including any form of government) unless transmitted over only the Internet. Promoted by three town councils, one from each partner country, Rádio Ás could be defined as a project on Luso-phone[8] culture and identity. Focusing on the idea of intercultural cooperation through sound, Rádio Ás appeared in the Portuguese context as a unique media project. To our knowledge, this was the first community radio station in the country promoted by a municipality but aiming at a Lusophone audience wider than the borders of that very municipality. The notion of community implicit in this profile is in fact not confined to the borders of a local municipality. In this sense, the shape of Rádio Ás coincides with Cammaerts' (2009, 639) thought, according to which "reducing a community to a local context or setting is deemed to be too limiting." Quoting Peter Lewis (1993), the author explains that "a community of interest can extend 'across conurbations, nations and continents' and thus bypass or transcend the geographically and spatially confined definition" (2009, 639).

Owned by the Aveiro city council, whose website it was embedded in, Rádio Ás was organised under two boards or committees. The management board was integrated by the three partners. The editorial board, however, included individuals from Aveiro only. This particular board was responsible for the selection of the programmes and counted on the collaboration of two local schools and two higher education institutions (the Communication and Arts Department of the University of Aveiro and the Institute of Information Sciences and Administration). Created to ensure the editorial independence of the radio station, this board was ultimately responsible for the 'design' of the programming.

According to its editorial mission statement, Rádio Ás aimed at: (a) "consolidating the mutual knowledge, the cooperation and the close relation between populations from the three partners"; (b) "fostering the value of the multicultural experience"; (c) "supporting the diffusion of the Portuguese language by intending to be a vehicle of 'Lusophony'; and (d) encouraging "innovation and creativity."[9] With the general objective of reinforcing the spirit of community and cooperation among the countries involved, Rádio Ás was meant to be a collaborative project.

In terms of resources, the radio was entirely funded by the Aveiro city council and by the partners themselves, since the authors of the webcast programmes worked on a volunteer basis. The project was extremely cheap, according to one of the station's representatives, Virgílio Nogueira, who holds a degree in Communication Studies and works in the city council.[10] Rádio Ás expenses were as low as around 500 euros per year. The equipment was bought with the support of patrons and no relevant duties were required, except for the regular fees of the Portuguese Association of Authors for music copyright.

In November 2012, Rádio Ás celebrated its first anniversary. On the occasion, the local daily newspaper of Aveiro, *Diário de Aveiro*, proclaimed that "the first year of Rádio Ás was a success."[11] According to a city councilman, Pedro Ferreira, referred to by the newspaper, the project had concretised its objective of involving the community.[12] By that time, according to paper, Rádio Ás would have registered more than 60 programmes and could count on around 100 collaborators.

However, it did not perform an education-oriented function in a strict sense, as some Brazilian radio stations do, because it aimed at creating a community-like public sphere oriented towards a more general associative and civic movement. Nevertheless, there were schools, libraries and students collaborating with Rádio Ás, which contributed to the pedagogical role that this station also played.

PROGRAMMING: DISCONTINUOUS BUT PLURAL

Although broadcasting daily, Rádio Ás programming was not based on a 24-hour system. Due to the editorial strategy, privileging content produced almost exclusively by civic institutions and individual citizens, programming was irregular, fragmented and made of diverse contributions. The Web radio station worked as a kind of sound-hub where productions coming from various origins combined to devise a singular composition of resonances in different Portuguese accents. People were therefore invited to participate by creating programmes and voicing ideas. Those who wanted to collaborate were asked to submit a proposal with the description of the programme (objectives, thematic, topics related to community life, approach to local cultures and identities, multicultural thematic, expression of Lusophony), information on the author or on the team, periodicity of the programme, schedule, duration and the public to whom the programme would be targeted.

Depending on the proposals received from the audience, programming was discontinuous. The broadcasting schedule concentrated on the evenings, between 8 p.m. and midnight. In the last version of the scheduling, Rádio Ás had no programming in the morning. There were only two programmes on Saturday before 2 p.m. The rest of the week, the radio station worked mainly during the afternoon and at night. Taking into account daily routines, it could be said that this webcasting schedule was more or less adapted to leisure time. Without specific apps for smartphones or iPhones, Rádio Ás was listened to mainly on its website. Some programmes, however, had pages on Facebook (like *A Idade (com)Vida*[13]) and specific pages where authors usually made available programming produced for the station (like *80 à Hora*[14]). Although rigorous studies on Rádio Ás audiences are not available, it was estimated that the station was accessed by listeners from more than 80 countries.[15]

Without pretending to examine the programming in depth, a simple and almost informal analysis of the programmes' technical data demonstrates that these were prepared almost exclusively in Portugal, by Portuguese listeners individually or by Portuguese institutions. Only one programme, called *In the Mix Brazil*, was produced outside Portugal, namely in Brazil, being broadcast by many Web radios in the latter country and supported each week by a DJ invited to animate this one-hour programme. Besides individual producers, there were also some programmes promoted by civil society organisations. *Environmental Education and Citizenship* was a one-hour programme promoted by the Portuguese Association for Environmental Education with the aim of fostering environmental citizenship and education through the implementation of the Lusophone Network for Environmental Education, deepening the knowledge of cultural and environmental diversity in Lusophone countries and exploring relations among culture, art and the environment. Due to including interviews with both experts and citizens, this programme was presented by volunteers from the association.

A programme on reading and literature also had a weekly edition, prepared by a group of school libraries. Focusing on Lusophone literature, *Ler + na Rádio* (Reading + on the Radio) had the following goals: to promote reading by teenagers, explore children's feelings on reading, develop relationships with the local community and other schools and disseminate literature for children and teenagers.

Another example of a more institutional programme was *Assembly Channel*. Promoted by the assembly of Aveiro's local government, the programme was designed to give a space of visibility to the activities of this assembly. Concentrating on the Aveiro county region, the programme aimed to promote engagement among citizens and improve civic participation; analyse the reality of the region in political, social and economic terms; and boost local cultural identity (e.g., gastronomy).

An association of immigrant support was responsible for a weekly programme on *Cultural Diversity*. More concerned with immigrants from eastern Europe than from the Portuguese-speaking countries, the main objective of this programme was to promote interaction between different cultures, to encourage the integration of Russian and Ukrainian immigrants into Lusophone culture and to invest in intercultural dialogue by inciting the listeners to learn about eastern European traditions and cultural practices.

Although produced in Portugal, the programme *Firkidja* was proposed by the Portuguese Association of Guiné-Bissau Friends. Focusing on the culture of this Portuguese-speaking African country, this programme aimed to discuss the social inclusion in Portugal of people coming from Guiné-Bissau, as well as contribute to the dissemination of the culture and dialects from this country. In addition to this set of more institutional programmes, Rádio Ás included various projects on music. Produced by single authors, in general, these programmes proposed to briefly span diverse kinds of music, such as jazz, hard rock, punk and avant-garde, amongst others. Music and literature were the main themes broached, more in terms of individual productions than of associations or more formal groups.

There were neither daily programmes nor news bulletins. Programmes had a weekly, biweekly or monthly periodicity, but many had an informational purpose. The daily newspaper *Diário de Aveiro* produced a series of biweekly programmes. *A Uma Só Voz* was a space dedicated to interviews mainly with politicians invited to comment on issues affecting the population of Aveiro. Besides, although promoted by the press office of the city council, the programme *Aveiro em Revista* aimed at the diffusion of information on activities carried out by the council. Revolving around the ageing theme, the programme *A Idade (com)Vida* was an informative rubric. It was meant to be a programme on the present demographic panorama, inspired by the 2012 European Year for Active Ageing and Solidarity between Generations.

Producers could be individuals interested in music, but a significant part of the authors were actually people working for organisations, schools and associations. No specific competencies were required. With no pretension to be a professional medium, Rádio Ás was created to mobilise people around a common interest for the empowerment of groups, no matter how qualified the productions. At least in theory, the project is in synchrony with Janey Gordon's (2012, 2) idea of such a station being able to "provide social capital, social worth and ultimately social gain to that community."

THE END: WHEN POLITICAL PRIORITIES CHANGE

Rádio Ás was online for 49 months. In January 2014, the project was suddenly suspended. The new mayor, who was a candidate from the same centre-right party, the PSD, was elected September 2013 and autonomously decided to put an end to this Web station, not recognising the communitarian identity of the project. According to the *Diário de Aveiro*,[16] the council cancelled payment to the website hosting the service. Producers were informed by email, at January 3rd. The unilateral decision of the mayor was founded on two reasons: (a) the council had no funds to support the station and (b) the activity of Rádio Ás was not considered of relevant public interest by the new municipal executive, which would reformulate the municipal policy of communication.

Collaborators and a few bloggers expressed surprise at the city council's decision. For instance, in reaction to the suspension, the spokesman of the Portuguese Association on Environmental Education declared that "this was a project of citizenship with lots of people involved, an activity of social interest."[17]

Rádio Ás had been announced as the first online radio station promoted by a municipality. And it was—in terms of its underlying rationale—a virtuous idea. Three main reasons contributed to the originality of this pioneering project: (a) the intersection of three partners from different countries; (b) the collaborative structure based on contributions from individual authors, associations and other social groups; and (c) the investment in audio content exclusively (besides the institutional information, the only other possibility offered by the website was that of listening to the streaming). The population seemed to welcome the initiative, as more than a half a hundred programme proposals were submitted for validation. Despite consisting in city council property, this project was able to gather the participation of many groups; nevertheless, the project seemed already doomed to fail due to governance having no space for bottom-up input, with too much power being held by the municipality.

In accordance with Nico Carpentier's (2011, 27) approach, participation is more than access and interaction. In his own words, "access and interaction do matter for participatory processes in the media—they are actually its conditions of possibility—but they are also very distinct from participation because of their less explicit emphasis on power dynamics and decision-making." From this point of view, Rádio Ás was not a clear example of participation. More than access and space for interaction, it provided listeners with the power to produce but not to take part in the decision-making processes. Programming was indeed essentially ensured by external independent entities and by citizens. Fuelled by the work of volunteer collaborators, Rádio Ás constituted a kind of spiral of communities: the community of producers, the community of those directly or not involved with the producers, the community of Aveiro inhabitants and, more widely, the community of Portuguese citizens living in foreign countries as well as the community of listeners in the partner countries.

Though there was initial enthusiasm, the project lasted only two years. Apparently it failed due to insufficient resources to support it and the weak involvement of the partners. The first reason, the most significant one for the mayor who ordered its closure, was that the project was funded entirely by the council, in the context that an effort was being implemented to reduce expenses as a part of the general budget.

Rádio Ás was a very modest project, certainly not the height of innovation on the Internet. Some weaknesses may have determined its end. The equipment for radio broadcast (or webcast) in general is relatively simple and inexpensive. Rádio Ás had the basic resources but suffered from technological limitations if it was indeed to be more ambitiously expanded. Moreover, as previously mentioned, there was weak involvement of the other partners. Based in Aveiro, the project did not count on much collaboration from other municipalities, although some programmes were clearly concerned with cultural production within the so-called Lusophone space.

Cammaerts (2009, 648) warns that "community radio movements had limited lobbying power and were usually positioned as rogue or unprofessional amateurs within the broadcasting community." In this light and in line with his thought, it should be recognised that Rádio Ás was generally composed of amateurs. Furthermore there was neither a clear editorial structure nor a hard core of collaborators who could assume part of the programming and ensure its coherence. As we said before, Portuguese legislation is vague regarding what community radio should be and how it should work. There is insufficient regulatory information on how these kinds of stations should be organised and funded. The lack of inspiring models in Portugal could also have justified some of the difficulties felt by Rádio Ás promoters.

However, as far as we can understand, Rádio Ás ended more because of a political decision than because of its undeniable weaknesses. The project was working. There were people committed to the ideals of the project. Funding was not very demanding. It would have been possible to keep Rádio Ás on the air if the municipal executive had wished to do so. A project depending on a political institution is nevertheless subject to changes in policy. Indeed, Janey Gordon (2012, 1) alerts us to the fact that "governmental and non-governmental authorities have found 'community' a convenient tag to give respectability to their favourite projects." The true defense of community, however, is not always practised.

Rádio Ás constitutes a convenient experience to discuss what is still missing in Portugal to allow for the flourishing of a new mediascape. To summarise, three lessons can be learned from this particular case:

Firstly, bottom-up processes cannot emerge without the participation of the community in the management of a media project: if nothing protects the project of community radio promoted by political associations from discretionary policies, there are no conditions to ensure a long-term project; the community should indeed be able to play a role in the decision-making processes so as to ward off excessive dependence on political power, which has its risks.

Secondly, a permanent staff with a clear management and editorial structure, independently or not of the former being composed of volunteer collaborators, is fundamental to promote balanced and continuous programming.

Thirdly, a clear regulatory framework with a greater degree of legal precision, would promote quality in terms of organisation and functioning, despite the non-professional and community-based nature of community radio apparently not requiring rigid normativity.

COMMUNITY RADIO AND THE EMPOWERMENT OF COMMUNITIES

Community media were understood as alternative media based on participatory and collaborative communication. Emerging as a kind of reaction to the communicative deficits of mainstream media in the local context, this communication model pins all its hopes on citizens and communities. In a context of historical uncertainty, economic insecurity and the failure of traditional media systems, participatory communication has been defended as a pivotal foundation for human communities of belonging.

Despite this general understanding—commonly subscribed to by researchers on media studies—community media in Portugal and community radio in particular are not developed or supported enough in regulatory terms. In countries like Portugal, where there is "a strong public service broadcasting tradition, community radio is only a fairly recently recognized distinct media space" (Cammaerts 2009, 649).[18] Unlike Brazil (and several countries such as the UK, Ireland, Canada and Australia), where community communication has been strongly developed for many years, in Portugal the marks of a long dictatorship, extended by the principle of the public service broadcasting system, did not favour the emancipation of such projects. But a movement towards this direction seems to be happening.

On the one hand, Kate Coyer (2006, 129) asserts that community radio "is a means of social organizing and representation coalesced around 'communities of interest' and/or small-scale geographic locales." Besides revitalising local and small communities of interest, there are many reasons for community radio to constitute an exciting idea for countries like Portugal. The emergence of such projects, FM or online, contributes to the recognition of radio as a resilient, flexible and still-passionate medium. In a hypervisual society, a growing concern over sound culture seems to be gaining relevance. David Hendy's (2013) book on the history of sound, as well as the sound mapping projects of many global cities, are significant examples of this new sensibility for sound. On the other hand, the creation of community radio has represented the emancipation of audiences, who are increasingly empowered to create and share compared with the past. The effects of media education programmes and of the emergence of more friendly and intuitive technologies, as well as the general liberalisation of thought that occurred in the second half of the twentieth century, are the factors that probably accelerated the impulse towards more creative and engaged communities. According to the World Association of Community Radio Broadcasters (AMARC), "community radio is not about doing something for the community but about the community doing something for itself" (Mtimbe et al. 1998, 34). Moreover, within community stations lie good chances to preserve the sound memory of a community and to promote intercultural dialogue. Used as the voice of the voiceless, community radio is associated not only with non-formal education but also with the expression of minority cultural groups. Cicilia Peruzzo (2006, 118) explains that "community radio's specificities are expressed in identity building, both at cultural level and at social values necessities field of each place."

Bottom-up media and community projects are not supposed to suppress traditional, commercial and professional media. However, as shown by Rádio Ás programming, alternative media also constitute a symbolic space of power. Owned and promoted by non-profit organisations, these media, radio included, do not have to follow strict economic principles. There is a new kind of editorial freedom in these projects, which probably dictates political resistance to their consolidation. From the political point of view, it can be risky to empower citizens to express their own feelings and ideas. But if getting listeners increasingly involved in the soundscape can be considered a cultural gain, this cannot be anything else than enriching.

NOTES

1. See http://iamcr.org/section-home-seccomm-201.
2. There was a public debate during the spring of 2013, in Portugal, on the role that local radio stations play in some Portuguese villages. This discussion was generated by the announcement of the end of a specific programme on a local radio station located in Northeast Portugal. The *Bom Dia Tio João* (Good Morning Uncle John) programme was on the air for twenty years early every morning, and the presenter became a kind of uncle figure around whom a large family gathered to listen to the programme, in the words of a Portuguese daily newspaper. In an interview in 2013, the person responsible for the programme commented that when he started speaking into the microphone in 1989, his first words were: "Good morning, I am Tio João and I would like to create the largest family in the world." Despite its tremendous success, this programme was temporarily cancelled when the local radio station was bought by a big radio broadcasting company. Popular protest led to the programme being on air again. The importance of the public debate that this case sparked and that was globally reported by newspapers resides in its having shown how listeners form a real community who listen to the radio with the same expectation of conversation that they would have in going to a café to meet friends.

3. NET Station: shaping radio for Web environment project, funded by the Portuguese Foundation of Science and Technology and developed by the Communication and Society Research Centre/University of Minho. The project applied for funding in 2010 and started in April 2012.
4. This legal statement identifies the general objectives of community broadcasters, the principles of their programming, as well as the legitimate owners of community radio. According to this law, only legally created and registered non-profit foundations and community associations, led by Brazilian citizens (or citizens who have been naturalised for at least ten years), are allowed to be owners.
5. This classification is decided by the Regulatory Board for Social Communication [Entidade Reguladora para a Comunicação Social] when the licence is assigned.
6. Once again, this classification is decided by the Regulatory Board for Social Communication.
7. See http://www.cm-aveiro.pt/radioas/RadioOnlineMissao.aspx?SelPg=1.
8. The notion of 'Lusophony' is usually associated with expression in Portuguese, embracing individuals who are culturally, historically, and linguistically linked to this Latin idiom.
9. See http://www.cm-aveiro.pt/radioas/RadioOnlineMissao.aspx?SelPg=1.
10. Some information on the functioning of Rádio Ás was obtained during an interview with Virgílio Nogueira, who worked directly with the team that promoted this Web radio station. The interview, conducted by telephone on April 2014, focused on three main topics: the origin of the project, the way the project was organised and managed and the reasons for the demise of the station.
11. *Diário de Aveiro*, November 28, 2013, 2.
12. *Diário de Aveiro*, November 28, 2013, 2.
13. See https://www.facebook.com/pages/A-Idade-comVida-Rdio-%C3%81s/148 816708587468.
14. See http://www.mixcloud.com/joaojgomes/.
15. *Diário de Aveiro*, January 8, 2014, 3.
16. *Diário de Aveiro*, January 9, 2014, 5.
17   *Diário de Aveiro*, January 8, 2014, 3.
18. In Poland, the situation is similar. There is no fully recognised non-commercial sector that could be a real supplement to commercial local broadcasting.

REFERENCES

Almeida, A. C. and Magnoni, A. F. (2010). "Rádio e Internet: recursos proporcionados pela web ao jornalismo." In Magnoni, A. and Carvalho, J. M. (eds.), *O novo rádio. Cenários da radiodifusão na era digital.* São Paulo: SENAC, 273–290.
Cammaerts, B. (2009). "Community Radio in the West. A Legacy of Struggle for Survival in a State and Capitalist Controlled Media Environment." *The International Communication Gazzette,* 71(8), 635–654.
Carpentier, N. (2011). "The Concept of Participation. If They Have Access and Interact, Do They Really Participate?" *CM: Communication Management Quarterly/Casopis za upravljanje komuniciranjem,* 21, 13–36.
Carpentier, N., Lie, R. and Servaes, J. (2003). "Community Media: Muting the Democratic Media Discourse?" *Journal of Media & Cultural Studies,* 17(1), 51–68.
Cebrián Herreros, M. (2008). *La radio en Internet.* Buenos Aires: La Crujía.

Coyer, K. (2006). "Community Radio Licensing and Policy: An Overview." *Global Media and Communication*, 2(1), 129–134.

Gordon, J. (ed.). (2012). *Community Radio in the Twenty-first Century*. Oxford: Peter Lang.

Hendy, D. (2013). *Noise. A Human History of Sound and Listening*. London: Profile Books.

Howley, K. (2005). *Community Media: People, Places and Communication Technologies*. Cambridge: Cambridge University Press.

Lewis, P. M. (ed.). (1993). "Alternative Media: Linking Global and Local." *Reports and Papers on Mass Communication*, 107. Paris: UNESCO.

Martin-Barbero, J. (1993). *Communication, Culture and Hegemony: From the Media to Mediations*. Newbury Park: Sage.

Mtimbe, L., Bonin, M. H., Maphiri, N. and Nyamaku, K. (1998). *What Is a Community Radio?* AMARC Africa: Panos Southern Africa.

Oliveira, M. (2013). "Sounds and Identity: The Role of Radio in Community Building." In Stachyra, G. (ed.), *Radio. Community, Challenges, Aesthetics*. Lublin: Maria Curie-Sklodowska University Press, 177–188.

Palácios, M. (1990). "Sete teses equivocadas sobre comunidade e comunicação comunitária." *Comunicação e Política*, 11, 103–110.

Peruzzo, C. (2006). "Rádio comunitária na Internet: empoderamento social das tecnologias." *Revista FAMECOS*, 30, 115–125.

Portela, P. (2011). *A rádio na Internet em Portugal*. Ribeirão: Húmus.

Rennie, E. (2006). *Community Media: A Global Introduction*. Oxford: Rowman & Littlefield Publishers.

Shannon, J. and Weaver, W. (1949). *The Mathematical Theory of Communication*. Champaign: University of Illinois Press.

Starkey, G. (2006). "Radio: Theorising the Future, Theorising in Future." *Recerches en Communication*, 26, 123–133.

13 The Value of Productive Publics in Radio

A Theoretical Frame on Value Creation in Participatory Culture

Adam Arvidsson

INTRODUCTION

Radio, along with television and other 'old media' platforms, is making increasing use of audience participation as a source of value. Radio might be perfectly suited to integrating such participatory culture, as the potential immediacy of the medium, along with its tradition of audience interaction, enables it to rapidly and creatively integrate audience-created inputs into its programming content. Indeed social media companies seem to be particularly keen to cater to radio stations, offering a host of services to mine and capture social media–based audience content for radio producers.

In recent years such appropriation of participatory culture has been criticised along the lines of the Marxian labour theory of value. Audience members are increasingly exploited, it is held, as not only their attention, which already Dallas Smythe (1981) understood as exploited by media companies, but also their productive interaction and agency are put to work. This perspective is particularly salient in relation to the critique of social media platforms and their ability to channel and commodify participatory culture with greater efficiency (van Dijk 2013). In this chapter I would like to put this critique within a broader perspective by providing a more general perspective on value creation in participatory culture.

VALUE CREATION IN PARTICIPATORY CULTURE

At a first glance, the term 'participatory culture' seems a bit awkward—as if not all cultural practice involves participation in some sense. If we look a bit closer at the term and its history, however, we find that the kind of participation intended is highly particular. Participatory culture entails popular participation in the creation, not so much of culture, values and traditions, as of economic value—or at least the creation of the kind of raw material that can, potentially, be transformed into economically valuable commodities. In this sense the term 'participatory culture' is part of a new condition of cultural practice: it describes the way culture, and in particular popular culture, works after its complete 'subsumption' within the relations of capitalist practice. Participatory culture, in this sense, is a symptom of complete inclusion of cultural practice within commodity production, which Frederic Jameson (1991) already saw as a key feature of what used to be known as 'postmodernity.'

Indeed, cultural 'participation' used to be considered quite differently. Within media studies, the emphasis on popular participation in the creation of cultural meanings developed chiefly within the postwar cultural studies tradition. As it emerged in the postwar years, Cultural Studies reoriented scholarly focus from high culture to popular culture, and the tradition emphasised the political potential of popular cultural participation. Through the study of working-class traditions, subcultures, audience activity and consumer reflexivity, the Cultural Studies tradition emphasised how ordinary people could carve out a space for subjectivity and resistance through the everyday reflexive appropriation of consumer goods and mass cultural products. However, in part as a reaction to the ever more inclusive 'subsumption' of everyday life on the part of consumer capitalism, the theoretical space afforded for such 'resistance' was progressively reduced: from youth subcultures redefining collective identities in the 1970s, to young women asserting alternative forms of individual agency in the 1980s, to more vague forms of bricolage and post-structuralist strategic utilisations of the cracks in a seemingly totalitarian consumer society on the part of ordinary consumers in the 1990s (McGuigan 1992). As Paul Willis (1990, 26) laconically concluded in his later work: "commercial cultural commodities [are] all that most people have."

This 'tragic' reduction of the space for consumer resistance was in part a result of a shift in theoretical focus on the part of cultural studies scholars. From having concentrated on class and collective identities in the 1970s, the focus shifted to individual identity and affect in the 1980s and 1990s. But it was mainly an effect of the expansion and qualitative reorientation of consumer culture itself. The sheer amount of advertising and commercial cultural products increased drastically as media deregulation opened up national media systems to global consumer culture in the 1990s. At the same time, traditional advertising was supplanted by branding practices that ever more relied on the inclusion of consumer activity and reflexivity within the value chain of commodities. Consumers were put to work, and precisely their agency and reflexivity, their ability to 'go against the system' and innovate was what constituted the most valuable aspect of their 'labour power' within a new cross media 'convergence culture' (Arvidsson 2006; Jenkins 2006). Conversely, in a highly mediatised postmodern consumer society, the creative appropriation of consumer goods within strategies of identity creation became normal practice. Previously marginal subcultures were replaced by consumer tribes, where consumer agency had been de-politicised and recast as a source of commercial innovation (Maffesoli 1996; Muggleton and Weinzierl 2003). With the diffusion of the Internet in the 1990s, such consumer agency appeared to have become a mainstream phenomenon, as online communities dedicated to anything from Harley-Davidson motorcycles to *Star Trek* and sadomasochism proliferated, seemingly tapping into a pent-up desire for brand community (Muniz and O'Guinn 2001).

What sort of value does consumer participation create? From the point of view of the consumers or audience members who participate, there are a wide range of use values—from a narrative experience via community to business opportunities. But where lies the value of participatory culture from the point of view of cultural industries like radio? From their point of view, ordinary consumers can create value in principally two ways: as the creators of content and as the creators of valuations. The former dimension is most straightforward: YouTube users upload videos that can be watched by others, the listeners of a radio show suggest the soundtrack by posting their suggestions and preferences to Facebook, *Star Trek* fans write fiction that can be appropriated by the owners of the *Star Trek* brand and transformed into storylines for coming films, gamers develop the gameplay of Counter Strike of World of Warcraft, thus making the gaming experience meaningful for others. However, in this chapter I will propose that both historic and current evidence suggest that to emphasise content production as the main dimension of value creation is misguided.

Granted, there are some instances, such as gameplay or the peer-based production of Free or Open Source software (rather a limited case of the kinds of participatory culture that we are discussing in this volume), where the creation of content is doubtlessly the main aspect of consumer participation. But in most other instances, consumer-produced content needs to be substantially processed and filtered before it can enter into the value chains of the culture industries. Street fashion has but a marginal and remote impact on the yearly looks presented by high-fashion designers at the Milan fashion week; most fan fiction is ignored or discarded by television producers, particularly in a television market that seems to be privileging high-quality *auteur* television series like *Mad Men*; and a whole new branch of cultural production—the creative industries—grew on the basis of processing and packaging a diffuse popular creativity so that it could be rendered fit for corporate consumption. It is significant in this respect that YouTube, the contemporary flagship of participatory content creation, only stopped losing money for its owner—Google—once it invested in channels for the distribution of professionally created content.

What about Google and Facebook? Don't they make money on the participatory production of content, seducing users to co-produce a user experience that can motivate them, in turn, to give of their time and attention to the platform so that this can be sold off as a precious 'audience commodity'? Apart from the fact that advertising sales are not a sustainable basis for the business models of Facebook or other social media companies (Arvidsson and Colleoni 2012), it would be more correct to suggest that

Facebook principally lives off the participatory *valuation* of content. That is, the valuable activity of a Facebook user lies not so much in the postings that he or she creates, as much as in his liking a particular post or posting something on her timeline. It is by making *affective* investments in media products—created by amateurs or professionals—and by participating in a platform-wide 'like economy' (Gerlitz and Helmond 2013) that the user becomes useful to Facebook. This is because what Facebook sells to advertisers is not undifferentiated audience time attracted by a co-produced user experience, but the ability to insert an advertisement or a message within a specific cluster of affective investments (likes, postings, friendships, visits, etc.) where it can be understood as valuable in relation to a highly particular and specific 'order of worth' (Stark 2011). Indeed, most present attempts to 'subsume' participatory culture are oriented towards such attempts to package and commodify networks of affective investments.

For example, Facebook's 'Edgerank' algorithm estimates the value of users' feeds by a combination of 'affinity' (a measure of the density of interactions), weight (a measure of the quality of engagements: a comment is more engaging than a like, for example) and time decay (giving priority to recent interactions over older ones), thus effectively valuing users according to their ability to engage with other users and make them endorse and re-transmit their communications: Edgerank is a measure of the potential of a particular user's feed to give value to content by placing it within the particular hierarchy of worth that prevails in the network within which he or she interacts. Similarly Twitter's advertising department has launched a service that puts monetary value on tweets allocated in users' streams according to the ability of these users to spread messages in their networks, or, which is the same thing, to confer value on them as content that spreads (Carmody 2013). The same tendency continues as social media companies are starting to market themselves as interfaces that allow for the direct mining of data produced by 'old media audiences' (it is estimated that in the UK 40% of all Twitter traffic at peak TV viewing time is about TV, and 60% of all Twitter users use Twitter while watching TV [Carmody 2013]). Twitter has recently struck an agreement with Nielsen to create a "Nielsen Twitter TV Rating" that will measure the total audience for TV-related conversations on Twitter, including both people who comment and people who are exposed to their comments. The system will enable advertisers to rank the value of users according to their ability to create attention and engagement on the part of others. In parallel, a number of applications like Hootsuite, Tweetdeck (bought by Twitter in 2011 for $40 million [cfr. Rosoff 2011]), SproutSocial, VerticalResponse, Sendible, Postling and Visual Revenue enable brand managers to explore the network of the followers/fans of the social profiles they manage. They provide brand managers with data about these networks polarised around the profiles they manage: once again the success of communication strategies is evaluated according to shifts in the reach of each follower/fan, the average klout score of the network, the most commented/liked/shared Facebook posts, the most clicked and re-tweeted tweets and the most important cities from which the clicks came. Start-ups like SocialGuide Intelligence, Viggle, TweetTv and GetGlue offer ratings and audience valuations based on social media traffic or data derived from smartphone apps and established actors, like Nielsen offers similar services collaborating with Twitter and Facebook and mining these social media giants for data on television audience behaviour. Once again the main category for the valuation of social media presence remains the influence of the communication networks thus generated. In other words, beneath vague terms like 'clout,' 'engagement' and 'influence,' there seems to be an emerging focus of value measurement of the ability of people watching to affect or create engagement on the part of others around a particular piece of media content, or, in what corresponds to the same thing, to confer socially recognised value upon it.

PUBLICS AND VALUATION

The valuable contribution of social media audiences is ever more that of singling out pieces of content that are valued differently from others. However, this valuating function of publics has a long history. Gabriel Tarde defined the economic function of publics as that of conferring value on otherwise anonymous goods. Tarde was the first social thinker to take the economic role of publics seriously. Already in his *Psychologie économique* (Tarde 1902) he underlined how publics played a crucial role in modern consumer society. Where people increasingly consumed goods that found no place in traditional structures of needs, the ability to define their value through public communication became crucial to commercial success. Indeed, the public sets the 'truth, beauty and utility' of mass-produced goods, celebrities or political programmes. What is more, he argued that such public value was determined collaboratively: it depended on "the greater or lesser number, the greater or lesser social standing (that is, their overall reputation and their recognised competence), of the people who support it, as well as the intensity of their belief in it" (Tarde 1902, 62). This definition was further operationalised in Tarde's call for a hypothetical 'gloriometer'—technically impossible at the time of his writing—whereby the value-creating potential of members of a public, their worth, could be calculated:

> A man's glory, like his credibility and wealth (. . .) is therefore a kind of social quantity. It would be interesting if, by means of some ingenious statistics, we could get an approximate measure of this singular quantity for each species of celebrity. The need for a *gloriometer* is felt with particular sharpness given how fame of every color has multiplied, how suddenly it comes and how fleeting it is, and how, despite its usual transience, it always goes together with formidable power, being a *good* for the person who possesses it while for the society it is an *illumination*

and source of faith. . . . *Fame* is one component of glory; it can readily be measured by number of individuals who have heard of a man or one of his acts. But admiration, a no less essential component, is a more complex matter to measure. We would have to count the number of admirers, to calculate the intensity of their admiration and also—here's the rub—take into account [the admirers'] sharply unequal social value.

(Tarde 1902, 70–71)

For Tarde, the value of public activity consisted in its ability to form a temporary association of strangers held together by a common passion and, importantly, by a common commitment to particular values or a particular ethos. It is the ability of this ethos to support a public definition of 'truth, beauty and utility' or, in more contemporary terms, a value convention, that enables the formation of monetary prices around 'ephemeral' goods like audience attention and brand values. Tarde's perspective thus opens up a different interpretation of the position of audiences and participatory publics in the political economy of the media system.

First of all, from a Tardian perspective the value-creating ability of the public primarily rests with its ability to *produce* a consumption norm: to create and sustain a particular way of interpreting the meaning and value of an object. By forming a public, the audience situates itself, so to say. It endows itself with a set of values, or perhaps better an *ethos* (Arvidsson 2013) that renders its behaviour, taste and preferences predictable. In a situation of complexity and data overload, it becomes increasingly valuable to construct the kind of directionality that allows for interpretation and prediction.

This is precisely the principle behind contemporary brand management. The growing importance of brands as marketing devices that has occurred since the 1980s has in no small part been a response to the problem of creating predictable consumer demand in a situation where such predictability can no longer be guaranteed by the institutional nexus of the media system. It is when the formation of consumer tastes escapes the overall control of the media industries that the brand develops as a vehicle for the creation and sustenance of publics that allow for a certain forward control of consumption. Apple, for example, can successfully predict how many iPhones will be sold, and above all what features the next version of the iPhone should have, because the public formed around the iPhone brand allows for such predictability. Crucially the value of a brand, its 'brand equity,' is understood to be based not only on the number of people who care about it, but also on the passion it is able to generate in the people who care, as this passion is what keeps the brand-public together.

Second, the creation of publics is crucial to maintaining value conventions. Once again, to brand has come to mean to create and maintain a convention that supports the idea that one product is different from another, yet functionally and aesthetically similar (Audi and Skoda are similar cars built on the same technical platform, yet the meaning and value of their brands are widely different; Apple and Samsung use similar technical solutions but are perceived as different phones). With the rise of a contemporary participatory culture, the responsibility for creating and sustaining such value brand conventions has come to rest ever more on the ability of consumer publics to create and support what in marketing parlance is known as 'customer-based brand equity.' In this way, the ability of the audience to form a public becomes integrated as a valuable step in the brand-centered commodity chain.

But brands do not simply operate on consumer markets. Rather, brands are principally financial resources that serve to justify financial valuations of companies that exceed book value measurements by a factor of 2–3. Facebook, for example, is primarily a brand-based financial venture. While its earnings amounted to about $1.3 billion in 2012, the company was able to raise capital on a financial valuation 130 times as high. This financial function of brands is particularly clear in the culture industries. Indeed, Michael Szalay's (2014) work suggests that the content and programming strategy of HBO can to a large extent be understood as directed at creating brand equity for financial investors, and not simply for consumers. This scenario is consistent with contemporary interpretations of financial markets that point at the conventional nature of value formation (Stark 2011).

From this perspective, public valuation has been integrated not simply in the value chains of the commodity economy but, importantly, as a crucial element of value creation in an ever more financialised bio-economy where the crucial value nexus develops between financial markets and the passions and affects of life itself.

CONCLUSION

As Jenkins, Ford and Green (2013) have recently argued, content does not simply spread because of its inherent 'memetic' properties, but rather achieves 'spreadability' as it is actively endorsed and given value by a public. To thus transform content from an undifferentiated mass of text—or, in the case of radio, audio piece—into something that can find a place within a more or less clearly ordered value hierarchy, allowing for both predictability of tastes and the formation of steady consumption norms, is arguably the most important role of audience 'labour' within a participatory culture. Indeed, it can be argued that this valuing function has been the most important dimension of audience participation ever since, sometime in the 1970s, pre-Internet, this activity began to be seriously included within the political economy of a new 'promotional' capitalism (Wernick 1991). As members of subcultures, some people created content, but this activity was fairly rare. Most members of subcultures contributed actively to value content, to determine what was cool or not, or politically correct or not, thus articulating value horizons that made it possible to sustain both forms of more or less political resistance and alternative and innovative aesthetic forms. Conversely, such participatory valuation was the most interesting dimension of audience activity to be measured and surveyed as the media and advertising industries began to take an empirical interest in the dynamics of consumer culture with the launch of psychographic surveys in the 1970s. And as I have suggested in this chapter, today audience valuations, rather than content creation, remains the most valuable aspect of participation.

Such a perspective obviously pushes us to rethink theories of audience exploitation. Most of the critiques of contemporary participatory culture have focused on content creation, casting audience members in the mold of Marx's industrial workers who are exploited as their productive labour is insufficiently remunerated (or not remunerated at all). But if their main contribution lies not with content creation but with content valuation, this analysis is less to the point. Rather than the realm of production, it might be the case that a critique of social media companies and of participatory culture in general might concentrate on the realm of valuation. That is, consumers are not so much economically exploited as content producers as much as their ability to set the values of a participatory culture might be subjected to invasive and subtle forms of control on the part of the biopolitical strategies of social media platforms. Foucault, rather than Marx, might by the most fruitful point of departure for a critique.

REFERENCES

Arvidsson, A. (2006). *Brands. Meaning and Value in Media Culture*. New York: Routledge.

———. (2013). "The Potential of Consumer Publics." *Ephemera: Theory & Politics in Organization*, 13, 367–391.

Arvidsson, A. and Colleoni, E. (2012). "Value in Informational Capitalism and on the Internet." *The Information Society*, 28, 135–150.

Carmody, T. (2013). "Better than Nielsen: Twitter Breaks Down TV Behavior by Demographics, Device, and Genre." *The Verge*. Accessed January 10, 2013. http://www.theverge.com/2013/1/10/3861954/twitter-uk-study-real-time-television-ads.

Gerlitz, C. and Helmond, A. (2013). "The Like Economy: Social Buttons and the Data-Intensive Web." *New Media & Society*, 15(8), 1348–1365.

Jameson, F. (1991). *Postmodernism, or the Cultural Logic of Late Capitalism*. Durham: Duke University Press.

Jenkins, H. (2006). *Convergence Culture. Where Old and New Media Collide*. New York: New York University Press.

Jenkins, H., Ford, S. and Green J. (2013). *Spreadable Media*. New York: New York University Press.

Maffesoli, M. (1996). *The Time of the Tribes. The Decline of Individualism in Mass Societies*. London: Sage.

McGuigan, J. (1992). *Cultural Populism*. New York: Routledge.

Muggleton, D. and Weinzierl, R. (eds.). (2003). *The Post-Subcultures Reader*. Oxford: Oxford University Press.

Muniz, A. M. and O'Guinn, T. C. (2001). "Brand Community." *Journal of Consumer Research*, 27, 412–432.

Rosoff, M. (2011). "Twitter Has Bought Tweetdeck, Says Report." *Business Insider*, May 2. Accessed December 27, 2011. http://www.businessinsider.com/twitter-has-bought-tweetdeck-says-report-2011-5.

Smythe, D. W. (1981). "On the Audience Commodity and Its Work." In Smythe, D. W. (ed.), *Dependency Road: Communications, Capitalism, Consciousness, and Canada*. Norwood: Ablex, 22–51.

Stark, D. (2011). *The Sense of Dissonance: Accounts of Worth in Economic Life*. Princeton: Princeton University Press.

Szalay, M. (2014). "HBO Flexible Gold." *Representations*, 126(1), 112–134.

Tarde, G. (1902). *Psychologie économique*. Paris: F. Alcan.

van Dijk, J. (2013). *The Culture of Connectivity. A Critical History of Social Media*. Oxford: Oxford University Press.

Wernick, A. (1991). *Promotional Culture: Advertising, Ideology and Symbolic Expression*. London: Sage.

Willis, P. (1990). *Common Culture. Symbolic Play at the Heart of the Everyday Cultures of the Young*. Boulder: Westview Press.

Contributors

Adam Arvidsson (PhD) teaches sociology at the State University of Milan, where he also directs the Center for Digital Ethnography (www. etnografiadigitale.it). Presently Adam participates in the EU-funded project P2PValue, which analyses forms of value creation in networks of peer production. He has published on the creative industries, on new forms of freelance or precarious labour, and the political economy of information in general, as well as, in an earlier incarnation, on the history of marketing and consumer culture. Overall, Adam's main research interest concerns the emergence of new forms of value creation in the information economy. Adam has written a number of scientific articles and is author of *Brands. Meaning and Value in Media Culture* (London; Routledge, 2006) and *The Ethical Economy. Rebuilding Value after the Crisis* (Columbia University Press, 2013, with Nicolai Peitersen). adam.arvidsson@unimi.it

Tiziano Bonini, PhD in Media, Communication and Public Sphere at the University of Siena, 2008, is a Lecturer in Media Studies at IULM University of Milan. He has published extensively on radio and new media. His current research interests are the intersection between radio, Internet and social media; digital ethnography; public service media; production studies; media and democracy; freelance work in creative industries; digital free labour issues. He has done research for the European Broadcasting Union (EBU) on public radio and social media and he is the Young ECREA representative for the radio research section. Since 2005 he has also worked as a freelance radio producer for community, national commercial and public radio (Radio Popolare, Rai Radio2, Radio Svizzera Italiana, Radio24 Il Sole 24 Ore). In 2005, he won the special mention at The Swiss Public Radio Documentary Award with a feature on life stories of asylum seekers living in Sicily. tiziano.bonini@iulm.it

Manuel Fernández-Sande (PhD) is Professor of Journalism and Media Management and coordinator of the undergraduate programme in Journalism at the University Complutense of Madrid. He is the author of *Los orígenes de la radio en España, Volumes I and II* (Editorial Fragua, 2006)

and numerous articles on media and broadcasting. Fernández-Sande is a member of the research groups Mediacom (UCM) and Midia, Cultura e Memória (Conselho Nacional de Desenvolvimento Científico e Tecnológico, Brazil). His research interests include the radio broadcasting industry, marketing strategies for radio, community radio and the history of broadcasting. He is a member of ECREA and AE-IC (Asociación Española de Investigadores en Comunicación). Manuel.Fernandez@ucm.es

Iliana Ferrer (PhD) is a researcher of The Image, Sound and Synthesis Research Group (GRISS, which is a consolidated research group at the UAB, recognised by the Generalitat de Catalunya, 2014SGR1674). She is member of the Catalonia Radio Observatory (l'OBS). She received her BA in Social Communication and Journalism at the University of the North, Barranquilla, Colombia (2003) and her PhD in Audiovisual Communication at the UAB (2012) with a dissertation on Spanish TV news. She has been a visiting (postdoctorate) scholar at the Center for the Study of Latino Media and Markets, School of Journalism & Mass Communication, Texas State University (USA) and at the Research Center in Communication and Information (CINCO), Division of Humanities and Social Sciences, Instituto Tecnológico y de Estudios Superiores de Monterrey (Mexico). Her research projects focus on television journalism, latino/a studies, radio and social media. Iliana.Ferrer@uab.cat

Golo Föllmer holds a PhD in Musicology and was awarded the "PD" post-doc status for successfully completing a 6-year Junior Professorship in Media Studies. In 2009 he founded the masters programme Online Radio, which he is still heading. Since 2013, he has been Project Leader of the 3-year HERA-funded European Collaborative Research Project *Transnational Radio Encounters*. He is Senior Researcher of the Medien- und Kommunikationswissenschaften Department at Martin-Luther-Universität Halle-Wittenberg. His research interests include sound art and contemporary art music; the use of media in all kinds of musical applications with a focus on impelling the listener to action; radio and its arts, as well as related questions on auditory culture. golo.foellmer@medienkomm.uni-halle.de

J. Ignacio Gallego is Lecturer and Researcher at the Journalism and Media Studies Department of the Carlos III University of Madrid and of the TECMERIN research group. He holds a European PhD from The Complutense University of Madrid. He has been a research fellow at the Glasgow Caledonian University and has also participated in the Interactive Cultures Research Group based at the Birmingham City University. He has been a member of the COST Action IS0906 *Transforming Audiences, Transforming Societies* (2010–2014). He is currently general coordinator of the permanent international seminar "Transformations of the Independent Music Sector in the Digital Era" (www.transformacionesmusica. com) and a member of the national research project "Cultural Diversity and Audiovisual Industry: Good Practices and Indicators" (www. diversidadaudiovisual.org). juanignacio.gallego@uc3m.es

Maria Gutiérrez (PhD) is an Associate Professor of Audiovisual Communication and Advertising at the Autonomous University of Barcelona (UAB), where she is also part of the academic staff of the Masters Degree in Audiovisual Communication and Advertising Content. She is a committed member of the Catalonia Radio Observatory (l'OBS), where she participates actively in research projects on radio programming trends, radio and digital space, radio content and synergies between analogue and online broadcasting and youth audience. She is also studying the use of young people of social networks in the field of transnational communication. Maria. Gutierrez@uab.cat

Stanislaw Jedrzejewski is Professor at Kozminski University and has been teaching in the area of Media and Social Communications. He is a Senior Researcher at the Communication and Society Research Centre at the University of Minho (Portugal), where he was also Invited Professor for two years (2009–2010). He is a member of the Project "NET Station: Shaping Radio for the Web Environment" (funded by the Portuguese Foundation of Science and Technology). He was Vice-Chair of the ECREA Radio Research Section and currently chairs the Supervisory Board of Polish Radio (Polskie Radio) in Warsaw. sjedrzejewski@kozminski.edu.pl

Josep Maria Martí (PhD) is an Associate Professor of Audiovisual and Advertising Communication at the Autonomous University of Barcelona (UAB), where he is also part of the academic staff of the Masters Degree in Audiovisual Communication and Advertising Content. He is a Senior Researcher of The Image, Sound and Synthesis Research Group (GRISS, consolidated research group at the UAB and recognized by the Generalitat de Catalunya, 2014SGR1674). He is the Director of the Catalonia Radio Observatory (l'OBS), member of the Radio Committee of the European Broadcasting Union (EBU) and the Éuropenne Radio Forum. He was the Dean of the College of Journalists of Catalonia. He is also the general secretary of the Ondas Awards. His research interests focus on promoting and improving the quality of Spanish and Catalan radio. JosepMaria.Marti@uab.cat

Belén Monclús (PhD) is a Post-doctral researcher at the Audiovisual Communication and Advertising Department at the Autonomous University of Barcelona (UAB). She is a Researcher of The Image, Sound and Synthesis Research Group (GRISS, which is a consolidated research group at the UAB recognized by the

Generalitat de Catalunya, 2014SGR1674). She has been the coordinator of the Catalonia Radio Observatory (l'OBS, GRISS-UAB) since 2007. She has been a Visiting Researcher at the Centre for Cultural Policy Research (University of Glasgow). Her studies are focused on the evolution of the radio sector, digital radio and the synergies between conventional and online broadcasting, the adaption of conventional media within the online environment, the use of social networking, youth audience and audience participation, as well as the measurement and investigation of the Internet audience. Belen.Monclus@uab.cat

Madalena Oliveira is Associate Professor at the Institute of Social Sciences at the University of Minho (Portugal), where she coordinates the Masters Programme on Communication Sciences. She is also the Vice-Chair of the Communication and Society Research Centre and the Principal Investigator of the Project "NET Station: Shaping Radio for the Web Environment" (funded by the Portuguese Foundation of Science and Technology). She chairs the Radio and Audio Media Research Group of the Portuguese Association of Communication Sciences and is the Vice-Chair of the European Communication Research and Education Association's (ECREA) Radio Research Section. Her research interests include journalism, meta-journalism, semiotics, sound aesthetics and radio. madalena.oliveira@ics.uminho.pt

Jan Pinseler (PhD) is Professor of Media Research at Hochschule Magdeburg-Stendal (University of Applied Sciences). He is also part of the research network "Radio Aesthetics—Radio Identity." His research interests include radio research, community media and queer media studies. jan.pinseler@hs-magdeburg.de

Xavier Ribes (PhD) is an Associate Professor of Audiovisual Communication and Advertising at the Autonomous University of Barcelona (UAB), where he is also part of the academic staff of the Masters Degree in Audiovisual Communication and Advertising Content. He is a Researcher of The Image, Sound and Synthesis Research Group (GRISS, consolidated research group at the UAB and recognised by the Generalitat de Catalunya, 2014SGR1674). He is a committed member of the Catalonia Radio Observatory (l'OBS), where he participates actively in research projects on radio and digital space, radio contents and synergies between on-air and online broadcasting and youth audience. He is also studying the design of apps in the mobile environment and transmedia storytelling in audiovisual productions. Xavier.Ribes@uab.cat

Salvatore Scifo (PhD) is an Assistant Professor at the Department of Public Relations and Publicity (English), Faculty of Communication, at Maltepe University in Istanbul and a Post-Doctoral Researcher at the Mediated Interaction and Experience Lab (MIXLab) at Koc University, Istanbul, for the EU-funded FP7 project "The Contribution of Social Media in Crisis Management" (COSMIC). He has previously taught at Marmara University, London Metropolitan University and the University of Westminster. His research interests include community media, media history and social media in the context of crises. salvatorescifo@maltepe.edu.tr

Toni Sellas (PhD) is Associate Professor of Theory and History of Public Relations at the University of Girona (UdG), where he is also part of the academic staff of the Doctoral Programme in Cultural Studies and Communication. He currently works as a Delegate of the Rector for Communication Policy. He is a Researcher of the CSiI research group (UdG) and was involved in the European Broadcasting Union's research project "Why It Works." His research interests include media and participation, new media and public relations, public communication, and social media and social network analysis. toni.sellas@udg.edu

Grażyna Stachyra (PhD) is Assistant Professor of Social Communication at the Maria Curie-Skłodowska University in Lublin and Lecturer at the College of Enterprise and Administration in Lublin. She is a Vice-Chair of the Radio Research Section of the European Communication Research and Education Association (ECREA) and a member of the Radio Section of the Polish Communication Association. She is also a trainer of voice emission, NGO consultant and former radio journalist (i.e., Head of the News Department at the Radio Centrum in Lublin). Her research interests include anthropological contexts of radio communication, radio aesthetics, theory of radio genres and convergence process in modern radio, among others. Gstachyra70@gmail.com

Guy Starkey (PhD) is Professor of Radio and Journalism at the University of Sunderland, UK. He was Chair of the Radio Research Section of the European Communication Research and Education Association (ECREA) (2008–14) and a member of the ECREA Executive Board (2013–14). He is on the Steering Group of the Radio Studies Network within MeCCSA, and the Comité Scientifique of the Groupe de Recherches et d'Etudes Scientifiques sur la Radio (GRER). A former radio producer and presenter who still broadcasts on Internet radio, his publications include *Radio in Context* (2nd edn., Palgrave Macmillan, 2013), *Local Radio, Going Global* (Palgrave Macmillan, 2011), *Radio Journalism* (with Professor Andrew Crisell, Sage, 2009) and *Balance and Bias in Journalism: Representation, Regulation and Democracy* (Palgrave Macmillan, 2007). guy.starkey@sunderland.ac.uk

Fredrik Stiernstedt (PhD) is Lecturer in Media and Communication Studies at Jönköping University, Sweden. His previous research concerns producers and production in a transforming radio industry. His other research interests are the material and ideological aspects of digital culture, media

and social class and questions of labour in the media and cultural industries. fredrik.stiernstedt@hlk.hj.se

Asta Zelenkauskaite (PhD) is an Assistant Professor of Communication at
Drexel University, USA. Her research focuses on the interplay between
mass media and social media. In particular, she is interested in ways that
mass media are shaped by social media content. Her research is based on
an understanding of online user behaviours, user-generated content contribution, content selection and value extraction by utilizing a theoretical
framework of interactivity. She is interested in the alterations that social
media bring to the mass media landscape by studying these phenomena
from a multi-method approach, so as to analyse the changing understanding of content, audiences and media companies. astaze@gmail.com

Index

For Product Safety Concerns and Information please contact our EU
representative GPSR@taylorandfrancis.com
Taylor & Francis Verlag GmbH, Kaufingerstraße 24, 80331 München, Germany